THE
TRUING
OF

Visions of Life
and Thought
for the Future

CHRISTIANITY

JOHN C. MEAGHER

DOUBLEDAY·NEW YORK·LONDON·TORONTO·SYDNEY·AUCKLAND

THE

TRUING

OF

Visions of Life
and Thought
for the Future

CHRISTIANITY

PUBLISHED BY DOUBLEDAY
a division of Bantam Doubleday Dell Publishing Group, Inc.,
666 Fifth Avenue, New York, New York 10103

DOUBLEDAY and the portrayal of an anchor with a dolphin
are trademarks of Doubleday, a division of
Bantam Doubleday Dell Publishing Group, Inc.

"Only A Shadow" by Carey Landry, copyright © 1971 from the
collection Hi God, available from N.A.L.R., 10802 North 23rd Avenue, Phoenix, AZ 85029. All Rights Reserved.

Library of Congress Cataloging-in-Publication Data

Meagher, John C.
The truing of Christianity / by John C. Meagher. — 1st ed.
p.   cm.
Includes bibliographical references and index.
1. Theology, Doctrinal.   2. Christianity—20th century.
I. Title.
BT78.M42   1990   89-34997
270.8'29—dc20   CIP

This book is dedicated to my sister, Anne Adams,
who took good care of me from before my earliest memories
and grows, with the years, more lovely in her caring;
and to Terry Miosi, who has brothered me and friended me,
far beyond what brother and friend could mean to me
before the grace of his strong inventiveness; and to
Roscoe Hill, who has taught me painlessly and gracefully
through the changes of thirty years, always with
winsome wit and inspiring faithfulness;
and to our various great-grandchildren,
now hidden in the womb of an unformed time
beyond our mortal days,
as a welcome
and an invitation to share
what gave us strength
and life.

CONTENTS

FOREWORD

Having lost confidence that anyone reads forewords except the people mentioned in them, I will be uncharacteristically brief with this one, apart from one general remark about the stance from which *The Truing of Christianity* is written.

My last few books (which not even the people about to be mentioned have read) were, in religious terms though not personal ones, relatively disengaged in that I did not spend much time being self-conscious about where I was coming from theologically, and attempted (probably unsuccessfully, though no one has yet pinned a denominational bias on any of the books in question) to neutralize the particularity of my background and biases by driving in my Objective Scholarship gear. In an earlier book, *The Gathering of the Ungifted,* although I expressly acknowledged my Roman Catholic background, I tried to treat the content with a focus on a general and denominationless Christian convergence. Apparently no one was fooled except me. Catholic and Protestant friends alike remarked how *Catholic* the book was. So this time I have decided to attend more explicitly (though by no means exclusively) to the Catholic situation, partly in the hope that friends will eventually tell me how *ecumenical* I managed to get this time, but mainly because (a) that is really where I am coming from, and going, and (b) to get myself more clearly situated gives what I say the best chance of being useful to those who are not of my specific tradition. (I have learned over the last fifteen years that I am less clever than I had thought about speaking to everyone at once, and you, the reader, are more clever than I had supposed about finding my case adequately analogous to your case if it seems worth your effort.) Consequently, this book is especially concerned with Catholic problematics. But it is nevertheless more general in intent and is addressed, often directly, to all Christians, ex-Christians, non-Christians who are interested in Christianity, and to my great-grandchildren, wherever they may fit.

Though anticipated and gestated for many years, this book became possible, like everything else in life, through the kindness of others. Most specifically, my extraordinarily generous professional host, St. Michael's College in the University of Toronto, which has been a good dream for twenty years; and the Basilian Fathers whose extraordinary dedication and generous wisdom have made it so; and the International Religious Foundation, whose fostering of interreligious discussion made it possible for me to try out some of the material in the central chapters on an unusual variety of religious sensibilities and in graciously comfortable conditions; and the Social Sciences and Humanities Research Council of Canada (whose grant supplemented the generous University of Toronto study-leave allowance enough to make possible my pilgrimage through the places about to be mentioned); Landrum Bolling and the staff and residents of Tantur in Jerusalem; Ignatius Hirudayam and Maria Jeyaraj and Miss Jane Louis and the sweet sisters of Aikiya Alayam in Madras; Bede Griffiths and the lovely people of Saccidananda ashram at Shantivanam; Tourism Secretary R. Kirubhakaran, a generous host who gave me both R and R and useful perspective by providing me with a memorable religious tour of Tamil Nadu and received me graciously into his warm family; Jan Van Bragt and Jan Swingedouw and Jim Heisig of Paulus Heim and the Nanzan Institute for Religion and Culture in Nagoya, who offered many of the basic good things in life in grand style, including beautiful accommodations, excellent study facilities, great conversation, and a helpful dash of attention-getting criticism. And to Toshiba, which for all its subsequent naughtiness about silencing submarine propellers produced the machine that made it possible to build the basic draft of this book in airports and on buses and in cafés and under trees on riverbanks in the sunshine as well as in various libraries and hotels and guest rooms; and to Dragonfly Software, who despite frustrating delay eventually armed said machine with *Nota Bene*, their splendid word-processing program that makes even the writing of footnotes simple and convenient, and does much, much more to make everything work better for typewriter-traumatized authors. And to St. Michael's again, and Toronto, and my superb and fascinating children, for being there to come home to when the basic work was done. And to those who read all or part of one or more of my successive drafts or their patchwork antecedents, and responded with reassurance and helpful advice: Roscoe Hill, Carol Ochs, Bill Speckman (with whimsically brilliant perceptiveness), Terry Miosi (doggedly attentive, supportive, and demanding), Barbara Walkden, Ardis Collins, Don Evans (generously and incisively), Anne Adams, Lee Cormie, Mary Ellen Sheehan, Nancy Hill, Theresa D'Orsogna, Michael Armstrong, Lee d'Anjou (modulating her professional rigor with admirably friendly restraint), and finally Roscoe Hill again (intervening gratuitously with self-sacrificing thoughtfulness and care).

And with that—but no, let me slip in two more brief points after all:

Aside from the ideas in this book, there are a couple of other features that may annoy readers by their unorthodoxy even though, like the ideas, they are intended to be helpful. One is a not-infrequent practice of giving key words special meanings that are assembled from quite legitimate dictionary meanings but not quite what might ordinarily be expected. I will say more, as I do this, about how and why I am doing it; but I give both advance warning that it's coming, and assurance that it is not either frivolous or uncareful. Your patience is solicited in this regard, as well as your attentiveness when I tell you the meaning I intend the words to convey (the index will help if your attentiveness wanes).

The other major deviance is in the signaling of endnotes, which are of three kinds. When the note adds mere documentation or slight additional relevant but dispensable content, it will be initiated with a normal plain superscript numeral, like this.[1] If there are further remarks in the note that I suppose are probably worth the trouble it takes to find and read them, the superscript numeral will have a plus sign after it.[2+] When the numeral is followed not by a plus sign but by an exclamation point, that means that I am outright pleading with you to look up the note and promising that you won't regret it.[3!]

—Toronto

Epiphany, 1990

1. The sentence is, I think, self-explanatory.

2. When in doubt, I omitted the plus sign. So please suppose, when I put it in, that I am definitely encouraging you to take the trouble to look up the note, on the grounds that what it adds is more than a trivial aside but was too much of an aside to work into the main text. All the remaining notes, after the very next one, will be found in the back of the book, in obvious and continuous numerical order. Try the ones with a plus sign, at least for a while. Please.

3. There are very few of this type, and this one was perhaps worth reading just for that reassurance, but I'll throw in a bonus in the form of a new definition of sins, suitable at least for scholarly adolescents: zits *im Leben*. Or, if that doesn't do anything for you, I have it on very good authority that Pope John XXIII once, upon receiving a portly cleric who was sucking in his belly for the occasion, bopped him on the stomach hard enough to make him drop the pretense (and the belly), and then turned to another priest in attendance and explained—this is real, mind you: I am only two removes from the scene via reliable reporters—"In our student days, we were in Paris together," then adding, as he patted his own ample front, "We are of the same *arrondissement*."

PROLOGUE

Among the poorest of the poor, Ali Hassan spent much of his time rummaging in the trash heaps of Cairo, looking for discarded goods that might, if cleaned carefully and perhaps patched here and there, be sold for a few piasters.

It was on one of these excursions that he found the lamp.

As he carefully brushed off the dried clay that clung to it, suddenly the genie poured out into the air, and announced in grand tones that the treasure was at his command.

"The treasure?" echoed the befuddled Ali Hassan.

"The treasure," repeated the genie. "The treasure that everyone dreams about; the treasure they make up stories about, though all the stories actually fall short of the truth. The treasure that genies are expected to deliver."

"I accept," said Ali Hassan, humbly.

There was a pause.

"So hand it over," said Ali Hassan, acceptingly.

"Oh come on," replied the genie. "You know that we don't just drop treasures in your lap. I go by the usual rules: we need some token effort on your part. You have to dig it up. I just tell you the instructions."

"So tell," said Ali Hassan.

"Okay," said the genie, "listen carefully, because I'm not allowed to repeat the instructions, and you have to do it just right or it won't work."

"Ready," said Ali Hassan.

"Roger," said the genie. "First, you need a pointed spade. Only a pointed one will do."

"I've got one," said Ali Hassan. "Bought it last week at the Wikalet el Balah. I don't usually buy, but I figured it was a professional tool, maybe tax deductible. Besides, it was dirt cheap. Pardon the expression."

"Pardoned," said the genie. "Are you free at midnight during the next full moon? That's the only appointment available at the moment."

"All clear," said Ali Hassan.

"Great," said the genie. "You know the big trash heap just north of Doqqi?"

"Like the back of my hand," said Ali Hassan. "My livelihood, you know."

"Fine," said the genie. "Take the pointed spade there, right at midnight. A few minutes either way won't matter, but try to be punctual. Do you have a red fez?"

"Fezes went out with Farouk," replied Ali Hassan, anxiously. "I could maybe get one."

"Sorry," said the genie. "Long time in the lamp; you lose track of fashion. How about a beige libda?"

"Will brown do?" asked Ali Hassan.

"I guess it's close enough," said the genie. "Be sure you're wearing it."

"No problem," said Ali Hassan.

"Right," said the genie. "So you go to the middle of the bank at the west side of the Doqqi trash heap, step out five paces, and dig. It may take you a couple of hours to get the whole thing out, since it's a pretty sizeable treasure, but you've got till dawn to finish the job, so that shouldn't give you any trouble."

"I can manage," said Ali Hassan. "Is that it?"

"That's it," said the genie. "Oh, except there's one thing more."

"Shoot," said Ali Hassan.

"While you're digging," said the genie, "it's very important that you do not, at any point, think about the sphinx—otherwise the treasure will disappear."

. . .

What Ali Hassan thought about the genie afterward is not recorded. It is, however, known that he did not bother to keep the midnight tryst with the putative and evanescent treasure, and that he managed to take permanent heart from his momentary lift of hopeful spirit, turning it into imaginative resolve. At last report, he owned a chain of hardware stores and had put seven children through college. Three of them are now teaching in Cairo high schools, where they are reputed to be particularly keen about cautioning their pupils against fanciful superstitions and encouraging them to make good use of every opportunity.

THE

Part 1

UNDERPINNINGS OF

THE PROBLEM:

DO CHRISTIANITIES

TRUE?

1

HOW
TO MEAN
"FAITH" AND "BELIEF"

For all I know, you are now browsing in a bookstore and wondering whether you will be interested in this book. You don't want to have to read this chapter in order to decide, and you may guess that the first chapter won't necessarily be typical of the whole thing anyway. So as a kindness to fellow browsers, and to help you make up your mind, I will drop some background information about it into this first endnote[1] and give you a sampling of its preoccupations and intentions in the next few paragraphs—not an abstract of the argument or a real outline of the procedure, but at least a taste of what comes after.

1. Traditional Christian assumptions are in serious trouble. From very early times, Christians have normally assumed that Christianity as they understood it is divinely revealed, unquestionably true, and manifestly destined to become the definitive world religion. These assumptions were powerfully reinforced by the astonishing success of Christianity's spread in its early centuries, the gradual consolidation of a European Christian culture, and the effective worldwide extension of Christianity under the protection of the imperial, colonial, and technological expansion of Christian-culture regimes. But the world has changed in important ways, and so have our ways of understanding it. Christianity no longer looks either as unques-

tionable or as ultimate as it once did, to Christians as well as to non-Christians, and its need for accountability has dramatically increased.

2. Christian accountability is in bad shape. Christian theologians and missionaries and pastors and parents have been used to forwarding traditional Christian assumptions as if no question need, or may, be raised about them. Questions are now raised, some from without the Christian fold and some from within. They are not usually answered well. The traditional answers are not adequate to the questions, because they repeat the traditional assumptions: but the questions are about whether those assumptions can be sustained. Christian accountability must face some deeply unsettling questions more honestly—and the honesty is bound to lead to more modest answers, and sometimes to the admission that some of what Christianity has been is wrong.

3. The leaders of the Christian churches have normally insisted on loyalty to what Christianity has been, with relatively little attention to what Christianity may become. References to "the Christian tradition" as a substitute for "Christianity" are common, but misleading: the definite article usually implies an exaggerated sense of unity in the Christian past, and—more important—the phrase is almost always used to describe only what is seen in the rearview mirror, the stuff of the past rather than the ongoing *process* of passing it on. The sense of obligation to support the faith of our fathers and mothers is admirably pious, but it is dangerously small minded: the sense of obligation to prepare the faith of our great-grandchildren is far more urgent and far too underdeveloped, and it does not work in the same way. We cannot honor Christianity adequately by merely reaffirming its past and present. Our responsibility includes assisting it to change, sometimes to retreat as well as to advance, to learn new ways of life and thought, to live more appropriately in order to live more abundantly and to think more critically in order to think more truly. We will fail our great-grandchildren if we pass on to them only what we have received. Already it is evidently not enough.

4. We do not know what is enough. If we think of Christianity as essentially finished already, the true lore and set of beliefs and way of life and rituals and sacraments that exhaust the ways in which God provides for our authenticity, then I think we misunderstand both Christianity and ourselves, and defraud our great-grandchildren in the process. If you used to find traditional Christianity totally satisfying, as I did, I hope you are, as I am, grateful for the experience and still practicing at it. But I also hope that you no longer find it totally satisfying, and are hopeful not just that more

practice will make you more proficient but that Christianity itself may be improved. There is much that Christianity ought to be that it has not yet become; there is much that it has been that will no longer do. There is more to all this than matters of faith and belief, but these are of great concern in Christianity and need special attention. In the next phase of its life, I think we should learn how to let go of beliefs that cannot really be sustained and to relocate Christian life within a faith that goes beyond beliefs and can allow us to restructure beliefs, or to retire them, when they collide with what we know or embarrass our sense of divine benevolence or compromise our purposefulness or retard our capacity to live in the presence of God.

5. I do not claim to exemplify what it is to live in the presence of God. I claim only that trying to abide firmly in that presence is probably the thing most thoroughly worth doing, and the most life-giving matrix for anything else that is to be done. All of this will come into question in the rest of this book: what "God" means, how to figure out what living in God's presence would be and how to go about getting there, why it matters, how it can be done honestly, what we can receive and give in doing it. I start with a candid admission of what I long suspected and feared might be true and hoped was not:

Not everyone needs to recognize God.

Some people get along quite well—not only seem to get along, but actually do get along quite well—without ever having a thought about God, or, after having thought a while about God, setting the thoughts aside either regretfully but decisively, as children come to drop thoughts about Santa Claus, or with the settled relief that comes with setting aside thoughts about vampires and boogeymen. In fact, those who still think about God have usually dropped a lot of thoughts with regret and relief—regret at the loss of the fanciful God who was expected to protect them from all hurt and stuff their lives with rewards and gifts, and relief at the loss of the equally fanciful God who threatened to punish them bitterly for offending him or for failing to live up to his (the "him" and "his" were always part of the original deal) unreasonable expectations. Over the years, I have thought, and then dropped, approximately thirty-seven successive editions of God. I have cringed before some of them, manipulated others, defied a few, ignored some, and in a few cases tried to think about it as little as possible, for fear that God would disappear if thought about much. And indeed, approximately thirty-six editions of God did disappear. I don't miss them. I now feel persuaded that God will not disappear, whatever may happen to my current and future editions, and I want to think about God in a way that will take that into account: what would it be like to think about God in a way that will not collapse under inspection, that can face up to everything and stand in all weather?

What will stand in all weather? If your reaction is to appeal to the Mighty Fortress, or even the Rock of Ages, then you are demonstrably wrong. The ancient fortresses, however mighty they may once have been, are now delapidated or long since dismantled to build more modest homes. Rocks endure longer, a long time indeed as human lives are measured; the same rock may seem essentially undiminished through generations. But it's only a question of time and perspective. We know that in fact all the rocks are being peeled off and scrubbed away all the time, wind and rain and sun and lichens all taking their gradual toll, so that eventually the bold cragginess of Alps and Rockies and Himalayas will be humbled to the green softness of the Alleghenies and the Maumturks and the Cotswolds, where sheep graze and crops are grown and men and women collect wood for their fires and build shelters against all weather. Almost all weather, that is: in the visitation of the rare but occasional hurricane or lightning bolt, the shelters are rapidly leveled, as what remains of the mountains themselves shall eventually be, and the fires are put out. What will stand in *all* weather?

To answer that, I must first say this: almost all Christians I have known or read about have been exemplars of a small-town religion.

I say that metaphorically, but the metaphor may be better understood if I clarify the way I mean it. I like small towns; I grew up in one and have occasional nostalgia about the coziness of small-townism. You all eat the same things for breakfast, get your hair cut in the same style (perhaps by the same barber), see the same movies, wear the same outfits, share the same values. The wonderful virtue of smalltown is that there is a deep security in knowing that everyone else is very like you—your loyalties are their loyalties, your ways are their ways, and everywhere you look, your life is guaranteed to be sound by the echo of it that comes from nearly all the others.

The discomfort of living smalltown is not the sameness. It is that there is always the knowledge that bigtown is out there, probably calling into question the adequacy of who and what you are. My smalltown swaggered patronizingly in the presence of the tinytowns nearby, but was apologetic and deferential to the nearest bigtown, and scarcely imagined itself to be in the same century (certainly not in the same league) with the national and international Hugetowns. And I am not talking about things like lacking the hotel capacity to host the annual meeting of the American Academy of Religion and the Society of Biblical Literature, or being used to doing without the convenience of having an international church's world head-quarters just down the street. I mean the feeling of incapacity to keep up in conversation with what AAR/SBL convention-goers would perhaps be saying, and the abashing thought of comparing religious notes with a president or chief moderator or archbishop or pope, which are feelings and thoughts that may readily arise in those who have never conversed with archbishops or redaction critics.

Most Christians, even generally well-educated ones, tend to live smalltown religion. That is, they stay in their own groups, reassuring one another that they are living the right way—but always ready to feel under the judgment and in the shadow of some imagined bigtown or even Hugetown alternative that is much more sophisticated, much more up-to-date, frighteningly *modern* in a way that may challenge smalltown religion far beyond its available resilience, as a Minnesota winter will challenge a California wardrobe. Remember that "smalltown" is here a matter of meta-phor and mind-set, not of geography: when I lived in Washington, D.C., and in London, I was smalltown Christian among smalltown Christian native Londoners and Washingtonians who were, like me, concerned about believing the right official things in the same correct way and occasionally glancing over their shoulders, wondering what bigtown Christianity—and even scarier, Hugetown ex-Christianity—might be like. We were usually just as glad not to exercise our curiosity about such matters, uneasy about what we would find and what it might possibly cost.

There is indeed something to be paid, I eventually discovered, but it does not threaten bankruptcy—at least not the bankruptcy of the real company we want to keep. This book is about the cost, and also about what can be bought by paying it. It publishes what I take to be bad news and good news about the standard Christian smalltown uneasiness over what goes on in bigtown religious thought, and about what the routines of belief and wor-ship really accomplish even at home. The bad news is that traditional smalltown Christianity, as it is believed and practiced in Good Thunder and in Manhattan, in the quiet streets of Podunk and in the midst of the whirl of Metropolis, is apparently, alas, almost as false as many of the participants sometimes restlessly suspect. The good news is that it is false not the way charlatans and hypocrites are false, but rather as affected accents and gaudy jewelry and shoes that are too tight for a comfortable stroll or too formal for a homey celebration are false. Those who fear that the semblance of truth would vanish from Christian belonging if we looked closely need not worry about it. That's not one of the things that collapses under careful scrutiny; it is more sturdy than the fear supposes. Truth and life are genuinely there, and it would not take as much adjustment as we may anxiously suppose to eliminate the falsity and thus to make that belonging better and more true. It may be made as true as Yes! as we give the inheritance to our great-grandchildren. It can be built to stand in all weather.

But there is work to be done. This book is meant to be about the work, and to be part of it.

THE TRADITION OF LANGUAGE: AN APOLOGY FOR CREATIVE UNORTHODOXY

Matters of belief and faith are hardly the whole of Christianity, but they are clearly of central importance in the Christian tradition and have been central from its very beginning. That does not mean that they have been well understood. I think that they have in fact been rather poorly understood, and that we need both to reconsider what we mean by "belief" and "faith" (that will be the main business of this chapter) and to reconsider the status of some of the traditional objects of belief and faith (that will be the task of Chapters 4–6). But before tackling those questions, there are a couple of still more elemental issues underlying them, and they are the focus of the next part of this chapter: care about our use of language.

These issues are reflected in the subtitle of this book's first part, "Do Christianities True?" This is not a misprint nor an aimless bit of playful provocation. It is a serious question put in an unorthodox form that is intended to be very much to the point. That is not to say that it is a heretical question. It is unorthodox in the sense of being odd, unconventional, not the way it's usually done—as when one says that Henry Ford's manufacturing technique was unorthodox, or that there was something unorthodox about Mao Tse-tung's way of conducting a communist revolution, or that Dick Fosbury developed an unorthodox style of high-jumping. I will attend later to the more orthodox question "Is Christianity true?" and will in the course of doing so offer some observations that may strike some readers as unorthodox in the other sense, i.e., heretical, illegal, dangerously wrong. But for the moment, I wish to linger briefly on the unorthodoxy of the question, not of the possible answer: "Do Christianities true?"

One part of the point of the unorthodox form lies in the use of the plural, Christianities, as a reminder of a fact that we usually suppress by using the singular: Christians do not now, and never really did, constitute a unified and harmonized body. To speak of "Christianity" is usually as misleading as analogous generalizations about "the Victorians" or "contemporary music" or "what women think." Decently well-informed people are quite aware that representatives of various Christian denominations have often demonstrated bitter disagreements and intense rivalries about what Christianity is, and that various Christian churches define themselves in terms of their specific rejections of the views of other Christian churches—and yet the same people are capable of speaking of Christianity, in the singular, as if Christians are essentially agreed and cooperative in matters of religion, or perhaps as if Christianity means my religion plus others' imitations (however distorted) of it.

The reality is of course much more various and disordered, and the language we use for talking about it should try to remember that truth. The singular will do when isolating what the various Christianities have in common that distinguishes them from other religious traditions, but in focusing on the Christian world, it seems to me better to stay explicitly aware of its multiplicity in order to think about it more accurately than the conventional singular invites, and I will accordingly use the plural whenever I think it important to remember the pluralistic reality it reflects.

Unorthodox language may sometimes seem unnecessarily playful or pedantic, but it should not too easily be dismissed as such. The words we use have a powerful effect on our understandings of the matters we discuss, and can create and preserve important inaccuracies or deformations of those understandings. This is not a trivial problem, and it is worth the trouble of struggling with occasional unconventionalities when the conventional blurs or distorts meaning.

Meanings are often distorted, disguised, or diminished by what gets imbedded in language by deliberate craftiness, or by wishful thinking, or by slow unnoticed change, or by ordinary carelessness. The formality of military jargon is notorious for disguise: "termination with extreme prejudice" manages not to sound like, and seems not to mean, "murder," which is exactly the illusion intended. We have now generally recognized and rejected the distortions embodied in racist language, and are at work on purging the analogous distortions of the sexist equivalents; we may eventually realize more adequately how unwholesome attitudes toward children are insidiously fostered and protected by the ways in which we customarily speak of, and to, them. And the diminishment of values that are casualties of cultural changes may be readily sensed by anyone with a feel for the histories of words. It is now, for instance, extremely difficult to express at all, and certainly impossible through the same words, as much as Shakespeare meant by "kind," or "natural," or "gratitude" (which is, I think, regrettable—not least because of how useful his senses of these words would be for thinking about religious tradition).

Unless we are more than usually careful with the way we use language, we cannot take adequate care of the realities we most cherish. And, ironically, even the way we use language in taking care tends to make it more difficult to be careful. It is partly to our credit, but a source of problems, that we spend our most important words generously, to buy attention and dignity for relatively modest realities. Words that reach to the grandest extremes our imaginations can propose get deployed across a spectrum so large that they become overextended, and begin to show signs of the verbal equivalent of metal fatigue—or at least they lose the brightness that belongs to the rarified atmosphere of their most exalted senses and begin to take on the tarnish that can't be avoided in the smog of the ordinary.

Take *love,* for instance. I cannot, after some reflection, think of a more sublime attempt with this word than the one supplied by 1 Jn 4:16: "God is love, and he who abides in love abides in God, and God abides in him." *Love* is a term whose natural habitat is at least the better side of the ordinary, and which has been much enhanced by the labors of poets, suitors, and the religiously devout. Here it is pressed about as far as it can go, to a place where it both picks up new grandeur and confers some of it on human lovers of some sort. But just *which* sort is rendered unhappily unclear by the fact that the key word is used rather promiscuously at the other end of the spectrum. Tammy's in love, I love Paris in the springtime, Sarah loves applestrudel. Worse yet, it is trivialized and distorted by giddy tumescence, unscrupulous guile, and coy euphemism, and is used to name what is more properly called lust, or exploitation, or what another euphemism calls "the facts of life." It would have been inconsiderate of Robert Browning actually to have asked his wife to explain how she loved him; but if he did, it is understandable that she might wish to clarify her sense of the term, given the possibilities for misunderstanding. He who abides in just *what* abides in God? And given how many and conflicting ways the word *God* is used, how much would we learn if we figured out the answer?

But let me go back to the original question, "Do Christianities true?" The plural is unorthodox for the purpose of bumping the language, and therefore the perception, closer to the reality, and that is a quirk that will appear from time to time elsewhere in the language of this book. The other unorthodoxy of the question is the use of *true* as a verb, and is meant even more pointedly to raise the issue that will be the major concern of the next chapter—namely, how we may appropriately use the word *true* when talking about Christianities and about our relationship to what they offer. For the purposes of the present chapter, let it suffice to note that *true* is a legitimate and important (though neglected) verb—meaning, roughly, "set right, make straight, shape up"—and that I intend to lean on it throughout this book. But now, back to "belief" and "faith."

ON NOT CONFUSING BELIEF WITH FAITH

In *The Gathering of the Ungifted,* I deliberately and explicitly chose to ignore distinctions between faith and belief, because I was dealing with specific problems that the intended readers shared with me, in which the traditional Christian tendency to use the terms interchangeably was not a serious difficulty and was best accepted as a given. In this book, I am addressing different problems, which have as much to do with the well-being of Christianity and of my great-grandchildren as with your well-being and mine, and in this case the difference between faith and belief is of paramount importance.

The Christian tradition has blurred the distinction between the two from very early times. Of course, any commentator on the earliest extant Christian writings, the letters of Paul, will rightly insist that Paul did not use the Greek word *pistis* to mean simply "belief," but rather employed it in close conjunction with his vigorous use of the verb *pisteuô* to indicate a form of self-engagement, a submissively self-giving obedience rather than an intellectual assent. Nevertheless, the Epistle of James, as it addresses a point about which Paul is very outspoken—i.e., the relationship between *pistis* (faith) and *erga* (works)—clearly uses *pistis* and *pisteuô* to mean something like "mere belief," observing that even the demons have it, and it is of little help to them (Jas 2:19). James treats the controversy about faith and works, which was a deeply divisive question in some parts of the early Christian world and probably in antecedent Jewish controversies,[2]+ as if it is obvious that *pisteuô* means "believe," and shows no sign of being aware that Paul's use of the terms is significantly different—and whatever your opinion of James (which is likely to be lower than it should be), this epistle is part of the New Testament and bears witness to an early Christian way of talking about what faith means.[3] In that epistle, it means "belief."

Most of the earliest Christians were religious Jews who saw their Christianity as a completion of their Judaism. Their basic ways of thinking about their Christianity naturally had much in common with the thinking of non-Christian Jews, but since the latter trusted in God but not in the Messiahship, resurrection, and eventual judgeship of Jesus, which kept the two groups apart, there was a natural Christian drift toward emphasis on articles of special belief. Subsequent Christian tradition attempted to preserve something like the Pauline meaning by distinguishing, e.g., between belief *in* and belief *that,* but in overall Christian religious culture, the meaning of "faith" continued to be absorbed into the meaning of "belief." Despite honorable attempts to keep the terms distinct, they were, and are, confused—sometimes deliberately, as Christian writers occasionally alleged that a faithful trust in God should entail accepting and believing certain specifically Christian claims.

Questions of belief have been a constant preoccupation in the Christian world since those earliest days. Now and again, there have been pivotal controversies about ritual, about the liturgical calendar, about legality or morality or discipline, but the dominant theme in Christian self-understanding has been the theme of orthodoxy, right belief. Corrective attempts to discriminate a sense of "faith" different from "belief" have not on the whole been successful.

The English language reinforces this equation between faith and belief through an unfortunate deficiency in its otherwise unusually rich vocabulary. English lacks a verb corresponding to the noun *faith:* there is no clean English way to translate Paul's use of the verb *pisteuô*. This deficiency is normally supplied (partly because of the theological and popular tendency to confuse the two) by using the verb *believe*. By simple linguistic habit, consolidated by theological bias, English-speakers,[4+] when they move from noun to verb, automatically register that their religious *faith* is, when they want to describe it in action, expressed by *what they believe*. English can, of course, express belief in persons, in causes, in ideals; but there is a tendency to move to another vocabulary for such things, and to speak of trust, conviction, belonging, identification. Religious faith thus becomes confounded with belief, and a standard synonym of "religion," enshrined in law as well as in high rhetoric, is "creed." A religion is accordingly defined by its beliefs, and most Christians, if asked to explain in what Christian faith consists, are likely to respond by listing articles of belief.[5+]

This state of affairs introduces two serious problems.

One is that this is not a healthy way of defining a religion, be it Christianity or any other. Beliefs are certainly part of the fabric of religious belonging, but they are not the substance of religious life. To make them central is, to my mind, as great an error as defining a religion by its styles of prayer or its ethical traditions, both of which surely must count in any sound description of its reality but should not be mistaken for the heart of the matter. Christianity is not its creeds: the creeds are merely instruments of Christian realization, along with other instruments, and they are not necessarily the most effective, stabilizing, or permanent elements of the Christian repertoire, nor are they necessarily the best way of locating what is important to be faithful to. A Christianity's truth, and its power to true, cannot be expected to reside exclusively, or even especially, in what makes it different from other religions or from other variants of Christianity. Belief is overrated in the Christian tradition.

The second problem is manageable if we resolve the first one, but it is otherwise almost overwhelming. It is that much of traditional Christian belief appears, in the light of the critical investigations of the last two centuries and in the light of a massive shift in Christian thought about other religions in the last few decades, to be unsound, unreliable, even untrue. There is no changing this result. It is not a mistake that can be corrected or a temptation that can be resisted. It is a realization that must be faced. We must learn how to take responsibility for it. And taking responsibility will involve changing some long-cherished beliefs and surrendering others.

That is why it is urgent that we reconsider what belief is, and how it relates to faith, and what kind of foundations it rests on, and what sort of claim its traditions have on us. If we can understand that loyalty to Christianity is not the same as loyalty to its customary beliefs, and if we can understand that loyalty to the Christianity of our great-grandparents is not more important than loyalty to the Christianity of our great-grandchildren, then we can perhaps summon the honesty and courage to do what needs to be done.

For this is not simply a time of threat for the Christian tradition: it is a time of opportunity, a transitional time that may turn out to be no less historically crucial than the patristic period, in which the tradition that we have received was consolidated, nor less crucial than the time of the Reformers, in which the tradition was importantly redefined, nor less crucial than even the apostolic period, in which the first interpretations of what had happened were laid down. Be that as it may, it is a time with tasks to be done, and some of the most important of the tasks have to do with the reconsideration of beliefs and of belief itself, because there is reason to think that these have been misunderstood and dangerously overrated in the Christian tradition.

In subsequent chapters, I will attempt to explain and to deal with some of the problems of specific endangered beliefs. In the rest of this one, I want to confront the key element of the overall problem by distinguishing belief from faith.

THE MEANING OF FAITH

Faith is not belief.[6+] Beliefs are often held with fidelity, loyalty, trust, and it is understandable that the term *faith* gets carelessly used where *belief* is the proper word. But the carelessness is regrettable, and the resulting confusion has caused too much needless pain, loss, and even death. Faith is no more identical with belief than loyalty is identical with opinion.

Faith is how one is in love with what is true and real, and is the foundation and matrix of the quality and meaning of one's life. It is not something that happens merely in the intellect, or merely in the emotions, or merely in the will, but rather a condition of the whole person. It is not the content of what one trusts, or of what one accepts or of what one loyally affirms despite opposition (although the nature of that content will certainly make a difference in the *quality* of faith), but rather the sustained habit of trusting, accepting, and loyally affirming. It is the vitality of the Yes! through which one engages oneself in a self-giving that at once affirms who one is, defines what one chooses to be, and establishes the nature of the reality to which one is committed. Faith is essentially an active receptivity and self-engagement, a responsive and responsible readiness to accept, affirm, value, and even love whatever is really given and whatever one invites into realization.

Faith is not belief; it is a total self-disposition that addresses everything real and true, the appropriate response to the notion expressed in Gn 1:31: God looked upon everything that he had made, and ah! it was good. Faith looks upon reality—or, in traditional religious language, upon God and God's creation, all that is—and welcomes it as good, however troubled or inconvenient or unfinished or crippled or perilous it may be. The welcome extended by faith is deeper than understanding; it is the ground in which understanding takes root. It conditions all the ways in which we appropriate reality and truth, and thus conditions our becoming real and true. Faith is the condition by which we belong to the real, and it to us. It is the proud and devoted patriotism of a consciousness that takes all of reality as its country.

Well, *ideally* proud and devoted: for faith admits of degrees. Everyone has it, but in the way that everyone has health—the best way to have it is robustly, but it may be shaky, precarious, enfeebled, close to expiry. The acceptance of reality can similarly be qualified, suspicious, skeptical, begrudging, even hostile; it can withhold assent from some things despite their credentials for claiming to be real and true, or withhold approval of realities out of spite because they are not what we might reasonably prefer. Faith can be small, weak, stunted, stingy, or paralyzingly (as distinguished from wholesomely and productively) discontent, but it cannot be altogether absent if there is consciousness at all.

Faith need not take a conventionally religious form; it need not include a notion of God even in persons whose openness to reality is generous and compassionate (though I will have more to say on that subject in later chapters). But faith is essentially religious in an unconventional sense: it determines the quality of one's engagement with life and thus one's capacity for life, and seems accordingly to be a better index of one's religion than an inventory of creeds and rituals. Your religion, that is, is more essentially determined by your faith than by your belief. It is in fact not improper to say that the nature and practical expression of your faith define your religion, whatever your beliefs may be. Even if one of your beliefs is that all religion is nasty, that belief is symptomatically expressive of your faith and indicative of *your* unorthodox religion, like it or not.[7]+

IMAGINATION

To put it another way, faith is the temperament of *imagination*,[8]+ the way we relate to what imagination brings; and imagination is how we enter reality and permit it to enter us.

Imagination is the primary act of consciousness, the enactment of our sense of what is or what has been or what may be, together with their interconnections. Imagination is structured awareness, the awareness of ourselves and of whatever is not ourselves: seeing with the mind's eye and dancing to the heart's music. It is the mode of consciousness by which we form our grasp of the real and entertain notions of the quasi-real and play with the fanciful—and stay aware of the difference. Imagination is how we have anything at all to think about, and it is how we relate these things to one another in a more or less coherent *world* that is at least partially thought through; it is how we have any content toward which faith may be directed.

It is in imagination that we hold, or construct, the reality to which faith attunes and addresses us. It is thus in imagination that beliefs are proposed, and in imagination that they are cherished, and in imagination that they are critiqued and dismantled. The imagination forms what faith embraces, while faith is what capacitates imagination to do its work of putting us in touch with reality and possibility, truing us to what is—and what may be —there, both within us and outside us. Faith is what allows us to experience in the imagination what is true and what trues, and to value this against what is false and what falsifies. It is by faith, acting through imagination, that we sustain belief that is true and that trues, and it is by faith, acting through imagination, that we discard belief that is false and that falsifies.

I consider this book to be primarily about faith, and about the imagination that is leavened by faith. I am firmly committed to the priority of faith over belief and concerned about the damaging effect that untrue, and untruing, belief can have on the clarity and vitality of faith. I mean to be respectful of traditional Christian beliefs, but respectful does not mean uncritical; and being critical means acknowledging that some traditional beliefs may no longer be honestly sustained.

All beliefs are best rented; to buy is to have too much stake in their market value. Even traditional beliefs are provisional, to be honored to the extent that they are true and true us in mind and heart, in imagination and faith. When they cease to true, and especially when they are a debilitation or injury to faith, faith requires that they be set aside, or reimagined in a different, and truing, way.

THE MEANING OF BELIEF

Belief has three common senses.

One is the sense in which we say "I believe that . . ."—Lizzie Borden did her parents in no matter what the jury said, or vitamin C cures colds, or Burma will win the next World Cup. It expresses conviction that something is or was or will be the case, in a way that can be rephrased as a claim about the truth of some proposition.

A second is the sense in which we say "I believe in . . ."—the work ethic, or the current prime minister, or municipal bonds. Here it is a question of trusting or valuing the object, in a way that can probably be turned into "belief that" propositions that will describe what the trusted or valued item can be counted on to be or to do. The word may sometimes be used simply as an acknowledgment that you are firmly committed or entrusted to something or someone without necessarily being clear about what will result ("I believe in vegetarianism," or "I believe in being candid at all times" may mean no more than "this is how I do things, period")—but under prodding, I guess that the one using it thus will acknowledge that it should either be explicable by "belief that" statements or replaced by a less misleading expression, such as "I heartily approve of," or "I've taken up," or "I'm into."

Third, there is the simple "I believe . . ."—my astrologer, my daughter's explanation, the star defense witness. I think it fair to say that this third variety really comes down to saying either "I believe that what she says is true" or "I believe that she is not lying," and that therefore this sense is also legitimately translatable into "believe that" statements. The second and third senses are thus just dense and explicable variants of the first sense. Accordingly, I will henceforth concentrate on belief as "belief that," which is at any rate the usual mode when *believe* is used in religious contexts.

Belief is, or should be, concerned with truth. It is simply silly to say that someone believes something that she knows to be false, or even that she deeply suspects to be false (she may assert it, even act in accordance with it, but it would be misuse of language to say that she believes it). Belief is a self-alignment with what one takes to be true, a way of truing oneself. The proper use of the word also implies a degree of technical uncertainty; what is self-evident, or rigorously demonstrable, or essentially impossible to question, is not a matter of belief, though the term is sometimes used in an elegantly precious way to cover such cases. One does not say "I believe that $6 \times 9 = 54$" or "I believe that eyes are helpful to good vision" or "I believe that rivers move more swiftly than glaciers." If you assent to what no reasonable person can doubt, you do not call it belief. Belief is a stance that is not inevitable, a judgment that is not simply compelled by what is given. Belief differs from knowledge, though both are ways of taking a stand on what is true.

Belief is not, however, a matter of choice or of feeling, though it is often confused with both. Advocates of particular beliefs not infrequently urge others to accept them, as if one were quite free to do so without further persuasion. But if it were as easy as this, Othello would not have got into so much trouble. Wanting not to disbelieve can conjure up considerable protective power for an established belief, but wanting to believe is feebly insufficient to bring one about. ("I have decided to grow a beard" or "I chose the job closer to home" will work; "I have decided to believe in palmistry" or "Tomorrow, I will choose to believe that children's rights are neglected" will not.) The use of "I feel that . . ." for "I believe that . . ." properly registers that feelings often enter into the formation of judgments, but improperly omits the judgment itself by which feeling is transformed into belief. Belief often takes place without such judgments being explicit: it is frequently experienced as just a happening, an automatic assessment, a disposition that circumstances simply bring about and that, once established, operates in a stable and regular and implicit, and often unconscious, fashion.[9]

Much of religious belief (though by no means all) is conscious, and most of it is originally far from spontaneous. One does not normally come to believe that God is a trinity of persons in one nature, or that the glorified Christ will return in judgment, in the same way one comes to believe that budgeting one's funds is desirable or that you *really* can't fool all of the people all of the time. Most of us are told what to believe at an early age, and do so because it is evidently important and no more difficult than the thousands of other things small people must take on trust, being ill equipped to make independent investigations. We are told by larger people who were themselves introduced to these beliefs in the same way, and who very likely have not raised any serious question about them since, or have deliberately resisted and rejected serious questioning. We, and they, usually hold these beliefs in a community of fellow believers who reinforce the sense that these beliefs are a deep part of our identity and are profoundly valuable possessions, threatened by the outside world and capable of being lost but also capable of bringing great reward to those who keep them faithfully.

What guarantees the truth of these beliefs? The question does not usually arise in full force for quite a while. The earlier experience is rather of their *propriety:* and what makes them evidently appropriate beliefs is that they are *ours,* a dimension of who we are, the heirlooms that we most solemnly share and treasure. We take them to be true, because they are beliefs, and that is what the term means; but we take them at all, in the first place, because we belong to them along with family and community. They, and with them the truth they are taken to express, are simply part of what we are given by being embedded there. Their truth is effectually guaranteed by the community of believers.

When the question does arise as to their truth, apart from their social propriety, other members of the believing community are likely to reassure the questioner that their truth is guaranteed by God, through his revelation in the Bible and in history, and especially through his incarnation and work in Jesus, confirmed in the church by the Holy Spirit. Such an answer is normally expected to close the question, an expectation that is not infrequently supported by the suggestion that further questioning would be impious, disloyal, and potentially dangerous.

I think that such a response is inside out, and I would like to turn it the other way around.

Such a response evades an important responsibility. Beliefs differ in some significant ways among varying Christian denominations, to say nothing of the differences between Christian and non-Christian traditions. If beliefs are our way of making contact with truths of the utmost importance, then we must be concerned about discriminating true beliefs from false ones. It is possible to claim that *our* beliefs happen all to be true, through God's mercy or our fidelity or whatever, while many of *theirs* are false; but what such a claim says about us, about them, and about God does not have an obvious ring of plausibility—and if it is, however implausible, true, then there is every reason to subject our beliefs to the kind of closer examination that will undoubtedly vindicate them, strengthen our confidence, glorify God, and provide illumination for those who are in error. And if, by chance, some false beliefs have managed to creep into our tradition, then surely they should be discerned and corrected. To avoid applying tough critical scrutiny to our beliefs, protecting them by taking refuge in a notion of faith that makes them self-validating, is impious, disloyal, and potentially dangerous.

BELIEFS ON TRIAL

Beliefs must stand critical trial, precisely in the name of faith.

The critical examination of a belief may confirm it and overturn the beliefs that oppose it, sometimes surprisingly, as when chemical analysis of what skeptics supposed to be the worthless quack remedies of superstitious and ignorant witch-doctor medicine reveals that the component herbs actually contain impressive amounts of effective medicinals, or a fair trial acquits someone who had appeared clearly guilty in the eyes of everyone but her husband. Archaeological evidence has rehabilitated more than one piece of biblical lore that serious criticism had given up as fictitious; Heinrich Schliemann was scoffed at for his naive trust in Homer's accuracy, unshared at the time by other scholars of the classics, but by following his unfashionable belief, he found Troy.

But if critical investigation sometimes giveth, more often it taketh away. No one now doubts that the Donation of Constantine is a forgery, but until Lorenzo Valla's probings punctured it, it enjoyed centuries of credit and deeply influenced the course of European law. Not everyone was happy to see it exploded. The disqualification of Piltdown man, the Kensington Rune Stone, the poems of Ossian, Hitler's memoirs, and Jesus' true shroud, were all discomforts to some people, but they are all discredited beyond retrieval. Beliefs are like possessions.[10] Even if they seem to have little psychological cash value, once they become even minor parts of our habitual landscape they become part of our stability, and it can be rattling to have to give them up.

It can be surprisingly rattling, in fact, even if there is no obvious way in which they matter much. As I recall, I experienced little trauma in surrendering Jack Frost or the Easter Bunny; letting go of Santa Claus was harder, and I thought up reasons not to; but the debunking of Veronica's miraculously imprinted veil was a decided shock that aroused all my defenses. The difference was made, I think, by whose credibility was eroded in each case, rather than by the intrinsic importance of the beliefs. But merely being used to a belief creates a loyalty to it, and it can be disturbing to discover that there are no penguins in the Arctic or polar bears in the Antarctic or tigers in Africa outside of zoos, even if these matters do not much impinge upon one's goals and values and no one's reputation suffers.

When, however, one is personally involved at a deep level in a belief that has life-shaping power, then the threat of its dismantling sometimes calls up desperate tactics. Leon Festinger's well-known Theory of Cognitive Dissonance[11] was especially inspired by a study of a small cult-group that believed they were about to be rescued from an earthly cataclysm by friendly aliens in a flying saucer. When the saucer did not appear, the believers restored their psychic equilibrium not by concluding that they had been mistaken, but by inventing an explanation for the nonhappening and becoming more public and zealous about their conviction that they were on the right track.[12] No Christian who knows Christian history should find such behavior surprising.

In summary: given the right conditions, we can acquire false beliefs that rest on completely inadequate grounds, without ever bothering to check their credentials; we can develop such intense involvements with and loyalties to these beliefs that to give them up may feel devastating; and as a result, we can show great creative ingenuity and impressive determination in our efforts to hold onto them, even when they are demonstrably unsound.

How do beliefs that are unsound, or at least unnecessary and unfounded, originate? People *do* care about truth, after all, and do not—probably cannot—deliberately persuade themselves that such-and-such is true when they know there is no good reason to think so. So where does the false step come in?

There are several routine ways of taking false steps, most of which are commonplace and relatively uninteresting. Some people lie to those who trust them, and the trusting ones wind up believing, falsely, that the president was not in on the dishonest campaign sabotage or that this brooch is made of 24-karat gold. Others misunderstand what was said in good faith, and are thus convinced (and sometimes convince their friends) that what they sincerely think they have heard carries the authority of the original source. (My friend Barbara, after a conversation with an Armenian priest, reported that he had disclosed that the Armenians have a sacred lake; investigation revealed that he had made a reference to papal authority, calling it by one of its customary names within Catholic circles, the Holy See. When I was a child, Bill Breer, whose father worked in construction, told me that a Caterpillar could knock down a brick wall: I, fascinated—and chagrined at having missed such a wonder in my searches through animal books— asked him where such caterpillars come from, and was the more impressed to learn that they came from a *plant.)* Or someone tells a playful story and the listener somehow fails to realize that it's play; or somebody is curious about where the word "tip" came from and another makes the wild (and inaccurate) guess that it may be the initials of To Insure Promptness, and into the folklore it goes, to be eventually propounded in restaurants all over the English-speaking world as a nugget of sophisticated knowledge.

But more interesting are the beliefs that arise from gradual changes that occur as things are handed down through tradition. People do things in a certain way because it makes sense, and then times change and the way it makes sense disappears but they keep doing it the same way because that's the way they're used to. And they show their children how to do it and their children do it the same way because that's how it's done. And *their* children may be told that it's the best way but they don't know why, and then somebody makes a wild but not totally implausible guess about what might be a good explanation, and eventually the receivers of tradition may be instructed that the now-traditional explanation shows that this is the only really right way to do it.

Sometimes we can catch this process before its origins disappear into unremembered time, and before it hardens into the shape of its invented justifications. A colleague of mine, endowed with the curiosity native to philosophers of religion, watched his wife cut off the end of a ham before putting it in the oven, and asked why she did it. She replied that it was to let the juices out. He remarked that this didn't make sense: surely one should want to keep the juices *in*. She recognized that he was right, and added that she had merely accepted this explanation from her mother, who had taught her how to cook hams. The mother was accessible. When asked, she denied that she had ever said anything about juices, admitting that she had simply picked up this technique from *her* mother, and had never understood why this was the way to do it. Her mother was still living, and the philosopher asked her whether she cut the end off a ham before cooking. "Usually," replied the Ultimate Source of the custom. "My baking pan is too small for most hams."

Modes of acting and modes of understanding get established in religious matters in a similar manner. It starts out making sense—or is done that way just because it has to be done *some* way, and why not like this?—and then it becomes a convention, and then a custom, and then a revered tradition that is solemnly passed on and reverently probed and speculated upon for meaningfulness. The process of transmission works much the same way as in the case of ham-baking and guesswork etymologies, except that in religious transmissions there's always an atmosphere of reverence and solemnity that makes the difference between something getting discolored and something taking on a patina. With hams and folk etymologies, nothing is at stake except convenience and plausibility if anyone raises a question about changing the tradition's mind, and if no one cares to do so, the conventions are often more casually passed on until someone has reason to blow the whistle. In religion, inconvenience becomes solemnized and unintelligibility is transformed into mystery; convention is preserved in reinterpretation, like a bug in amber, and becomes too precious to tamper with.

Thus when it became customary to make the sign of the cross, it had to be done *some* way, and in some places it became customary to use three fingers to make the relevant touches on the forehead, chest, and shoulders. Like most Christian threesomes, this got associated with the Trinity. Those who came from a different tradition that had conventionalized using two fingers were accordingly accused of being heretics[13+]—and the

Monophysites, in defense of their doctrine that Jesus was of divine nature only, adopted the practice of doing it with one finger.

Or take another example, which you may have puzzled over in times past: the Apostle's Creed tells us, and asks us to profess, that Jesus "descended into hell" after his death. Christians may be excused if they find that a bit startling the first time they run into it, and perplexing ever after. It evidently originated in the utterly routine assumption that between his death and his resurrection, Jesus' personal locus was where any traditional Jew would have put it, in Sheol, the biblical place of the dead. This is properly translated "Hades" in the Greek translation of the Hebrew Scriptures, the Hades of Homer's *Odyssey* being in fact very like Sheol. "Hell" was originally a good translation, it having meant "the hidden place," i.e., the underworld, which was presided over (at least in Old Norse) by the goddess Hel. It then got confused with the place of punishment that is called Gehenna in the Gospels and elsewhere, "Hades" too being often reinterpreted in the same way by that time, and Christians started imagining Jesus among the flames. What was he doing for those three days (actually one and a half, if we go by the standard accounts rather than the traditional number, which is put into Jesus' mouth with unreflective literalness in Mt 12:40)? Fairly early in the tradition, it was assumed that he took advantage of the opportunity to preach the good news to those in storage in Sheol (or in torment in Gehenna), to give them either a chance or a reprieve or both. The classic New Testament locus for this supposition is 1 Pt 3:19, on which later commentators especially built. It shows up in a creed in 359, but was probably present in earlier Syrian creeds that have not survived; it then makes desultory appearances in other creeds over the next couple of centuries, and finally gets firmly ensconced in the Apostles' Creed, whence it made its way into Christian profession all over the West.[14] We were supposed to believe it, and mainly still are, though hardly anyone I know gives it much emphasis anymore, or really cares about it. Nor should they: however officially creedal, its foundations are as flimsy as the wispy inhabitants of Sheol were thought to be.

The ways we make false steps of belief are also, in short, the ways our predecessors made them, right back to the beginning. We may like to think that the original Christians were privileged to be proof against such mistakes, but the evidence indicates that they too followed the same paths of transmission and stumbled over similar roots and rocks. They were rather like us, and subject to the same missteps. Then, as now, a false belief could be produced in a moment, spread abroad in an afternoon, and lodged in a literal Time Immemorial in the space of three or four uncorrected generations.

It is therefore a mistake—yet another misstep in believing—to suppose that reliably secure foundations for belief can be built by going back to our roots and presuming that whatever was apostolic is true.[15] The teaching of the Apostles does not give us the real roots of Christianity. The real roots are the career and the gospel of Jesus, and apostolic teachings are only *interpretations* of Jesus, some of them of doubtful appropriateness.[16+] They have a partial advantage in lying close to the roots, as tubers do, but should not be mistaken for the roots themselves. Most apostolic beliefs are more like potatoes than carrots, and the plant can live healthily even if some of the tubers are carefully cut away. It is therefore entirely appropriate to subject inherited beliefs to critical reassessment; like many life-sustaining medicines, they should be shaken well before swallowing. Believing, whether in religious or secular matters, is a tricky enterprise and should be pursued with caution.

Since beliefs and practices can be formed without genuinely adequate foundation, it is important to have a mechanism for checking the process and arresting it when it starts generating potentially damaging or divisive falsehood, just as the cellars for maturing and mellowing wine need to be monitored to catch it if the aging process begins to produce expensive vinegar. If the damage is already done, it should be identified and assessed. Expensive vinegar makes good salads, but it is not good form to decant it into the glasses of family and friends to accompany the main course.

We have, at least in our parts of the world, a fairly satisfactory mechanism that is already in place for detecting what should be reconsidered and for undoing what has been falsely done: free critical inquiry, combined with uncensored publication. Budding silliness and blossoming error and blooming idiocy can be spotted and spotlighted in time to warn us away from their ability to do heavy harm; traditional errors and misinterpretations and unfounded speculations can be corrected and the tradition rerouted on a better track.

It doesn't always work that way, as history shows, but it at least can. That is a significant advantage over the cultures in which the Roman Empire rose and fell, and Christian religiousness was originally interpreted and classicized. They did not have newspapers in which reports of significant events of many kinds from all over the world, sometimes searchingly analyzed and usually held accountable by interested and informed writers of letters to editors, could be found daily at the store on the next corner, in a couple or half a dozen alternative forms, and bought by child-tenders and bricklayers preparing to vote in the election of their leaders and lawmakers, for the cost of less than two minutes' wages. They did not have universities through which the children of butchers and seamstresses (and the seam- stresses and butchers too, if they prefer adult-education courses to TV situation comedies and bowling) could learn the skills and techniques of critical thought and be introduced to its best current results—and, if they have appetite and aptitude enough, be trained to be agents of public curios- ity and given the leisure and opportunity to learn and teach and write for enterprising publishers about the formation of traditions two thousand years earlier, in order to help us understand them with a discernment that was not available even to those who were on the scene when they were formed. The people who formed and handed on early Christian tradition did not have such advantages. We, who now have the job of re-forming it and handing it on, do.

We have advantages that may be exploited to undo falsities and fixities that were innocently, but not innocuously, perpetrated long ago and honor- ably—but onerously—handed on by tradition ever after. We have the equipment and procedures for identifying beliefs that should be let go, showing that they never really earned the right to be kept, exposing their unsteady foundations, and dismantling them before someone else gets hurt by colliding with them.

We have what it takes to do the critical preparing. But that is only the first part of the unlearning process, and arduous though it sometimes is, it's the relatively easy part. The hard part is actually learning to let such beliefs go.

LETTING BELIEFS GO

Letting go is not easy, even for trivial beliefs. Important ones may be wrenching to abandon. And no one who can do it easily should suppose that others can casually follow suit. People differ not only in their readiness to let go but in their very *capacities* to do so, even when it seems plain that this is what they ought to do.

The psychological study of individual differences is still in a relatively rudimentary state, but has already produced some helpful results. One rele- vant accomplishment is the distinction between field-dependent and field- independent styles of cognitive processing—which roughly means that in- vestigations indicate that some persons think in terms that relate intensely but narrowly to the apparent context of the here and now, while others are more ranging and versatile in what they bring to bear on a given matter, able to overrule the immediate context through an appeal to wider considerations.[17] The latter are not superior—they do better at some tasks than the former, but less well at others—but it appears that they have a greater tolerance for ambiguity, an easier capacity to suspend or surrender belief, than the former. In one set of experiments, designed specifically to check this out, subjects were given tasks and provided with evaluations of their performance that were really arbitrarily and randomly distributed without reference to how well they had actually done—and then taken aside and told the truth: that the ratings were phony, artificially assigned as part of a psychological experiment. The results showed that field-dependent subjects, unlike the field-independent, tended to persist in believing the truth of the ratings *even after learning that they were unreal.*[18]

The psychological term for such persistence in a behavior or a belief even after one has discovered that it doesn't really work is *perseveration*. Perseverance is a virtue; perseveration is not. It is a caricature of perseverance, since it involves being counterproductively loyal to something that has simply lost its right to loyalty. Our culture has perseverated in sustaining superstitions, luck-lore, and what used to be called old wives' tales, despite (in at least some cases) centuries of consistent opposition by the Christian churches and concerted efforts by generations of reasonable critics. The churches, in their turn, have doggedly protected various beliefs despite their having been called powerfully into question by competent and authoritative investigation. All this is understandable, and may be forgiven. But it is not reasonable to perseverate in discredited *credenda*—the outmoded stuff of critically impeached creeds—let alone to continue to demand such perseveration as a condition of authentic belonging.[19!] The practical question is: what is to be done about it?

It may well be that some persons with a certain kind of psychological structure simply are not free to abandon their personally important beliefs without undergoing disorienting disturbance—possibly (though not probably) not free *at all*. If this is the case, then I should think that it at least behooves the interpreters of belief, especially the pastors, to attempt to make sure that such *credenda* are interpreted so that they can be understood in a way that is fit for human consumption. But it also behooves the theologians and the teaching authorities of the churches to be more concerned than they have traditionally been not to retain unqualifiedly on their agenda of instruction beliefs that have been critically unsettled. The authoritative promotion of a belief is not like assessing loyal parishioners with an additional psychic pew tax that may be canceled without difficulty if it proves inconvenient: for many of them, it will be like creating a physical dependency that can't be overcome without a painful process of withdrawal.

Let those who influence the next stage of tradition be wary. What was good enough for your great-grandfather is not necessarily good enough for you, and may be offensive or pernicious for your great-grandchildren. No belief should be passed on without critical scrutiny. Longevity and persistence in a belief-tradition is certainly an argument in its favor, but hardly a sufficient argument. At the very least, the official inventory of Christian teaching needs to be reviewed and adjusted.

But whatever may take place at official levels, individual Christians have their own weeding out to do if they care about their truth. And for individual cases, among persons who feel anxious about following through with their honest conclusions that this belief, though traditional, is probably wrong, and that one, though cherished, is highly doubtful, I offer a little calculus of detachment that has been found helpful by people with whom I have used it.

Suppose you know, or discover, that belief X (which you happen to be fond of and loyal to) has fallen under such unsettling critical question that it is now largely discredited and possibly untenable. You are reluctant to allow yourself to disbelieve, though it appears that it might be dishonest or cowardly to cling to this belief in the circumstances. What do you do?

I suggest that one helpful response is to follow a procedure consisting of four—or five—brief steps.

1. Ask yourself what value you attach to this belief, what you instinctively think it implies. (Take, for instance, Matthew's popularly cherished tale of the visitation of the Magi to the infant Jesus, which biblical scholars now quite generally think a romantic fiction based on reverent piety but not on real history. Are you used to believing that it happened and to supposing that it shows that Jesus was the Messiah? or that he was both human and divine? or that the Gentiles were invited to salvation? Find out what you personally are used to thinking about its implications, and move to the next step.)

2. Look at belief X closely: does it really imply what you are used to getting from it? (It usually takes a surprisingly short time to realize that, while you have habitually associated belief X with implication Y, X does not in fact mean or entail or in any way prove Y. Real historical visiting

magi do not in fact prove Messiahship or imply divinity or lead to any conclusions whatever about Gentile salvation. If you look closely at Mt 2, you can see that not even the original author draws such conclusions.)

3. Is there any other way of arriving at Y without depending on X? (Again, it normally requires less than a minute to discover that conclusion Y, which is where the real goodies are, can be arrived at by a route that is quite independent of belief X. There are other grounds on which Messiahship, divinity, and salvation of Gentiles can be argued. If that's where you want to go, you don't need magi, with or without camels, to take you there.)

4. What would it cost to put belief X on hold, register it as doubtful, or simply accept it as nothing but a pious invention? (By this time, the price is likely to seem trivial, however great it may have appeared three minutes previously. So maybe the Magi are a piece of romantic fiction: big deal. They are, as Mary Meagher observed in a precocious reflective moment many years ago, "too cute to throw away," and may be kept as a witness to early pious invention and modern pious playfulness even if admitted to be otherwise unhistorical.)

This is perhaps far enough to take the process for the purpose of reducing or resolving the tension arising from threatened belief. But for the thorough and the curious, there is one more step:

5. What does it cost to keep belief X?

This is a more demanding question. We are often mistaken about the implications of a given belief, valuing it either consciously or unconsciously for other things that we wrongly suppose it to entail, and may be surprised to discover that belief X does not automatically give us result Y. But we are also mistaken in another way.

Beliefs often *do* have implications that we don't consciously notice, and if accepting belief X does not really take us to the desirable Y, it may nevertheless leave us embarrassingly stuck with an undesirable Z. If I seriously believe that I have a lucky number, I must eventually, if I take responsibility for thinking it through, face questions about how the numbers are assigned and how they are endowed with the power of luck and how this power manages to circumvent randomness and lotteries' security procedures. If I manage to think up a world where all of this would work, it will probably not resemble the world I live in, nor be a world that I would like to inhabit. I have a friend who believes that Arnold Ehret's fruit diet has made her much healthier, which may be true; but when she goes further and insists that its success can be credited to Ehret's having made revolutionary discoveries about how the human body *really* works, I observe that if she believes this, she must lose confidence in all of modern (and most of ancient) physiology, since if everyone before Ehret failed to discover that blood is pumped through the system by the lungs, the heart being only a valve, we can hardly trust their reports on anything.[20]

Beliefs do have implications, and we should be careful about them. They cannot be responsibly acquired and retained as if they didn't cost anything. Religious beliefs that at first seem to be appropriately pious may, after a little closer inspection, turn out to be quite the opposite. The rush of gratitude in someone who unexpectedly recovers from a malady that had baffled the doctors leads readily to the belief that God stepped in to accomplish what was beyond human means. Family and friends may reverently concur. But if they push their thinking beyond the boundaries of this happy case, they must make the awkward discovery that to see this recovery as God's intervention means that they must see the unhappy death of the young mother next door as a case in which God declined to intervene. You can't have the one without the other. Accept the recovery as miraculous, and you're stuck with the withholding of an intervention. The resulting image of God is not obviously an image to stir up extravagant praise for the quality of infinitely generous mercy. Such a miracle may turn out to cost dearly if responsibly entertained.

Those who do not care about theological coherence or the deeper practicalities of piety may settle for saying with a shrug that we can have such a miracle without awkward consequences if we merely acknowledge that God's will is inscrutable and his ways not our ways. Those who wish to take more responsibility for their thinking are obliged to raise a question about whether it is fair to suppose that God intervenes in such cases, given what this must imply about the divine morality if an apparently still more desirable intervention is withheld elsewhere. Immediately on its heels is another question about whether it is possible to respect, or even to credit, the image of a God whose selectivity of action results in the withholding of interventions that no decent or respectable person would withhold. It is not edifying piety to acknowledge that God's ways are not our ways if it results in making God's ways seem morally outrageous. To give serious credence to such an image of God is bound to have an effect on one's faith, and I do not suppose that it would be for the better. Please do not dismiss this as simply a small-minded objection to the way God works, uttered by a person who has no sense of the divine grandeur and mystery: it is the expression of a profound doubt that God in fact works that way, and a plea for a reconsideration of some of our routine and casual beliefs about God that in fact defame under the guise of piety. It is a plea entered against some kinds of belief, in the name of faith.

BELIEVING AS BELOVING

The adjustment may properly begin with a reconsideration of what we ought to mean by religious belief in the first place. *Belief* is, in fact, one of those words that have quietly shifted in meaning between the time that they became important and the time in which we now wrestle with what they demand of us. Wilfred Cantwell Smith's investigation of the meaning of "belief" in various religious traditions[21+] resulted in some surprising and illuminating discoveries. His own summary of the central substance and fundamental contribution of his *Belief and History* is the demonstration "that the words 'belief,' 'believing' have drastically changed their meanings since they were used as central religious terms," and that "until recent times no one affirmed that it was religiously important to believe" various notions that are now matters of contention, since they were taken as known, or presupposed, or simply neglected.[22+] That is, we were originally asked not to become loyal, and stay loyal, to beliefs that were difficult, but to get on with what we accepted on apparently good authority to be the case, to be true to what is given in reality—to be faithful to what faith, not belief, asks of us.

It would be an exaggeration to say that the usual Christian sense of belief is a modern invention. When the fourth-century Nicene Creed enjoins faith in the consubstantiality of Jesus Christ with the Father, it is evidently proclaiming that this is a truth commanding our allegiance and our belief, and it clearly means to rebuff as untrue the alternative belief of Arius and his followers, who held that Christ, though almost unimaginably great and glorious, was metaphysically subordinated to the Father.

Were the Arians totally persuaded by the council's decree, thinking that they had been proved wrong rather than just officially disqualified? Probably not, in most cases: they had arguments as good as those who won the final vote. But just *how* such a belief was held in the fourth century is not the issue,[23+] since we are concerned not with imitating the ancients but with honoring their views appropriately from our own time, in which we cannot share all their suppositions about what is true. If we should no longer find sufficient grounds for confidence in the affirmation by the Apostles' Creed that Jesus descended into hell after his death, what is the best we can do in coming to terms with this honorable but no longer quite credible element of the tradition?

The etymological root of *belief* is the lost Indo-European *lubh*—,[24] "to hold dear," whence we get such words as *lief* and *love*. The root notion seems to be to cherish, to "belove"—a word now regrettably gone from the living language, except in its past participle, beloved. That is a rather attractive alternative potential sense of "believe," and I would consider it a great gain in religious health if we could restore more of this sense to a word that has, in its more restrictive meaning, caused so much grief. There are historical assertions in the creeds and other professions of belief that will not hold up as the facts they purport to be, and nonhistorical assertions that seem both arbitrary and polemically high-handed (and thus unnecessarily divisive) as official truths. I think some of them should be changed, and others abandoned, when it comes to what we affirm as true; but even these articles may be *beloved* in their original form, entertained respectfully as having claims to dignity even if not to truth, honored for their having been manifestations, however imperfect, of sincere faith. One can still affirm them as such in good faith, even when belief in the usual modern sense is impossible to conjure up.

We may reverently approach the caves of Lascaux and Altamira to admire the prehistoric paintings on their walls, without supposing that we could be comfortable living there; we may contemplate with awe the remarkable and long-useful astronomical achievements of Ptolemy without wishing that they be substituted for the post-Copernican version now in place; we may treasure an early Christian ivory that shows Jesus' feet poking earthward through a cloud at his ascension, or pray before an icon depicting Jesus' celestial crowning of his mother, without being constrained to think that these scenes actually once took place; and we may cherish what the tradition of belief offers us without being bound to affirming its truth.

The Turin shroud was long revered by many Christians, Catholic, Orthodox, and Protestant, as a true relic. Many believed that it was the shroud in which Jesus had been buried and through which he burst forth into resurrection. It has now been disqualified, having been dated to the Middle Ages by the most rigorous of modern carbon-14 tests. What is its status now?

I suggest that it may still be religiously beloved as an icon of the entombment of Jesus in death, the most widely cherished image of that event that the Christian tradition has ever produced. It would not be right to continue to suppose it a true relic of that event, but it would surely be appropriate to continue to revere it for what it has become through the devotion of the faithful, an image that objectifies what that event means. Many traditional beliefs are like the Turin shroud, hallowed by their history even if no longer able to inspire confidence in their truth. Although disqualified as facts, they may legitimately survive as icons. We may, and probably should, continue to belove them. More should not be asked.

I am told that Bishop James Pike said of some questionable portion of doctrine, "I'll sing it, but I won't sign it." That strikes me as not a bad formula for according proper respect to what may have nourished our forebears but no longer feeds us. We should honor what once inspired the church precisely because it did so, because it was once near the center of the religious life that has been passed down to us and close to the roots even if not really part of them. We should honor it not patronizingly, but with faith's awe at how precious it was, how it was fought for, how many lives were spent in its defense, how many lives were edified by contemplating, savoring, and preserving it, and how many lives may still find a way of being helpfully touched by it. But we should not suppose ourselves required to imitate the imaginations that held to be true what we can no longer find so. We honor the faith that supported traditional beliefs, and look to it for guidance and inspiration, but we must do so with an integrity that will not require our own provisional beliefs to be set aside merely because they disallow beliefs of our predecessors. The faith that animates us makes its own demands, and the imagination that is built with care may not properly be required to defer to another with inferior critical credentials.

Christianity is now in a state of bad faith. Experience, both critical and personal, tells us something different from traditional belief. And "this gap between belief and experience can become a limbo of unreality that is only too easily institutionalized. It can even attract us in the way unreality does, because it is well-populated by those who have agreed not to tell the truth to each other—the world of complacent piety or of intolerant self-righteousness. A place of slow dying and protracted suffering, it defends the half-life that masquerades as truth."[25] Despite the stern rigor with which the tradition has demanded that we persevere (or perseverate) in "unchangeable" beliefs, we must, in the name of faith, recognize that the more authoritative voice of truth may call us to a different stance. "The forms in which our beliefs exist and in which they are expressed are always in the process of passing away—the mind has here no abiding city; only in the heart can we find the enduring reign of God. Whatever has form, like our beliefs or bodies, is always in transition to a new form."[26+]

The Christian tradition is always in transition. That is what tradition means: a transition, a handing-on, from one time to another, from generation to generation, the transition from one Christianity to the next one in the succession of time. In tradition, there is always stability; but there is also, almost always, a measure of change, adjustments and adaptations that keep the tradition from becoming opaque and fossilized. The adjustments are rarely quite sufficient to keep the tradition entirely alive: hardly anyone now remembers that "goodbye" was originally a blessing, or sees much meaning in tossing rice at a wedding, or is clear about the appropriateness of eggs and fancied rabbits at Easter. But those traditions are too marginal to matter. Change is vastly more important in a tradition that is intended to be the matrix of our deepest and fullest life.

We are the present stage of Christian tradition. We have the opportunity of attending to its sense of faith and of belief as we hand it on to those who come after us. We have the task of discerning what is true and what is truing according to our judgment and experience. And we have the responsibility of trying not only to keep it alive, but also to make it life-giving and to transmit it with vitality. We have the chance of passing on to our great-grandchildren a Christianity that will stand in all weather, as the Christianity I received will not. There is much reconsidering to be done. It must be done now. And it must be done in good faith, for which bad belief is no substitute.

2

TRUTH,

AND SOME

CONSEQUENCES

There are two ways to visit a zoo.

I have never outgrown the way I learned as a child among the modest collection of cages in Sibley Park, where I pondered the odd name and shape of the coatimundi, admired the disdainful nobility of the lounging lion, and thrilled with safe terror at my glimpses of the reputedly dangerous bear who usually lurked in darkness and mystery in the recesses of his den. Behind their fences, the sullen deer and antelope did not play and the mangy bison did not roam, but they conjured up visions of the mythical home on the range all the same. I secretly longed to have one of the monkeys as a pet, even though I had often heard the solemn and scary tale of one having bitten my aunt's finger long ago. And sometimes my sister and I took home a couple of the white rabbits for the summer, gave them improbable names, and held out carrots to them as we cuddled them or followed their slow hopping across the lawn. I read all the books I could find on the animals of the world, fascinated by their names and appearances and habitats and diets, and wished that our zoo were more lively and inclusive. But at the zoo, I did not study the animals. I watched and savored them as wonderful things, imaginable pets, dim windows to an incomprehensibly vast and varied world.

It was only many years and zoos later that I learned that *zoo* is short for *zoological garden,* and that to some of those who visited behind the scenes it was a laboratory for seeing animals quite differently. I eventually dipped into zoology in a formal way, and learned how to get beyond contemplating the mystery and fear and potential pets, but I never got behind the scenes in the zoological garden. I never quite learned to see its animals more technically and systematically in a place where the range is not home and there is many a discouraging word about fatal diseases and endangered species and failures to breed in captivity as the zoologists study what the beasts are really like beyond the romance, and what may be done to ensure their survival.

In the meantime, I had learned two ways of knowing Christianity.

The first, and by far the more important to me, was as one who belonged to it, who had been graciously and mysteriously transformed in baptism before all memories and who prayed and believed and hoped, and tried unsuccessfully to love well, in accordance with that blessed calling to more abundant life.

The second was as a theologian, attempting to understand the origins and foundations of Christian belief and hope and to find ways to refine and consolidate that understanding for my own mind and for the minds of my students, my colleagues, my children.

It is not altogether obvious how these two ways of knowing Christianity are related. One may be a Christian without being a theologian. It is also possible to be a theologian without being a Christian. One may be an animal fan without being a zoologist, or a political theorist without belonging to a political party, and vice versa.

But if you are a serious member of a political party, and aspire not only to electing a few of its representatives but also having its values and ideals prevail, then it should matter whether those values and ideals are politically realistic. You have to become, or at least team up with, a theoretician who can think through the systematic implications (however inept she may be at systematic implementation). A dream of simultaneously reducing the national debt, lowering taxes, and expanding government spending on welfare, housing, and defense is a dream only. Any one of these taken alone could, if promised, become embarrassing if the party is elected and must deliver. But genuine concern for the ideals and goals of the party does not wait for the test of power: it thinks out the possible in advance, and makes its hard choices. It does not promise what is unreal, and does not dream about what cannot be done.

Theology has regularly, in times past, undertaken to articulate and defend the beliefs and hopes of the Christian tradition, including its uncritical claims and promises. Now it seems progressively clearer that theology would serve better by helping to make those promises and claims less uncritical and more realistic.

As theology has increasingly pursued that course, it has become steadily more evident that the traditional understandings of Christianity—be they the understandings of the New Testament or of the Reformers or of the Roman Catholic magisterium—can no longer be sustained by a theology that is intellectually honest. Theologians must choose whether to invest their loyalty in the preservation of what is traditional, orthodox, customary, or in the discernment of what is viable, accountable, reliable. The difference grows increasingly stark.[27+]

The pattern of assumptions the Christian tradition is used to is no longer credible enough to guarantee the survival of its honest respectability. Over the next chapters, I will deal with this in greater detail; for the moment, I want to say three things about the situation in general.

First, I am not claiming that it is impossible to sustain traditional Christianity, or that it has become absolutely unbelievable. Hardly anything is absolutely unbelievable. Despite the difficulties that have been raised, it is still possible to sustain traditional Christian belief—so long as one is willing to pay the price it will exact from the coherence and integrity of one's understanding of everything else.

Second, I want to argue that the price required for supporting traditional Christian understandings is too high. Theologically, traditional Christianity is on the verge of bankruptcy and requires massive infusions of implausible belief to keep it from collapsing. Even if Christians on the whole can still come up with the necessary payments, they should—and Christian theologians must—be concerned about the solvency of what is passed on to coming generations. Christianity needs to be intellectually refinanced in some fundamental ways.

Third, I think that a viable Christian understanding can be successfully brought about, though perhaps not painlessly. But it will involve some important changes of habit and orientation. To be loyal to the Christian tradition must now mean to be loyal not to what the churches taught our great-grandparents, but to what they should teach our great-grandchildren. They should not teach distorting untruth as if it were true, or call healing truth dangerously false, and must learn to know, and tell, the difference. Much will have to be surrendered in order to make that transition, and it will be hard to let go. But that can be done, and a stronger faith can take its place. Not a stronger belief, but a stronger faith. And faith is especially dedicated to the cherishing of what is true.

THE MEANING OF TRUE

True is another of those versatile, elusive, chameleon words that merit careful use and close attention. Let me try to sketch some of its anatomy.[28]

The commonsense basic meaning of *true* is "a matter of fact," i.e., how it really is, or was, or will be. For example, $3 + 3 = 6$, P comes after J, Dostoyevsky wrote *The Brothers Karamazov,* I will be retired at sixty-five, and Lizzie Borden was not guilty of murdering her parents.

But common sense is in a bit of trouble if it fails to sort out the differences among these "matters of fact." Let me count the ways.

1. It is true that $3 + 3 = 6$ because it is an automatic implication of what we mean by 3 and by 6. It follows from the system of numbers as a logical inevitability, and simply cannot be imagined to be otherwise.

2. It is true that P comes after J because tradition has conventionally arranged the Roman alphabet (though not all alphabets) in that way. There is no logic in the arrangement to dictate that what we mean by P requires that it come after what we mean by J (quite unlike the case of 6 and 3) and there is no reason in principle why the order could not be rearranged. But until it is, you will not have done your job in a true way if you put the John Jameson folder in your employer's filing cabinet behind the folder on Paddy's. Their true order is their conventionally accepted alphabetical order, no more—but, until further notice, no less.

3. We may say that it is true that Dostoyevsky wrote *The Brothers Karamazov* if and only if he really did it. No one doubts that he did: there is ample evidence to make us comfortable about that. But it is at least playfully *imaginable* that we are mistaken about this, and we can entertain the notion of a vast and clever hoax that allowed Dostoyevsky to pass off as his own something that was actually written by his niece. If convincing evidence of such a thing came forward, we would admit that it is not, and never was, true that Dostoyevsky wrote that book. It could never be doubted within the boundaries of usual arithmetic, even playfully, that $3 + 3 = 6$, and it is impossible to suppose that P never came after J (even if we get a revised alphabet, that was at least true for a while). Dostoyevsky's authorship stands or falls on the evidence: we admit that it (unlike the previous cases) *could* turn out to be utterly untrue, but we have good reason

to think it true. In historical cases like this, evidence and good reason are all we ever get for settling the matter, so the matters are settled with varying degrees of confidence. When we get beyond a reasonable doubt, it is fair to say "true," until reasonable doubts arise with further evidence or other good reasons to support them.

4. If everything goes as presently planned, it is true that I will be retired at sixty-five. But the future, unlike the past, has not taken place, and the intentions and events that we presume will form it may not in fact work out as expected. The laws may change; I may get into another line of work where retirement is not required; I may fall ill and retire early, or die short of sixty-five. Talk about the future is not talk about matters of fact, but rather matters of probability. The varying degrees of confidence with which we can speak about future events resemble our varying degrees of certainty about past events, but the resemblance stops there. "True" is not properly used of the future at all, and when it is used, it should be understood only as a metaphor for "expected." But if the expectation is so firmly grounded that it seems virtually inevitable, it's not too misleading to say "true."

5. It is true that Lizzie was not guilty, because that's what the jury found. The jury gets to say, and neither historians nor deathbed confessions can make any difference, because "guilty" is here a legal term rather than a moral one, and the matter is decided by decree. If the umpire rules that it's a home run, then it's true—and it goes on the scoreboard and into the record books even if the cameras prove that the ball was just a tad on the foul side as it went over the fence. Maybe it shouldn't have been made true, but it was: the umpire's decision can't be overturned by the evidence of the cameras or by popular demand or even by the regret and repentance of the umpire herself. Accepted authority may decree what is the case in certain matters, what is true within the embrace of its jurisdiction. Such authority can be invested in big sisters, teachers, umpires, popes, academies—wherever it is created by a general allegiance that gives it such decision-making power with either explicit or implicit rules to define it. The most obvious case is the legal one: laws and governments and courts can designate the true heir, the true length of a meter, the true value of a dollar, the true boundary line.

. . .

This preliminary excursion gives us five different senses of how to say something is true as "a matter of fact." 1. It is logically inescapable. 2. It accords with received and accepted custom. 3. The evidence dispels all doubt that it is so. 4. We have good reason to be confident that it will come to pass. 5. The authority has decreed it. I will turn shortly to other primary ways in which *true* is used, apart from various types of matters of fact, but it is time to pause in order to apply to the Christian case what I have sketched so far.

What Christians, as Christians, consider importantly true in this general sense of the word is especially encapsulated in, though by no means confined to, the creeds and confessions of the churches. These contain items of differing kinds. Not much attention is given to the logically inescapable (though many have assumed that only the muddleheaded could doubt the truth of the creed's proclamation of one God), or to merely conventional matters (though many would concede that Jesus' being seated at the right hand of the Father is more a matter of customary metaphor than of literal locale and posture). But the remaining three senses are amply represented in creedal articles.

Some are expressly issues of historical fact ("born of the Virgin Mary, suffered under Pontius Pilate, was crucified, died, and was buried") for which the early tradition has taken some pains to provide convincing evidence: disinterested historians may decide that the available evidence is inadequate to persuade them that these things are true, but will doubtless admit that persuasive evidence is at least imaginable and may once have been available. Some are predictions of future happenings (the resurrection of the dead, Jesus' coming to judge) which the Gospels attempted to show had grounds for being thought reliable: non-Christians will presumably agree that the happenings of the future could prove these true even though not expecting that they will do so. Some are explicitly matters beyond history (e.g., God's omnipotent paternity, the unique Sonship of Jesus from before all time, and the procession of the Holy Spirit from the Father and the Son) for which it is not possible, even theoretically, to offer to non-Christians and disinterested critics either decisive evidence or convincing argument: those who are not committed to believing such things are likely to be puzzled about how to evaluate them at all.

The creeds affirm that all these things are true, despite the varying degrees of difficulty in making a case for them. They are affirmed to be true not by the presentation of argument or evidence but by decree. We are thereby asked, or commanded, to bypass the limitations in provability and to be unqualifiedly confident because these things have the backing of some authority that officially proclaims them true.

There is a difference between officially proclaiming something true and proclaiming something officially true, just as there is a difference between saying that God forbade adultery because it is wrong and saying that adultery is wrong because God forbade it. The former assumes that the proposition would be true with or without the decree, and that the decree only endorses and promotes what was already the right way to settle the matter; the latter, by contrast, self-consciously legislates a truth that *originates* in the decree, creating a new fact rather than merely canonizing an old one. The former is what happens when the appointed authorities examine your credentials and confirm that you were legally married in 1977; the latter is what happened in 1977 when the voice of authority pronounced you man and wife and thereby made it legally happen.

Traditional Christian creeds and confessions are evidently intended to do the former, confirming with authoritative voice things that were already true; but under critical scrutiny, they may appear to behave more like the latter, bestowing a legislated truth by transforming conjectures, speculations, hypotheses, possibilities, and fancies into official facts. This appearance arises from two features of the creeds looked at from the peculiarities of a modern perspective.

First, there are some articles in the creeds that clearly ignore the kind of accountability to evidence that is characteristically, and in some ways peculiarly, modern. Those who formulated them can hardly be faulted for that: they did not aspire to modernity, and probably would not have done so if offered the choice. When the creeds were formed, the ground rules were different, even for science. The truth of scientifically sound assertions was understood to be guaranteed not so much by evidence as by authority. What we should hold to be true was determined by what the authority held to be correct, orthodox, right opinion—right because true, and known to be true because authority affirmed it. For understandable reasons, the procedure for finding out what is true did not resemble modern scholarly or scientific investigation as much as it resembled the workings of modern law. What is legally true (he has a right to a share in her estate; if you cross that river, you will no longer be in Ontario; if you are in England, laws about cattle apply automatically to geese) is established by precedent, legislation, contract, formal decree, and court decisions. Similarly, the Council of Nicea concluded not with a report evaluating the evidence and arriving at provisional conclusions, but with a verdict, embodied in a creed that decreed what we are to consider true.

But the verdict was not a mere legal convention, like the canonized kilogram in the Bureau of Standards: it was intended to state what is the case, in a sturdy scientific way, and it is not unfair to raise questions about whether it still seems to be an appropriate verdict when probed with the tools of a different scientific investigation. When a verdict of this kind deals with matters of historical fact, for instance, we may reconsider the evidence and the ways of assessing it, and may conclude that the earlier decision was not well founded, that it was based on a misunderstanding, and that it was almost certainly wrong opinion no matter how authoritatively it was pronounced.

That is where the second appearance of merely legal or official fact comes in. If its historical standing is undermined to the point that it is no longer recognized as true according to critical standards, it may still continue to be formally held within Christian churches, not merely as decorative antiquity (like traditional nuns' habits and priestly vestments, relics of the ordinary fashions of long ago) but as a fact that one is not permitted to question (e.g., that Paul wrote the Epistle to the Hebrews, a proposition that no trained and dispassionate scholar would now support, though still an article of required belief in many churches). Those who belong to such Christianities have generally been expected to say that it really is true even if it appears to be false—but many are unable to muster the necessary confidence in the authoritative churchly view by which to override their confidence in critical historical procedures. This conflict will, of course, arise again in subsequent chapters. For the moment, note that there has been an important shift, over the history of the Christian tradition, in the nature and role of authority in determining what is true, and that part of the traditional inheritance is caught awkwardly between the ancient and modern views, officially true but otherwise quite doubtful. Beliefs that are established by creeds and confessions as *officially* true (i.e., in sense 5) may once have been therefore taken as *demonstratedly* true (i.e., in sense 3); now many of them are sufficiently doubtful by critical standards that they are often taken as being, for that reason, at most *conventionally* true (i.e., in sense 2), in that they are true in an official way but not necessarily in any other, and thus are treated as true only in special circumstances for certain formal purposes.

And since they are officially true only within the jurisdiction of the authority that decrees them, they may have a starkly different status elsewhere. A few pages back, I mentioned three items from the Nicene Creed that point to truths beyond history and beyond definitive argument. The first two (the fatherhood of God and the unique sonship of Jesus) have been rather consistently accepted by Christians. Even if we are still far from achieving adequate explanations of just what they mean, there has been general agreement among Christians that they are true. The third item, however, the procession of the Holy Spirit, has been a point of deep contention between major Christianities for centuries. The form in which I mentioned it (procession from Father and Son) is a specifically Western form, fostered by the Latin church. It is rejected by the Eastern Orthodox, who hold that the Holy Spirit proceeds from the Father alone.

Which is true? That is, which is *really* the case? We cannot possibly check it out: how then do we decide? That the Western church inserted its view into the original creed at a relatively late date is notoriously true, a matter of historical record.[29] But that does not resolve the problem. Was the insertion right or wrong? Was it a falsification of a true statement, or a proper correction of a defective one? Or neither? This is not a case that can be submitted to the bar of evidence or of probability. Two different Christianities have decided it by decree; for the individual Christian, it is accordingly decided by *belonging,* either to the Western or to the Eastern Christian tradition. What we take to be the case, at least officially the matter of fact, is determined by our allegiance.

Now, there are two quite different ways in which allegiance may determine what is true, and they may be called general allegiance and special allegiance. The former belongs to the last of the types I have been discussing; the latter is a new meaning of *true.*

General allegiance, like the case just mentioned, is a voluntary belonging to an overall jurisdiction and accordingly accepting as true whatever the authority of that jurisdiction prescribes, taking it as a matter of fact in sense 5 of the previous discussion. Either the positive law of decree or the common law of ordinary practice can do the prescribing: if you are a law-abiding citizen of the DDR, the true rate of exchange between West German marks and East German marks is set by the government, whether you like the results or not; if you ally yourself with the black market instead, a quite different true rate is set by market forces, and there is just as little that you can do about it. In either case, the matter of fact is a function of the turf you belong to. The powers that rule the turf decree what is true for those who choose to walk on it.

Special allegiance is a different kind of belonging, and what it makes true is never independent of whether anyone likes the results or not, nor is it dependent on a changeable jurisdiction. It is our individual self-engagement with realities so as to transvalue them, as when the first ten-mark banknote your new store took in is so dear to you that you would not part with it for a hundred times what the government or the black market or a wealthy banknote collector or anyone else would make it worth. In special allegiance, values are determined by inside rather than outside powers, and the defining authority and jurisdiction are both one's own.[30] One of the values affected is the value of "true," in the sense that your future legal spouse was already your true love in 1976, because—and only because—you realized that this was the one to whom you were self-given. Special allegiance thus gives us another basic sense of *true* beyond the varieties of matter-of-fact: "true" as *realized,* i.e., both recognized and made real, by personal engagement.

What is true by special allegiance may be essentially individual (my maternal grandfather was a true Lutheran, whatever the Wisconsin Synod may have thought) or essentially cooperative (Terry and John are true friends, but only because they see to it together). Cooperatively, special allegiance may operate on a grand scale to establish and sustain dependent truths. For instance: as a child, I participated at school in that rite of civil religion known as the "Pledge of Allegiance," in which we were required to assume reverent poses and recite solemnly our dedication to "one nation, indivisible, with liberty and justice for all."[31!] This is quite obviously a sort of creed. In what sense are its characterizations true? I will not go into whether the nation in question did, or does, have liberty and justice for all, but I would like to have a closer look at "indivisible."

The inclusion of this word was substantially motivated by the armed conflict arising from the secession of the southern states, still referred to (significantly) as the "Civil War" in the North (home of the victorious "Union" forces, operating in the name of "the United States of America") and as the "War Between the States"[32+] in the South (then calling itself "the Confederate States of America"). It turned out to be true that the nation was not successfully divided, though it appears to be true that it was divided for a while.

But that is sheer history: the word in the pledge is not "undivided" but "indivisible," and that makes a claim of another order. It is not merely a matter of recorded fact, nor is it just the way we happen to do things, since it doesn't pertain to what *was* (the nation had in fact been divided in some significant ways) or merely to what *is* (that it isn't now divided is only a trivial, and possibly temporary, truth that doesn't mean as much as the pledge obviously intends) but rather reaches out to limit what *may be.* On the other hand, it is hardly something so given in the structure that it could not imaginably be otherwise (it is not intrinsically impossible for the other forty-nine states to secede collectively from Idaho). Nor is it simply a prediction. One could argue that its claim to be true is legal—that is, that the contracting parties who founded and defined the nation abjured for themselves and their successors in perpetuity the right to withdraw from it. But, aside from whether it is possible to bind the political self-determination of future generations in such a way, more is meant than even this.

"Indivisible" is here a point of principle, an ideal to which the Pledge of Allegiance is itself a commitment. The kind of truth it has could not be either secured or altered by strategic legislation, and is quite independent of whatever the founding fathers may have had in mind. In effect, it is true by the citizens' renewed act of making and keeping it true, and in no other way; it is true as a function of their being true to it, something that they conjointly determine *shall* be true. Truth is here moral rather than legal, not a given but a gift, a quality bestowed upon a notion by an allegiance of self-involvement.

This special type of allegiance is significantly different from the allegiance of general jurisdiction, as becomes quite clear when the two take conflicting stands. Even if the law allows divorce, a given marriage may be truly indissoluble—not merely undissolved, but indissoluble—if it is created and sustained as such by the commitment of the partners; if your labor union, or your political party, is repudiated by most of society and outlawed by the legislature, it may still be real and you may still be a true member of it, even though you are denied the privileges of legal unions or parties (McCarthyism implicitly, and ironically, conceded this in asking whether people were members of the Communist party; I don't recall whether anyone successfully evaded the question by pointing out that it was legally impossible). What is legally or officially true is determined by what authority decrees. But public authority doesn't necessarily have the last word when personal authority disagrees.

So far we have glanced at two basic varieties of "true." The first is "matter-of-fact," with its five subdivisions: what we know to be the case because of necessity or convention or evidence or inevitability or authoritative determination (i.e., what everyone must acknowledge to be the case whether or not they are pleased to accept it). The second is the sense of "true" as applied to a condition or a quality that depends on a personal engagement of allegiance and would cease to be true if the engagement were withdrawn or significantly altered (i.e., what can be the case only insofar as the key people still care to make it so).

There is obvious overlap among the various dimensions of "true" established by these two main varieties, especially given the subdivisions of the first of them, but it is useful to distinguish their different properties. It is often helpful, and sometimes indispensable, to attend not simply to *whether* something is true but rather to *in what way* it is true—and in what way it is not. A saying attributed to Jesus that made its way into one of the earliest major manuscripts of the Gospels makes the point with stunning force. Jesus sees a man plucking grain on the Sabbath—a deed that was widely supposed to have been decreed sinful by God—and says, "Blessed are you if you really know what you are doing; but if you don't, you are accursed and a breaker of the law."[33]+ Is it true that the man was sinning? Yes, according to some important religious authorities of the time; yes, according to some important ways of understanding and evaluating the Scriptures. But be that as it may as matters of fact, Jesus relocates the question in the second main sense of "true," and says that if the man personally accepts that it is sinful, then yes, it is sinful—but no, it isn't if he *realizes* that God permits it. It depends on whether he makes it true by the way his mind and heart are invested and by where and how his treasure is laid up.

In addition to these two basic senses of "true," there are two other basic senses that ought to be looked at. I will treat them briefly, not because they are less important—they are potentially crucial in the exploration of religious questions—but because they are somewhat less tangled and do not require as much sorting out.

A third basic sense of "true" corresponds to the ethical and personal ideal of self-consistency. "This above all, to thine own self be true" formulates memorably its basic principle of self-coherence, truth as integrity; and the next lines, "And it must follow, as the night the day,/ Thou canst not then be false to any man," add the interpersonal corollary, truth as honesty or sincerity (in their traditional deeper senses), authentic relating.[34]+ What is true, in this sense, is what accords with deepest conscience in its awareness of who and what one most basically and fundamentally is, along with what coheres with reality as one knows it—what is in tune, rather than dissonant, both within the self and between the self and all the rest.

This proper fidelity to self and to others is closely related to the truth grounded in special allegiance that I have just been considering, but differs from it in some important respects. That kind of truth has to do with special ways of giving or pledging oneself where one happens to belong or where one chooses to belong; they can affirm and strengthen what was already true, or create new truth, by redefining allegiance. But the truth of integrity is more elemental and offers fewer options. This is where one comes closest to experiencing what is inescapably and essentially true of oneself, including one's relation to other truth. It is the most intimate expression of that ultimate allegiance to truth that ideally governs the forming, sustaining, and withdrawing of all other allegiances. Its starkest test is perhaps that of conversion, where the resettlement of the true self in a newly discovered home of truth often results in the radical revision of previous belongings and values and understandings, but its usual mark is the stable steadiness of high fidelity.

The self is where one *must* belong. Once we cross the border between *what* we have come to be and *who* we have always been, we are dealing with a belonging that is neither by happenstance nor by choice. Receiving, acknowledging, and honoring the self is the rhythm of the self's reality and profoundly affects the receiving, acknowledging, and honoring of any other reality. There is a great deal at stake in how well it is done—that is, in whether one is finally true or false.

My fourth, and final, instance of the basic uses of *true* is its use as a verb, as in Do Christianities true?

The use of *true* as a verb has long been established, even if it has been largely neglected or confined to the sort of mechanical applications I recall from my childhood in farming country ("Get a saw and true these ends up," that is, make them all correspond to one another in uniform length, or "Let's true that wheel, so it won't wobble," i.e., set it right, adjust it to what it is supposed to be and how it works properly). To true is to bring about the best integrity of something, to verify, to *adjust* in both the rudimentary mechanical sense and in the more ambitious sense of *make righteous.* It means, in general, to bring something, or someone, closer to an appropriate ideal, to a sounder condition: to put in tune, set right, fix up. It is an important and extremely useful verb, one that says what no alternative will quite say. I will want to take advantage of that frequently in the rest of this book, and I ask you to be patiently ready for more talk about truing and about what trues.

TRUTH AND CHRISTIANITIES

We have, accordingly, four questions to pursue.

1. Is Christianity true? That is to say, are the claims made by the various forms of the Christian tradition about what can be counted on as reliable matters of fact genuinely reliable, each in its own order? Here we must

contend especially with various types of fact and likelihood, from the trival to the momentous (was Jesus born in Bethlehem? was he divine? will he come again in glory to judge the living and the dead? is salvation only through him?).

2. Are you keeping Christianity true? Do you think and live in ways that are faithful to and sustaining of the Christianity you espouse, and is that Christianity properly faithful to the Christian tradition? Is the shape of your mind and life a clearly Christian shape, consistently expressive of your loyalty to what Christianity is supposed to be and of the effectiveness of that way? Do you *realize* Christianity? Here, the question is whether we in fact incarnate the religion we profess well enough both to experience and to exemplify its rightness and thus to help maintain it as a sound and life-giving tradition—whether we are genuinely Christian and whether the genuineness of Christianity shows in us.

3. Are you, as a Christian, true? That is, are you *sincerely* Christian? Is your integrity consistent with Christianity as you understand and try to live it, your deepest sense of reality fully compatible with a Christian vision? Can you profess and practice it with an easy grace that is without serious doubt, misgiving, divided mind, reservation? The previous question is concerned with whether we profess and live out what Christianity seems to call us to think and be and do; this one is concerned with whether we find our best attempts to think and do Christianity satisfying and uncompromising in our deepest sense of honesty. Here we are concerned with what Christians are expected to believe and to disbelieve, to do and not to do, and how confident we are that these expectations would truly fulfill us[35+] if we truly fulfilled them.

4. Does your Christianity true? When you try to imagine what it would be like to know reality square-on without falsifying, and when you imagine what you and the world might better become in the next wave of changes, are you satisfied that Christianity as you know it is the right way to get from here to there? This time, the issue is how closely our Christianity resembles our serious convictions and heartfelt ideals about reality, and how effectively Christianities work as agents of transformation toward truer and better selves and a truer and better world—to what extent the problems that concern us would be effectively dealt with through specifically Christian solutions, whether what is wrong would be put right by being Christianized, how well the Christian answers address the most important questions.

. . .

Hardly anyone would answer all four of these questions with confident affirmatives. The first question is likely to produce at least some wavering in all but the most doggedly conservative quarters, since it is notorious that serious doubts about elements of traditional Christian belief have steadily increased over the last few generations. Traditional humility requires a negative reply to the second one as part of the routine self-indictment common to various Christianities, whose members regularly lament that they have not become Christian enough. But I think that Christianity is in deeper trouble on these two fronts than is usually realized, largely because these questions are not often faced honestly. The last two questions, along with the senses of "true" that they represent, are less frequently considered, but they need to be taken very seriously. There are things they can show us that we urgently need to know, including mistakes that may still be corrected.

The standard assumptions have been that Christianity as we have received it is completely true, and that the main problem is that we are not completely conformed to it. Any failure to conform has been assumed to be our fault, the result of our pride, sinfulness, ignorance, weakness. If the received Christianity seems incompatible with our integrity—if it asserts as true something that careful inspection makes seem false, or if experience suggests that sometimes its labeling of what is sinful and what is virtuous gets them backwards—then we are expected to disregard our sense of integrity. If it doesn't seem to work well, to be obviously life-giving and liberating and redemptive, then we are supposed to assume that we are asking the wrong questions or pursuing the wrong values. In short, we are always to call ourselves into question, but never our Christianity.

Such assumptions are untrue, in every sense of the word, and it is irresponsible to make them.

We should not, to begin with, assume that the Christianity we have received is Christianity rightly understood. Some aspects of it are sufficiently doubtful that it seems quite likely that we may have got it wrong, and that those who gave it to us may have got it wrong from the start. It can hardly be a good idea to conform completely, in Jesus' name, to a mistaken version of what Jesus was trying to accomplish. There are good reasons for arguing that we *ought* to doubt, rather than believe, some of what has been traditionally taught, and that we still have a great deal to learn and to question when it comes to what we are called to be and to do.

It is entirely possible that we have only a rudimentary understanding of the truth toward which Christianity points—that our present grasp falls as far short of the real thing as alchemy fell short of chemistry, or even as astrology falls short of astronomy. At any rate, learning what Christianity should be is an unfinished project, and whatever the extent of its unfinishedness, we can proceed only by using all the resources at our disposal; and one of the most important of these is our honest sense of integrity, especially where we experience collisions between what our lives and minds find true and what we are asked to find true on traditional religious grounds.

It is arrogant to suppose that the integrity that arises from a tiny pocket in time and place can stand in easy judgment over centuries of accumulated affirmations. Still, it is irresponsible to suppose that matters of the utmost importance ought to be decided by a tradition that, by all historical evidences, was founded on and sustained by understandings that were no less provincial and biased than our own, and in many respects less well informed. Increasingly, Christians express misgivings about the sufficiency of the tradition to take adequate care of the problems of the world and of its persons, noting that environmental rapacity has seemed to be authorized by a traditional understanding of the commission to subdue the earth (Gn 1:28), that concentration on heavenly reward has retarded the striving for earthly justice, that the tradition's attention to sin has distorted our judgments, our attitudes, and our sense of self-worth.

It is quite possible not to care about all this, and to say "I will believe as I am told," or "What was good enough for them is good enough for me," or "My country, right or wrong," or "God's ways are not our ways." But if we take such a stand, we ought to be clear about the fact that we are abdicating personal responsibility and redefining what our integrity means now and can ever mean again as long as we stand there and can, or will, do no other. And if we decline to abdicate, our truth must deal with some sobering realizations about what has been traditionally thought to be true, and truing.

This book is especially addressed to those who incline to answer each of the four questions—and the general summary question, Do Christianities true?—with "not really," or even a simple "no," and find that answer regrettable, uncomfortable, perhaps even alarming. The remainder of the book is written with these questions, and that answer, always hovering in the background and sometimes directly scrutinized; its overriding concern will be how we may appropriately deal with that spontaneously negative reply in order to discover a better and stronger way of affirming. It is intended to offer good news, but does not undertake to be comfortably reassuring. It is the sharing of my own attempts to deal with problems that are to me of urgent importance. They are problems that I do not think we can honestly solve in the traditional ways. They require an improved style of tradition if we are to be able to pass the best of the old tradition onward to our great-grandchildren. The remainder of the book will therefore be preoccupied with questions about what is true and truing, beginning with the traditional sense of Christianity's finished and superior truth, which is where we turn now.

FACING [Part II]

THE PROBLEM:

ARE CHRISTIANITIES

TRUE?

3

THE
SUPERIORITY
OF CHRISTIANITIES?

To the extent that the Christian tradition is perceived as demanding that we accept as true all the beliefs that it has handed down, or even just the principal ones, we are in trouble. Some of us simply cannot sustain that kind of belief, and it is no use requiring of us what we cannot do. Where belief has failed to rise spontaneously to the occasion, or has faded with experience and closer inspection, it is not a matter of lack of good will, or even of good faith, any more than in the case of allergies, or being unable to carry a tune.

Nor is it a mere lack of confidence, derived from associating with a skeptical and critical disbelieving environment, which might be cured by Christian immersion in a setting and an atmosphere where doubt does not penetrate—or at least is not admitted. To one who does not believe, the belief of others may seem impressive, but it is not likely to appear persuasive. It is no more accurate to think of unbelief as a deficiency in faith than to consider belief an excess of credulity. Faith and belief go hand in hand, but they are not the same—and if it is important in this case not to let the left hand know what the right hand is doing (I think not, but if it is) I suggest that it is time to think of belief as the left hand. We have tried it the other way, and it does not seem to work well.

The unbelief of sheer ignorance can be corrected: with enough time and patience, one can give a convincing demonstration of the existence of Zimbabwe or show that the stars are considerably farther away than may appear to the naked eye. Some unbelief can't quite be transformed into belief, but may at least be nudged into a middling state of *undisbelief:* I may be persuaded out of my flat dismissal of your testimony into a place where my imagination at least entertains the possibility that you may be right. But the religious situation of those I referred to in an earlier book as the Ungifted is such that they can't always manage even undisbelief for some of the traditional dogmas. They have to deal with some honest unbelief. And at least some of it is a function neither of ignorance nor of stubbornness but the contrary: the misgivings are grounded in experience and familiarity and serious but unsuccessful attempts to conform, and further information and thoughtfulness tend to confirm rather than dispel the doubts.

Many—probably most—of those who have been given the privilege of being able to spend much of their time investigating the bases of Christian beliefs have found that they cannot sustain many of the traditional beliefs as confidently as they once could, and must relinquish some of them altogether. This is almost certainly an irreversible shift, and it has also occurred in many of those who do not enjoy such investigative advantages, as the results of those investigations have been publicly shared and made communal property. As the word gets out further, a similar shift is sure to follow in many others who have not yet heard about these goings-on except in a caricatured version. Once one arrives at this condition, there appears to be no turning back from it to where one was before. Some kinds of belief are vulnerable to knowledge and to unscrupulous deprogrammers; the corresponding grounded unbelief is not.

But even if it were, that would still not solve the overall problem. It is not only those with misgivings who are in trouble from a traditional orthodox perspective. Christianity itself is too, to the extent that the Christian tradition is perceived as committed to the truth of beliefs that have no strong warrant for being thought true, and some of which seem more likely, if judged by the evidence, to be false.

Conventionally, Christian thinkers have regarded undoubting belief as a gift of God and as something that may at best be artificially imitated, not genuinely acquired, by those to whom the gift has not been given. It was assumed that the gift is God's only, to bestow or withhold as God sees fit, and that the Ungifted can do nothing to change their condition except repent, pray for true belief, and wait patiently. In the meantime, they can learn to live with their ungiftedness within Christianity. In *The Gathering of the Ungifted,* I attempted to explore one way of living with it: accepting that the views of the faithful believers are normative and authoritatively expressive of the true content that is divinely given in the gift of faith, and then proceeding to live out Christian life in a state of loyal undisbelief.

Now I wish to investigate the other way of living with ungiftedness, once it is clear that belief is not the same as faith. This other way is to take as normative not the inheritance of beliefs or the convictions of believers, past or present, but the priority of faith and the primacy of what is true and what is truing.

THE GIFT OF FAITH RECONSIDERED AND REDISTRIBUTED

All of us have the gift of faith properly so-called, a gift that is given to all along with the gift of human life. All are empowered to develop the quality of that life and of that faith. But belief is not given to all. Indeed, belief is not given *at* all, in the sense in which faith is given, as a concomitant of human life and thus as much a divine gift as existence itself. Belief comes, to use the terms used by the early rabbis to distinguish their own pronouncements from what had been given to Moses on Sinai, not "from heaven" but "from men," i.e., from the social communities that determine one's original ways of imagining reality. If you had been born into a Muslim community, your belief would have been formed according to a Muslim imagination; if you had been the offspring of a Buddhist community, so would your beliefs have been.

The beliefs that come as one's familial and communitarian birthright are the gifts of circumstance. Whether you wish to call the circumstance luck, or chance, or fate, or providential design, is a matter of choice. If you wish to express your gratitude for the beliefs in whose midst the accidents of your birth placed you, you may choose to maximize circumstance's divinely guided or divinely determined purposiveness and call it providence, or you may choose to accentuate the unmerited gratuitousness of such good fortune and call it grace. To express gratitude in such ways is entirely appropriate, as long as one remembers (a) that pious Jews and Hindus are also grateful that they were originally nested in the best religious community, rather than being born to a family that was Christian or even worse; and (b) that it is only fair to be evenhanded about putting a theological seal of approval on the contingencies of birth and rearing, so if yours was providential or gracious, one ought to extend those terms to cover all other births and rearings as well, unless one is able to find good reason not to do so.

What would constitute good reason? If those who happened into other religions universally groaned about having suffered such misfortune once they learned about a Christian alternative, and converted to some brand of Christianity at the earliest opportunity, one might be able to build a case. But in fact this is far from being how things are. Other religious traditions are apparently altogether as capable as Christianity is of inspiring reverence and gratitude in those who belong to them, and their members do not usually feel the need to find something else or to recognize Christianity as superior when introduced to it.[36]

If there were something clearly deforming in non-Christian religions, rendering their devout practitioners obviously spiritually grotesque when compared with Christians, an argument about selective grace might be pulled together. But this too simply will not wash, being ludicrously far from the observable realities. It is appropriate to be grateful about having been born into Christianity, and it is appropriate to leave it at that, without manufacturing explicit or implicit invidious comparisons. It is good to be Christian. It could become better to be Christian. Let our concern be not that Christianity be thought superior to alternative religions, but that the Christianity of the future be superior to what we now have.

Augustine apparently says somewhere[37] that it's not how you got there that is important, but why you stay. People stay for all sorts of reasons, of course, some of them self-serving, cowardly, ignorant, unimaginative, and arrogant. The more interesting ones are those who stay because they find the pulse of a deeper life, the glow of holiness, a sense of centeredness and reality, and a source of welling joy enough to drown all sorrow. That sort of reason is admittedly not bad, and might well be thought a thorough justification for staying, whatever one may have to put up with in doing so. And testimony of this kind can be found in every religious quarter, from the Psalmists to the Sufis, from Aelius Aristides' love of the now long-vanished Aesclepius to Sri Ramakrishna's devotion to Rama, from the Hasids of Jewish orthodoxy to the Pentecostals of Christian enthusiasm. Every principal religion has demonstrated its capacity to nourish faith into strength and delight and generosity and peace. They all give reason to stay.

And they all have produced exemplary and saintly persons, admired and revered by both coreligionists and outsiders. To judge from their apparent results, all religious ways have a potential for truing the faith and the lives of those who follow them. They all seem to work beautifully when they are done well.

Doing them well seems to involve doing them faithfully and truly. Characteristically, the persons who have been seen as saintly, even by those who have known them most closely, stayed true to their inherited ways by following them faithfully in their traditional forms, urging and inspiring others to do the same. Being trued was for them closely related to staying true to the tradition. This is the sort of life for which the debased expression "true believer" would most appropriately be reserved, a life in which faithfulness to the tradition releases and enlarges and strengthens faith, and belonging begets truth.

But a true believer, in this most saintly sense, is not likely to be committed either to the falsity of all alternatives or to the truth of all understandings of her own tradition. The early Israelite position appears to have been not that there were no other gods but theirs, but that any others were out of bounds to them; worship at another shrine was like adultery rather than fantasy. The later Israelite position concluded that there is one God only, who presumably loves Gentiles as well as Jews, at least enough to want them to see the error of their ways and accept the Jewish God. The deeply experienced Hindu devotee of Kali does not accuse the Krishna-worshipper of idolatry or foolishness, or absolve all Kali-worshippers of the charge of superstition; the advanced Buddhist will acknowledge that his conformity to the truth of the Buddha falls far short of the true ultimate, and that some Sufis are undoubtedly closer to it than many Buddhists.

Let me give two quite different, but equally instructive, examples from antiquity. Both Socrates and Apollonius of Tyana were revered both in their time and in subsequent centuries, and by persons of various religious persuasions, as saintly religious models. They were both concerned with helping others to become more truly religious. Their circumstances and specific projects were somewhat different, however.

Apollonius[38] traveled widely, and encountered a wide variety of religious traditions and ceremonies. Occasionally, he rebuked or exposed a fraudulent prophet or a religious charlatan, but for the most part he spent his time encouraging people to honor their traditions, performing the sacrifices with reverent care in accordance with the way they had been ordained and understanding the modes of worship as well as they could, re-forming them to their original condition. His accent, that is, fell upon how being true to oneself carries over into being true to one's religious tradition and making it more true to itself.

Socrates[39] remained in Athens, except for a brief period of fighting wars heroically on its behalf, and while he continued to honor traditional piety (his last recorded act before his death was to provide for a sacrifice to the god Aesclepius), he dedicated his life to the pursuit of a more critical truing, convinced that being true to oneself is better accomplished if it entails an avoidance of falsity in religion and in religious thought. He was condemned to death for disrupting the traditional religious views of Athens, and accepted the sentence; he had certainly been guilty of challenging the adequacy of the traditional views in the name of a better faith and a higher truth.

Apollonius evidently realized that to believe in—to belove, to belong to —one religion does not entail scoffing at others as false. Consider a modern analogue:

In the world of psychotherapy, there are many competing views. Freudians propose one way of understanding the workings of the human psyche, Jungians another, and so on. There is no privileged independent point of view from which the truth of competing theories can be evaluated. But it is possible, at least in a general way, to assess the results of applying different views. The result is intriguing. What appears to be the case, from comparative studies that have been made, is that each of the various principal views works about as well as any other, provided that both the therapist and the patient have confidence in it.

How far can one extrapolate from this to the comparison of religions? Undoubtedly, Apollonius was right in supposing that virtually any religion can help to true those who belong to it without calling the value of other religions into question, just as any language can meet human linguistic needs satisfactorily without thereby proving other languages false. If the people believe and belong, let them honor their own truth by honoring its religious heritage well.

But honoring it well does not mean honoring it just as it is and was, preserving it quite unchanged from earlier generations. Socrates was also undoubtedly right in supposing that some kinds of believing and belonging are spiritually retarding, falsifying, even downright pernicious, and that to become properly trued as we move from what we have been to what we may better be, we must often change some of our allegiances and beliefs. He was, to his death, a loyal Athenian who wanted to help in the truing of Athens, including the critical improvement of its religious tradition. The way in which his offer was definitively rebuffed seems to be fairly good evidence that Athenian religion needed improving.

Apollonius emphasized the positive reconciliation with received tradition and the importance of practicing it devoutly; Socrates emphasized the confronting of its falsities and a devotion to what is more true. These two ways are not mutually exclusive, and the choice between them must depend on an assessment of the values of conformity and of correction in a given instance. Does it falsify or does it true?

Sometimes the answer is clear and simple, but more often it is ambiguous, yes-and-no. Relating to it appropriately may require a more complex tact. Apollonius encouraged people to be faithful to their ancient ancestral rituals, but he also encouraged them to adopt a symbolic understanding of the rituals and the myths, so that the *meaning* of what they were doing might true them, however unedifying their religion might have been without such reinterpretation. The lessons offered by Apollonius and Socrates are not obsolete. It is still the case that what is ultimately true about you will include your religion, and your further truing must include coming to terms with it. It is still the case that coming to terms with it is bound to include some forms of change and reinterpretation as well as reconciliation and acceptance. It is still the case that another religious way is not necessarily false, and that one's inherited way is not necessarily true. It is still the case that it's not only why you stay that matters: *how* you stay is even more important.

Christians, however, are not well prepared by their tradition to entertain the possibility that their claims to truth should be much more modest, and their sense of superiority taken much less seriously, than has been customary. Christianities have traditionally resisted reinterpretation for the honorable if naive reason that their leaders have thought the established interpretations unimprovable, and have operated according to a possessive and exclusivist notion of truth that is much more reminiscent of the Athenian authorities than of Socrates or Apollonius.

In the early centuries of Christianity, it was commonly assumed that non-Christian religions were damnably false. Many Christians still make that assumption, and would readily dismiss all other religions as superstitious delusions, their spiritual heroes being graceless dupes. Other Christians would now at least allow that the evidence suggests that God is at work even in non-Christian religions, at least to some degree, and that salvation is possible there despite the absence of Christian belief. But in general, the Christian view is still that Christianity is the true way, and alternatives are correspondingly false: this is the way chosen by God to deal most intimately with human possibilities, and it is the way ordained by God for human beings to understand and worship rightly. Anything else is at worst diabolical and damned, and at best misguided, even if tolerably capable of producing impressive results. To the non-Christian saint, respectful of but quite unpersuaded by the Christian invitation, even the more tolerant modern Christian has inclined to say, "Let us then part, and go on to love and serve God—you in your way, and I in His."

Christians commonly suppose that their Christianity is both necessary and sufficient, because they suppose it to be definitively true, in a way that another religion cannot compete with and that cannot be much improved upon by further Christian development. That kind of definitiveness is, in traditional Christian thought, the source of Christianity's unquestionable superiority and the key argument for why one should become, and remain, Christian. The tradition of attempts to demonstrate that Christianity is the definitive religion—and specifically that the definitive truth is in the classical set of beliefs that have been mislabeled "the faith" and misidentified as the essence of Christianity—is the overall enterprise of Christian apologetics. The next chapter will therefore take a general critical look at the traditional foundations by focusing on the apologetical tradition of foundation-building.

4

CHRISTIAN

APOLOGETICS

Why should one be a Christian? is not a question much asked over the history of the Western world, where almost everyone was Christian. (Fifth-generation residents of Sydney probably rarely ask "Why should I be an Australian?" or "Why should I speak English?") To the extent that the question came up, it was normally answered in the same way as the more frequent and specific modern question: "Why should I be a Roman Catholic?"—or a Lutheran, or a Jehovah's Witness, or an Anglican, or a Baptist. The conventional answer has traditionally been something like "Because that is what we are," or "Because my family has always been." The possibility of conversion to another Christian group presses the question more demandingly, and the answer then becomes a bit more theological: "Because it is the way in which God has revealed that he wants to be served and honored," or "Because this is how God has offered salvation," or "Because it is the true way." A world-class theologian may combine all three of these together, as Karl Barth did in his succinct pronouncement that "the Christian religion is true, because it has pleased God, who alone can be the judge in this matter, to affirm it to be the true religion."[40]

CLASSICAL APOLOGETICS

There are two periods in the history of Christianity when the question about the rightness of being a Christian has been especially urgent.

The first one was the earliest days of Christianity, when Christians needed an answer not only for the potential converts addressed by the apostolic mission, but also for the authorities whose suspicions of the church had to be allayed and whose persecutions needed stopping. The latter need gave birth to apologetics, the presentation of a reasoned argument for the propriety of being Christian—the forensic case for the defense. The defense eventually won the case so thoroughly that it ran out of importantly threatening opposition. Apologetics then got bolder as it got less practically necessary, and turned mainly to proving Christian rightness to Christians for the sheer satisfaction of it. For the most part, it stayed in that condition until the second urgent period arrived.

The second period is one in which we now live. Over the last several generations, serious challenges to Christian belonging have arisen from *within* Western society for the first time since the fourth century; and much more recently, Christian thinkers have begun for the first time to face in a concerted and considerate way the issues posed for theology by the existence of other major religious traditions, which can no longer be easily dismissed in a world that has grown both much larger in its possibilities and much smaller in its density of relations. On both counts, apologetics has been put to a much more demanding task than it had learned to handle.

Despite these novelties in the modern Christian situation, the traditional form of apologetics is still carried on largely unchanged. A few of its classic themes have fallen into disuse (such as the moral and philosophical superiority of Christianity to all alternatives, and the evidence of world history as a confirmation of Christian claims), but most of them are still around,[41] and the objective is still to demonstrate that Christianity is the way in which God has revealed that he (the traditional "he" is usually employed by traditional apologists) wants to be served and honored, the way God has offered salvation, the *true* way. The standard strategy is first to prove the existence of God, and then to establish that God has truly revealed a way of salvation in the Bible and in Jesus Christ, and that Christianity (or some particular form of Christianity) is it. I will bypass for the moment the first step, proving God's existence and capacity to reveal, and consider the way apologetics goes about the next step: proving that God *has* revealed, and that what God has revealed is the truth of Christianity.

One style of approach to this question is by way of an argument from decorum. An omnipotent and loving-merciful God, says the apologist, would *want* to reveal his will, and would of course do so truly and intelligibly: any alternative would be inappropriate. This motif seems to be muted in recent apologetics. That is understandable, since it is both a weak and a dispensable argument.

It is weak in that it depends on assumptions about how God would be *bound* to act. But traditional apologists are inconsistent about applying consistency to God. When confronting other features of Christianity that are difficult to rationalize, they often remind us that God's ways are not our ways, and that we are therefore not in a position to say that they must make sense to us in order to be thought true. Logically, it then follows that God may not want to reveal, or can choose to do so in a form that we can't grasp. Besides, if rational appropriateness is the basis for judgment about revelation, we can make a better case for the Qur'an than for the Bible, and universal natural revelation may well seem a more plausible and effective tactic for revealing than Jesus Christ.

And this form of argument is dispensable if one can show, as traditional apologists think they can do, that the Bible is supernaturally inspired. If that can be pulled off, then obviously one does not have to meddle with matters of decorum and probability: if you can show that this is in fact what God did, it is unnecessary to persuade me that God would have considered it inappropriate to have done otherwise.

The traditional arguments for this position are neatly summarized and reaffirmed in a recent book on classical apologetics:

(1) It is virtually granted that the Bible (not assumed to be inspired) contains generally reliable history. (2) The Bible records miracles as part of its generally reliable history. (3) These miracles authenticate the Bible's messengers and their message. (4) Therefore, the Bible message ought to be received as divine. (5) The Bible message includes the doctrine of its own inspiration. (6) Therefore, the Bible is more than a generally reliable record. It is a divinely inspired record.[42+]

I would like to comment on these points, one by one.

1. It is certainly fair to say that the Bible contains generally reliable history, in the sense that it is not essentially a work of imaginative inven-

tion, like *Pilgrim's Progress,* or *Gulliver's Travels,* or *The Lord of the Rings.* It is used by archaeologists for practical clues, and archaeological results prove that it contains them. Where its contents overlap with secular chronicles, the secular chronicles are frequently confirming. And even when its versions of what took place may be questioned, it often gives information that proves reliable enough to be used in an alternative reconstruction that makes good historical sense. But it is equally fair to say that if we leave aside the question of inspiration (as our authors ask us to do at this stage of their argument) and treat the Bible as a set of documents to be used in reconstructing history, these documents prove to be of highly variable historical value. Some of them are evidently pure fantasy (e.g., Jonah), some a mixture of fantasy, legend, and approximate memory (e.g., Genesis), some demonstrably unreliable in many historical particulars (e.g., Acts). "Generally reliable history" is a vague and relative term, and its appropriateness depends on how much one wishes to claim as a result of affixing this label. The qualified general reliability of biblical history is not enough to guarantee its reliability in any given instance.

2. The Bible presents stories of miracles. Some of them are set in the midst of historical accounts that are in some other respects apparently generally reliable. Mussorgsky's *Boris Godunov,* Borodin's *Prince Igor,* Glinka's *A Life for the Tsar,* and Rimsky-Korsakov's *Ivan the Terrible* also contain generally reliable history; and they also present arias in the course of unrolling their generally reliable history. What logical conclusion can be drawn about arias? Historical reliability is not infectious, and the fact that miracles are reported adjacent to reliable material does not establish that the miracle-reports are themselves reliable. A considerable skepticism about *all* miracle-reports has developed progressively since scientific investigation put an end to the supposition that God manages creation by direct manipulation. I will return to this point a little later. In the meantime, one may not conclude that the miracle-reports necessarily share in the general reliability enough to be themselves specifically reliable.

3. There are two difficulties with the assertion that the biblical miracle-reports authenticate the messengers and their messages. One is, as I have just mentioned (and will clarify later), that we have good reason for doubting that the miracle-reports are trustworthy. The other difficulty is that even if the miracles really happened, it simply does not follow that the messengers or the messages are thereby authenticated. The Bible frequently reminds us that people may expect miracles as the guarantee of authenticity for messengers and messages (hence the demand for signs which Jesus interestingly

rebukes as evidence of wickedness and impiety on the part of the demand-ers[43]), but it is also quite prepared to acknowledge that miracles do not always provide such credentials. Pharaoh's sorcerers perform the miraculous trick God taught Moses, and do it every bit as well as he (Ex 4:2–5, 7:10–12); and Simon Magus puts on a show sufficient to bring the Samaritans to think him the Great Power of God (Acts 8:9–11). Anyone who thinks that an apparent miracle proves that its performer is divinely authenticated ought not to be allowed to go to the big city unaccompanied.[44+]

4. Even if the messages of apparent miracle-workers had to be accepted, which is not the case, it is a great leap in argumentation to say that this confirms anything about the Bible as a whole, or "the Bible message" pure and simple, whatever that may be. That would be rather like saying that Pär Lagerqvist's 1951 Nobel Prize established that all Swedish literature is of a high and inspiring quality, or that if someone offers to sell you a packet of currency at a bargain rate, and shows you that the top, bottom, and middle bills are genuine, you need not worry about any of the rest being counterfeit. What miracles can be credited to Luke, or to the authors of the Fourth Gospel, whoever they were, to validate their messages? But this blends into the next point.

5. I will deal in chapter 5 with the fallacy of a self-validating Bible. To anticipate the argument presented there, the Bible as we now have it did not exist when someone (most New Testament scholars think that it was probably not Paul) wrote that all the Scriptures are divinely inspired (2 Tm 3:16).[45+] There is no reason whatever to think that this text refers to itself, or even to the Gospels, as included in the category "Scriptures," which at that time meant what is now called by Christians the Old Testament (usu-ally, in Greek-speaking circles, including also what the Protestant tradition calls the Apocrypha and occasionally other books as well[46+]). Neither is there any strong reason for supposing that this random verse deserves to be accorded the authority to establish the truth about what is or is not inspired by God, even if we knew precisely which texts it envisages.

6. The conclusion that the Bible is divinely inspired is here derived from a reasoning that is consistent if and only if (a) we pretend that "generally reliable" means "totally reliable," (b) we assume that all wonderful happen-ings are miraculous, (c) we take for granted that workers of wonders all speak for God, (d) we accept that inspiration is so infectious that it spreads to everything that is placed in the same container with a sample of it.

This will not do.

It is, however, a representative case. The authors of *Classical Apologetics* are in fact faithfully presenting a classical apologetics: this is not an egregiously botched job of thinking, but the way apologetics has been reasoned for centuries. It has long since been demonstrated by experimental evidence that faulty logic is much more likely to slip undetected past even those who are trained in logic, if it is used to come to conclusions the readers want to believe. Apologetics in general has been a sterling example of this. Although, as "the reasoned defense of the Christian religion,"[47] it is ostensibly directed to non-Christians, it has in fact been conducted mainly as an in-house exercise, where its conclusions are congenial enough to hide its logical faults.[48+] Rather than being set up to stand or fall on whether nonbelievers are inexorably persuaded, apologetics is usually attuned (though often unconsciously) only to satisfying the believers that their beliefs seem to be firmly encouraged by dispassionate reason. The crucial word is *seem*. Apologetics of this classic variety has mainly been conducted as an art of illusion, of a decidedly nonmiraculous kind.

THE DIALECTICAL ALTERNATIVE

Classical apologetics is committed to rational argumentation, and attempts (however unsuccessfully) to assume as little as possible as it builds its case by the force of public evidence and logic. (The first description of apologetics I ever heard still roughly describes the ideal of classical apologetics: "You start out assuming that there is no God, and then bit by bit prove by reason alone that everything we believe must be true."[49+]) Hence it begins with "natural theology," the sort of theology that can be done without reference to any privileged revelation, and tries to establish that the Bible (or, as one finds frequently in Catholic apologetics, the Church[50!]) is supernaturally revealed and infallible; and then it can proceed to reason from the Bible (or Church) to determine just what God has revealed and what its implications are—how God wants to be served and honored, how salvation has been offered, what the true way consists in.

There is another approach to the defense of Christianity, however, that works quite differently and is hostile to the rationalism of classical apologetics.[51+] Its ancestry goes back to very early times, when Christianity was in competition with philosophy and general culture rather than in league with them, and Christian apologists argued from the salutary effect their religion had on the heart and mind so as to justify it against culture and philosophy.[52] This occasionally resulted in a stark rejection of philosophy and of the type of thinking that produces it, and begat that bald antirational commitment to received belief that is properly called *fideism,* in which the unreasonableness of a belief does not count against it. The most notorious example of this in antiquity is Tertullian, who asserted that the Christian doctrine of the Incarnation, scoffed at by cultured unbelievers, is "believable because absurd, certain because impossible."[53]

Christian thought soon allied itself with philosophy and rationality, however, and eventually became thoroughly comfortable with natural theology. Blaise Pascal reacted against this in his celebrated distinction between "the god of the philosophers" and "the God of Abraham, Isaac, and Jacob," and in his equally celebrated preference of the latter on grounds that he thought should not be held to rational account: "the heart has its reasons which the reason does not know."[54] The subjectivism that Pascal sponsored remained undeveloped in published circles until the work of Søren Kierkegaard at the end of the nineteenth century, and since then this nonrational mode has become widely adopted, especially in the wake of Karl Barth and Cornelius Van Til, whose highly influential work is firmly set against natural theology and the rational approach to Christian belonging. I will refer to this general stance by what is probably the most widely used label attached to its more recent forms: dialectical theology.

Dialectical theology takes its point of departure from the conviction that natural humanity, operating under its own power, is too beset by the effects of sinfulness, ignorance, willfulness, and limitation to undertake a search for the utterly transcendent God without bungling the job monstrously and fully defeating its own purposes. The only possible source of authentic relation to and knowledge of God is therefore God's self-giving and self-disclosure. Hence the attempt to prove the existence of God, traditionally the first step in apologetics, is repudiated by dialectical theology. The initiative must come from God, not from humankind. If we are born again (in the presuppositional theology of Van Til), if we submit obediently and with faith to the graciously and gratuitously given Word of God (in the theology of Barthian neo-orthodoxy), then we can begin to theologize from what is given in the transformation of understanding that results. But this transformed state and the pretransformed natural mind are discontinuous; apologetics can be only a description of Christian faith (in the believing sense in which they use the term), not a rational argument that induces it.

There is something grand and inspiring in dialectical theology's dogged determination to resist not only the domestication of God within the small and cozy shape of comfortable piety but even all attempts to think toward

God by means of human resources. And doubtless there are persons whose experience of being born again in Christ, or of falling under the judgment of the inbreaking power encountered through the Bible whose center is Christ, makes human reasoning seem trivial. Such a believer neither needs nor wants any supplementary reflection to defend and justify the beliefs that are somehow brought about in the course of such a transformation. Rational evaluation, criticism, or readjustment of such beliefs must seem an outrageous mistake. If Paul is rapt to the third heaven and hears words that may not be spoken aloud, it is pointless for him to attempt to persuade the Corinthians that it happened and was appropriate; if the folks dancing around the Golden Calf are skeptical of what Moses reports about his conversations on Sinai, there's not much he can do without further assistance; if Abraham believes in his deepest integrity that God has summoned him to kill his beloved son, he should probably not bother trying to convince Sarah that he cannot be mistaken or that it makes good sense.

Dialectical theology starts from axioms that are different from the axioms that ground traditional apologetics, and the two can have little fruitful interchange on the subject of the proper way to arrive at Christian belief. The end point seems to be much the same, but the mode of access is different, as with two happy marriages in which one couple fell in love at first sight and the other first met on their wedding day through the carefully negotiated mediation of a marriage broker.

But what if you don't fall in love at first sight? Nor want to put that much of your future into the hands of a matchmaker? Is marriage then out of the question?

Those who do not have the kind of belief that classical apologetics tries to justify, and that dialectical theology settles for confessing, are not likely to arrive at it by either route. Whether the beliefs of classical apologists and dialectical theologians are finally identical, despite their disagreements about how to think about them, does not matter much to one who cannot start with a conviction that they are true. Those who happen to belong to the jury may recognize that the prosecuting attorney has tried to present the strongest case she can make, and may be struck by the evident sincerity and feeling of her star witness, but deciding what is right involves more than being impressed. The question for many Christians is not how to prove the truth of traditional Christian beliefs, or how to proclaim it most effectively, but how to decide whether it is there at all.

From this perspective, the belief promoted by classical apologetics is inaccessible. What is more, it is, when the matter is thought through, also *unacceptable,* and not to be encouraged in one's great-grandchildren. There is too much about it that appears to be false, and too much that seems to be falsifying, to inspire a longing for the belief that is not already there in the heart and mind or a hope that one's descendants may acquire it. Whether others arrive at their obedient and trusting convictions by a reasoned justification of traditional authorities, or by a once-for-all transformation of understanding, or merely by accepting without question what they grew up with, the place where they arrive looks, from the kind of critical sense of truth that informs much of current Christian reconsideration, far too arbitrary and unlikely, much too provincially dependent on doubtful notions of revelation, and altogether too gnostic in its confidence in beliefs that cannot be adequately reconciled with the supposition that truth looks like truth. In short, it does not appear to be intellectually and spiritually responsible.

Dialectical theologians are of course not concerned to seem intellectually or spiritually responsible to those who do not already believe, but only to be responsible to what is revealed. Classical apologists are concerned about being intellectually responsible up to the point at which the key authority is shown to be, and turned over to, a Bible and a specific tradition of interpreting it, or a church that solves all important problems. But if the chain of reasoning is faulty, and the authority claimed for a particular way of reading a Bible (or thinking about a church) lacks plausibility, the crucial question is begged rather than answered: why should we conclude that these beliefs are in fact authoritatively revealed?

THE UNDERMINING OF APOLOGETICAL AND DIALECTICAL FOUNDATIONS

Classical apologetics and dialectical theology, although they are deeply opposed to one another in procedure, come to agreement when they get to what they finally profess: a conviction that in the Bible, and especially in Jesus Christ as disclosed in the Bible (or specifically in the Bible as interpreted officially by the Church), we are to find the locus of the ultimate truth about human possibility before God. Classical apologetics tries to prove it; dialectical theology tries to bear persuasive witness to it. Those who are not convinced, by either the arguments or the confessional witness, about this sense of the Bible's (or the church's) privileged place and this confidence in its Christology, may wonder whether it makes good sense to entertain such ideas at all.

There is little room for discussion across this barrier. Paleontologists, struggling to discover what can be learned from the evidence of fossils, cannot discuss the matter fruitfully with creationists who maintain that the fossils too were created a few thousand years ago; those who were impressed with Mesmer's famous early demonstrations of hypnotism could not profit in their attempts to understand it by talking with those scientists who were convinced that Mesmer was nothing but a clever fraud. No matter which side may turn out to be right, you can't argue people from one side to the other by appealing to assumptions that they refuse to make and consider inconsistent with their reason, faith, experience, and integrity.

A few centuries ago, when the Christian world on the whole could dismiss Judaism as obsolete and superseded, Islam as an especially virulent heresy, Hinduism as a jumble of polytheistic pagan superstitions, Buddhism as a program of atheistic spiritual calisthenics, and agnosticism as a cowardly betrayal of faith, there was only one serious candidate for the office of True Revelation. Apologetics set forth its rational credentials and affixed its satisfied Q.E.D. at the end, without having to wait for the approval and authorization of those who were not already convinced that these conclusions *had* to be right. Dialectical theology subsequently affirmed that such conclusions could be *experienced* as right. Both classical apologetics and dialectical theology seem to me to be essentially vestigial remnants of those days, which will come again no more.

There are four major ways in which that world has broken down, irrecoverably. And if the breakdown does not necessarily mean that no one can any longer believe in Christianity—or, more precisely, in the traditionally understood Bible and the classically formulated Christ to which it has seemed to point—in the old way, it at least means that the old way is in parlous straits for those whose sense of truth emphasizes personal integrity.

The first breakdown is in the first step of classical apologetics, the proofs for the existence of God. Controversy on this matter remains alive, especially about the "ontological proof" introduced by Anselm of Canterbury, which argues that our capacity to conceive of a being that exists by necessity demonstrates that such a being must really exist. This argument may satisfy minds that process reality in a certain kind of idealist or Platonic fashion (some people would say that numbers are real only within the mind, while others think that they have reality outside it), and such a mental style is by no means to be dismissed as either wrong or inferior; but not all minds work this way, and the ontological argument is for the most part found unpersuasive, and is impeached by its critics as depending on a faulty logic and a confusion between concepts and realities.[55] The other traditional proofs have all been faulted[56+] and have largely fallen into disuse as proofs, though acknowledged to have a degree of retrospective supportive value for a belief in God that has been arrived at in another way.[57+] Given the total body of critical reflection on this question, it may be fair to conclude that the results leave us free to claim that God exists, but not to claim that we can prove it adequately. This is apparently no longer a viable apologetical enterprise. The loss is not momentous or even particularly significant, except for its effect on apologetics, since there are many realities that cannot be *proven* real; but it may be important to recognize that this is not an available way for the mind to get sturdily to God, so that we can concentrate on other ways. I will attend to this problem in Chapters 8 and 10. In the meantime, it seems that Pascal was right about the inadequacy of the god of the philosophers.

The second breakdown is in the central step of nearly all forms of apologetics, including the antirationalist apologetics of dialectical theology: the establishment of a universally definitive Christian revelation. There is no longer an intellectually honorable way of accomplishing this.[58+] The naive Christian supposition that the Bible is authentic revelation and the scriptures of other religions are not, simply cannot be supported by serious argumentation. For reasons that I will advance in Chapter 5, the traditional assumption that the Bible is composed of the infallible and inerrant words communicated by God to humankind is now an endangered species that seems destined to dwindle steadily. The same is true of more modest promotions of the Bible as definitive revelation. Virtually unanswerable critical questions have left the status of the Bible so much in doubt as to unsettle its relationship to theology altogether and call forth such an uneasy statement as this: ". . . one wonders how long the Bible can meaningfully serve as even a second source of theology equal to experience if it cannot be conceived (in some sense) to have God's commission behind it."[59] The various retreat actions designed to save the principle by reducing the audacity of the claim—e.g., the more moderate position that the revelation lies in God's deeds as reported by the Bible, especially those accomplished through Jesus—face another difficulty that is likely to overwhelm them, and that is my next point. In the meantime, it may be said that there is still a way of arguing qualifiedly for the Bible's divine commission, in that it is an expression of the divinely empowered Godwardness of human aspiration (more on this in the next chapter); but there is no clean way of excluding the scriptures of other religions, or even nonscriptural writings, from an equivalent commission—and no obvious way of defending all biblical texts as equally successful in fulfilling it.

The third breakdown: the problems entailed in supposing that God intervenes selectively in history are so considerable that theologians are increasingly disinclined to promote this traditional view. In a nutshell, "The idea of a God who acts has become so problematic today that it receives scant attention."[60] The reasons for this are various.[61] One of them is the readiness with which putative acts of God may and should be accounted for by other means. The Bible itself offers an utterly superb example: 2 Sm 24.1 says that God inspired David to commit the sin of taking a census; 1 Chr 21:1, evidently realizing that this would hardly be worthy of God, says that the inspiration came from Satan. Would anyone want to defend the earlier version and put the responsibility on God's direct intervention? (Most of us would perhaps be inclined to take the correction a step further and opine that the inspiration probably came from David's financial ambitions, in consultation with his tax department: no need to look further than that.) Another reason for the waning of an intervening God is that a scientific understanding of the natural order offers thoroughly reasonable alternative explanations for some of the purported divine interventions, raises doubts about the reality of others, and leaves open the possibility of finding noninterventional ways of accounting for any remainder. We now know, as our distant predecessors did not, that making the sun stand still for Joshua is not like making a parade pause for a while; a literal and astronomical version of the happening would involve too many complications and repercussions to be thinkable—unless we accord God the power to manipulate reality as easily as we manipulate our fantasies, which leads to theological disaster and spiritual stultification. We also know that reports of more localized wonders with less disruptive consequences are more reasonably accounted for by imaginative inventiveness. Or the misapprehension of witnesses. Or the embroidery of tellers and retellers. Or (if one can get over those high hurdles) the possibility of a still-undiscovered systematic explanation, or at least the isolation of imitable techniques that work, as in the way that hypnotism was rescued from its initial reception as either wonder or fraud and made a readily replicable parlor game. But perhaps the most prominent and decisive problem, putting all miracle reports and other direct divine actions into deep question, is one I touched on in Chapter 1: the idea of God's selective intervention is protected only by dangerously selective thinking. If we are more thorough and consistent in our thought, we must face the implication that a God who deliberately intervenes to save a party by changing water into wine is also necessarily a God who deliberately declines to intervene when vastly more is at stake, which is intolerably inconsistent with any sane notion of divine benevolence. I will sketch an alternative notion of an acting God, one that does not involve selective intervention, in later chapters. I will have no further words in appreciation of the God of selective intervention, who seems to me an irredeemably false conception and best abandoned in all theological work and in almost all practical piety.

The fourth point of breakdown in the old order of thought is the dissolution of the reflex Christian condemnation of other religions, and its replacement by a steadily increasing tendency to take them seriously. It is no longer possible to consider it obvious that they are inferior to Christianity in their thought, ways of life, sources of revelation, or sense of God. This is possibly the most important theological development of the last few generations—perhaps of the last few centuries—and I will enlarge on its implications in chapter 14. Between here and there, I will take it for granted that reasonable Christians will accept the change of heart and mind mentioned in this paragraph.

I suggest that the balance sheet, when all this is added up, tells us that the Christian tradition can no longer be expected to develop in the shadow of the framework of thought represented by classical apologetics, nor in the lightning flash of the dialectical counterposition. There is a need for a stronger and steadier light than these approaches provide. When examined by such a light, the received tradition of Christianity's self-understanding is simply inadequate. Those who see it in such a light offer a challenge that should not be refused. The received form of the tradition, as I have previously suggested and now reiterate in this context of failed apologetics, needs to be theologically restructured if it is to be saved from intellectual bankruptcy. It is not enough that there are still millions of people who stand ready to grant it endless credit: the critical insolvency is larger than their resources can cover, and they are not entitled to mortgage the future credibility of the tradition to make ends meet temporarily.

That evaluation, even if accurate, does not imply the future demise of Christianity. Nor does it mean that the only future Christians will be those who can accept the dubious arguments of classical apologetics and those who can bypass reasonable accountability with a leap of belief. There are, after all, many people at present who remain loyal to a Christian belonging despite their inability to assent to the official beliefs of their churches. It is likely that their numbers will increase before they start dwindling out of discouragement, but they will not disappear altogether. Those whose general trust in the claims of the tradition is disciplined and qualified by an insistence on holding them critically accountable will reconstruct their Christianity according to different principles, with or without churchly hospitality. I do not think that Christianity could thrive if such people were excluded, and there is no means of keeping them out, even if they may be repudiated by particular churches. There is a need now, and I guess that it will steadily increase over the next couple of generations, to provide a theology and a piety that will honestly address not only the precarious state of undisbelief but also the positive disbeliefs that critical inquiry inevitably begets. And there is a need to provide an interpretation of the Christian tradition that will stand in all weather, that our great-grandchildren can gladly embrace as their home.

I think that an authentic general reinterpretation, sufficient to provide a foundation for such a theology and such a piety, is possible as well as desirable. The Christian tradition is inexhaustibly rich. It is endowed with resources that reach well beyond the limits of the customary creeds and catechisms and fumblings at proof and testimonies of personal or communal belief. If the conventional ways of abstracting the essential doctrines of this tradition contain much that is either untrue or uncomfortably doubtful, then we need not conclude that Christianity must be jettisoned or that it can be sustained only by self-deception or bad faith. We may rather conclude that we have been mistaken about some doctrinal particulars, and mistaken about how essential they are to Christianity itself. We may conclude that we still have a lot to learn about Christianity.

There is real life in the Christian way, however incomplete and malformed its habitual self-description may be, and there is room and nourishment there for faith that can stand in all weather and does not need to lie. We have not yet learned very well how to go about the needed reconsiderations and reconstructions, or how to articulate them theologically. Let us get better at it.

John Henry Newman, grand exemplar of a great tradition of honest believing theologians, reassured the anxious and troubled faithful of his time that a thousand difficulties do not make a doubt. Those who can no longer follow the lead of his kindly and stalwart light may be given a different reassurance: a thousand doubts do not make a difficulty. We need good honest doubting now, as much as we then needed Newman's good honest belief, to clear the theological air and give us a new start.

Newman tried, with admirable success, to be faithful to early Christianity while acknowledging that its doctrine could develop without being fundamentally changed. We too can, and should, be faithful to early Christianity: but we should recognize, in a way that Newman did not, that if we allow ourselves enough hope and perspective, we should suppose that *we are still in early Christianity,* looking to thousands of years of its future; and therefore we have, like it or not, the task of helping to shape it according to the requirements of faith and truth.

The next two chapters are a pair of steps in that direction. They turn to the reconsideration, and the reconstruction, of Christian thinking about the two key preoccupations of Christian apologetics: first, the Bible; and then, the idea and the person of Jesus, surnamed the Christ.

5

THE

BIBLE

The place of the Bible in Christian theology has been, with rare exceptions, sturdy and unchallenged from virtually the beginning. It has been like the constitution to which all subsequent law must conform, the body of scientific knowledge from which technology is derived, the blueprints which the builders must follow faithfully. But the content of the Bible has varied from age to age and from group to group, and the understanding of the nature of that content has varied even more—and the character of the Bible's specific role in theology has varied with it.

THE FORMATION AND DEFORMATION OF THE CHRISTIAN BIBLE

To begin with, earliest Christians did not quite have a Bible. They had writings that they understood to be divinely inspired, but there was still some unclarity, in earliest Christian times, about just what did and did not belong to what the Jewish tradition called then (and still calls) "Torah (or The Law), Prophets, and Writings."[62] Greek-speaking Jews (and subsequently, Greek-speaking Christians) used a collection that included works not recognized as true scripture by the Rabbinic movement; the rabbis themselves still disputed, well into the first Christian century, the status of the Song of Songs; the Epistle of Jude cites, as if scriptural, a writing attributed to Enoch that failed to survive in any extant collections of the holy books (though it was obviously in collections that have perished). Earliest Christians had holy scriptures, but not a Bible.

The scriptures to which earliest Christians appealed therefore contained some variables; but they did not contain what we now call the New Testament. The scriptures of the earliest Christians were the Hebrew Scriptures, with or without Enoch and the Song of Songs and the Wisdom of Solomon (depending on which early Christian community we're talking about), and were used by Christians to establish how God had been and still was at work, creating an elect people, regulating their behavior, and foreshadowing the redemptive events that had now taken place through Jesus Christ.

Some of the early Christian writings, including several that witness to these attempts to see in the Hebrew Scriptures a prophetic anticipation and validation of Christianity, were eventually gathered together, in stages, and gradually accorded a status like that of the scriptures to which they appealed. Thus was the New Testament created, and the scriptures of the Christians enlarged to include a record of the doings and teachings of Jesus and the doings and teachings of his early followers. Scriptures, including the new Christian scriptures, gradually became Bible,[63+] but with some wavering of boundaries, a few of which are still with us. Marcion, early in the second century, attempted to repudiate the Hebrew Scriptures altogether as a source of true revelation, but with only temporary and limited success; the Fourth Gospel was rejected for a time in some parts of Asia Minor, and the final book of the present New Testament was not universally accepted as scripture by Christian churches until the tenth century.[64] The reformers of the sixteenth century eliminated from their Bible some books that had belonged to the Bibles of their childhood (an inheritance from the scriptures of Greek-speaking Jews and early Greek-speaking Christians, passed on in Latin translation through the medieval Western church), and as a consequence those books now form part of the Bibles of Catholics but not of Protestants. The Latter-day Saints added to their Bible the Book of Mormon and other books still not recognized as authoritative by other churches. The actual contents of the Bible still remain variable in the Christian world.

The theological importance of the Bible, however—no matter which Bible is in question—remained steady. The Reformation tended to promote the view that the Bible alone held divine revelation; Catholicism claimed revelational authority for understandings passed down in tradition, even if they were not recorded in biblical books, but maintained the authority of the Bible as the primary and most substantive source of revelation and therefore of theology. In the present state of Christian theology, the Bible is still held almost universally to be normative for Christian theology. It is held to be the word of God, inspired and authoritative, and the record of a definitive revelation that is not to be altered or augmented until the end of the world. Theologians have generally treated it accordingly.

But "accordingly" has never been, and is not now, an obvious matter. Given that the Bible is inspired and authoritative revelation, how does a theologian use it to think out how reality is to be understood?

In early Christian times, the Hebrew Scriptures were combed for possible prophecies of Christian events. The rules for finding such prophecies were rather loose. For several centuries, the Hebrew Scriptures were perceived by Christian exegetes as a sort of code through which God had offered a revelation different from what it appeared to be on the surface; to read them "spiritually" was to go deeper and to find a revelation of Christianity and of the Christian way. Ingenuities in breaking the code to get helpful Christian results knew hardly any bounds, and some of the results are, from a modern perspective, curious and somewhat embarrassing. In Mt 2:15, a text in Hos (11:1) is read as a prophecy of the return of the child Jesus from a temporary exile in Egypt; it is evidently of no concern that in its original context it quite obviously refers to the Exodus. The author of the Epistle of Barnabas, noticing the number of the circumcised in Abraham's household (Gn 14:14 conflated with Gn 17:27), points out with considerable satisfaction that the letters used to form this number in the Greek numeral system can be understood as referring to the cross and to Jesus Christ (Barn 9.9); it is evidently of no account to him that this interpretation does not work if the text is dealt with in its original Hebrew, or that no non-Christian could ever have come up with such a reading, no matter how piously and thoughtfully she pondered the text. The First Epistle of Clement (chapter 22) casually assumes that the voice of Psalm 34 is that of Christ speaking to Christians, which could not have entered the mind of any sane reader a century earlier.

Early Christian exegetes read the Hebrew Scriptures allegorically, typologically, and with queer senses of prophecy, apparently supposing that getting supportive Christian results essentially validated what they did, no matter how they got them. Evidently, it simply did not matter how the text would be read by those who approached it with a trust that it is to be understood to mean what it seems to mean, rather than as a hidden Christian message. Technically, this is not *exegesis,* getting the meaning out of a text, but *eisegesis,* putting a meaning in where it is not invited; it may less technically be called *interpretive forgery.*

The Bible came to be seen as a highly complex structure of prophecies and fulfillments, allegories, typologies, and veiled disclosures, a grand open-ended riddle by which nearly any theological opinion could be supported. Its historical origins were never forgotten, but were neither much understood nor much studied. They didn't count for much. The Bible was held to be God's words, dictated into human history but from beyond it; its writings were addressed only ostensibly to Israel, Theophilus, or the church at Rome, and were really written to all Christians at all times.

This view remained largely unquestioned and unchallenged until the fifteenth century. In the meantime, a gradual shift occurred in overall ways of thinking about reality that must eventually call that kind of Bible into question. Natural philosophy (i.e., protoscience) increasingly saw happenings in the world not as caused directly by God but as products of "second causes," built-in regulatory influences that worked as if God had designed the world to be at least somewhat self-determining rather than requiring constant divine intervention. Some theologians complained about the impiety of this view, wanting to maximize the ways in which creation depended immediately upon God, but further investigation sustained the notion that God had endowed the universe with regular principles of happening (thus making science possible, as the investigation of those regular principles). The same habit of thought gave rise to an altered sense of what counts as evidence and what may be learned from considering it, and an altered sense of the appropriate ways of reasoning and understanding. Changes occurred in the map of the world and in the map of the heavens; history was reconsidered and rewritten; political and philosophical and ecclesiastical traditions were challenged and occasionally overturned.

The Bible continued to hold its theological place, but it was read in a different way in the European churches. The historical contexts of its books were given new attention, along with the original Hebrew and Greek languages that underlay the received Latin translation; allegorical, typological, and other coded readings fell out of fashion. New theological conclusions were argued from this newly read Bible, challenging the interpretive forgeries that had supported earlier conclusions. Early in the sixteenth century, John Colet reported the surprise and thrill he experienced in learning to read Paul's epistles as the writings of a specific historical man to specific historical churches, rather than as God addressing Christians of all times and places through the superficial occasion of Paul's history. But although the Bible's human dimension rose to greater prominence, it was still seen as the words of God, a text whose origins and character were unlike those of any other text and whose authority was absolute.

It was only a matter of time, however, before such assumptions had to be challenged. When studied from the perspective of the historian, according to the rules that are applied to other ancient documents, the Bible put up little resistance. It began to look rather like other ancient documents. There were ways of accounting for it that did not require an assumption of supernatural origin, and ways of reading it that made it look as if it was not free of ordinary human limitations after all. Over the last two centuries, there has been a gradual and largely reluctant drift toward compromising, and even surrendering, the traditional sense of its infallibility and inerrancy. The Bible began to be dethroned from its celestial seat and placed on earth, firmly in the midst of human history.

In this human setting, how much of the Bible's divine right was to be sustained? Some theologians resisted this apparent demotion altogether and vigorously opposed its supporters; other theologians accepted this proposed change of address and set about trying to minimize the cost of the move, finding new ways of explaining and justifying the Bible's authority, claim to inspiration, and status as definitive revelation. Protecting the privileged place of the Bible, securing its position in Christian theology, became a major theological enterprise. It still is.

PROTECTING THE BIBLE

How shall we go about it?

First, it should be recognized that how to go about it is entirely a matter of choice. We are not forced to historicize and humanize the Bible, and neither are we forced to continue to think of it as inspired revelation at all. Despite the impressive results of historical researches and historical criticism, we are still free to see the Bible as infallible and inerrant. The styles of thinking that are most in fashion now and given privileged places in our universities—scientific, historical, psychological, sociological—are no more likely to lead to an inerrant and infallible Bible than chemical analysis is likely to lead to a definitive interpretation of *Hamlet;* but no decent scientist, historian, psychologist, sociologist, or other specialist in the advancement of human understanding, will be likely to claim that there are no other viable ways of thinking or to deny that the present results of their enterprises are only provisional, capable of being overturned by further advances. They are not in a position to refute the claim that the Bible is a privileged exception; they can only observe that their disciplines can produce no good grounds for asserting that it is so exceptional and that they are able to offer other ways of accounting for the texts in question. The choice remains open. On what basis should it be made?

It should not be made, surely, by pretending that there is really no choice —by alleging that the Bible is obviously or demonstrably infallible and inerrant, or by asserting that it claims to be so and therefore must be, or by maintaining that to think of it otherwise is mere pride and impiety. All of that is untrue. Neither should it be made *simply* out of pious obedience to God, or because such is the basic assumption of one's religious tradition. To be piously obedient to God does not automatically entail supposing the Bible to be what a given religious tradition says it is, and to belong to a religious tradition is not to pledge never to try to alter it for the better.

Other ways of thinking about the Bible raise doubts about its inerrancy and infallibility, pointing out inconsistencies, historical errors, and general signs of ordinary human weaknesses; and while much intelligent Christian ingenuity has been dedicated to arguing that these are not really inconsistencies and errors, quite a bit of thoughtful industry is given by others to the job of arguing that the Bible may be allowed to contain minor untruths without robbing it of its authority as divine revelation.

Bible traditionalists may legitimately ask, with legitimate impatience and even anger at what may seem to them to be faithless cowardice and capitulation to modern fashionable unbelief, just what revelational authority is the Bible allowed to maintain under such a skeptical regime? I will try to describe the choice that is left.

It is difficult to render such a description to anyone who supposes that revelation can occur only when benighted humanity is visited by a power well beyond human reach. That not only begs the question, it makes at least two other theologically suspect moves: (a) it leaves quite unaccountable the ability of human beings to recognize revelation when it arrives (a child can recognize an adult's shouting as being important, but an adult must eventually discriminate good shouts from bad, and distinguish the small still voice of helpful suggestion from the small still voice of seduction); and (b) it presumes, on inadequate grounds, that God has left us with infantile incapacity to carry on the most important aspects of life *while,* simultaneously, requiring us to recognize the divine voice even when it issues from such a bland and self-effacing mediator as Luke in the preface to his Gospel, writing without any claims beyond his own sense of responsibility and the quality of his research.

It is not, I submit, unfair or impious to suggest that God is not likely to leave God's own image and likeness caught in such a crunch. It is (whether traditional thus far or not) at least as likely that God has empowered those who carry such image and likeness to discover what has been revealed and promulgate it as a discovery of God and God's ways. Paul, being careful to establish his theological credentials with a Roman community whom he had never visited, says as much about the case of the Gentiles: they did not have the revelation given to Moses on Sinai, but they had the world at large from which to read the truth and glory of God, and have no excuse for having blown the opportunity.

If we push Paul's thought about the Gentiles far enough, we come to a mediating position about revelation. It is better, by far, to receive it directly through a divine intervention. But we are not entitled to wait until that happens. God has provided revelation in the very structure of God's creation—not as lucid as dictated words, or inscriptions with a burning hand, but enough to go on—and we have no right to complain if we are aware of nothing beyond this level of divine disclosure.

It is with this style of piety—not impiety or mere skepticism, but rather a reverence for God as the universally benevolent provider—that theological revisionists approach the Bible. We (well, I and many others: I can't speak for the whole spectrum) are not despondent to find no spectacular evidence of heavenly dictation, or discouraged to imagine that everything contained in the biblical books has been thoroughly filtered through limited human imaginations, or bothered by the thought that everything in those books may have been invented by representatives of God's image and likeness who were devoutly in search of God and told the results of that search as well as they could. We rejoice in the results: the books of the Bible are among the most encouraging and inspiriting writings that human beings have ever produced, and a testimony that God has given ordinary mortals —probably even us—the capacity to discover and pursue a belonging to God that overflows in such zeal, wisdom, challenge, infectious enthusiasm, and sheer delight as we still find in the records of two thousand years ago and more. If this should turn out to be the only way in which God has arranged for revelation to happen, we are not complaining. It is generous, and enough. We would of course be grateful for still more, but we think it would be unappreciative—and perhaps unrealistic—to be dissatisfied when so much has been made available.

The choices are now there, available. Taking any option is a choice against the alternative options. Such an important decision ought to be recognized as a choice, and ought to be made responsibly, in the light of other possibilities.

Of course, the decision is not always deliberated and conscious. You may simply accept the views of your community or your tradition as part of the package of belonging to them; or you may feel seized by a text (or by the happening it reports, or by a power that breaks in through it) as by the presence of a charismatic leader, and experience the encounter as if you are being judged and decided by this Word rather than the other way around, and can only submit and assent. But even in these cases, you must eventually decide, when the question comes up, whether and why and how to continue to entrust yourself to this sense of belonging. For the quality and truth of such belonging depend not on how you got there in the first place, but why and how you continue there.

There is a firm tendency against the more conservative option among well-informed people, and for good reasons. One reason is that many of the Bible's apparent inconsistencies, errors, and contradictions are difficult to explain away and even more difficult to account for in a body of related documents that, by conservative theory, could be expected to be unusually free of even *apparent* difficulties of this kind. Another reason is that the documents that form the Bible have been extensively studied according to the techniques normally used for the investigation of any ancient documents, and they seem to present no serious problem to the investigator who wishes to understand them in those terms. They behave like regular documents. They use known ancient languages, in accordance with the habits of style and vocabulary prevailing at generally identifiable historical periods; they conform to known characteristics of specific historical and cultural contexts; and in general, they present nothing to the historical critic that requires their being given exceptional status. No pressure arises from within historical criticism that makes it necessary to accord to them a quality of inspiration significantly different from that found in a respectful reading of Homer or Pindar, of Dante or Blake.

Of course, that does not prove that they are not exceptionally and supernaturally inspired; but it shifts the balance of proof to those who wish to claim that they are. Much scholarly energy is dedicated to accounting for the remarkable happenings in the texts of Homer, Pindar, Dante, and Blake, and much still remains to be accounted for; but no serious scholar would claim that the accounting must appeal to a form of inspiration that is beyond gifted human capacities. If the books of the Bible seem to the eye of the historical scholar so thoroughly like books that are not of the Bible, and if the study of what looks human about them produces no nonhuman leftover as evidence of a supernatural origin, what grounds do we have for claiming that they are divinely inspired in a way that human life itself is not?

Christian incarnational theology offers a basis for explaining how Jesus could have all the characteristics of human flesh and blood and still be genuinely divine: true God and true man, at once. Respectful biblical scholars, intent on honoring the special authority of the Bible, have increasingly tended to acknowledge that whatever revelation is offered there is offered incarnately, through processes and texts that are fully human. Even if also expressing revelation that is genuinely divine, the Bible expresses limitations that are authentically human: instances of ignorance, superstition, bigotry, brutality of mind, desensitizing arrogance, and self-serving credulity can be found as readily as errors, inconsistencies, contradictions. The analogy of the Incarnation makes it possible to admit this without scrapping the authority and inspiration of the Bible. In the general spirit of what Paul quoted to the Philippians about Jesus' having humbled himself to human limitations (Phil 2:6–8), it is possible to suppose that God's revelation was humbled to the shape of God's image and likeness as embedded in human history.

Possible, but not altogether comfortable. Christians, including Christian theologians, have generally been wary about the human side of the Incarnation, and have been slow to accept the implication of Phil 2:6–8 that Jesus may have been approximately as culture-bound, provincial, and generally limited in his understanding as his neighbors; and theologians have been equally slow to accept that the same may be said of the biblical texts. Christians have usually wanted a Jesus who thought with the mind of God, not of man, even if one of their most central and cherished doctrines makes it not only acceptable but appropriate that he should have learned and thought about the world in the ordinary human way; Christians, even while acknowledging that the human voice may be an authentic vehicle of divine communication, have usually wanted a Bible that speaks with the voice of God, not of human beings.

Admitting the humanity of biblical texts does not mean giving up claims to the Bible's special inspiration and authority—but it does put those claims on the witness stand, where the cross-examination reveals them to be vulnerable. One may say that the Bible only *appears* to be of human origin, but is in fact exactly determined, word by word, by the will of God. There is no way to refute such a claim; it could, in fact, be entirely true. But the same claim has been made for the Qur'an, and could imaginably be made for the works of Vergil, or Luther, or Swedenborg, or Werner Erhard, or even for the 1984 Saskatoon telephone directory. How may such a claim be founded and tested?

Here and there, a claim like this is made overtly within the Bible. The prophet says, "This is the word of the Lord," or the narrator says that God wrote these words with a burning hand. But why should we believe the prophet and the narrator, when similar assertions are made by others whom we do not believe? And in any event, how can occasional localized claims of this kind be stretched to include the Bible in general? One may hear, from time to time, that the Bible validates itself as extraordinarily inspired through 2 Tm 3:16, but this both begs and misses the question: this verse is itself a claim that may be doubted, and there is no good reason to think that it refers to what was later to become, through the gradual decisions of Christian communities, the New Testament.

The Bible, as such, does not make such a claim for itself, and cannot—for the Bible, as such, is not self-constituting, but is a collection stocked and authorized in different ways by the slow development of Israelite piety, by the work of compilers and editors during and shortly after the Babylonian exile, by the inventiveness of Alexandrian Hellenist Jews, by the Rabbinic movement toward the end of the first century, by the Christian movement gradually over the next 900 years, by the work of sixteenth-century reformers, and by Joseph Smith in the last century. The Bible, in short, is something historically made by human decisions, and there is still no universal Christian agreement about what belongs to it. Its exact boundaries are still, right now, not agreed even among Protestants, let alone among all those who accept Genesis as Holy Scripture. The question therefore remains: Why should any one of the collections of texts revered as Bible by Samaritans, Jews, Protestants, Catholics, or Mormons, be held to have a privileged quality of inspiration and be treated accordingly as the major, or even an important, source of theological authority?

The answer is somewhat disappointing and disconcerting. It should be held as inspired revelation and theologically foundational because it *has been held* as inspired revelation and theologically foundational. Neither more nor less. At the simplest level, this means that we are used to doing it this way and do not wish to reconsider. At a more complicated level, it means that when we reconsider, we reaccept it as the way we want, because, like our language, our values, our family, it is where we were formed and where we feel we belong and where our reality is given the shape and guidance we prefer to all other options.

None of the possible places is uninhabitable. If you wish, you may have an inerrant, infallible Bible that gives you God's indispensable instructions for just what you should do and not do, tells you how everything began and where it is going, resolves all the major questions, and puts you among those who are graciously saved. The catch is that you must be prepared to pay what it costs. Nothing comes free in theology, any more than in any other means of ordering and structuring a system. To have that kind of Bible, you must have the kind of God it implies—a God who communicates in such a way as to make the ultimate divine communication indistinguishable from the communications of earnest (and sometimes not so earnest) human beings, a God whose infallible and inerrant words look for all the world like fallible and errant ones, and therefore a God who hides celestial communication from, and perhaps damns, those whose honest inquiry concludes in the judgment that a divine revealer would be highly unlikely to offer the decisive revelation in a fashion that makes it look so unlike what it really is.

God's ways are not our ways, we are frequently reminded. But what does this theological principle tell us? It tells us, I think, that no theological place is uninhabitable. We may imagine a God who deliberately baffles attempts at honest inquiry. We may imagine a God who rewards the gratefully smug and punishes the curious inquirers. We may imagine any sort of God at all, including a malevolent one. We can therefore take the Bible any way we please, including Marcion's reading of the Hebrew Scriptures, which offers a God who is a moral monster, tyrannical and deceptive. The recognition that God's ways are not our ways is a blank check and is not a helpful general principle for reading the Bible. It allows any possible way of doing so, and therefore does not assist us in deciding just what the Bible is or what allegiance we owe to it or how it ought to be understood. We are therefore thrust back into the received traditions of thinking about the Bible, which have eliminated Marcion's ways not because they are impossible and unthinkable but because we have other ways that we prefer. We must fall back, finally, on our sense of appropriateness.

SITUATING THE BIBLE APPROPRIATELY

Appropriateness is a slippery theological principle, because it can appeal simultaneously to received tradition, present cultural norms, aesthetic patterns, and philosophical analogy, in varying combinations and weightings. Still, it is a powerful principle, its strength aphoristically registered in Duns Scotus' pronouncement about the doctrine of the Immaculate Conception of Mary: *"posuit, decuit, ergo fecit"*—God was able, it was appropriate, so he did it. But arguments from decorum may be turned around. If one really holds to the truth of the Incarnation, it may be argued that for God to take human form through a prostitute would be at least as appropriate as to be born of a woman who was free even from Original Sin.

And so it is with the Bible. Traditional apologetics has been swayed by the sense of decorum according to which it seemed appropriate that God reveal his work and his will in ways so clear and reliable as to be inerrant and infallible. God was able, it was apt, so he did it. But there are two deep problems with this view. One is that the Bible, when studied through the techniques of historical investigation, does not appear to be any more clear, inerrant, or infallible than other texts. The other is that it is not obviously more appropriate for God to offer a divine self-disclosure through a privileged verbal inspiration than to empower those who seek God to report according to their best lights what they suppose God has done and is doing, and who or what they understand God to be.

If theology continues to be based on the Bible, it is necessary to be clear about which Bible is being used.

When I ask which Bible, I am not this time talking about which books are included. I am asking about what the given theologian's Bible *is,* what kind of authority it has and where the authority comes from. The infallible/inerrant Bible is losing ground, simply because it looks improbable. It is not impossible, but its plausibility has been eroded, I think decisively and irreversibly, by the force of historical criticism, whose investigations have situated the biblical books within the boundaries of the human possibilities of their time, and have found no remainder to be accounted for only as divine inspiration. For the traditional theologian, this means that God works in human ways, through human history: as if the traditional understanding of the Incarnation, which Christians have never really quite believed, is in fact a good guide to God's willingness to work in terms, and within the limitations, of real human stuff.

It is quite legitimate to object that the historicizing of biblical texts falls importantly short of what they are as biblical texts—that is, to treat Luke's work as if it were a somewhat romanticizing account of the backgrounds and early days of Christianity is only to deal with the first portion of its career, which was later transformed by its being given the status of Holy Scripture. I agree that this matters. Literary theorists generally acknowledge that a text's umbilical cord to its author is severed at birth, and thereafter the author is no longer in charge of how it is allowed to mean. It is released to what tradition will do with it, and the custodians of tradition have choices about how much to know, and how much to respect, the intent and context that determined its original meaning and status.[65+]

A good paradigmatic example is the inscription at Delphi, *gnôthi sauton,* know thyself. Plucked out of ordinary Greek speech—perhaps having become a proverb, which is already a transformation of meaning and authority—it was hallowed by being formally inscribed at one of the most important shrines of the Hellenic world. What did it mean there? The best historical guess seems to be that it was intended, and taken, to be a reminder to mere mortals that they should take care to remember, in this holy place, that they are mere mortals. But once this simple saying or randomly useable proverb had been thus enshrined, it took on a special radiance that made its possible meanings more interesting than whatever meaning was intended by those who carved it in stone, and the next phase of research was conducted not through documents and interviews leading back to the inscribers, but through peising the weight of these two words within new imaginations. By the time of Plato, their resonance had come to be a reminder of the task of discovering truth by introspection, learning who you are as an instructive dimension of the philosophical journey. By Plotinus' time, they were taken as an invitation to discover the hint of divinity disclosed within every reverent self-searcher, and had become much better news than was probably intended by those who set these words up as Scripture.[66]

The original authors are no longer in charge; the original meanings are no longer in charge. Texts have no life of their own, but are infused with the life of their readers, reciprocally, like batteries whose power is awakened only when engaged by an implement with the right wattage and voltage. A text may empower any interpretation that hangs together, and the demoralization that has resulted from a century of relentless historicizing of the Bible[67] is currently being lifted by an appeal to this truth, especially as it is grounded in theory by Hans-Georg Gadamer and Paul

Ricoeur.[68] The Bible, accordingly, can mean new things undreamt of by its original authors, without abusing the texts themselves.

This is good news and bad news. The good news is that we are not confined to the historicist warrant for legitimate interpretation. We can ignore history altogether, and use the canonized texts to acquire and consolidate new meanings and new confirmations entirely foreign, and even opposed, to the understandings they originally purchased. The bad news is that if we take this step, we are no longer in continuity with the historical grounding that has traditionally been taken to be one of the most important guarantees of Christianity's stability and authenticity.

Christianities have characteristically prided themselves on being rooted in history and thus being significantly different from religions founded on myths: in the unmythical Christian case, it has been traditionally argued, what our forebears pledged themselves to was not a good and guiding dream but *something that really took place.* What really took place therefore had a defining authority to which later understandings had to be submitted and disciplined. What happened then, at that foundational time, is the basis of Christian truth. What was said and meant then, in the texts that became the Bible, is the basis of the tradition of Christian understanding. If Christianities are prepared to cut the traditional tie to those foundations, a whole new world of possibilities opens up in the interpretation of their classic texts. But the move is costly. It means surrendering what tradition has understood to be what makes all the difference, what authorizes its claims to being true.

There are defensible reasons for altering the traditional Christian pledge of allegiance to historical grounding. One of them is that serious question has been raised about what really took place, and about the adequacy of early Christian interpretations of it. If the classic texts can no longer buy on the historical market what they once seemed able to afford, they might be spent elsewhere to good effect. But it cannot be pretended that we can retain the right to claim historical grounding, other than in the history of our own receptive interpretation, if we take such an interpretive liberty with the Bible. To try to have it both ways at once is merely a more sophisticated form of interpretive forgery, and it renders Christianity a mythic religion built upon a repudiation of historical integrity and a disdain for honoring the meanings of other Christians.[69]

It is simply not true to say that the biblical texts do not mean what their authors intended them to mean. One may say that they can be read to mean something else, but that is quite a different proposition, and requires a more qualified statement. The "know thyself" inscription at Delphi did not originally mean what Plotinus meant by the same words, and Plotinus cannot outvote its inscribers enough to authorize us to trash what they meant, even if we prefer to think of the words his way. Genesis does not mean that living creatures developed by evolution or that Jesus was part of God's plan from the beginning. Matthew does not mean that sincere Muslims are assured a place in heaven or that the Pharisees' teaching was false. Paul does not mean to call us to Heideggerian authenticity. If we don't like what they *do* mean, the honest response is to disagree with them, not to pretend that they agree with us. If we wish to propose a different interpretation of foundational Christian events or of present Christian life, let it be clear that we are differing, and that we are no longer under the shelter of apostolic authority. If we wish to say, as the Advent liturgy said on the evening on which I write this sentence, that all the prophets announce the coming of Jesus Christ, let it be clear that this is the rhetoric of celebration, with no more literal authority than the wild gestures of political nominating speeches and toasts at wedding banquets: a genuinely respectful reading of the prophets will not support such a claim. Nor will a respectful compact with history validate all that the prophets really predicted, on their own terms. If we wish to keep the traditional Christian pact with history, and faith's commitment to truth, let it be clear that we must simply give up some of what the Bible supposes really happened, and some of what the Bible offers as interpretations of the happenings.

What then becomes of the Bible? Some of its privileges being taken away, in the name of intellectual honesty and in the honor of God's apparent respect for the relative independence of creation (together with its capacity to misjudge, misunderstand, and be misinformed), the Bible then becomes what it always was, played now in a different key: *it is the record of human perceptions of who and what God is, and of what God has done, and of what God wants us to be, and of what God offers for our future, even beyond the grave. It remains one of the world's most illuminating and steadying exemplars of faith turned toward God. It is our best starting point and deserves to be honored as such. It is not necessarily the finish line.*

Some of its privileges cannot be taken away. It remains the formative source of the grammar and vocabulary of our religious understanding, without which we could barely know how to think or hope in the ways we find most fruitful. It remains the most luminously inspiring of all our millions of books, and part of any definition of what we mean by wisdom. It remains our chief religious link with one another and with a hundred generations of predecessors who have revered it and shaped themselves to its steady and enduring form while languages and civilizations and cultures have risen and fallen around them. These are established truths that have not been shaken and need not be lost even if the traditional notion of the divine inspiration of the Bible must finally be abandoned.[70]+

The acute problem that arises when we make this reverent adjustment is that we cannot any longer move beyond what biblical authors say that God has told us to a confidence that God has really told us what they say. The truth of the Bible—not in every sense, but in the most traditionally important sense—is accordingly called into question. That is the essence of the fight that now goes on between those who promote the inerrancy/infallibility of the Bible and those who no longer understand this to be the way God works. We crave divine reassurance, reliable knowledge beyond our usual means, and we have been enticed by a long tradition into supposing that it has been given in the Bible. In the meantime, we have lived with the Bible as a reliable source of such information. Now we are offered a Bible deprived of such privilege, a Bible that is no more than one of the greatest available examples of the dedicated and impassioned human faith toward, and search for, God. That is in fact where we now are.

We do not want to be quite there (though if you reread that next-to-last sentence acceptingly, it may not sound like such a bad deal), not so starkly abandoned by what we want from God's direct guidance and intervening participation. But that is largely because we have not thought the matter through very far.

Christians who gaze upon the dismantling of the Bible's divine authority rarely realize what good news that dismantling is. Think about it: now we have a book that contains what is no less than one of the greatest available examples of the dedicated and impassioned human faith toward, and search for, God! The guidance it gives to our own search is invaluable, and in the meantime we no longer need to make excuses for its bigotries and ignorances, explain away its errors and occasional absurdities, contrive symbolic or "spiritual" reinterpretations of what cannot be swallowed at the literal level, or puzzle painfully over its apparent divinely inspired valorization of contempt for women, Gentiles, non-Christians, heretics, Jews, and people who think that the world is likely to last beyond the reign of Trajan. We can give it proper respectful use as a major and virtually incomparable resource for strengthening faith, reflecting on belief, forming and correcting a way of imagining God and a world under God's creative care, and generally profiting from profoundly important and influential religious advice—and all this while remaining ready and able to take responsibility for our integrity by saying, on occasion, no, this is not true; that will no longer do; I cannot believe these claims; I will not accept the implications of this way of thinking; it is impossible that God could have done or asked such a thing. The demystification of the Bible, if only we would make a less defensive assessment of the matter, is probably the best thing that has happened to Christian culture since it (or at least parts of it) gave up the conviction that God will roast non-Christians forever.

But in the meantime, while we gather our collective wits to appreciate the good news in what is happening to the Bible, theologians try to pick up the pieces of our damaged confidence in it by offering other ways of thinking about the locus of its authority, ways designed to be respectful of the achievements of historical criticism while preserving a sense of biblical privilege. The place of revelation is relocated, away from the words of the prophets and historians and priests and philosophers who wrote the biblical texts, and relegated to a place beyond. Inspiration and divine intervention, it is now often alleged, lie not perhaps in the words of Scripture but rather in the events that it witnesses to, or the encounter with God that may be experienced through it, or the personal and existential decision into which one may be thrust by taking its authors' invitations (or orders) seriously. The words are no longer God's words, but the deeds they report are divine. The new central theological locus is therefore not the text, but the saving events they report, and especially the saving events seen in the career of Jesus Christ. That is where we must go next.

6

JESUS
THE CHRIST

The words of the Bible no longer command the confidence they once enjoyed as a foundation for belief and theology. The *subject* of the Bible is another matter.

As critical developments have made it difficult for theologians to rely on the texts of Scripture, theology has turned increasingly to what lies behind the texts. In one obvious sense, what lies behind the texts is God—but in the Christian tradition, it has been taken mainly to be God prefiguring, acting through, and disclosing the meaning of the career of Jesus. A recent reflection on consensus in theology refers to "the common conviction, shared by all Christians, that the revelatory and redemptive center of human and cosmic history is to be found in Jesus Christ, as attested by apostolic tradition and by the canonical Scriptures."[71]

Four things about this statement are especially notable. The first is that it partially detaches the locus of revelation from the biblical account, which is here made a witness rather than the source. A second is that it identifies Jesus Christ as the unique pivotal point for belief and therefore of theology. A third is that it balances two items in the boldness of the claim, the totality of human and cosmic meaning and redemption on the one hand and Jesus Christ on the other—as if it were to be taken for granted that revelation and redemption are notions that belong to any proper conception of the cosmos (which is not the case) and as if "Jesus Christ" has a clear and coherent meaning (which is not the case) and as if these two notions can be easily and coherently correlated (which is not the case). Fourth: "shared by all Christians" is also not the case.

THE BIBLE AND THE UNDERSTANDING OF JESUS

Making Jesus Christ the center and procedural norm of theology entails problems. One is the problem of access. There are some who suppose that they have immediate access to Jesus Christ, through an illuminative personal relationship. Be that as it may, theology must proceed by an appeal to less private sources. A theological appeal to Jesus Christ is necessarily an appeal to the Bible, for the most part: what can we know about Jesus is mainly what we can know from the Bible, since the information that can be gleaned from other sources is slight and doubtful.

The problem with the Jesus known from the Bible is that there is so little to rely on.

Rudolf Bultmann, surely the most influential New Testament scholar in this century, opined that while the Bible gives us considerable evidence about the early church's sense of the risen and glorified Christ, it can tell us "practically nothing" about the historical Jesus of Nazareth, since the Gospels' accounts are so deeply infiltrated by the postresurrection beliefs through which his story was recounted.

That opinion, dominant among scholars a generation ago, no longer holds sway. It is now generally granted that we can know something, but for the most part it is admitted that we cannot know nearly as much as we used to suppose. Virtually any trained biblical scholar will acknowledge that the Gospel narratives and quotations are colored and leavened by the convictions of the early church, and that to find who Jesus was and what he said and did requires careful critical sifting. Those who have devoted the most labor and care to evaluating the available evidence can offer precious little as unquestionably reliable evidence about the Jesus we seek. Once we have carefully discriminated what he is likely to have said and done from what has been attributed to him, and distinguished between what he was thought to be and what he truly was, and differentiated the events of his earthly career from the interpretations given them by early writers, the picture of Jesus that remains is sketchy and disappointingly uncertain.

Modern researches have discovered that the gospel *about* Jesus, the gospel of the Apostles, is in many respects strikingly different from what can be reconstructed of the gospel *of* Jesus, the one that he himself proclaimed. The two are conflated and fused in the written Gospels, and it appears that early Christians did not much care about, and perhaps did not really notice, the difference between the Jesus thus portrayed in the first four books of the New Testament and the more strictly historical Jesus sought by modern critical research.

Here theology is faced with a potentially awkward choice. If Jesus is to be held the "revelatory and redemptive center of cosmic and human history," he is clearly to be placed at the heart of theology. But which Jesus? The historical Jesus who can be *glimpsed through* the apostolic tradition and the canonical Scriptures, or the Jesus who, elaborately embroidered with early Christian interpretive belief, is *presented by* Scripture and tradition? The question is peculiarly modern, since the two were not distinguished until modern times. But it has arisen and may not be ignored.

How was the difference obscured for so long? It is largely through the role of Scripture, in two senses: one is the role of the Hebrew Scriptures in forming the early Christian interpretation of Jesus in the first place, and the other is the role of the New Testament in imposing this interpretation authoritatively on subsequent Christian generations.

Earliest Christianity appealed to the Jewish Scriptures not only to confirm, but sometimes even to found, its claims for the content and authority of its new gospel. For although the fact of Jesus' crucifixion was public knowledge, and the fact of his resurrection attested by witnesses, the *meaning* of neither of these events was given along with the fact. Despite the Gospels' attempts to represent Jesus as having given instructions about the proper interpretation of both events (and both before and after they took place), the balance of evidence seems clearly to indicate that Jesus' followers had no such help, and had originally to find a way of understanding these things all by themselves (though subsequently faulting their hesitation and crediting Jesus with what they had eventually come up with).

That is, all by themselves with the help of Scripture. Paul gives in 1 Cor 15 one of the oldest surviving evidences of how this was done, as he presents to the church at Corinth a brief summary of the established Christian position on the fact and meaning of the crucifixion and resurrection of Jesus.

And now, my brothers, I must remind you of the gospel that I preached to you; the gospel which you received, on which you have taken your stand, and which is now bringing you salvation. . . . First and foremost, I handed on to you the facts which had been imparted to me: that Christ died for our sins, in accordance with the scriptures; that he was buried; that he was raised to life on the third day, in accordance with the scriptures; and that he appeared to Kephas, and afterwards to the Twelve. Then he appeared to over five hundred of our brothers at once, most of whom are still alive, though some have died. Then he appeared to James, and afterwards to all the apostles. In the end he appeared even to me.

Two features of this summary stand out importantly.

The first is Paul's use of the phrase "in accordance with the scriptures," twice. Obviously he does not mean "as the New Testament says," but "as the Hebrew Scriptures prophesied." With this phrase, he is claiming scriptural authority as a guarantee of the Christian reliance on these facts and interpretations as the works of God; but he is suggesting still more. The burial and third-day resurrection of Jesus might theoretically have been established by apostolic witnesses and then confirmed by Scripture as having indeed been on the providential agenda; but the interpretation of Jesus' death as having been "for our sins" lies beyond the capacities of a mere eyewitness, and it is very likely that Paul is here indirectly bearing witness to another important historical fact—that this interpretation of the crucifixion's meaning *was derived from seeing it as a fulfillment of Scripture.*[72]+

The second striking feature of Paul's summary is that he introduces it by remarking that in presenting it, he is repeating what he has already taught and what he himself had received. Since the summary includes a catalogue of witnesses to Jesus' resurrection appearances, he is evidently summarizing not what he had received from special personal revelation, but what he had received from earlier—it would have to be nearly the very earliest—Christian tradition. If so, then the use of Scripture as an instrument for interpreting Jesus and thus forming the gospel about him, as well as for guaranteeing the truth of this gospel, was apparently a general tradition among those who preceded Paul into the Christian Way. Jesus as revelatory and redemptive center was, from the earliest times, Jesus as interpreted through the Scriptures.

This practice of seeing Jesus through and in the Jewish Scriptures is clearly pervasive in earliest Christian documents, and was readily extended to a massive claim that what took place in the career of Jesus was not merely anticipated in the Scriptures: it was their major preoccupation. For

Paul writing to the Galatians, this is what the information about Abraham's wives and sons was really about; for Paul writing to the Corinthians, this is what was foreshadowed in the creation of Adam, and what was hiddenly at work as Moses guided his people through the wilderness and parted from them to receive the revelation on Mount Sinai. The Epistle to the Hebrews sees in Jesus the real Melchizedek and the perfect realization of the pre-scribed cultus that the Israelites could only approximate. The career of Jesus, as interpreted in the Gospels, became precisely what attentive readers of Scripture ought to have *expected* was in store. Luke's Jesus berates his followers for not having seen that his death and resurrection were *required* by what all the Scriptures revealed (Lk 24:25–27, 44–46); the Jesus of the Fourth Gospel insists that those who revere the writings of Moses should be able to see that they are all about him (Jn 5:45–47).

The attempt to correlate the career of Jesus with the Scriptures had two faces. Looking one way, it used the Scriptures to interpret who Jesus was and what he accomplished, or what was accomplished through him; looking the other way, it used Jesus' career to interpret the meaning and intention of Scripture. But looked at from the side, it was each testing the other —and, as in many two-faced enterprises, the correlation began to break down under testing.

The Scriptures, after all, were not the exclusive property of Christian interpreters. Many Jews who revered them did not think that they could rightly be read as testimony about the Christian gospel; and not even all Christians agreed about how far and in what ways they could be pushed to tell about Jesus. On the other hand, there were various non-Christian ways of interpreting who Jesus was and what he accomplished, some of which pointed to the Scriptures to oppose him, to justify his execution, to disqualify the Christian claims about him, and to deny his resurrection. Even Christians continued to have disagreements about whether or not certain reports about him were true and about which ways of interpreting him were apt. If grand claims about Jesus could be supported by appeals to prophets and psalms, doubts about those claims could also be argued to be "according to the Scriptures."

It need hardly be added that from a present perspective, the limitations of scriptural authority and the limitations of early Christian interpretive technique must be taken into consideration as one evaluates any appeal to "Jesus Christ, as attested by apostolic tradition and by the canonical Scriptures" as the reliable foundation of Christian belief and Christian theology.

JESUS AND THE BIBLE: CONFLICT AND PRIMACY

Even before Paul's conversion, Christian tradition had already pledged itself both to the authority of the Scriptures and to the authority of some sort of gospeling interpretation of Jesus. In cases of apparent conflict between the two, how should the ruling be made? When Scripture is not helpfully supportive of what one believes about Jesus, does one adjust the gospel to more faithful correlation with Scripture, or set the Scripture aside (or distort it to make it fit)?[73+]

This problem still haunts Christian theology. It started at the very beginning.

Ignatius, Bishop of Antioch in the early years of the second century, wrote to the church in Philadelphia about it, stating boldly what he thought should be the Christian ground rules about the primacy of Jesus over the Scriptures. "For I heard some," he reported, "who were saying, 'If I do not find it in the Charters,[74] I do not believe in the gospel.' And when I said to them that it is written,[75] they replied to me that this is what is in question. But for me, the Charters are Jesus Christ—the inviolable Charters are his cross and death, and his resurrection, and the faith through him."[76]

Evidently, Ignatius has had dealings with some who measured the credibility of Christian proclamations by whether they were adequately predicted or foreshadowed in the Hebrew Scriptures, and found the evidence wanting. But for him, the gospel is not to be evaluated on such a basis. It is axiomatic, arrived at not primarily through scriptural interpretation but through belief in its immediate claims about Jesus, whether or not they can be convincingly argued from Scripture. If Scripture and the gospel should collide irreconcilably, it is Scripture that must founder.

The echo of Paul, especially as Paul's usual habits of mind may be distinguished from his sense of tradition, is clear. One begins with belief in the good news of the saving events through Jesus. Scripture is to be reinterpreted in the light of this belief, and is presumed to be thoroughly supportive; but appeal to Scripture is secondary, and is in the long run dispensable. Belief is more importantly invested in an interpretation of Jesus than in an interpretation of Scripture. What God has done through Jesus is more definitive than what God has done through Moses and the prophets. Jesus is more important than Scripture.

From such conclusions came a revision of what it meant to be "according to the Scriptures." Increasingly, the Scriptures lost their power to challenge the development of Christian interpretations of Jesus, especially as the church absorbed Gentiles with little or no history of loyalty to the independent authority of those Scriptures or knowledge of their non-Christian interpretations; at the same time, there grew an instinctive market for specifically Christian Scriptures that could tell the new, or at least newly realized, truth more plainly. The reverence that had once been attached exclusively to the received Holy Books was extended, or displaced, to Christian writings that displayed Jesus' career directly, together with its gospel interpretation. Paul's epistles were gathered, and with them their testimony that through Jesus the Law had been abrogated and the Covenant revised; accounts of what Jesus did and taught formed into new holy books. What eventually became the New Testament began to be gradually canonized as superior to the traditional Scriptures, or at least equal to them (and, being more recent, bigger news than they). What had been unconditionally revered as the Holy Scriptures was in the process of being demoted to being only the Old Testament.

The new tendency had its one extreme in Marcion's total rebuff of the Hebrew Scriptures not only because they were dispensable in their lack of support for what he wanted but also because he judged them to have been given under malicious auspices, the disclosures of a false god from whom Jesus had been the rescuer. (By the same logic, Marcion seems to have been extremely selective about what he would admit to be authoritative among the Christian writings: only what would support his case—cf. the way most Christians select the New Testament verses that deserve great attention and the verses that deserve little attention.) At another extreme, the notion that the Christian revelation made everything else obsolete supported gnostic movements purporting to know what had *really* been revealed through Jesus, passed down through the elite while the public Christian Scriptures kept others in the dark.

But two extremes do not exhaust the list. Events like this are multidimensional, and allow room for more. It appears that other Christian extremists, the Ebionites, resisted some of the more ambitious Christological interpretations of Jesus, largely out of loyalty to traditional Jewish interpretations of Scripture, and were eventually marginalized, ignored, and dismissed as heretical distorters of the true gospel. The Fourth Gospel developed an extreme interpretation of Jesus that came under deep suspicion for a time, but eventually carried the day. Another movement from within the Christian fold apparently denied at least the Messiahship of Jesus, and perhaps Jesus himself.[77] The variety of interpretations of who Jesus was and what had really happened through him was extraordinary. It is a marvel of history that there came to be a way of sorting it out.

We have almost no idea of how it happened, or who took charge at the crucial moments, but eventually there was a successful equilibrium achieved that established a catholic (i.e., essentially universal: one may think of a compromise that works) representation of Jesus by endorsing enough interpretations together that nearly everyone could be satisfied that the result was good and fair and inclusive. (It does not seem to have been much noticed that the resulting compromise consensus was neither consistent nor coherent.) The primacy, even ultimacy, of the gospel was preserved, but also found to be in complete harmony with the Scriptures; the two could therefore be used to interpret one another, with the gospel understood as the Scriptures' perfect fulfillment. Jesus became the new locus of salvation that was continuous with what God had offered to Israel and now was transformed into a New Covenant offered to absolutely everyone, including Israel if they make the necessary adjustments. Jesus was really human—including human birth and death—yet also divine, descended from heaven to take human form. What had taken place through him was a continuation of God's promise to and covenant with Israel, yet significantly different. All was well: it was a new era, and almost every Christian opinion was valid in some way, and could be accommodated formally if necessary; Jewish opinion no longer counted.

This was the approximate state of affairs by the time the basic contents of the New Testament had become conventionally accepted as the Christian holy books. From then on, the fundamental stability of Christian belief is impressive. There were deep and wrenching controversies—the Arian question deeply troubled the church, and the Monophysites broke away a portion of it, that still pursues its independent course—but even in these cases, it is remarkable how much agreement surrounded the points of contention.

And so it has remained ever since: despite the bitterness of Orthodoxy's alienation from the Western church, and the even greater bitterness of the Reformation and Counter-Reformation, Christian understanding remained remarkably similar even across deep denominational divides, as the various formal interdenominational dialogues are in the process of realizing now. That is largely because it remained loyal to the Jesus Christ who is set forth in what is more or less the same New Testament for all churches. Christian theology now usually leans upon this same set of reconciliations, wonderfully but implausibly achieved, of the interpretations of the meaning of Jesus' career as understood by early Christian writers and communities. Not very much has changed in almost two thousand years except the strategies of defending this artificial and pluralistic consensus.

DISTINGUISHING JESUS FROM CHRIST

Who then was, or is, Jesus Christ?

The very question has a tinge of incoherence. "Jesus" is a proper name, not uncommon in first-century Jewish circles, and is in this case the name of a Nazarene whose birthdate is uncertain,[78+] who was crucified in Jerusalem under Roman authority, on an unestablishable date and on unclear charges,[79+] and who in the meantime had caused a considerable stir through teachings and deeds of an extraordinary and inspiring, if controversial, character—and whose resurrection from the dead was subsequently reported by witnesses. "Christ," on the other hand, is the Greek translation of *māshīah,* anointed, a title derived from an epithet applied to the high priests and kings of the Israelites, and specifically a title that was popularly supposed to denote one who would reestablish the vacant throne of King David's dynasty and reign with great success.

The popular modern Christian assumption that Jews in Jesus' time understood "Christ" or *Messiah* to mean an expected incarnation of God in human form, or at the very least a personal religious savior, has no foundation whatever. The title is simply never used with anything like such a meaning in extant pre-Christian writings, and there is every reason to suppose that these senses were a Christian invention.

As for what pre-Christian Jews really meant, it may be added that while there was a popular first-century Jewish assumption that the Scriptures bore witness to God's promise of a politically liberating kingly Messiah, that assumption was by no means universal and had almost no foundation. This piece of popular lore was not derived from careful attention to Scripture. The Hebrew Scriptures never use the absolute expression "the Messiah" at all; the few long-range future-oriented uses of such expressions as "the Messiah of the Lord" are vague, pointing only generally to a restorer of the Davidic throne. The only clear and specifiable messianic text in the Hebrew Scriptures is Is 45:1, which identifies "God's Messiah" with one of the author's sixth-century contemporaries: Cyrus, King of Persia.

The classic messianic lore about a Davidic king to come developed primarily in the post-scriptural or intertestamental period. It was linked to scriptural texts mainly by eisegetical interpretations that well-informed readers are very unlikely to credit now, and did not universally credit then.[80] It is sometimes suggested that Jesus reinterpreted the title *Messiah* and applied it to himself in a religiously salvific rather than a political way. It is evident that such a reinterpretation took place, but it seems equally clear that it was the work not of Jesus but of the early Christians. It is doubtful whether Jesus applied the title to himself in any sense.

In short, a clean reading of the Hebrew Scriptures will not sustain the myth that they show any preoccupation with a Messiah, or that on the rare occasions when such a notion is present they envision more than a pious and able king whose reign would bring sovereignty and the Davidic monarchic dynasty back to Israel.

It need scarcely be added that this has still not happened. This is clearly one of the things that Jesus did not do. It seems to me difficult to argue that it was on his interrupted agenda. From a respectful historical viewpoint, Messiah, or Christ, is not an appropriate title for Jesus.[81]+

The incoherence of the expression "Jesus Christ" is typical of the problems that one must confront in dealing with early Christian interpretations of Jesus. To this real and overwhelmingly impressive person was linked a series of speculative notions that do not seem to have been well-rooted in Jesus' own self-presentation, but derive rather from early Christian attempts to honor him and to maximize the significance of his career. Naming him Messiah was an early step, soon to be dwarfed by making him the agent of the forgiveness of sins, appointing him as the final judge of humanity, and assigning him Lordship over all creation. Endowing him with preexistence, identifying him with the Logos, and proclaiming his divinity followed soon after, and took early Christology about as far as it could go.

But on what grounds was this journey made? What are the warrants for such claims?

It will not do to say that they are guaranteed by having found a place in the New Testament, because that simply begs the question. They are in the New Testament because the journey and claims were made before there was a New Testament, and interest in the truth requires that we care about how this happened and on what basis. The evidence weighs against supposing that Jesus disclosed these things about himself either before or after his resurrection. Nor does the resurrection itself establish them, although it has been so interpreted: the resurrection of Lazarus (Jn 11) is not thought to have constituted Lazarus as either Messiah or divine. No argument can be made from the universality of these beliefs among early Christians, since they were not in fact universal (the Synoptic Gospels appear to be entirely innocent of any sense that Jesus was the Fourth Gospel's preexistent divine

Logos) and since universality does not confer the kind of truth that is in question (the early Christian belief that the final apocalyptic judgment would come soon seems to have become nearly universal, and was wrong).

Christological claims for Jesus are, quite simply, ill founded. They cannot be safely rooted in Jesus' own teachings, and are at least as likely to be the arbitrary extravagances of grateful piety as the inspired discernments of previously undisclosed truth.

RECONSIDERING CHRISTOLOGY

There has rarely been any doubt in the history of Christian theology that Jesus Christ is its source and center. There is now considerable doubt about the authority on which this derivation and centering are based, and about how much can responsibly be said about who he was and what he accomplished. In contemporary theology, a new circumspect language registers this with care: "A Christian community is a community of persons for whom the life, death and resurrection appearances of Jesus of Nazareth, taken as an interconnected whole, is at once: (a) the *inauguration* of God's promised kingly rule, (b) the *promise* of its full actualization eschatologically, and (c) a *call* to live in the world with companions in forms of life (i) that are appropriate to the fact of the inauguration of the kingdom of God in precisely that peculiar way, (ii) that serve the community's mission."[82]

The author of this thoughtful "formulaic characterization of the Christian church," the theologian David Kelsey, acknowledges that its "full explication would probably yield a fairly comprehensive systematic theology." Undoubtedly true. What I wish to note especially is that it is a systematic theology that begins not with statements of cosmic truth or claims about ultimate revelation, but with the situation of the Christian community. The allegation is not that this is the nature of the cosmos, but that this is the nature of Christianity. In the words of the first quotation in this chapter, the center "is to be found" in Jesus Christ, not that it was bestowed by or through Jesus Christ. It is found there by those who define themselves as Christians by finding it there. They stay true to it and they keep it as their truth, in special allegiance, like one nation indivisible. This is not necessarily the kind of truth that is there without their efforts.

Kelsey's definition shows a modesty that represents a diminution of Christian confidence, by comparison with most earlier definitions. I think it an appropriate diminution of confidence. We should not, indeed, be confident that what has been the traditional interpretation of Jesus is true all by itself (though it may be so, beyond our ability to expunge reasonable doubts). Nor should we necessarily be confident that it deserves to be protected, sustained, or repeated (though we should respect arguments for treating it thus). But I think we may, and should, be confident that Christian belief and Christian theology have been overbold and almost certainly wrong in some important respects—just as I think we may, and should, be confident that both sides in World War I were overbold in supposing that God was for their cause and almost certainly wrong in thinking that God wanted them to conquer and humiliate their enemies.

As I argued in the last chapter, this recommended shift in confidence may well be applied to some dubious traditional assumptions about the Bible. The struggle to put our views about the Bible on a sounder footing than the traditional one is far from being over, but Christians have in fact begun to learn how to revise their understandings about the Bible and to live with the results: and so far, this shift, however painful, has been much less traumatic than it once threatened to be. We have not yet done as much to face the problems that lie in wait at the center of traditional Christian understanding, in Christology. But if we are more carefully honest, we will have to stop handing on much of what the tradition has claimed to be true about Jesus the Christ, or at least learn to do it more qualifiedly.

Let me glance again at David Kelsey's definition. Appropriately, it does not attempt to correct or reject any alternative notions of what a Christian community is, but presents in positive terms a way in which such a community might understand itself. More interestingly, its positive statements include almost nothing by way of creedal claims about facts. Nothing is said that may be called into question in the way that traditional creeds may be challenged. The title "Christ" is not used, there is no mention of the divinity of Jesus, and "resurrection appearances" (i.e., the clearly attested experiences of Peter, Paul, et al.) is diplomatically substituted for the expected reference to Jesus' resurrection. Nothing is said that can be disputed as factually insecure; the heart of the matter is shifted to a special way of seeing the meaning and implications of some undisputed facts, and to the engaged communal living-out of these implications.

There is one apparent exception, the reference to "the fact of the inauguration of the kingdom of God in precisely that peculiar way." But this proves on closer inspection not to be a claim that Jesus inaugurated the kingdom of God. It is an acknowledgment that those who see Jesus' career as such an inauguration and undertake the mission of living out its apparent implications constitute and define by their doing so just what is meant by "the inauguration of the kingdom of God"—that is, the community makes it a fact *in precisely that peculiar way.*

This definition, in short, is a splendid example of a wholesome direction for Christian reconsideration. It denies nothing of the Christian tradition: it does not exclude belief in Jesus' Messiahship, divinity, resurrection, miraculous birth, miracles, salvific death, or second coming in judgment—but it affirms none of these. It says nothing that is untrue, and makes no claims that can be denied by any reasonable critic. It concentrates almost exclusively on what Christian special allegiance can honestly make true, and offers a route for the living-out of faith that is open simultaneously—and communally—to the traditional believer and to the most unpersuaded of Christian doubters.

I have two reservations about what this definition says, but they can wait until later. Right now, I want to address some reservations that many Christians are bound to have, not about what it says but about what it fails to say: its failure to offer a Christology, and indeed to say anything at all about Jesus of Nazareth beyond the bland facts that he lived, died, and seemed to have been resurrected.[83+]

READJUSTING CHRISTOLOGY

There are two principal reasons why I do *not* think that this definition is deficient in its statements about Jesus.

The first reason is that it is a concise definition of a Christian community from a deliberately neutral standpoint. It is not an attempt to define Jesus, or to evaluate biblical testimony; it is not a Christian creed or a catalogue of standard popular beliefs. It is a streamlined abstract of what the author takes to be the essential objective characteristics of a Christian community, put in a way that would allow non-Christians to assent to it without qualification. In short, it does not promise to be any more complete than it is, and in no way suggests that there is anything untrue about even the most extravagant Christological statements.

The second reason is that I do not think that a basic Christology should go much further than this. I think that there is probably quite a lot that is untrue, and certainly much that is ill-founded, about the most extravagant Christological statements. I do not think that belief beyond this level should be required of Christians, even though it may be tolerated in them, and occasionally celebrated. Morever, appearances are deceptive even in Christology: what is implied by this seemingly modest view is not necessarily less significant than the more familiar alternatives, nor is it less traditional. To say this much, to arrive at this level, is already to go far—possibly further than seemingly bolder claims would take us.

This last remark may seem odd. But it is not mere careless rhetoric. It means especially two things. The first is that Kelsey's concentration on the disposition of a Christian community and its practical living-out of the implications of that disposition actually registers a greater claim on Christian life than a mere catalogue of extravagant Christological titles could do: like the demons' beliefs as glanced at in the Epistle of James, an elaborately high Christology may be held without it making any behavioral difference whatsoever. The second is that a closer look may disclose some surprises about traditional Christologies, and show that there is less meaning and less implication in them than may seem to meet the habituated eye, and that some alternative—but still underdeveloped—Christologies have considerably more promise than has usually been accorded them.

Let me illustrate what I mean, by looking at the understandings of Jesus associated with the Christian tradition through its four greatest ancient liturgical feasts. These four feasts—(in English alphabetical order: Christmas, Easter, Epiphany, and Pentecost)—were the occasions for specialized remembrances within the large continuity of popular and official Christian understandings of Jesus. Feasts having been deep good occasions in earlier days, these became the gathering-places for rich biblical, ceremonial, theological, partying, and folklorish reflections through which we may take soundings on what the tradition once gave, and still gives thus far.

1. Pentecost

Pentecost may seem an odd place to start in an exploration of the tradition's sense of Jesus. It is preeminently the feast of the Holy Spirit, to whom (or which) Christians have often thought that too little explicit attention is paid: it is the one feast that attends to what many consider to be the most neglected and least understood member of the Trinity, and should be appreciated as such. I agree. Still, there is no feast dedicated specifically to the Father, and Pentecost is no exception to the general liturgical assumption that Christian worship is given to the Father through Jesus Christ as the Son, in the Holy Spirit. Pentecost traditionally celebrates the Holy Spirit through Jesus.

Pentecost was traditionally not an isolated feast dedicated to a special topic, like the later-invented feasts of the Holy Trinity and Corpus Christi.[84] It was the conclusion of the Easter season, rounding off the remembrance of that culminating sequence of events that began with Jesus' last supper, proceeded through his passion and death and resurrection and ascension, and reached completion through his sending of the Holy Spirit to initiate the apostolic mission and the life of the church until such time as he comes again in glory. As the feast of the Holy Spirit, Pentecost was the feast of the fulfillment of what Jesus had come to establish in this world.

Consequently, the traditional liturgy of Pentecost, while filled with joyful celebration of the Holy Spirit as such, was full of remembrances of Jesus as the sender of the Holy Spirit, the Eucharist as bread from heaven, the institution of baptism in Jesus' name, Jesus as the Good Shepherd, Jesus as healer, the initiation of the mission to proclaim the good news of Jesus, with readings from the Fourth Gospel's accounts of Jesus' promise not to leave his followers orphaned, and even a prominent proclamation of Jn 3:16: God so loved the world that he sent his only begotten son.[85]

In short, Pentecost celebrated the Holy Spirit much in the way that the Apostle Paul did so: as the happy ending of the next-to-last chapter of the Christian story about what God had accomplished through Jesus. It therefore embraced, in a somewhat scattered way, a recapitulation of what Jesus had done, how this had fulfilled God's promises of love and rescue, what Jesus himself had promised, how he had fulfilled all but the last details of the promise, and how thoroughly he had equipped the members of his church to understand and carry out their calling in this world until he comes again.

The Pentecost view of Jesus is as the astonishingly successful accomplisher and keeper of promises, the one who has emboldened his followers to a confidence that all shall be well and has (in totally cooperative fulfillment of the Father's abiding and saving love) provided a permanent gift that will see them through everything that may befall them. The gift is the Holy Spirit; but it is not clear, in the course of the liturgy, that the Holy Spirit is a Significant Other. The readings from the Fourth Gospel repeat the intriguing shift that takes place in Jesus' Last Supper references to the Holy Spirit that can come and abide only after Jesus has left this world: at times it is clear that the Holy Spirit is something quite other than Jesus, sent either by himself or by the Father at his request, but at other times it appears that the Holy Spirit is to be Jesus himself in another mode, returning to his followers to abide with them until the end, giving them strength and understanding and joy.

The authors of the New Testament were sometimes uncertain about how to understand the Holy Spirit in relation to Jesus. The First Epistle of John

(2:1) uses the term *Paraclete* (traditionally translated *Comforter* or *Advocate*), as does the Fourth Gospel (14:16, 26; 15:26; 16:7), but in 1 Jn it is clearly identified with Jesus; the Fourth Gospel shifts between identity and non-identity, while making the Holy Spirit a surrogate for Jesus in the noniden-tity passages, a power that will remind them of what Jesus said, give them courage to know who they have become through the intervention of Jesus, and show them Jesus' true glory;[86] Paul shifts in a single verse (Rom 8:9), referring to the Holy Spirit as both the Spirit of God and the Spirit of Jesus. Pentecost is about the Holy Spirit, but it is mainly about Jesus. Its dominant message is that Jesus has accomplished astonishing work, and that the abiding evidence of the accomplishment is the presence of the Holy Spirit, and that we now have everything we need to become trued to God and to help true the world.

That is the other way in which Pentecost leaves it unclear whether the Holy Spirit is a Significant Other: the Holy Spirit has come to abide so deeply that it—or she: Semitic languages always treated the Holy Spirit as feminine—becomes a dimension, the best dimension, of ourselves. It is not a dimension of ourselves that we are entitled to have, or use, or feel pleased about, when we think of ourselves as isolated entities. She is what happens to transform us when we belong firmly to God. To the extent that we allow ourselves to be so transformed, it no longer matters much whether the Holy Spirit is male or female, Jesus or his surrogate, something God has given or something God has allowed to happen: the Holy Spirit is how, and where, we are called to live in honor of what Jesus has fulfilled among us.

The unclarities of Pentecost are part of its good Christology. That is perhaps why it has never been much attended to by Christologists. The precise ways in which we are empowered are left open; the difficult ques-tions about whether the Father sent the Holy Spirit at Jesus' request, or whether Jesus sent the Holy Spirit on his own, or whether the Holy Spirit *is* Jesus in an invisible but life-giving way, are not resolved. Whether the Holy Spirit proceeds from the Father and the Son or from the Father alone is a question that simply does not arise: the concentration is on the comple-tion of Jesus' work and the empowering of his followers to do theirs. It is theologically very indecisive, apart from its general suggestion that every-thing needful has been done except what it is our task to do.

Pentecost has had little effect on the Christian sense of Jesus, because Christians have mainly concentrated on its attention to the Holy Spirit as someone or something significantly different from, though closely related to, Jesus. I regret that. I guess that some good reconsideration could come about if we were to retrieve the spirit (no pun intended) of the early-traditional Pentecost. But that spirit is not now very lively—much to our disadvantage—and I will therefore put Pentecost aside, remarking only that it is one of the two major ancient feasts where more good Christology is offered than regularly gets appreciated. I will return to the other after some remarks on the two more prominent feasts where *less* good Christology is offered than is regularly appreciated.

2. Easter

The highest-ranking of all Christian celebrations, according to the traditional liturgical calendar, is of course Easter, the feast of Jesus' resurrection, celebrating that event as the culmination of all that God had done from the beginning of time to prepare and accomplish the salvation of human beings.

Anyone who knows the New Testament will recognize that the liturgical primacy of Easter was virtually inevitable. Earliest surviving Christian tradition shows differences of opinion on who Jesus was, and different interpretations and evaluations of his origins, his teachings, his deeds, his crucifixion—but it manifests massive agreement that his overcoming of death showed the purposes of God and decisively changed the possibilities of human life. Earliest Christian texts affirm the resurrection of Jesus as the most important truth of God's new work and also of God's old promises, since passages of the Hebrew Scriptures were interpreted as prophecies of this event (and also of the death of Jesus, to which the resurrection is the definitive answer: see, for instance, Acts 2:24–31 and 13:33–37). Paul goes so far as to insist that without the resurrection of Jesus, Christian faith is in vain and Christians are the most pitiful of all men (1 Cor 15:17–19). Easter (taken together with Good Friday) is of the essence of traditional Christianity.

Who and what is the Jesus of Easter?

The basic answer is that he is the Savior and the Lord, the one through whose death and resurrection it becomes possible for our sins to be forgiven and the gates of heaven to be opened to us.

Easter does not necessarily imply any more than this. That is not to say that more has not been claimed. The argument proposed in Acts 2 is modest, concluding that Jesus' resurrection established him as Lord and Messiah (interestingly, in that order) who now somehow presides over the saved. Most early Christian writers on the subject went further. Paul repeatedly refers to Jesus as the Son of God, and evidently supposes that his special sonship was what qualified him to be the agent of salvation through dying and rising. Others have argued that the expiation of sin through the Easter happenings was possible only because Jesus was fully divine, and still others have claimed that the resurrection proves his divinity.

But although Christians have commonly understood that the one who was raised was in fact the Messiah, miraculously born of a virgin, divine, the same one through whom the world was created, these beliefs are not indispensable to the basic traditional meaning of Easter, which is that Jesus is Lord and Savior. The Jesus of Easter is our rescuer from doom to glory, and he is so because he cooperated with what the Father ordained, and he is accordingly ensconced in heaven as Lord and Savior. Nothing beyond that brief abstract is really required to fill out the basic meaning of the Easter Jesus (see Peter's first evangelical pronouncements in Acts 2–3), though much more has been ornamentally offered by the tradition. Theoretically, the Father could have appointed virtually anyone to fill the role. We celebrate the one thus appointed, and thus acknowledged. But then, out of good gratitude, we elaborate the occasion.

Since very early stages of the tradition (I offer Acts 2–3 as still earlier), Christian astonishment at what Christians had come to realize spilled extravagantly into the elaboration of gratitude by heaping all available laurels on the Jesus who had been their hope and who had again become, despite their temporary discouragement, their salvation. They seem to have supposed that their recovery from discouragement was an entry into salvation, and that what had happened with Jesus was the key. I think that they were right. But I think also that they misinterpreted their experience.

Jesus' crucifixion must have been a profound blow to those who had thought that he would bring instant relief and had not adequately heard his repeated reminders that to belong to God does not guarantee an easy path, but that it is in itself what we can best mean by salvation. For Jesus, I think, the God to whom he instructed his followers to pray was the Savior and Lord. I guess, from the surviving evidences, that he tried to make that clear in a variety of ways. I also guess that the gratitude of those who had been promised salvation and kindly Lordship somehow shifted to the bringer of such good news. Anyone who has heard wisdom from another can understand that: we are grateful to the vehicle, as we should be, and fall a bit short of appreciating that the vehicle is not the ultimate source.

Jesus had introduced his listeners to their Father and their Savior. They had got the idea, but they hadn't distinguished between the message and the messenger. Their gratitude to the messenger was appropriate. When he was junked by the world, they overcompensated. When they realized that he was no longer dead, they rejoiced that he had been resurrected. And then that he had risen. And then that he had risen to glory. And then that he had risen to assume the glory that was his entitlement. And then that he had reassumed the glory that had been his from the beginning of time. All of that is entirely understandable as the expression of the dazzled gratitude of those who had grasped for the first time his message that they were taken care of by ultimate power and inexhaustible love. The practical question is: should it be imitated?

Should the fantasy that I have just expressed be imitated? That is a similar question, differing from its predecessor in that it is not backed by centuries of traditional elaborative piety. Does it differ in any other way?

We suspend that question, and turn to the Easter Jesus of traditional elaborative piety: fundamentally, Lord and Savior, the one who now newly rules the world and through whose death and resurrection we are, if we enlist in him, available to God and God to us. That is the traditional Jesus of Easter.

There are two difficulties surrounding the traditional Jesus of Easter.

The first is that closer scrutiny has raised some extremely awkward questions about the facts of the matter. In earlier times, the New Testament's consistent emphases left no doubt that Jesus had indeed been physically raised, and exalted to the right hand of God in glory and Lordship. But the reliability of New Testament documents is no longer so thoroughly taken for granted, and those who study them critically are inevitably struck by the lack of agreement among them concerning the particulars of Jesus' resurrection. They differ significantly in where the appearances took place, to whom, in what circumstances, over what period of time, with what results, in what form. Was the reported risen body made of flesh and blood, capable of being fed and felt, or was it untouchable and able to pass through locked doors and vanish suddenly? In which of their conflicting particulars, if any, did the authors of the Gospels get the story straight? Were the original witnesses really in a position to tell the difference between physical event and hallucination, between the seeing of the eye and that of the spirit's intuition? Are *we* really in a position to be confident that Jesus was actually seen alive by human eyes after his crucifixion?

Added to this set of uncertainties is a change of mind about the appropriateness and necessity of the resurrection, at least in its traditional understanding. It is now widely argued, by Christian theologians and scholars and clerics and teachers, that nothing really important depends on things having happened as they are reported by the Evangelists. It does not really make a difference how or where Jesus resumed life in order for the benefits of Easter to be provided. Paul's elusive version of the resurrection is as adequate for theological purposes as Matthew's or John's: the conflicting details of the various accounts are unimportant if all that really matters is the stark fact that it was realized that Jesus lives again. It is therefore now widely admitted among scholars of the New Testament and Christian theologians that there may have been no revivified flesh, perhaps no empty tomb, probably no conversations or touchings or shared meals or instructive explanations—in short, that the traditionally elaborated image of the Easter Jesus possibly does not correspond very much, if at all, to historical reality, and that the particularities of that traditional image are not indispensable prerequisites to God's accomplishing salvation through Jesus. If this seems to you a form of theological cowardice, please reconsider. It is an attempt to honor the importance of what has happened as well as we can, both what importantly happened—the realization that we live within an embrace of salvation under beneficent governance—and what happenings we cannot establish in good detail or interpret with any certainty.

The second difficulty with the traditional Jesus of Easter is that there is a substantial gap between the event of resurrection and what it has been taken to imply. It is often taken to be proof of Jesus' divinity, but that does not really follow: the early tradition says not that Jesus rose from the dead, but that he was raised by God; the emphasis is on his obedience to the divine plan, his instrumentality and leadership in carrying out the Father's work, his *appointment* to the role of Lord and Savior. Not even the Gospels propose that Easter shows Jesus to be divine. And although they *do* claim that Easter marks his transition into Lordship, it is not obvious what this claim really means or why it should be trusted. If Jesus had proclaimed his own Lordship, we would have a solid place to begin. But critical investigation suggests that it was his followers, not he, who made the claim, and that they had surprisingly little to go on in making it.[87]

What grounds are there for believing that the resurrection of Jesus establishes his Lordship and makes possible the forgiveness of sins? Once we set aside contrived arguments from peculiar readings of the Hebrew Scriptures, and artificial representations of Jesus' postresurrection teachings, it is no exaggeration to say that the only real grounds we are offered for believing this is that it came to be believed by Jesus' earliest followers. If you do not find that grounds enough, you may reasonably conclude that we are stuck in the same place the disciples found themselves in a few days after Jesus' crucifixion, experiencing the first Easter: Jesus is alive beyond death, and we do not know what that implies. It is not at all clear what the difference is between the pre-Easter and the post-Easter world, or what is really revealed to us in the Jesus of Easter. The greatest of the Christian feasts celebrates a mystery that is much more enigmatic than it has seemed to be. We do not really know what it means.

3. Christmas

At the popular level, the Feast of the Nativity, celebrating the beginning of Jesus' earthly career, has far overshadowed Easter's celebration of the end of that career, even though it occupies a lesser place in the traditional liturgical ranking. It had a certain situational advantage, being placed in the calendar in a privileged spot that had been marked for high holidays since well before the Christian era. But its poaching on the Roman Saturnalia and the winter solstice festivals is not sufficient to explain the extraordinary attention given its key themes by artists and the proliferation of the popular carols that have no Easter counterpart.

Somehow, the whole idea of Jesus' conception, birth, and early infancy has seized popular imagination from very early times, in a way that virtually no other aspect of Jesus has quite managed to do. The Gospels of Mark and John quite appropriately bypass the nativity of Jesus, which none of the Gospels show to have been remembered as impressive by anyone at all during his adult days, and move directly to the beginning of his public ministry, the beginning of the preached gospel; but it is Matthew and Luke whose stories Christians remember and elaborate in plays and pageants and songs and paintings and elaborate manger scenes.

Christmas has had a powerful command not only over the general Christian public, but over the attentions of some of the most serious Christian artists, poets, preachers, and thinkers. We cannot account for all this by appealing to the time of year or to a cultural fondness for infants. A substantial part of the special attention given to Christmas derives from its close association with the doctrine that perhaps comes closest to being the central doctrine of Christianity: the Incarnation. Christmas is preeminently not the feast of Jesus the Baby, but of Jesus the Word Made Flesh.

The Incarnation (along with other subordinate ways of affirming the divinity of Jesus along with his humanity) is so central to traditional Christian self-understanding that it is generally presumed that no one can possibly call herself Christian who does not assent to it. It is so revered that in the reading of the prologue to the Gospel of John at the end of every Mass in the pre-Vatican II Roman Catholic liturgy, everyone present was to genuflect at the words "and the Word became flesh." It is so important to the Christian tradition that very few Christians have ever noticed how little is written in the New Testament that would support it.

Early in the second century, after almost all of the books of the New Testament had been written, belief in the divinity of Jesus had become so firmly established in some Christian circles that his humanity had come into question. Ignatius of Antioch wrote against the Docetists, who denied that Jesus had real human flesh, to emphasize that although he was divine, he was nevertheless genuinely human. A few places in the Johannine literature show a similar emphasis on the flesh of the divine Jesus, most notably Jn 1:14.[88]!

But for the most part, establishing the humanity of Jesus is not a characteristic problem of early Christian writings. Most of them merely take it for granted. If the Docetists held him to be divine and not really human, the Synoptic Gospels evidently assume that he was human. They do not expressly deny his divinity, apparently for the same reason that they do not deny the divinity of John the Baptist: the possibility of such a thing simply does not seem to have occurred to the authors. Even Matthew and Luke, for all the dazzlement in their portrayals of the birth and infancy of Jesus, do not go further than making him the chosen Messiah and Savior, the true king of God's providence for Israel, even though they apparently had free rein to say whatever they pleased—for hardly any serious scholar of the Gospels will credit the nativity and infancy accounts with having much to do with real historical events.

Who then is the Jesus of Christmas? He is a divine Jesus, taken from a tradition about Jesus that seems to have been unknown to the very earliest Christians, imposed upon a human, though august, portrayal of the infant Jesus that is taken from some stories in Matthew and Luke that are not to be trusted. He is, like the celebrated definition of the Council of Chalcedon, a startling combination of two natures that do not readily seem to be capable of being fused together in the proposed way. He is the central Christian Incarnational paradox, made the more emphatically paradoxical by being celebrated in the humble, vulnerable, powerless, and undeveloped state of infancy.

It is a paradox that is hard to balance.

For most of Christian history, the weight has fallen mainly on the divine side: Jesus' divine knowledge and divine power have been so emphasized that it has almost seemed as if the Docetists had won. For if he was, in the dignity of his divinity, not really subject to human limitations, then in what sense could it be said that he was truly human?

More recently, the humanity of Jesus has become far more prominent. Theologians have learned to acknowledge that the genuineness of his participation in the human condition meant that he had the knowledge and the ignorance and the power and the weakness that might be expected in any other first-century Palestinian Jew. His humanity was real, and in no way overwhelmed by his divinity. But this counteremphasis has not restored the balance. It has inevitably led to the alternative question: if he was firmly embedded in the specific forms and limitations of historical and physical human life, then in what sense can it be said that he was truly divine?

That is not an easy question to answer. Christians need to get used to it, since the humanity of Jesus is much more obvious than his divinity, and it is likely to be the latter that will consistently come into question. But there is another question, much less frequently asked, that may usefully be put first:

What difference does it make?

This is meant not flippantly (as in "Who cares?!") but earnestly: if we start with the assumption that Jesus was authentically human, then what is added to the meaning or accomplishment or significance or value of his life if we suppose that he was also the Second Person of the Trinity? At first blush, it seems obvious that it makes an enormous difference. But, at second blush, *what* difference?

If you start making a list, you are likely to find that its items will change value under closer inspection. At first, it may seem that (to use a standard example) only a divine person would be able to expiate human sin by becoming a sacrifice, and therefore that Jesus' divinity was necessary for our redemption. But surely this must mean that God either would not or could not forgive human sin without the payment of a huge price in a primitive fashion. If the divinity of Jesus makes a fortunate difference in our sense of redemption,[89+] it must make a very unfortunate difference in our image of God. Or one may say that divinity would guarantee his trustworthiness; but if he was subject to human limitations, and to an uncertain process of others' reporting of his words and deeds, the advantage of a divine Jesus over an inspired prophet vanishes rapidly. Does a divine Jesus affect the significance of Jesus' resurrection? Yes—insofar as it diminishes the potential implications for me and you. That a divine man did not stay dead is neither very surprising nor particularly encouraging to those of us who do not have his unusual advantage. And so it goes. I frankly cannot think of a difference that does not fade away or sour under scrutiny.

I suggest that the end result is that the traditional Jesus of Christmas, Jesus the paradoxically Incarnate Deity, is built on no sounder foundations than the Jesus of Easter, the Lord and Savior—and that in both cases, there is good reason to be skeptical both about the reporting of events and about the drawing of implications. Things probably did not happen that way; and if they *did* happen that way, there is no compelling reason to suppose that the conclusions traditionally drawn from them would really follow.

And furthermore, if these traditional conclusions *did* somehow follow, it would not necessarily be good news. I mean that in three ways: in the first place, some of the traditional conclusions turn out not to make any real difference even if they are true; and in the second place, some of them turn out to be good but not news, merely other ways of proclaiming an old welcome truth; and in the third place, some of them turn out to be bad news masquerading as good.

Let me give instances:

a. It is generally conceded that after Jesus died on the cross, though much disputed where and how, he showed himself alive again. But if we give the tradition the benefit of the belief, and assume at least some version of the resurrection,[90+] it does not necessarily follow that Jesus is now in some sense at the right hand of the Father, enthroned as Lord, somehow in charge. If he is somehow in charge, it is by no means clear how that fact makes a difference, or how the world with Jesus in charge differs appreciably from a world where that is not the case.

b. Very early Christian tradition evidently maintained that Jesus died for our sins in fulfillment of the Scriptures. It does not seem quite reasonable to say that the Hebrew Scriptures prophesy such a thing, or prescribe it, or in any way establish it as part of the providential agenda. If they did, it would not necessarily follow that Jesus' death was in fulfillment thereof, or that as a result our sins can be washed away through baptism in the name of Jesus, and only in that way. If our sins *can* now be forgiven, that is good but not news: any reader of the Hebrew Scriptures, or of later pre-Christian Jewish religious texts like Sirach (Ecclesiasticus—which seems to have been received as scripture by at least Greek-speaking Jews), or of the reported teachings of Jesus, will find it repeatedly emphasized that God's mercy stands ready to forgive the sinner any time she or he repents and turns Godward.

c. On the other hand, Paul maintains that if Jesus is not risen our faith is in vain and we are still in our sins. As I observed in the previous point, that clearly does not follow if we put trust in the Scriptures, general Jewish religious tradition, and Jesus' teachings. But suppose Jesus and the others are wrong and Paul is right. What does that give us? It denies the Father of inexhaustible mercy, and substitutes a God who is evidently incapable of forgiving at all if there is a hitch in the mechanics of the sacrifice-and-restoration of his son, and apparently unwilling to forgive anyone who is not enlisted as one of those who believes that this is how he works. Does anyone out there think that it would be good news to learn that the real God is not the former but the latter?

A Christology built on the Jesus of Easter and the Jesus of Christmas presents some difficulties. It runs the risk of being unfounded, unreliable, untrue, unconvincing, unimportant, and unwelcome. But those are only the celebrations of the private—and artificially reconstructed—beginning and end of Jesus' earthly career. There is one more feast to be discussed, traditionally ranked higher than Christmas (just after Easter and Pentecost)[91] in the Western church though now much neglected both popularly and ecclesiastically, and bearing on the central and public part of Jesus' biography: the Feast of the Epiphany.

4. Epiphany

Unlike Easter and Christmas, which begin with specific moments in Jesus' life and enfold them with meanings and implications and consequences, Epiphany—"manifestation," meaning divine shining-forth (the feast was also called *Theophania*, "manifestation of God")—begins with a view of Jesus, a realization about him, a Christian experience of him, and gathers in a few illustrations from the stories about his career. The fundamental idea is that the glory of God was manifest in him. Whoever he was, whatever the other purposes or accomplishments of his work, those who beheld him directly could see that he was the real thing, one through whom the work and presence of God took place, and if they failed to see this, it was there all the same.[92+]

Traditionally, three examples are selected for specific remembrance on the Feast of the Epiphany: the visitation of the Magi (even Gentiles, if attentive, could detect that something important was happening), Jesus' baptism by John (including the Holy Spirit, descending and resting like a dove, and the acknowledging voice from heaven), and the miracle at Cana (which the Fourth Gospel reports to have been the first occasion on which his disciples glimpsed Jesus' glory).

I do not intend to make a case for the reliability of the examples, or for their appropriateness were they by chance historically real. Even if the

Magi visited, which seems vastly improbable, they are reported to have honored Jesus as king of Israel, which was a mistake. And besides, they were bumblingly naive on their entrance to Israel and thoughtlessly evasive on their exit; their failure to take adequate responsibility for what they had stirred up seems to have cost some infant lives in Bethlehem and an inconvenient Egyptian exile. Whatever they had learned, it wasn't enough. Jesus' taking John's baptism is an apt candidate for an epiphany, but that is not where the emphasis falls: it is rather on the dove (though it is not clear if anyone but the narrator recognized it as the Holy Spirit in disguise), and the voice (though the texts are inconsistent about what it said and who, if anyone, heard it). The Cana miracle is rather silly at the physical level, being little more than a show of power in a trivial cause, and it is unfortunately to that level that the received text settles, the more interesting symbolic level being obscured by too much literalism. The disciples seem impressed for the wrong reasons, and are not to be emulated. *These* ways of claiming that the glory of God was manifest in Jesus do not deserve promotion.

But Epiphany is dedicated not to these three random and badly chosen[93] instances, but rather to the general principle that God was manifest through Jesus. Not that Jesus was God playing a human dramatic role (deity in disguise) nor that Jesus was a human being enlisted as an agent of God's purposes in a sacrificial redemptive scheme (the Suffering Servant raised to the highest power) nor any combination of the above elements that would result in saying that there was a mysterious secret about Jesus that only the privileged were allowed to peek in upon to see the divinity hidden from the others. *Manifest. Epiphany celebrates the openness of God, the public character of God's presence and self-disclosure, the unsecret unhidden unreserved unlimited unrestricted self-givenness of God as shown forth through the public* (presumably also in the private, but that is perhaps none of our business) *life of Jesus.*

I have no doubt that some readers of this chapter, which has spent so much time complaining about how bad the received Christology is, are likely to have formed the impression that I would like to expel Jesus from Christianity. Quite the contrary. I would admittedly be glad to see bad Christology expelled, but that is hardly the same thing. I am against bad Christology because it is false, foolish, distracting, and religiously retarding —and especially because it obscures, with its Easter and Christmas Jesuses, the Epiphany Jesus that is the original inspiration, and is still the most profoundly captivating example, of the tradition that I take to be the most unquestionably true within the complex of Christian handings-on.[94]

I would like my great-grandchildren to be initiated into a Christianity over which the Jesus of the Epiphany presides. I am basically attempting to follow what I take to be the deepest Christian theological insight, namely that *Christian faith and Christian belief*—and please remember that they are far from being identical—*should be formed in accordance with what Jesus proclaimed, and who and what he manifestly was,* as distinguished from the dysfunctionally extravagant and ill-founded beliefs about Jesus that have ironically distracted Christians from the truing power of Christianity's ultimate source.

Beliefs are always to be called into question in the name of faith. That is not because beliefs are trivial but because they are subordinate and provisional. They are subordinate and provisional because we do not know reality very well, and should always be ready to change our minds about it if the love of what is true eventually calls us to do so. In the meantime, we should also work with our best understanding, however provisional it may be, and face what it tells us. We are allowed to lose heart, but we are called not to do so. So if our beliefs, however cherished and respected, compromise our faith, they must be quarantined and examined. They will often prove unreliable under inspection, but we can learn to live with that without losing faith. Not infrequently, our deepest beliefs will be vindicated as well founded and truing, and faith, even if startled, must readjust acceptingly. Faith, after all, is dedicated to what is true and truing, and belief is not always wrong about that.

But belief is sometimes wrong, even old and venerable and traditional belief; and although the ways in which belief is wrong are sometimes of little consequence, sometimes they are importantly damaging. Some beliefs offer far less good news than they seem to promise, and lead to unwelcome consequences: when such a belief is also ill founded or false or inferior to a more plausible alternative, it costs far too much to keep.

Christian faith cannot afford to sustain all of the classical inheritance of Christological belief. That is not bad news. It may at first seem so, because it is not yet generally realized how little it would cost to let classical Christology go, or how much it really costs to keep it artificially alive. It is even less generally realized what advances in truing might be brought about by bringing Christianity closer to home—facing the doubtfulness of traditional beliefs honestly, and readjusting the tradition toward the faith of Jesus. Christianities have been much too preoccupied with Christ to pay adequate attention to Jesus, and far too devoted to Easter and Christmas to see clearly the truth and glory of Epiphany. Christianities are, as a result, in a state of bad faith.

Bultmann's skepticism about reconstructing a reliable picture of the historical Jesus has now been set aside by contemporary scholars, but the latter still cling to the distinction by which Bultmann assured his readers that what he claimed to be the inevitable failure of their quest for the historical Jesus did not finally matter. The Historical Jesus of Nazareth, said he (following the lead of Martin Kähler a long generation before), is not the real object of our belief: it is rather the Historic Christ of Faith to whom we are pledged.

And that, I think, is not right side up. Nor is it upside down. It is exactly sideways. The mistake we need to renounce is neither the search for the Jesus of History, which appears to be adequately rewarded after all, nor the failure to realize that traditional belief has really been in what Bultmann calls the Christ of Faith, which is the case. What we should renounce (I think) is the assumption that the Christ title, with all its historically accidental accretions of beliefs, is an appropriate object of faith or an authentic source of revelation. I frankly think that we should consider it an early, and unfortunate, mistake. I also opine that we should reconsider the concomitant assumption that an undivine and unexpiating Jesus cannot be both an authentic source of revelation and an important occasion of—indeed, probably our best mediator of—faith.

In short, what we should set aside is the Historical Christ of Belief, an explicable but false construction, and what we should replace it with is the Historic Jesus of Faith—the Jesus whose faith may still reveal to us the way to an authentic faith in the God whose reign he unremittingly and joyfully proclaimed. The faith of Christians would be best guided by an Epiphany Christology, which can true it to Jesus' founding example at long last and bring Christian Godwardness into its appropriate focus and condition.

An Epiphany Christology will help to turn and true our faith as Jesus tried to do, by reminding us that Jesus was preoccupied with turning us to God, and that his gospel[95] consistently showed forth the glory of God as the forgiver of sins, the merciful and caring Father, the savior and redeemer and lord and judge, the one whose kingdom is peace that passes understanding and joy beyond imagining. Christianities do themselves, and their founder, small credit in transferring to Jesus the titles and attributes that he rightly insisted belong to God alone, or in neglecting to recognize that the heart of his epiphanic mission was to give glory to God, to get his hearers to be attentive to the glory of God, to bring them to see and celebrate

God's glory everywhere, to make the living of human life a feast of epiphany.

Epiphany Christology may seem to be a mildly self-contradictory phrase when used by one who has spent the early part of this chapter complaining about the impropriety of saddling Jesus with the misleading title *Christ.* It might be less misleading to say *Jesuology,* but it would be no less awkward —and besides, if behaviorists can live with a name like *psychology* and reflective scholars can speak of *death-of-God theology,* we can handle yet another ironic label. But there is a better reason for keeping the term *Christology,* if we keep it carefully. It is this:

Christ no longer quite means "Messiah," even though it was originally nothing more nor less than the best Greek literal translation of that Hebrew term. *Messiah* is still a solid and meaningful term in Jewish religion, but *Christ* is not. Christianity has taken it over, and has changed and de-Judaized its meaning. It no longer points primarily to a prophetic revelation in the Hebrew Scriptures that has been or will be fulfilled. It points instead to Jesus himself, precisely as The One Who Is About His Father's Business— but no more precisely than that. It is used to designate the baby Jesus ("for Christ is born today"), the proclaimer of God's Dominion ("as Christ said in the Sermon on the Mount . . ."), the one who died on the cross and was raised from the tomb, the one who is Lord, and the eastern Orthodox Christ *Pantokrator* who presides over the cosmos as the one who, in his prehuman mode, was also the agent of its creation. It can also mean the spiritual principle operative in individual Christians, linking them to God and God's Dominion, or the collectivity of the Christian community (the "Mystical Body of Christ") as a society in the process of realizing God's Dominion. It can mean all these things, because it can mean whatever you intend to mean by The One Who Is About His Father's Business.

"Christ" is, in short, a wild card waiting to be assigned a specific value for the purposes of playing the best theological hand. Christology is the critical discernment of how to play the best Christian theological hand, and the assignment of the optimum—not the maximum, but the optimum— value to "Christ." I am arguing that *the optimum value is found in Christ as Epiphany, the manifestation of God's glory found in and through Jesus and, mainly because of that, found and lived by Christians where Jesus pointed.* I am suggesting that *Christians are those people for whom the project of life is living out a feast of Epiphany in Christ—that is, under the leadership of the epiphanic Jesus and in dedication to their own pursuit of God's business, whatever they may understand that to be.* Epiphany Christology is the unpacking of the implications of these last two sentences.

Further suggestions toward an Epiphany Christology will emerge as this book progresses. But to close this already lengthy chapter, I wish to address one more point, and to make one more claim.

Changing one's beliefs about Jesus may at first seem outrageous, impious, disloyal, faithless. But my argument is simply that traditional beliefs may be importantly wrong, and that it may be faithless, disloyal, impious, and outrageous to keep them, especially when they distort and distract our faith from what ought to be its mainstay if we wish to be followers of Jesus.

Changing one's beliefs about Jesus may also seem to be costly, giving up too much. But my argument is that it may cost too much *not* to change them, and that to change them for the better and more truing is a decided improvement even if it means getting rid of old habits and going through some emotional withdrawal symptoms for a while.

My summary claim, which I leave it to the rest of this book to defend, is this: *nothing really important is lost if Christians change their beliefs in Jesus from traditional Christology to Epiphany Christology.* What deserves to be valued in the traditional promises is only transferred and relocated more truly, not surrendered. Whatever you may have thought attached to the Easter or Christmas Jesuses, and available only through them, can be received at the hand of the one to whose glory Jesus bore witness. It is in losing our received Jesus that we will find him, and in finding him truly, we find the way to all that can really be imagined.

Part III of this book will begin, and Part IV will continue, to unpack this claim and to try to deal with how reinterpretation of the tradition can put it on a sounder and truer footing for my great-grandchildren than the one on which it is now precariously balanced. But please do not expect me to produce, in the pages ahead, anything like a full description of what I think should come about in the next phase of what I hope is still early Christianity, let alone offer a developed systematic theology. I do not aspire so high, at least not in this book, which will be long enough as it is.[96] I proffer only a preliminary exploration of how we might be well advised to understand what we are doing and how we may best do it as we go about taking responsibility for the place we occupy in the tradition, the handing on, of Christianity.

We are not especially well equipped to do the necessary work of being the current, and perhaps an especially decisive, stage of Christian tradition. The next chapter will be mainly given over to how and why this is so. But being inadequately equipped does not excuse us from the task, any more than it excuses me from writing something about it.[97] The rest of this book will accordingly be concerned with making suggestions about how the job may be properly and effectively addressed. If you read further, I therefore ask you to be especially mindful not of what our Christianities have been, but on what they may become in the course of becoming more true and more capable of truing.

DEALING [Part III]

WITH THE PROBLEM:

CAN CHRISTIANITIES

TRUE?

7

GETTING

PRELIMINARY

BEARINGS

The last few chapters have, among other things, repeatedly made attempts at the general point that the credibility of Christianity in all its present forms has been deeply eroded for almost anyone who will acknowledge that belief is accountable to good evidence and sound argument. If this is true (I not only think it is but also insist that it should be, as a step toward the eventual truing of Christianity), not everyone has to be concerned about it. Non-Christians may be indifferent or pleased; Christians who decline to accept this kind of accountability, or who resent what it would do to cherished beliefs, may shrug and carry on almost as usual.

Some people seem to be well endowed with what has traditionally been called "the gift of faith" (more accurately, the state of confident belief), and can smile unconcernedly when the Ungifted (more accurately, those who do not in fact believe everything they are told they ought to and do not suppose this to be a mental or spiritual deficiency) trot out their problems and difficulties. There are lots of Christian believers who are confident that the measure of truth is in their belief, and that when belief collides with history and science and philosophy, it is the latter that are wrecked, while belief chugs on unhindered as a juggernaut.[98] Others, perhaps less confident of the invulnerability of belief but thoughtfully persuaded of its legitimacy, represent their position as a deliberate choice, the self-commitment to a community that defines its identity in Christian terms, pledging to keep it their truth.[99] The rest of this book will have little more to say about either, and will be concerned with a third way, which might be called the way of Reconstructive Ungiftedness but might more accurately (and at least a little less jargonishly) be styled the Christianity of discriminating accountability.

This way begins in gratitude to Christianity and attempts to conclude in union and reconciliation with it; but the route in the meantime travels over rough terrain. It proceeds according to the recognition that, for some of us, the present state of the Christian tradition is at best not quite true, and that it is not appropriate or even possible to believe as if it were. It continues with the acknowledgment that traditional Christianity does not quite true, and therefore should not be given unqualified submission. It assumes that the best way to be faithful, true, to Christianity is by attempting to make it true—not through loyal conformity to it despite its weaknesses, and still less by pretending that the weaknesses are strengths, but through decreasing its falsity. It undertakes to exercise its position in the process of tradition by handing on a sounder and more truing Christianity than it received.

No one has to belong to this way. I write for those who happen to do so, or who are in the process of discovering that they ought to—especially those who are concerned not only with the integrity of their own belonging, but also with the Christian belonging of future generations.

The initial demurrer of this way of being Christian, the recognition of untruth and the disinclination to validate it by conforming to it, is only a first step, a step backward from a traditional perspective but really a forward step in a new direction. The steps that follow are not yet on established maps, but they are arranged so as to come home, back to another part of the same fertile and gracious Christian valley, entering by another route where the toll in truth is less costly, and where one may homestead on firmer ground. But before we can do that, we must become clearer about where we are starting from.

SOPHISTICATION AND ITS DISCONTENTS

We are starting from an age that is much more sophisticated than the times in which Christianity was founded and the times in which the present state of its tradition was consolidated.

I do not intend that statement to be taken as self-congratulatory. Our time is indeed unnaive in many important ways, and skillfully knowledgeable in others; but it is appropriate to remember that the original meaning of *sophisticated* was "denatured, adulterated, falsified." We—and here (and for the next few pages) I mean by "we" the bulk of the sophisticated inhabitants of our time, not especially but not excluding Christians, Ungifted or otherwise—are that too.

Some of our most important falsity lies in what we think we see in the mirror. There is, in our time, an enormous failure of imagination when it comes to self-assessment. Educated Europeans of the sixteenth century routinely assumed that they lived in a diminished and deteriorating world, on the brink of its irreversible senility. Educated Westerners of the twentieth century routinely suppose that they are privileged to live in the most enlightened period of human history, and think themselves generous if they pay patronizingly appreciative homage to the now-obsolete accomplishments of earlier times. Many of them, and perhaps even a greater proportion of the less educated, see little point in looking back at all, supposing that there is little for a sophisticated century to learn from its less sophisticated predecessors.

That supposition needs to be corrected.

Our self-image is dominated by the dazzling advancements in science and technology, which have created a new form of provinciality.[100] In our sophistication, we guess that there is no place that is remotely as accomplished and satisfactory and complete as where we are used to living. I have asked many people how much they habitually—not after critical reflection, but in the routine structures of their habitual imagining—suppose we sophisticated people (including the world's laboratories and universities and professional societies) now collectively know of what may theoretically be known. The usual response is high: usually at least 30 percent, often 50 percent, not infrequently 70–80 percent.

No competent scientist would support a tenth of that in even the main and most tilled scientific fields,[101+] and in more traditional and less specialized undertakings like fathering, making a marriage good, or getting through adolescence with aplomb, it is obvious that we have vastly more to learn than to offer.

The instinctive exaggeration is significant. It symptomatizes not only habitual self-ignorance but also a premature jadedness in imaginations that presume that we can't go much further in learning, because—like Kansas City in the musical *Oklahoma*—we've gone about as far as we can go; we are nearly complete, and the excitement of venturing and discovery is just about over, except for filling in the last few blanks. I think of Joseph Conrad's Marlow in *The Heart of Darkness,* fascinated by one of the few blank spots remaining on his globe, which represented to him the chance of an adventure into Darkest Africa; modern globes cover all the inhabitable turf with national colors, and there are no intriguing blank spots left.

Many people seem to assume habitually, in their ordinary unexamined imaginations, that significant darkness has been eradicated from the earth, like smallpox. When I ask what grounds there might be for future historians (if our management of our world permits them to exist) to find a century in recorded history in which there was more darkness than in the twentieth, the thought usually strikes people as novel; but the question, which usually goes unanswered, is earnest, and the public record suggests that it is also very serious, and possibly urgent.

We have succeeded in bringing about two kinds of darkness, of very different qualities. The first is helpful, like the darkness of a room where films are developed. Each scientific and technological advance opens new vistas on the still-unknown, and one of the inevitable by-products of further investigation is an expansion in our *realized ignorance,* which is already huge but undoubtedly dwarfed by the still-unrealized ignorance that lies beyond it. But realized ignorance is creative darkness, the kind that leads toward light, and its discovery is to the credit of modern times. More to the point is the expansion of uglier and less promising forms of darkness in our age.

We live in a century whose wars are of unprecedented frequency, scope, brutality, and carnage; whose wealth is obscenely squandered on the acquisition, protection, and abuse of power, self-indulgence, or of further wealth; whose reverence is directed toward rock stars and film stars and sports stars (who form a religiously disappointing constellation) or toward fast-food gurus and salvific therapies and long-weekend personal transformations; whose sense of security is measured by the number and sizes of missiles, armies, insurance policies, and locks; and whose hospitality allows poverty to abound as never before—not only among the hundreds of millions of the physically undernourished, but also among the well-to-do, beset by the maladies of spiritual malnutrition: boredom, depression, cynicism, suicide. Spiritually anorexic, crippled, adrift, dismayed, our spokesmen quote over and over, like a mantra of hopelessness, the stinging, if poetically unexceptional, lines of W. B. Yeats:

Things fall apart; the centre cannot hold;
Mere anarchy is loosed upon the world, . . .
The best lack all conviction, while the worst
Are full of passionate intensity.[102]

To judge by the symptoms, we are in bad shape, deluded by how much we know and innocent of wisdom. The inspiring dream of endless progress that animated our predecessors has vanished, and we have spiritually dozed off in a darkness that is progressively engulfing us. Caught between the grim counsel of despair to which sophistication leads and the shrill cry of desperate belief which sophistication cannot support, our sophisticated age grimaces cynically and slips slowly down the drain of darkness.

It can be a perverse kind of fun to enjoy such a situation. "I love to taste my tears," says the girl in *The Fantasticks*. Our civilization has long and often unreflectively thought of tragedy as much more profound than comedy, and likes being grim as if that were a more sophisticated condition than delight. We live in a small corner of the imagination, stuck in a preoccupation with individuality, personal accomplishment, survival. We revere sobering realities like loneliness, frailty, and death as if they were somehow more important and more true than the inebriating realities of friendship, strength, and life.[103!] We instinctively suppose that grim solemnity is profound, and that profundity must be solemnly grim. To be serious excludes being jolly. Cheerfulness is taken as a mark of superficiality. Hell, even though no longer credible, is somehow taken to be at least more credible than heaven;[104+] the slogan "Life is a bitch, and then we die" appears with increasing frequency among the scrawled graffiti of customary places; Kurtz's final words in *The Heart of Darkness*, "The horror, the horror," are savored like an advance epitaph on all we are.[105+] In short, we take our sophistication much too seriously.

The general public collusion in the self-indulgence of our solemn self-preoccupation keeps it from being exposed and dismantled, and the provincial lack of imagination deprives us of insight into alternatives and a properly robust sense of humor. We are unfortunately too invested in this state of mind not to feel threatened if it is called into question: it is so deep a habit that we confuse it with our dignity. We seem to enjoy the poignancy of playing out the collective fantasy role of the lonely success who has nothing to look forward to, and to have lost the ability to laugh at our role-playing except with a bitter irony that refuses to let it go. With the

133

breakdown of traditional belief, a necessary casualty to our greater sophistication's loss of childish innocence, has come an unnecessary enfeebling of faith, as if the collapse of false confidence must sweep away the confidence of truth as well, or at least require it to retreat to defenses of pretended but unconvinced belief, which is further compromised by being consciously derived from the views of an earlier and less sophisticated era from which we accept absolutely nothing else as intellectually respectable. With diminished and anemic faith, we address life dishonestly, ashamed of our need to hide in its color supplements from the bad news we think it publishes on its front page. Quite apart from our uneasiness about our explicit smalltown religion, or the marginally nostalgic headache that comes from having abandoned its comforts without replacing them with something we can count on, our general habits of thought as we live out our numbered days put us in bad, as well as insufficient, faith that seems to invalidate creative hope and paralyze genuinely outgoing compassion. We need a shift in perspective.

SHIFTING THE PERSPECTIVE

Contemporary Christians share in varying degrees the sad condition of this larger "we," and that is part of the problem of imaginative retardation whose impingement on religious faith is one of the main themes of this book. But now I return to the more specifically Christian problems, which need their own shift in perspective. I will suggest a way of making at least a partial shift, admittedly playful but worth serious consideration.

In a brilliant stroke of imagination, Jean Piaget decided to explore the development of the moral sense of children by investigating the game of marbles.[106] He found that the six-year-olds tended to understand the rules as eternal and inviolable, as if handed down from Adam, or at least from Moses on Sinai; the ten-year-olds had grasped that the rules fell partly within their jurisdiction and could be adjusted if that were desirable and convenient; and the twelve-year-olds knew that the rules were entirely within their control and could be totally rearranged.

Adults, I propose, fall basically into three groups: ages six, ten, and twelve.

The six-year-old adults are those who perseverate in the inherited forms of whatever game they play, including all its rules of belief, because their imaginations allow them to go no further. Six-year-olds dominated the First Vatican Council (eventuating in the magnificently six-year-old proclamation of Papal Infallibility, among other things), and prepared initial drafts for the opening meetings of the Vatican II (the drafts were mainly rebuffed by the assembled bishops, and redone); it is mainly six-year-olds who become televangelists, readers of Hal Lindsey, and recruits to moral majorities.

Ten-year-olds know better and seize the opportunity to improve the game by adjusting some of its rules, being careful—or at least conscribed by the responsive judgments of the other players—in what they offer to change and how they offer to change it. It was ten-year-olds who won the day at the Second Vatican Council, despite the original six-year-old position papers, and brought about a change in the World Council of Churches' views on non-Christian religions, and rewrote the catechisms.

Twelve-year-olds rediscover the game with new enthusiasm once they see how much better it can become with some substantial imaginative changes, knowing that "Everything is allowed, every individual proposition is, by rights, worthy of attention," although innovations can be introduced only "by previously persuading the other players and by submitting in advance to the verdict of the majority."[107] For twelve-year-olds, the project can become vigorously alive as only twelve-year-olds can understand vitality, with the challenge of finding a way that will take us to far greater truth, reforming the religious imagination to what it has never been before, as it embraces the viable remains of what once was, in the course of creating what ought to be next.

I am, I guess, ten, aspiring to be twelve. I am deeply grateful for what was given to me in the Christianity I received, which was my life and truth for many years before I discovered ways in which it was untrue and stifled life. I wish dearly for my great-grandchildren to have a taste of what I received, but uncontaminated with the falsities and darknesses that marred what I was given.

I am inevitably accused—especially, I think, by six-year-olds—of betraying my Christian inheritance. In reply, I acknowledge that I lack the belief of my accusers and do not regret lacking it; and that my faith is not to be dismissed as less Christian than theirs. I espouse a Christianity that is very much alive and aspires to life that is still more abundant. I pursue a Christianity rooted in the ways it has been conducted within the imaginations of the traditionally loyal but animated by a faith that trusts in the truth we have not yet learned to belong to, a faith that does not shrink from the prospect of radical transformation. Christianity does not belong to us, or to those who preceded us; but we have as much right and obligation as they to try to say how it belongs to God, and how we belong to God in and through it. Let us proceed.

8

SEARCHING

FOR GODOT,

ILLUSIONS AND ALL

The examination of a religion may begin almost anywhere—with its beliefs, its customs, its forms of worship, its social relations, its philosophical styles, its scriptures. The construction of a religion may likewise start almost anywhere. But the best place to begin, at least when one is dealing with either a past or a future religion in the tradition of Jesus, is with its sense of God— with faith's relationship to God, and with the imagination's sense of the God to whom, or to which, faith is especially directed. Any authentic form of Christianity, and especially a reconstructive Christianity, must be concerned with the search for an adequate imagining of God.

THE EXISTENCE OF GOD

"God is" may seem like an affirmation, but it is really an incomplete phrase, like "vitamins can" or "chickens don't." We are used to supposing that it is complete, having to do with the affirmation or demonstration of God's existence. But there does not appear to be a satisfactory way of demonstrating God's existence,[108] and it may be importantly misleading to affirm it.

I do not mean to suggest that it is misleading to affirm God—only that using the notion of *existence* is perhaps not a viable way of doing so. To exist is not the only way of being real. If you are accused of something that I know you did not do, I will affirm your innocence; and in doing so, I am affirming something true, but not something that can properly be said to *exist*. The events of the past are real as past events, and we can speak both truly and falsely about them; but they are not still going on as events and thus cannot be said really to exist anymore. The future does not exist. It isn't there. It is a temporal emptiness in which things will eventually take place, but not yet—and until they do, we cannot know them but can only guess in their direction with various degrees of probability. But to behave as if the future were as unreal as the world of *Peter Pan* and could be as safely ignored would be decidedly unrealistic.

Reality has to do with what makes a difference. Existence is one of the most important departments of reality, but not the whole thing. It appears that God's existence can not be demonstrated. The failure of proofs for the existence of God has been a disappointment, but it is time to recover from the disappointment and to be instructed by the failure.

The failure evidently means that proving is not one of the available ways of getting to God. It also suggests that perhaps the brave affirmation of God's "existence" may take us down a false trail of expectation and imagining, and that existence may not be a useful category for enabling the imagination to pursue the presence of God. It is clearly not a useful category for the pursuit of the future, which does not exist but is nevertheless real and partially present, though its reality and partial presence would probably be obscured if we busied ourselves with the impossible and frustrating task of trying to demonstrate that it exists. The various imaginings of God in terms of an existing being seem to be badly off the mark, and the implications drawn from them are likely to be falsifying. "It is as atheistic to affirm the existence of God as to deny it," wrote Paul Tillich.[109]+ We are probably stuck with being unable to offer "God is" as a complete sentence. The failure is instructive about what doesn't, and what probably won't, work, and eventually it opens new options about what might.

But there is also instruction available in discovering why theists tend to be so bothered and uneasy about such a state of affairs.

THE ELUSIVE DEITY

The way John Wisdom's parable on God[110] has been bandied about among philosophy-of-religion types suggests that it touched a sensitive cultural and intellectual nerve. It deals with two men coming upon an unexpected garden in the midst of the jungle. One of the men opines that the garden is clear evidence of a gardener. The other is skeptical. They wait and watch, and no gardener appears. The first man revises his thought: the gardener must do his work at night, while they are sleeping. They watch through the night, and no gardener shows. The believer concludes that it must be an invisible gardener. Through various other tests, it is established that the presumed gardener must be not only invisible but incorporeal, and that his work is so subtle that it cannot be directly detected. The skeptic quite properly ends by wondering whether a gardener so elusive and qualified really differs from no gardener at all. Antony Flew's equally celebrated verdict[111] is that the hypothetical gardener accordingly dies through a thousand qualifications, and is rendered simply imaginary.

The history of Western thought about God is complex and tangled, but Wisdom's parable isolates one pattern that is especially impressive to modern minds and helps to account for both the expansion of casual atheism and the discomfort of being unable to prove that God is. Science has eroded the false but strong sense of God's immediate activity that used to be attached to both the regular and the irregular events of the world. Happenings that used to be explained by an appeal to God's management or intervention are now accounted for in quite another way, and this has been received generally as bad news about God.

This dialectic is not a modern novelty. The recognition that we do not have to call upon the name of the Lord to describe how the world works is already centuries old; but so is the resistance movement. Piety has been jealously protective of God's power and has traditionally attempted to see it manifested vividly in the created order. It has only hesitantly and reluctantly conceded, by slow stages, that the divine hand is not necessarily evident in the concrete processes of the observable cosmos, and it was quite unprepared to handle the overwhelming accomplishments of recent scientific explanation. The basic content of Wisdom's parable is more succinctly played out in the well-known exchange between Laplace and Napoleon. Surveying Laplace's account of how things work, Napoleon is said to have asked "But where is God in all of this?" and to have received from Laplace the reply, "I had no need of that hypothesis."

Laplace was right. We do not need to hypothesize God in order to explain rainbows, or eclipses, or the diversity of human languages; God need not be mentioned in accounts of volcanic eruptions, revolutions, famines, or in accounts of the stars, the seasons, the fertility of the earth.

Traditional piety was mistaken, though on the right track. The Psalmist's beautiful and devout praise of God as the indispensable intervener is courtly rhetoric, as fulsome and false as the adulation that King Canute is said to have refuted by sitting in the tide. The traditional piety that honors God by ascribing unqualified omnipotence and confirms its faith by concentrating on God's wondrous deeds is naive, as well as subtly self-serving. But when the naiveté remains canonized for some three thousand years, and then the wondrous deeds are whittled away until one has no need of the hypothesis of their doer, there is an understandable scramble to put up a desperate defense. We want to make God exist, be substantial, somehow—if not in directly causing the world's routine, then in its less routine happenings. And if divinity cannot be demonstrated through the disruptions of routine that insurance companies amusingly but libelously call "Acts of God," then it is easy to suppose that we must somehow subtilize the gardener in order to hold on to the vestiges of what systematic investigation has stolen from the traditional grounds of confident belief. Traditional piety has almost the right idea, but not quite. It needs to reorganize its good instincts and face the defectiveness of its thought—and then turn a little.

If proofs don't work, and retrograde belief only postpones the full shock to a later generation, and assertions of existence can't be backed by any decisive evidence at all, and progressive subtilization seems to result in total evaporation, then what is to be done? Where do we turn?

IMAGINING GOD

To begin with, we may acknowledge what has been going on all along, disguised by our insistence on hearing what we wanted to hear. There is one way, and one way only, of reaching the mind to where God may be found. It is by *imagining*.

There is no way of getting around that fundamental truth. If your God is drawn from the Bible, then you must be clear that he is drawn thence by your imagination. If he—or she, or it, or they—should happen to arise from the Qur'an, or from Meister Eckehart, or from the Bhagavad Gita, or from Scholastic theology, or from the intimations of your own meditative experience, or from sheer experimental inventiveness,[112+] the God your mind proposes is what you have imagined.

That does not make God imaginary: it makes God imagined. So, admittedly, are elves and banshees and bandersnatches and Middle Earth; but so also are the quarks of subatomic physics, the workings of the psyche, the essential personal reality of the person you love most, and how you will spend tomorrow. God can be brought into consciousness only by an act of imagination. But what is there in your consciousness that got there by another route? Consciousness itself is an awareness of imagining and of the imagined. And the imagined is not the imaginary: it includes the imaginary, but it includes everything else as well. To establish that a gardening God is, for all practical purposes, merely imaginary does not mean that God is not real: it merely means that it is not useful to imagine God as a type of gardener.

Imagination is the way in which the mind enacts and appropriates reality, in order to belong to it and to participate in it. The constituting of the imagination is therefore the supreme moral and cognitive act—cognitive, because it is the way in which we admit to consciousness whatever is to be known and the ways of knowing it; moral, because all our being and doing is a reflex of how we have imagined reality.

How we decide to imagine, how we let ourselves imagine, how we refuse to imagine, determines what makes a difference to us. It is through the structure and quality of our imagining that we establish what is real and what sorts of reality we are involved in, including imaginary reality. Raw imagination imports goods lavishly, but with the realization that they are on approval and must be sorted out. What doesn't fit in or can't be afforded must be sent back or traded for less expensive models. We cannot finally pay the cost of everything we may wish to imagine, and any new imaginative acquisition may make a difference in what else we can keep, or how we can keep it. Everything has its price, and the bills cannot be ignored. But we get to decide what our priorities are.

GOD AS IMAGINATIVE OPTION

God is an imaginative option.

It has been demonstrated repeatedly in the lives and imaginations of capable persons that it is quite possible to exclude God from one's sense of reality. No attempt to show that God is a logical necessity has been adequately persuasive. God is not imposed upon our minds; the only way for God to be there in our reality is to be invited—or, if smuggled in with the rest of our cargo, dutifully claimed.

Why should we issue the invitation, or accept what the invoice so teasingly and often implausibly appears to name?

To begin with, it is important not to be too impressed by the fact that there are things that we can get along without, that we can afford not to imagine. Western traditions of technological efficiency were long preceded by the cognitive efficiency of William of Occam, who observed that it is much more mentally tidy to clear out all unnecessary imaginings. The principle of Occam's razor, shaving away the dispensable, is important, but it is only one of the two major disciplines of the imagination.

The other may, in honor of the author of the lovely Psalm 133, be called Aaron's beard.

Aaron's beard is technically dispensable. It may be shaved with Occam's razor. Aaron, and we, could carry on much as before without his beard. But to stop with that recognition is to make a serious blunder about the imagination, and about Aaron. It is good to call imaginings into question, to weigh beliefs and notions and superstitions and assumptions in order to assess their credibility and usefulness and potential dispensability and their compatibility with what we would rather have. But to discover that something is dispensable is not to discover that it should be dispensed with.

Friendship is theoretically dispensable, and so is trust: we can get on in the world without supposing that other persons are to be relied upon, or that they can become the anchorage of our deepest sense of ourselves. But to impoverish our reality by slicing off trust and friendship in the name of economical efficiency would be supremely silly. Aaron's beard is dispensable, but it is expressive of his dignity and supportive of our respect for what he stands for. It may be shaved, but should not be if things work out better when he is bearded. We can dimly imagine a world that does not offer the possibility of friendship and, with sufficient cooperation, we can even make such a world come to pass by the assiduous expunging of unnecessary relationships and the careful discouragement of their occurrence among the inexperienced young. I would not like to live there. I prefer a world where Aaron keeps his technically unnecessary but effectively dignifying beard.

The imagining of God may be virtually impossible for some people. It may be inescapable for others. Those who have imagined reality primarily in terms of scientific mechanisms may have no room left for a divinity; those who experience life as a gift may be incapable of imagining reality without a divine giver. We are put together differently, and what trues one person may not true another. But to the extent that we are unfinished, and can choose, I recommend Aaron's beard over the undiscriminating application of Occam's razor. It offers more.

This may well sound like a stark reversal of my earlier remarks. Much of this book has so far been preoccupied with various forms of Aaron's beard that I have called into question. If the imagination is free to entertain the unnecessary and optional, then why cavil at beliefs of doubtful foundation? Why not simply accept the venerable Aaronic beard of the Christian tradition's customary beliefs, recognizing that their truth cannot and need not be proved, and that their ticket of admission to the imagination does not depend upon the success of the attempted demonstrations of classical apologetics?

I have tried consistently to admit that we are indeed free to accept traditional belief; nothing imaginable is excluded from the possibilities of structuring the imagination. But there is a price that must be paid. The imagination is an ecological system, and whatever is allowed to make its home there will eventually affect the other elements. We are free to accept virtually anything; we are not free to have that acceptance make no further difference.

The trimming and grooming of the imagination is an enterprise that is full of cognitive and moral implications. To shave it with Occam's razor is clean but costly, and one should be aware of the price paid for such tidiness. To open it to what is not required, to the optional, has its own price. But the price varies according to what is being bought. My argument is that we cannot any longer afford the cost of traditional belief, but that there are alternative ways of enhancing the faith with which we imagine reality that are not only within our means but beneficial to the tone of the whole economy.

The fundamental enhancement that I now propose, to agnostics and atheists as well as to troubled Christians, is the transformation of imagined reality, and of the faith with which we experience it, by imagining God as best we can (not just as vigorously as we can, but as *best* we can) as the primary object of faith. This is not necessary; it is only desirable. In the meantime, God is an option, the most important single option that confronts the imagination.

ILLUSIONS AND TRUTH

The moral and cognitive difficulty with the option of imagining God is that it runs the risk of being an illusion. Let us consider that threat.

Is it a good or a bad thing to be disillusioned?

It depends.

The word refers, in normal usage, to two quite different conditions. The primary one is the state of having an illusion dispelled, and the usual assumption is that if it was indeed an illusion, it is good to be rid of it. But the secondary reference is more often the main focus of the word: the state of disappointment that occurs when one loses the comfort that the illusion gave.

We don't enjoy being disillusioned, in the latter sense, even if we know that it's good for us. We don't use the word to refer to the loss of discomfiting illusions: if you expect that your new job will be a dreadful bore but find it in fact exhilarating, or if you suddenly discover that a person who seemed aloof and pompous is actually warm and congenial, you may describe yourself as pleasantly surprised, but you are not likely to say that you are disillusioned. The word specializes in disappointment, leans in a cynical direction. T. S. Eliot's well-known summation, "human kind / Cannot bear very much reality,"[113] suggests the standard underlying assumptions. Illusions are supposed to be false and desperately comforting protections against reality. To come closer to the real is to undergo disappointment, or worse. Reality is presumed not to be user-friendly.

But the actual state of affairs is not worthy of so pessimistic a style. Reality may not conform to our greediest and most self-indulgent fantasies, which is undoubtedly a blessing, but what it has to offer by way of spiritual nutritional value is only qualified and disciplined, not spoiled, by its grimmer side—and our failure to be constantly delighted by it is largely due to our perverse inclination to generate illusions that get in the way, making us shortsighted, wary, and untrusting. We all, or almost all, suffer from forms of spiritual hypochondria, haunted by the illusion that we cannot be adequately happy until something more is given us or something present is taken away, feeling that we are too old or too young or too poor or too inadequate or too unnoticed, dreading what might happen but won't, troubled by the fantasies that feed jealousy and envy. Illusions prevent us from experiencing the graciousness of reality more than they protect us from its harshness. It is a positive gain to lose illusions that threaten or inhibit us.

Illusions are not the same as delusions. Illusions are potentially distinguishable from nonillusory reality, but they are not necessarily opposed to it. Many of our nonpernicious illusions are disinhibiting, encouraging, motivating, and others are vehicles of demonstrable truths, functionally necessary for putting us in touch with reality and not to be casually rebuffed. One kind of desert mirage gives the appearance of an oasis where there is none, but in fact does us a favor by telegraphing, via an optical illusion, a falsely located image of a truly existing refuge hidden beyond the interrupting horizon. The face I seem to see on the other side of the mirror is not really there, but it shows me realities—and obviates some potential delusions—if I focus on it as if it were, as I distribute my sparse hair more decorously and steer my razor around vestigial pimples. The way you imaginatively "see" yourself in future situations is an illusion that helps you solve problems, make decisions, and experience the reality of your continuity more adequately. Illusions, like bacteria, are not all impediments to our well-being. Some of them are dangerous, even potentially fatal; but others are symbiotically cooperative and convenient, so much so that we fall ill if we lose their assistance. There are bacteria, and illusions, that we simply cannot do without if we are to thrive, or even survive, in body and spirit.

To describe someone as "thoroughly disillusioned" is usually to point to a deeply unhealthy condition—a sterility, not as in hospital operating rooms but as in crippled digestive tracts and the inability to be fruitful. To bid someone to have no illusions is therefore not to wish her well, but rather to invite her to the meanest form of life. Indeed, to be utterly without illusions would undoubtedly prevent one from functioning well and probably make it impossible to function at all. Hopes envision illusions to which one pledges allegiance, and are the bridges between present reality and the preferable but still-illusory reality that may be brought to be. My habitual sense of the reliable stability of my health and life circumstances is an illusion that could be readily canceled by various possible disasters, but I would have little psychological equilibrium without it. I do not wish anyone to be disillusioned. I do wish everyone to be responsible about illusions, and to choose and edit and critique them with care. That entails changing or abandoning those that harmfully falsify but it also means cherishing those that make the imagination, and the one who inhabits it, more true.

Truth, after all, is not simply the abstract of the way things really are. It is a condition of human being, like health, to be measured not by a binary yes-or-no but in uncountable gradations from moribund to robust, from utterly wrong to splendidly wise. As "health" points to the optimum functioning of the organism in itself and in its interaction with its environment, so "truth" points to an optimal adjustment of a person in collusion with reality. Truth and falsity are not simply properties of propositions. They are properties of human beings. The "troth" pledged in marriage is simply another form of the familiar word, and the qualities it promises—fidelity, honesty, reliability—are qualities we aspire to promote in our relationship with reality. The false is that which makes me untrue; the truth is what trues me, aligns me more adequately with reality, improves my fidelity to what is and was and is to become. Illusions, well chosen and well honed, are part of the process and of the condition of being true.

For reality itself is not simply that which is ultimately inescapable, divested of all illusion. It is the imaginatively entertained (including the ultimately inescapable) as we have seasoned and flavored it with illusions that do not falsify, but true—illusions that true us and true our encounter with what is not us. Our grasp of truth is not passively receptive but cooperatively creative, and our imagination's table offers both salt and pepper, the one indispensable for survival and enhancing to what would otherwise be insipid, the other a way of rendering more palatable and lively what we might otherwise incline, detrimentally, to do without. There is no need to skimp. Our nourishment is best taken in the recognition that humankind cannot bear too little reality.

THE RESPONSIBLE IMAGINATION

It has long been recognized among both philosophers and psychologists that perception, although naively experienced as merely receiving what is actually there, is a responsive and inventive act. What we call optical illusions are concrete reminders that we *enact* what we see, and do it in a way that is often (perhaps always) beyond the call of duty, and sometimes demonstrably false. On the one hand, what may be dutifully described as lines on a surface may be legitimately seen as a representation either of a solid cube or of a hollow box; on the other hand, when a special construction in a psychology laboratory is viewed through a peephole, it will be seen as a chair, although investigation from other perspectives will show it to be a set of unconnected and unchairlike pieces designed to produce just that illusion.

But in fact, *all* seeing is optical illusion, enacted with corrective imagination. The oak tree I see in the distance appears smaller than the birch close at hand, and the image cast by the oak on the retina of my eye is in fact smaller than that of the birch; but in the enactment of my seeing, I use this illusion to grasp the truth of the oak's distance and thus to register also its greater size. The illusion mediates truth rather than confounding it, because the imagination knows how to read it and respond to it aptly. With such speed and habituated ease that I am not aware of what a complex task I am performing, I imagine the truth about the messages passed along my optic nerve, unconfused by the fact that the visual images are projected upside down on my retina,[114+] instantly constructing and enacting the invited vista in a way that will prove consistent with what I will see as I stroll past the birch to the oak. I am not even aware of the illusions I have used in order to see what is true, until I think about them and realize that without such illusions I could not see at all.

We can construct illusions that fool us; we can analyze illusions that put us in tune with what is true. But it is not always obvious which is which. If you play the characteristic harmonic patterns related to middle C into a mildly experienced human ear, blocking out the specific frequency of middle C itself, the ear's wearer will hear middle C, even though it may be technically absent. Has she been fooled? Or has she made a constructive imaginative leap to discern the truth that this *is* intended to be the sound of middle C, recognizable despite the absence of an element that we might have thought indispensable? We perceive reality by constituting what it evidently implies as well as what its authority inexorably forces upon us. Even when we are being fooled, we are not necessarily being altogether fooled: if I mistake shoe polish for jam, my imagination has led me astray; but if I suppose your ingeniously flavored tofu to be cottage cheese, haven't I accurately understood exactly what you intended?

The imagination invents as it responds, and responds as it invents. When it is at work producing a poem or a dream, it gives from the store of what it has received, and when it is at work recognizing or understanding, it receives through what it gives. Its accomplishments are always provisional and subject to reconsideration. They may, as we advance in experience and discrimination, require considerable revision to improve the adequacy of what they were intended to accomplish, to become more accurate or profound or comprehensive or funny—to become more true and more truing. But they are all illusions, illusions confected for the purpose of putting us in effective tune with ourselves and what is not us.

Imaginings are amazingly complex acts of creative responsiveness, whether they be fairy tales or chemical theories or geometries or systematic theologies or glimpsings out the kitchen window. Their value depends upon how well they work and how important their work is to our becoming more true. A responsible imagination is aware of the provisionality of its illusions and deliberate in the distribution of its loyalties among them. It is animated by a faith that above all respects what is true.

The responsible imagination is the collector, critic, and curator of illusions. It takes charge not only of the illusions registered upon my brain through my sensory equipment, but also of all the other illusions offered to my mind and heart. It allows me to see the shape as a tree, as an oak, as a large and distant oak; it also allows me to see the oak as potential timber, as a problem for plowing the field, as a place to hang a swing, or a noose. It allows me to see the oak as not merely big, but grand as well, and mortal, and beautiful—none of which is inescapable or inevitable in the plain bald truth of my vision, but all of which are legitimate enhancements that belong to my larger truth when I enact their belonging. I can edit my imagination so as to see differently. I can, with some effort, withhold the sense of grandeur, or impose a sense of unbeautiful grotesqueness.[115] The oak itself will not change if I do so, nor will my vision become false. But *my* oak will have changed, and my truth will have shifted slightly because of the shift in my alignment with it.

I play with such shifts, jockeying for good results. Like the lines upon a surface that may be seen as box or cube, my bungling of yesterday may be seen alternately as painful or funny. Seeing it as funny may help ease the pain, and then seeing it again as painful may help me take it seriously enough. Seeing it as a moral lesson or a speculative parable or the first act of a potential play or a barometer of my mental health may all be useful; seeing it as evidence of malicious plotting against me or a symptom of the cruelty of fate or the work of demons or a confirmation of my superiority will probably do me no good, but these too are imaginative options, available through the same versatility of imagination that gives me access to the more wholesome alternatives. I do not have to be equally hospitable to all the possibilities, and such versatility demands discrimination and discipline if it is to be exploited toward more adequate truth.

The responsible imagination has a lot of critical work to do. Much of what is at first hospitably received by imagination must later be ushered out the door by critical tact if the credentials are not in adequate order. There are many incursions that imagination is forced to consider but needs finally to dismiss, illusions that barge in and make strident but illegitimate demands for recognition. An itch is a feeling without a referent, falsely presenting itself as if it were a response to an external irritant. Jealousy is often a disposition without a referent, projecting a gratuitous illusion to validate itself; the squared circle is a notion without a referent; anxiety is a fear without a conceivable referent. Our psychic pockets are stuffed with self-referrals in search of justifying external referents, and the imagination readily supplies illusions that offer to complete the circuit. They bid competitively against imaginings that offer to put us in better alignment with what is true. The responsible imagination must sift through the lot and learn to say no firmly. It probably must say no more often than yes, until discriminating taste becomes habitual. It will make mistakes in both directions. Some of them will be costly. Most of them will be corrigible, if faith is vigorous enough, and if we can absorb some wisdom from experience and from each other.

An illuminating illustration (if that is not too redundant) of this may be discerned through the application of Rorschach psychology. Presented with large multicolored inkblots, subjects are encouraged to "read" them, to describe what they "see." This characteristically releases an account of the image as a sort of picture, with thematic content and moods. Clearly, the content is not there in the image; it is in the subject, who accepts the optional invitation to project into the image some of the habitual content of imagination, objectifying it in such a way that some of those habits can be discerned and analyzed. (Those who reply merely that it is a blot of ink are perhaps quite sane, but unlikely to learn much that is helpful.) One typical disclosure arrives in the form of a "vista response"—i.e., some subjects perceive the projectively imagined scene (experienced, of course, as depicted rather than imagined, but nevertheless *known* to be a figment) as seen from a considerable distance, as if from a high bridge or a hilltop. Such subjects turn out, when looked into further, apart from the blots, to have feelings of inferiority, often including guilt, and to lack confidence in self-appreciation.[116]

Now: even if you suppose that some people are inferior, guilty, and ought to have little appreciation of themselves, you will probably concede that many who carry this kind of tonality in their habitual self-awareness have defective or distorted imaginations and that it would be good to get them reconstructed. Once this is discerned, there is a great deal of reimagining to do at a fairly basic level. A responsible reimagining may learn to say no to an imagining of God that valorizes a sense of anxiety, condemnation, guilt, and worthlessness, even if it includes a partially compensating sense of provisional expiating redemption, gratuitous if grudging divine acceptance, and official theological hope. If the whole package is finally dysfunctional, the good news is that it is based on inadequate authority, no matter how many fellow travelers the sufferer may be able to locate within the Christian tradition and among the writers of the New Testament. This does not, after all, look like the God of Jesus; nor need it be the God of anyone. The responsible imagination is entitled to say a clear no, and start over, to find something more truing.

I would of course recommend that it start over by reconstructing a more appropriate imagining of God. Often, alas, it starts over by tossing out the very idea of God. That is entirely unnecessary—rather like being soured on the opposite sex altogether as a response to a bad marriage—and it is bound to make the job of acquiring self-esteem more difficult rather than easier. But it would be far too glib to call it irresponsible to say no to the imaginative option of God. Overly hasty, perhaps, and unnecessarily expensive, but not downright irresponsible. One may go as far as to say, however, that it would be less responsible than an exploration of alternatives.

Which alternatives? That is not so easy to say. But there are lots of alternatives available, and any searching conversation can bring some out. You and I don't habitually mean the same thing by "God," whoever you may be; the imagining that you summon to your imagination is different from the one I produce, though we may be able to have a long and mutually profitable conversation without noticing that the differences are there. "God" is initially just a password to get us into each other's conversation; if we had to agree on the exact dimensions of the imagining it evokes, we could never even get started, since our imaginings are different, bent to the shape of our personalities and mental history, and both of them are defective. Talking about God is therefore, in the early stages, rather like an exchange I had with Margaret Meagher many years ago: she turned her kaleidoscope until she got an image that especially pleased her, and then thrust it vigorously into my hand so that I could appreciate it too. But once we get through that initial illusion of common meaning, and begin to explore what the Rorschach device "God" turns out to be when filled out by your imagination and mine, then we can do some serious business. The business may usefully include which previous editions of "God" we have rejected, and why.

For you and I both say no to various other alternative imaginings of God, including some to which we once said yes. We may say no to each other's. You may find yourself shifting your answer and your imagining daily after your second cup of coffee. Between us, we may scare up sixty-eight possibilities from what we have entertained and rebuffed, what we have read about, what we have experimented with, and what we now fear, revere, or pray to. But we would like to help each other arrive at something sound and stable, ideally something that works well, is appropriate, and will stand in all weather. What is it to be imaginatively responsible in such circumstances?

IMAGINING RESPONSIBLY

Perhaps the first act of responsibility is to be discriminating about who we are and why we are seriously entertaining—or declining to entertain—the imaginative option of God.

The second half of this is the easier one. However we may have started to entertain the option of God (upbringing, fashion, experiment, personal crisis, envy, instinct, boredom) and in whatever fashion we do so (tentatively and on approval, or committedly as a dimension of our self-definition and truth), we now stay at it for the same reason that sponsors our other seriously entertained options: we want to become trued. Imagining God seems to us truing, at least potentially. We may differ in how and why we find it truing—it makes more satisfactory sense than is otherwise available, or it honors and brightens the restless heart, or it enlists us in what seems the best wisdom of the ages, or it is experienced as bringing wholeness and faith, or it seems simply inescapable—but in some way we recognize that it offers to true us. Or, if we decline to imagine God, we are doing so for the same motive: we suppose it more truing to do without.

And who are *we* in all of this?

First—not necessarily in importance or in chronological sequence, but in my random shortlist—we are you and I. Significantly different projects. This is a truism that merits mention not only because it is a matter of fact but because it is inadequately respected despite its obviousness. Each of us recognizes, and most of us are occasionally terrified by, the otherness of others, but history provides ample demonstration that we love to imagine them otherwise—that is, *not really* "otherwise" but only variants of ourselves, more accomplished or younger or temporarily wrongheaded or differently acculturated, but *essentially* the same. Therefore you should try to be more like the norm, which is me. "Why can't a woman / Be more like a man?" sings Henry Higgins, obviously meaning that Eliza should be, and that it may be taken for granted that if he and Colonel Pickering are cut from the same cloth they must also be tailored alike. We chuckle at his insensitive generalizations and go home to fret over the unaccountable failure of our teenaged children to embody the proper values, or smile inwardly at the amusing accent and grammatical inventiveness of the man who runs the corner store. We may know better, but hardly anyone ever sheds the instinctive assumption that basic personal differences should ideally be ironed out, flat. The next chapter will return to this theme to explore some of the permanent wrinkles.

Second, we are we. If the differences are deeper than our reflexes acknowledge, so are the commonalities. I refer in the first place to our ability to get along with one another, the social and political necessity of doing so, the evident congruence of our separate nervous systems, the common tendency to want to be happy, secure, and taken seriously, and the universal reality of death (all of which we forget in practical ways, more frequently than we notice). But I also refer, in the second place, to our spontaneous expectations of sympathy and our equally spontaneous recoiling from those who appear to have none, and to the neglected fact that nobody, not even the government, *makes* money but merely gets it from someone else; and to the indebted obligation we have to predecessors whose genes are responsible for our talents and whose transmission of human culture is the indispensable condition of our even being able to think an intelligent thought—not to mention our obligation to our great-grandchildren, whose world we casually deform as if it were ours to tinker with as we please. (There will be more of that in the next chapter as well.)

Third, I am we and so are you. We habitually imagine that each of us is a unitary personality, some more complex than others but all under firmly integrative control by an ego that may sometimes get out of hand but is always in charge except in pathological cases. I do not quarrel with the crude truth of this view, but I think we need to attend more to its crudity. It is true that a healthy person tends to hang together in a coherent manner, but it is not at all obvious that this personal unity is more like the unification of a high-level physical organism than like the unification of Italy in the nineteenth century—or perhaps even the fourteenth. Our self-imagining, and in a different way our imagining of others, tends strongly to slip away from our intimations of real pluralism in individual personalities, in a way that is analogous with our failure to consider the implications of treating names like "United States" or "United Nations" as if they were combinations of a given name and a surname, to be used with singular rather than plural verbs. Natural, perhaps; possibly inevitable; certainly understandable. But misleading. (This too will reappear in Chapter 9.)

These different versions of who we are have direct bearing on the responsible imagining of God in several ways that will be addressed in subsequent chapters. For the moment, I wish only to make a few observations about the religious and theological implications.

Individual differences, if acknowledged steadily enough, mean that my imagining of God is bound to be different from yours, and that neither of us can expect the other to conform to, or even to find personally viable, the best and most truing God we can separately imagine. Nor should we be alarmed, surprised, or suspicious if we discover further differences in the theory and practice of religion—what is central and what is marginal, what is moral and what morality has to do with it anyway, what an authentic saint would be like and how to get there, how, or whether, we pray—and yes, of course, how much orthodoxy counts and what it ought to contain and how we should go about forming, holding, evaluating, and criticizing beliefs. If all this is so, it is obvious that a unifying theology will be difficult to come by unless it makes generous provision for variables in content and pluralism in structure. One might be tempted to conclude that theology as such must be impossible, and that everything must be relegated to the jurisdiction of personal piety, except that the fact of *we,* properly appreciated, means that it will be useful to both of us to attempt to reconstruct a theology together, since a search for agreement will refine our own imaginings and thoughts and unearth for each of us some possibilities that we could not discover without the other's help.

It also means that we are *obliged* to theologize, since a failure to do so would be a failure to recognize the fundamental truth of our mutuality, which will perforce have religious dimensions that it would be as irresponsible to neglect on the level of reflective thought as on the level of shared celebration. But we don't stop with the discovery of common denominators in celebration and thought: we honor our mutuality only if we press on to a sharing and participation even in the more alien and uncongenial modes of the other. You have to give serious consideration to my interest in integrating the erotic into religion even if you think it bizarre; I have to honor your advocacy of the Protestant work ethic or your insistence that saying a daily rosary would solve my problems, even if it makes me gag a little. We do this both for the symbolic honoring of the unity that exists in difference (and not just despite it) and for the chance of enlarging the experience of unity: we may eventually pick up some useful tactics from one another, once our serious efforts at understanding manage to overcome the initial distaste. By the same token, the full acknowledgment of human community should extend to tradition, coming to terms with and appropriating the legacy of the past and taking responsibility for and preparing the life of the future.

The inevitable tensions between the vectors of difference and unity, each with its demanding claims to integrity, highlight the importance of distributing our sense of personal reality into pluralistic forms. Personal pluralism means that irreducible differences do not have the last word, and that authentic mutuality need not compromise individual identity and integrity. It means that the individual can acknowledge the reality of others not merely by tolerance or respect or acceptance, but by genuine participation, incorporating and embodying and internalizing these realities within the imagining of the self. Obviously, the full integrity of the other can never be completely grasped or assimilated sympathetically; but it is possible to appropriate a genuinely self-transcending sense of another without dissolving or denaturing it, and it appears that our capacity to do this is much greater than we are used to thinking. The resulting worship and theology become pluralistic in a much more than token way: one can learn to pray and to think through the internalized presences of others, imaginatively accepted as aspects of oneself.

So we, being who we are, undertake (or at least ought to entertain) the imagining of God, because although it is technically optional, it takes us closer (or at least *may* turn out to do so) to where we want—and ought—to be. Because we are who we are, we keep it provisional, with any given edition of the imagining of God being subject to revision even if the faith that animates it is settled with steady loyalty to the life project of continuing to imagine God as well as we can. Depending on who we are and where we want to be, we imagine ourselves as belonging more or less thoroughly to the God we imagine and the God toward whom we move in doing so. Because we are who we are, and in order to improve in the truth of our imagining of both ourselves and God, we supplement the piety of our personal imaginings with the shared and disciplined imagining that is theology. And in order to be who we are as well as possible, we construct theologies that honor traditional forms of God as far as they carry us toward truth, and change them when they can be made more corporately truing.

What we mean by "God" will be different for each of us personally; but we try to agree on what we mean by *God* theologically. What do we mean at the place where these two projects especially intersect—where they both express who we most basically are in saying what we imagine as "God"/ *God?* What I mean at that place, and invite you to mean as well, will be elaborated further as this book goes on, but this is the abstract (though not the heart) of it: it is the imagining that best animates my faith toward my becoming true.

The imagining that is meant here is an illusion, because it cannot be otherwise: the only way God can be meant, however transcendent or immanent God may be, is by forming imaginative illusions that express our faith in a way that keeps us truing and Godward. I, being constituted in a peculiar and particular fashion, must imagine God differently from you, in a small, provisional, limited set of ways. I know this imagining to be an illusion, but it is an illusion that is shaped to fit my present state and designed to take me beyond it. I know that it is only by passing through careful illusion that I may get beyond that illusion, and replace it with one that is better, more truing, even if equally provisional. At the same time, I, being constituted in a fashion profoundly like and interwoven with your own, must pursue with you a way of imagining God that we can share, one that expresses the mutuality of our Godwardness and the best critical responsibility of our conjoint imagining. We know this imagining to be an illusion, but it is an illusion that formulates or abstracts the truest communal imagining we can now have of God, at least until we can improve it.

We: that is, you and I, you vs. me, I as I and you, all working together and apart in responsible imagining. But that too is for the next chapter.

9

PERSONAL

VARIABLES AND THE

TAILORING OF TRUTH

God is addressed, received, and realized through acts of imagining. But we don't all do it the same way. What does that mean?

It means that our backgrounds, traditions, religious cultures, styles of prayer, and habits of understanding differ. But that is well-known, and only gets the husk off the coconut: there is still something between us and the meat of the question, something much harder.

What is not as well known, though probably of equal importance, is that we are wrong to suppose that we can learn to do it the same way. To a considerable extent, we *can,* of course: education or cultural transplantation can pry us loose from the provinciality of where we now are, and give us new ways of thinking, valuing, understanding, praying, assuming. But there is a limit to personal reconstruction. We instinctively overlook this truth, generously (and ungenerously) assuming that a fundamental human identity underlies all important differences; but the assumption, though not entirely wrong, is misleading. There are very substantial differences among us in the basic ways in which the imagination works, and some of them are fundamental and foundational differences, based on the irreformable and snowflake-unique organization of each person's central nervous system.

PERSONAL STYLES AND WIRINGS

It is generally conceded that color blindness and tone deafness are limitations built into the brain and passed on genetically. Those who have them cannot be taught to see the full spectrum of color or hear the complete range of sound available to those who do not share the defect. Of course, none of us can see or hear the *full* spectrum: ultraviolet and infrared are invisible even to those with high-quality standard nervous systems, and there are tones too high and too low for any human ear and brain to make hearable. We all can imagine infrared and ultraviolet, and we can build instruments to detect and measure them as a disciplining guide to our imaginations—but we cannot *see* them. My father couldn't see blue or green either (I eventually learned how to interpret an instruction like "just follow that gray car"), not because of a faulty imagination but due to limitations in the neural equipment by which his senses presented the raw material on which perceptual imagination works.

The fact of irreducible basic differences is obvious, sometimes painfully obvious, at one level of physical performance. Most of us have had to bear the chagrin of investing vast amounts of time, labor, and discipline in an unsuccessful attempt to run fast, sing sweetly, bowl perfect games, or dance divinely, while watching talented others accomplish far more with effortless instinctiveness. It is not that we lacked dedication or proper diet or competent instruction. It is simply that we lacked the Right Stuff that is supplied to some as part of their basic equipment and never quite adequately simulated by the others.

Aptitude may often have something to do with acculturation, or previous training, or the workings of the unconscious—but it probably has much more to do with the ways in which our synapses are physically organized. This is likely to be equally true of more specifically mental aptitudes, such as those for acquiring fluency in new languages, or mastering chess, or painting arrestingly fine portraits. It is at least imaginable that there are genuine feats of extrasensory perception, occasionally brought about, like epileptic seizures, through peculiarities in the basic arrangement of some people's nerves.

To what *extent* are our differences in imagining due to differences in the physical underpinnings by which our imaginations are supported?

We know far too little about this. It is clear that significant alterations in imagination will take place, at least temporarily, in a given person who ingests certain chemicals. It is clear that other chemicals produced naturally within the body—adrenaline, hormones, endorphins—usually produce analogous temporary effects in the way reality is seen and imagined. Such phenomena produce interesting problems in evaluation, for although the one who experiences them will usually be able to distinguish between her normal, or basic, or usual state on the one hand and her exceptional states on the other, she is not obliged to conclude that the truth belongs more to the imaginings of the former than to those of the latter. The unusual states of imaginative apprehension may disclose a world that is not only more congenial but even more true, a world to which one may wish, and feel entitled, to belong permanently, as when medication (or an unidentifiable grace) causes a temporary lift in the midst of chronic depression. Some people apparently *are* born two drinks short of the truth. Rose-colored glasses may sometimes appropriately compensate for a rose deficiency in one's normal vision, just as rosy memories may have a thoroughly legitimate place in one's bureau of standards for assessing what is true.

But I do not right now want to attend to the fluctuations within our vivid imaginings, though I will eventually return to them. Right now, I want to turn to basic differences among us in our characteristic styles of seeing and imagining.

A fascinating series of experiments was conducted in England in the 1940s to correlate brain-wave evidence with styles of imagining. It was noted that experimental subjects could be divided into three groups, according to the behavior of the alpha waves registered in their electroencephalograms. The largest group, called R (for "responsive"), characteristically produced broad alpha waves when their eyes were shut, but the waves narrowed considerably when their eyes were open. A second group, P (for "persistent"), produced similar broad waves whether their eyes were open or closed. The alpha waves of the third group, M ("minus") never took the broadened form, but remained at all times like the narrow waves of the open-eyed R subjects. What makes the experiments especially fascinating is that the members of the P group were found to think with little or no use of visual imagery, while the M group's thought processes tended to take place though vivid concrete images. (The R group, as you might have guessed, used a mix of image and abstraction.)

If you do not have an electroencephalograph handy, there is a shortcut diagnostic device developed by the experimenters:

Shut your eyes. Think of a cube like a child's block. It is painted. Now imagine that you cut it in halves across one side, then cut these halves in halves, and then cut them a third time at right angles. Now, think of the little cubes you have made. How many of their sides will be unpainted?[117]

Read that through again, and arrive at an answer. I will explain in a moment how the diagnosis works, but assure you in the meantime that it is not a matter of superior or inferior powers, not a question of adequacy or deficiency. It is, apparently, simply the discernment of different satisfactory styles of mind-functioning, different effective modes of imagining—as if comparing an appliance that runs on AC with one that runs on DC, or a rotary engine with a fixed block, or Chinese with Arabic.

Hoping that you have come up with an answer, I now acknowledge that if you concluded that each small cube must have three colored and three uncolored sides, you are quite right, and if you did not so conclude, you can easily prove to yourself that it is so. But the answer is not the point. The point is *how your imagination did the job of working toward an answer.* The more important questions are accordingly these: what color was your cube? what was it made of? how did you make the divisions in it (e.g., with an imagined instrument of some kind, or by making it come apart in your mind's eye, or by some form of unvisualized geometrical abstraction)?

I have tried this diagnostic instrument with hundreds of people, and the results are intriguing. The statement of the task did not specify a color, but it is common for subjects to imagine a particular color for their cubes, and not unusual for them to be later under the impression that I had in fact named that color in the original instructions. The substance of their cubes is sometimes unclear, sometimes very definite (I suspect that the popularity of Rubik's cube accounts for the relatively high incidence of plastic ones in recent years)—and sometimes nonexistent. My most abstractive subject replied somewhat testily that I hadn't asked for the cube to be of a *specific* color, or to be made of anything, so his was an insubstantial geometric construct, abstractly registered as having color on the external surface. At the other extreme, my most imagistic subject was so eidetic in his imagining as to posit a wooden cube, paint it blue with a brush and a can of paint, and saw it into eighths, complete with sawdust.

This general example is potentially misleading in some respects. The imagining of my abstractive extremist was not just interestingly different from that of my concrete extremist, but technically more true, in that it imported fewer optional and uninvited illusions that might perhaps impede other ways of thinking adequately about the cube I had asked them to imagine. But his parsimony in sticking to exactly and only what was given was not more *truing* in the task at hand: it was not more successful in solving the ostensible problem.

Eidetic imagining (i.e., imagining that makes use of vivid images) in fact seems to offer an advantage in the production of a sound and confident answer to the official question in this test, since high-eidetic types can simply lift up the small cubes, inspect them with the mind's eye, and count the painted sides. It is the eidetics, not the abstracters, who appear to have the gifts of versatility demanded by various kinds of creative mathematical imagining as well as the more obvious matters of visual aesthetics; the capacity to imagine a vivid blue or a vivid magenta, and to shift rapidly from concrete wood to concrete butter in the course of exploring possibilities, offers chances of discovery that are more difficult to come by in an imagination that remains steady in an abstractly colored cubicity—for instance, if we ask what color cube would go best with your living room drapes if you want one for the coffee table, or what mathematical properties would change if we deform the cube into a doughnut-shaped torus ring.

But of course the abstracters have their own day in other situations that happen to favor their style. Consider another playful puzzle that has been in circulation for many years:

A prominent surgeon is being chauffeured to the hospital by his son, when their car skids out of control and crashes. The surgeon father is killed instantly; the son is critically injured, and is rushed to the hospital for emergency surgery. But the surgeon on duty, when about to operate, recognizes the patient and announces to the head nurse that "I cannot treat this patient: this is my son!"

Eidetics are likely to be initially spooked by the apparent paradox. Abstracters may be, but will not linger there in bafflement as long. For obvious historical and conventional reasons, the second surgeon will routinely be imagined as a man, and the head nurse as a woman. Those are decent probabilities, but they are not inevitabilities; and the solution to the puzzle lies, of course, in being able to imagine this surgeon as the patient's *mother*. Now: if your style of imagining tends toward the abstract, you will be able to recognize instantly that this is a simple and totally satisfactory way of meeting the requirements, and you may have come upon it before I offered my assistance. If your first imagining contained a tentative man as the second surgeon, you can, without much difficulty, make the adjustment to cancel him in favor of the necessary woman. But if your style is highly eidetic, the initial masculinity of the second surgeon will not be as tentative and as easily dislodgeable. You will probably enact a man for the role with such concrete vividness that his transformation to a woman is not a ready imaginative option, even if hints are offered for your aid.

Puzzles like these are potentially useful in discerning one dimension of talent in the individual differences that go into our ways of grasping reality, but we still have no clear idea about how many other dimensions may be in question. Work is currently in progress on other varieties of cognitive processing. One undertaking investigates the differences between cognitive simplicity and cognitive complexity.[118] Another pursues the nature and locus of personal consciousness,[119] and differentiates types of consciousness.[120] Still another attempts to map significant variations and differences in the intermeshing of specific cognitive and affective styles.[121] Further investigations are underway in attempts to achieve a more precise understanding of the properties of extraversion and introversion.[122] And so on.

In short, there is a lot of work afoot in the study of individual differences and their peculiar advantageous and disadvantageous properties. I have only sampled what has been done, and mention here only a sample of my sampling, in order to underline two points.

One is that current investigations suggest that when it comes to how we appropriate, enact, and generally imagine reality as well as how we interact with what is thus brought into our orbits, not only do we differ radically from one another in significant ways that are *not* culture-bound, *not* eradicable, but also that these radical differences are likely to be increased rather than decreased by our getting more in tune with ourselves, becoming more truly who we are. It seems to me to follow obviously that no single programmatic fashion of being religious can possibly true us all; our most effective ways of imagining God are likely to intersect only at the highest common denominator, and our best ways of relating to the imagined God will differ accordingly. No single formulaic way of imagining or relating to God can possibly be adequate to all persons, even—perhaps especially—when their imaginations are most reasonable.

The second point is that if we are limited not merely by the boundaries of our time, our culture, our education, but also by the styles of our nervous wirings, the Faustian dream of the lone individual coming to understand all that may be understood is even more absurd than we had supposed. It's not just the impossibility of one person's taking it all in that makes communal understanding indispensable: it's that even if this were possible, that person would still be singing it all in a particular and limiting key.

We have to adjust our imaginations to incorporate a more vivid awareness of the radically pluralistic and communal nature of human understanding. We cannot approach an adequate grasp of reality—including the reality of our individual selves—by relying on our own capacities alone. But however humbling that realization may be, it does not leave us stuck in mere relativism and mutual isolation. The sympathetic imagination has the capacity to annex an empathic grasp of others' styles as a supplementary and complementary enlargement of one's own limited primary equipment. (I will return to the sympathetic imagination's enhancement of the reasonable imagination shortly.)

The application of the lesson is fairly plain for task-oriented situations. We need to lean on eidetics when the problem is to recall the exact words of a text or a statement (abstracters can paraphrase their sense of what it meant, and may be more accurate than eidetics in this, but eidetics are more trustworthy in remembering the precise wording); or to cut away the unnecessary marble from a block, so as to disclose in stone the image in the mind (abstracters look on with awe as the eidetics chip away with authority and sometimes a success that was to the abstracter literally unimaginable); or to find your way back to camp in confusing terrain (eidetics remember landmarks, twists in the path, intimate details that abstracters have generalized beyond usefulness as clues). Who is more likely to produce truth when the question is intimately involved with concrete particulars? Not the one whose imagination registered mainly the overall sense, but the one in whose mind the sounds and letters are faithfully fixed. The one who thinks in firm lines and solid substances. The one who has built, turning by turning, an imagined model of the entire landscape.

But we need the gifts of abstracters when framing just and effective laws (eidetics will probably come up with something insufficiently comprehensive), or editing a novel to make it more coherent and coordinated (eidetics are good at appreciating its present draft but are not as versatile in appreciating what it *could* be with some reorganization), or figuring out how to survive when the supplies run out and the camp is five days' hike away (eidetics are likely to overlook important variables such as the dispensability of costly but weighty equipment and the discernment of edible plants).

Different styles of imagining have differing types of advantage in the work of truing. Ample communal truth cannot afford to give the advantage to either one or the other in general. Both are required, as the amphibious R group knows best but cannot effect well without the special talents of M and P colleagues; the Rs can thus make good mediators between the Ps and the Ms, according to the nature of the problem—which is ultimately to true the community at large, all the members of which limp a little.

Other differentiations follow a similar pattern. Field-dependent persons, who tend to discipline their understanding of things to the context in which they are presented, seem to make better novelists and psychiatric nurses, and are generally better endowed with interpersonal skills than the field-independent (who tend to detach things from their presented context and tinker with them), who make better architects and surgical nurses and are more skilled at reorganizations and restructurings of various kinds.[123] This is another Jack Sprat complementarity: "field dependence and field independence are not inherently 'good' or 'bad'; each style can be adaptive in a particular context."[124] For circumstances demanding empathy and social sensitivity, send in your field-dependents, but substitute the field-independents when the situation is ambiguous and unstructured.

And just whom do we call in when the question is about how to be appropriately religious?

There are two ways of answering that. You will have anticipated the second answer: I will give it later, to confirm it. My guess at the first answer is that we tend to call in the eidetics and field-dependents, and that this is both good news and bad.

The good news is that what we then get are people who are empathic and socially sensitive, endowed with interpersonal skills: good pastoral types. The bad news is that we do not get people who are particularly talented at dealing with ambiguity.

I remind you that I am only guessing, but I think the guess more tame than wild. Consider the probabilities. We are talking about a religion that from its earliest days has been concerned about unwavering belief, denouncing doubt, celebrating martyrs, valuing submissive docility. For something like sixty generations, it has tended to have zealous leaders of such a style promoting zealous beginners of similar style as their successors, grooming and culling according to their instinctive sense of what was best to protect and developing, accordingly, a church that was preoccupied with orthodoxy, strong belief, discipline, pious self-abasement before the will of God. The result is bound to be not only that a certain model and image (probably literally, in the eidetic sense) of the church and its religion will be fostered and will prevail, but also that the people in charge will be consistently ill equipped to entertain the possibility that there could be any appropriate alternative.

It is likely that Christianity has not developed in a truly communal fashion, but has been primarily in the hands of eidetics and field-dependents all its life—producing wonderful counselors and spiritual directors and compassionate pastors who defined the tradition in unrepresentatively narrow ways. It is likely, that is, that the process of self-selectivity and other-selectivity in the tradition of its leadership has resulted in a distorted transmission of the Christian tradition, and that another whole dimension of it has yet to be honored with an adequate hearing.

Well, that of course is the second answer. Whom do we call in when we *really* want to find out about religious appropriateness? We call in everyone. We recognize that Bishop Joaquin's doctrinal strictness is in part a quirk of his personal wiring, and that Mme Claudette's incapacity to share his confident belief is not a moral failing but a signal that there's more to the matter than his instincts take in. We see that Ann's shocked response to Pastor Albert's hesitations about the inevitable damnation of unconverted Catholics is not necessarily a vindication of the truth against an unworthy waverer. We acknowledge that when Ruth's steely clarity in condemning abortion in any circumstances collides with Lynn's uncertain willingness to entertain the possibility of exceptions, it means that perhaps the matter is not fully decided after all; and that Richard's detestation of icons, despite the reverence with which his family and (as far as they admit) the rest of his parish regard them, may be a true index of their value when observed with religious seriousness from within a certain kind of central nervous system.

Once we weed out misunderstanding, ignorance, silly arguments, self-serving, confusion, and the stultifying force of mental habits, there is bound to be an irresolvable set of differences still tangled at the bottom of the garden. We process reality differently. Nobody should be allowed to have the last word on what is appropriate, because there is no last word.

We are still startlingly primitive about realizing this. Almost no one really believes that one man's meat is another man's poison: deep down in our often uninspectable hearts, we figure that anyone who feels poisoned by what another relishes is faking, perverse, or educable. Each of us instinctively supposes that the others would all come round if they could only see things truly. It is inconvenient and unwelcome to think that communal truth is communally distributed, not the choosing of one melodic line against its competitors but an orchestration of differences into harmony.

The community at large must be deployed and appreciated according to what their members are capacitated to contribute. To engage with reality other than pluralistically is to diminish both truth and truing, on every level. To uniformitize any dimension of life, including religion, is to falsify. We have, collectively, the necessary equipment; but only collectively. We must learn how to make use of it, collectively. There is a lot of work to do before our traditions can arrive at a just equilibrium.

THE SYMPATHETIC IMAGINATION

Much of the work in question comes under the jurisdiction of the *reasonable* imagination, which undertakes to sort itself out by way of a careful appreciation of what finally makes sense and what doesn't, once the implications of individual imaginings are adequately scrutinized and assessed. But there is a complementary task that is equally important, and it enlists the other side of imaginative responsibility: the *sympathetic* imagination.

Given the various facts about irreducible personal differences, the reasonable imagination will recognize that its own instinctive and favorite style of constituting reality is not the only appropriate way of doing it. It is truly one's own way, but does not necessarily mean that competing alternatives are false or falsifying. So far, so good. But the next step is not just to avoid forgetting that this is the case. It is rather to stay ready to honor alternative imaginings by taking them in, sympathetically, on their own terms rather than sifting out what is uncongenial about them.

The ability to imagine sympathetically is an extraordinary resource that we use to much too limited an extent. But it is on ready call, however rusty, and is often employed so automatically that we don't notice (87 percent of the fun of a surprise party, and at least 36 percent of the practical arrangements, derives entirely from the participants' ability to anticipate just how it will be experienced by the one who is to be surprised). I have strained your patience and sympathy from the beginning of this book by asking you to adopt imaginings you aren't used to. I realize that most readers habitually imagine *faith* in terms of beliefs, but they have to suspend that habit and substitute another if they are to understand what I am trying to say; I have proposed more ways of understanding *true* than normally spring into imaginative action; I have argued for specific ways of imagining our time in history, the Bible, Jesus, and the way we think about God, and am now in the process of forcing upon you a provisional reimagining of how persons are constituted. You may not find all that worth the effort (which I would regret, because I want to communicate: I just can't think of how to do it adequately without requiring some imaginative unorthodoxy that takes work)—but the main point is that you and I both know that you can do it if you want to. When someone is furious with you, you *can* go beyond feeling unjustly abused and acquire a genuine appreciation of where she's coming from. When your favorite team trounces its old rival, you *can* imagine how the other side feels. This is an impressive capacity.

But still more impressive is the ability to build alternative imaginings into our own imagining system and respond to reality not just in our basic routines but from points of view that are not our own. Let me give an example from yesterday, simple and commonplace in initial appearance but astonishingly sophisticated, and thrillingly promising for the human future, when examined more closely. As I walked along the sidewalk, I saw just ahead of me a young woman conclude a conversation with a friend and take a step backward—right into the path of another young woman's bicycle. The biker swerved just enough to avoid a full collision, but there was enough of a bump to stop them both in their tracks. The one promptly asked the other (I don't remember who spoke first), in a voice expressive of genuine concern, "Are you all right?" and got as an immediate reply, in a similar tone, "Yes, are you all right?"

No damage had been done. If it had, and I had been called as a witness, I would have testified that the fault was equally distributed. The pedestrian was careless to step backward on a busy sidewalk without looking; the biker was careless to be pedaling so close even at her modest speed. Either one of them would have been justified in objecting to the carelessness of the other. But instead of reacting with indignant self-righteousness out of her experienced botherment, which is a normal and culturally acceptable response in such circumstances ("Why the hell don't you look where you're going!" is customary), each of them had instantly appropriated the other's right to be thought justified, and at her own expense.

There was no indication that they had ever met before. The instant mutual generosity of mind that sponsored the generosity of manner was evidently a function of these ladies' (and I choose the title advisedly) habituated readiness to leap spontaneously out of the limitations of the primary personal mind-set that presides over our actions, and relativize its righteousness by an instant appreciation of where another is, in this case literally as well as figuratively, coming from. Imagine what we could be and do if such habits of sympathetic imagination were cultivated by everyone!

There is no good excuse for not cultivating them, and a proper understanding of who we are would certainly encourage our doing so, quite apart from the personal and general convenience that would result. And in religious terms, the ideal of both deliberate and spontaneous sympathy of imagination (an ideal more or less within reach of anyone who works at it) is a genuine appropriation and appreciation of substantive alternatives to one's own religious imagining, not so as to derail or compromise it but enough to honor legitimate versions of who we aren't—and to assimilate them as adjunct extensions of who we are.

If you suppose that I will try to move from there to an argument that what is true of the collectivity of the community should also be made true in some sort of collectivity in the individual self, you are entirely right. I will get to that toward the end of the next subsection, but first I want to resituate the individual self in its environment and in its imagination.

IMAGINATION, INTEGRATION, AND COMMUNITIES

The two most important properties of imagination are that it constitutes and that it coordinates.

The world in which I live is, in a deep sense, a world of my own making. I have to enact it for myself, or it is not there. In a deeper sense, it is not of my making, but is an experienced other that is constituted through a tradition that I receive, like the language through which I think about it and the habits of savoring and valuing through which I appreciate it. If I wish to enact the world amply (and I do), then I must surrender my control to the tradition; if I wish to enact it truly (and I do), then I must surrender the control of the tradition and take personal responsibility.

In *Sleeper,* the character played by Woody Allen is warned that the thought police are after him, intent on destroying his brain. "My brain?!" he gasps: "That's my second-favorite organ!"

I am sympathetic with the basic sentiment, but, to begin with, the count is potentially misleading. Our organic equipment is not merely physical. More honorable than the brain, because already stocked with the imponderably rich resources that the brain needs in order to do more than low-level work, are the language that permits the assimilation of reality well beyond the bounds of an individual brain's independent possibilities, and the culture that empowers us to be creatively at home in this reality.

We are organisms vastly more complex than we routinely imagine. The widespread illusion of independent individuality bears witness to that.[125+] It is a tiny truth, only the size of a brain; it is unfortunately often allowed to stray beyond its proper limits, and to masquerade in garments that it is ludicrously far from filling. Our names, with which we brandish our sense of our own concrete particularity, are usually thought to be as isolatedly individual as our social security numbers, but that is only because they are so truncated, slicing off everything but the family that nurtured us and the specific difference of our individual selves. Some cultures (e.g., Hungarian and Japanese) wisely put the family name first, a reminder of our true cultural ontogeny. A dozen names would represent us more accurately, starting with one that everyone shared and ending with the specific individual difference only after registering how totally we belong to, and are functions of, a series of larger belongings and inheritances.

We are all public property, by the nature of the situation. Your brain is not your best, or even second-best, organ, if you entertain a wider sense of your organic connections with all the humanizing forces that have shaped who you are and what you can do with it. We must not define ourselves in physically organic terms as if we were separate beings, except in specialized medical circumstances: even general medical circumstances require that we remember the social and environmental organism we belong to (e.g., dealing with cases of hypertension or measles or asymptomatic typhus-carriers).

Our major equipment for dealing with life, whatever may be the physical equipment necessary for having it in the first place, is social. What you are reading now is a function of a language to which neither you nor I have contributed significantly; the questions we are dealing with are matters of importance to you because of what you have inherited from the tradition, not from your brain or your liver or your heart, however indispensable these may be for the underpinnings of the process of transmission. We exist not (as we like to fancy), as important individuals, but as moments in a grander music of human happening. The rudeness of sociobiology interrupts our complacency at one appropriate point: all that we have of importance has been given to us, and we function within the system primarily to make it possible for it to be passed on.

To make a difference is not as important as to keep the whole process going. We have a disproportionate view of heroes, leaders, change makers, and an inadequate appreciation of those who sustain the whole process so as to make it available to the next in the hungry line. Our history books tell us about kings and wars and the dramatic rise and fall of empires. But the usual history books tell only the more sensational part of the story, and from the parochial viewpoints of those who could afford to specialize in large-scale difference-making and to leave (or to commission) records of what happened at that superficial level. The basic stuff of history took place not in that specialized and ephemeral arena, but in the huts where children were made capacious persons by being given language and culture and love, and in the public marketplaces where new ways of doing things were shown and shared among people whose names have long been lost. Even for the treatment of the sensational surfaces of history, the nineteenth-century cult of heroes and the twentieth-century cult of progress are false if they make us forget that ripeness is all, and that ripeness is what is bestowed upon human time by the unheroic faithful.

Underneath the divisions of kingdoms and the conquests of heroes, underneath even the technological revolutions that have made modern history superficially so different from what went before, real change is usually slow. And it needs to be slow, because we are not very malleable stuff. That becomes especially clear when the external social change is rapid, and disorients the social interior. You who read this are likely to be a member (or, more likely, an uneasy resident) of a city that is overwhelming and rather overwhelmed, no longer quite in political control of how it happens or how it is to happen. You don't like that, but it sometimes seems as if there is nothing to be done. The naive rapacity of entrepreneurs is naively fostered by those in political charge, because what is good for business is supposed to be good for everyone. But achievements in one area do not spill over automatically into others. Prosperity begets conditions for fostering Olympic medalists and Nobel Prize winners. The way prosperity is spent makes a difference and changes some of the possibilities. The society in question gets to decide whether it wants to spend its prosperity here or there. Worldwide prosperity enlivens further possibilities. Relatively inexpensive computers make it much easier to write a book. International business competition guarantees that the manufacturers will keep the computers relatively inexpensive. But the quality of life resides in more elemental places, where our estrangement from each other and our estrangement from God make a much greater difference than purchasing-power, refined technology, steroid-stoked athletes, breakthrough physicists, and even improved public transit.

Caught in this stiflement and gasping for relief, the modernized people of our time ask increasingly, What is the meaning of life? A dignified but ultimately unprofitable question, analogous to, and possibly identical with, the question Who am I? These are not necessarily appropriate questions to ask; they are almost certainly not appropriate questions to answer. Not because we should not pry into the deepest mysteries, but because we should not ask for meaning, in the way that these questions usually do, where this kind of meaning is not available at all.

Try another: What is the meaning of a rainbow? We may invest it with symbolic or fanciful significance, and think of a divine promise not to flood life away or a pot of gold or the threshhold of a land dreamed of in lullabys. But those are meanings *lent* to rainbows, not meanings they *own*. A rainbow is simply not endowed with the capacity to *have* meaning. In itself, it is a meaningless phenomenon, like a sudden shower that makes it possible. What is the meaning of the sudden shower? What is the meaning of weather? "Meaning" is simply not the right instrument for probing their reality.

There is no intrinsic ultimate meaning in what is ultimately random, and these happenings are random. So are you and I in our given uniqueness—but we are empowered to acquire meaning by becoming meaningful. The answer to "Who am I?" is "What do you mean?"—first as an inquiry into the purport of the question, and then as an inquiry into the purport of how the questioner enacts and realizes her life.

Ambitious people generally want to be special—not only with the specialness they actually have, as uniquely situated and uniquely wired agents of the realization of the world, but with the specialness that singles them out among the rest, a special specialness that commands fame and unusual honor (cf. W.H. Auden's haunting lines, "For the error bred in the bone / Of each woman and each man / Craves what it cannot have, / Not universal love / But to be loved alone").[126]! But to squander ambition in a longing to be that kind of special, rather than investing it in a determination to enact well the specialness that is given with life and faith, is falsifying, and tempts us to cheat on who we are, and to cut the corners of integrity and sincerity in order to make a big impression. It also conjures up out of inadequately socialized ego a false sense of how the world works.

The big splash is not normally where the most important contributions are made. The real flow of the world works differently, though we grow restless with it and impatient of ordinariness. Relief maps exaggerate mountains to accommodate our sense of how much difference they make when we try to climb them or travel beyond them. We don't feel satisfied by the picture as it really is, where the apparent stark differences are, in global terms, minor irregularities that are very unimpressive.

All the same, the individuation of any person, while usually exaggerated, is the locus of a unique reality, and ought to be conducted with a measure of independent care. It would be one kind of folly to pretend that the world I imagine is my own invention and possession; it would be another kind of folly to suppose that I am either obliged or entitled to appropriate what has been given me without taking responsibility for the peculiar shape it takes in me, who am—like you—a unique if tiny instance of and contribution to the great inheritance. The faith with which we receive and enact reality also calls us to pass it on with whatever marginal improvements we can offer.

The imagination constitutes. It forms the reality in which we live. It contains places where I have lived and places that I have never even visited. It contains the past and the future, the dead and the living, people I have never met along with people I have met often; it contains attitudes and aspirations that I have considered and rejected, and others that I struggle to acquire. It stocks my reality with content and tone. Some of the content and tone is false. Part of my task is to increase the truth of what my imagination enacts.

And the imagination coordinates. It makes the elements of its content belong to one another as members of a world, rather than merely an inventory of disparate realities. It brings into apparent coherence and mutuality the divergent parts of various congeries of realities, so that I can generate the convenient, if potentially misleading, illusion of grasping my highly diversified city as an entity encompassed by a single name, or think of Asia as such, or the 1960s, or children, or, in very much the same spirit, me.

What I mean by "me" is a function of both phases of imagination. On the one hand, I have watched myself and have recorded, with undoubtedly rather indifferent accuracy, what I have done and how I have reacted and even glimpses of how I have been perceived by others. This goes into the mix of relevant data, for me to be responsible for in any version of my self-image. But the urge to coordination tends to overwhelm the disparate data, and as a result I edit, adjust the balance, reinterpret, and generally jimmy it all into an artificial coherence that an outside observer might find difficult to credit, except for the convenient (or inconvenient) fact that the outside observer also looks for, and for the same reasons will find, a coordinated sense of who she is and who I am, and we will therefore agree on the principle however much we may disagree on the specific interpretations. We are in collusion to minimize the incoherence, and thus we both falsify both of us by imposing too much coherence, and the task of self-knowledge is accordingly difficult.

The question of the unity of personality is intimately connected with the question of the search for God,[127] and the shadow of Descartes still falls across the heart of both questions. Descartes' admirable attempt to found understanding in total indubitable certitude is an ideal that still haunts the mind, like the ideal of a perpetual motion machine. But it doesn't work. Descartes' project of demonstrating the self, God, and external reality comes close—my impression is that if we grant him any two of his points, the third will follow—but close is still too far away. It is less consistently realized that his most celebrated demonstration is flawed, flawed in very much the same way as demonstrations of God, and quite relevant to them.

"I think, therefore I am" registers Descartes' *cogito, ergo sum* (or his original *je pense, donc je suis*) adequately. Like other forms of apologetics, this one works only to the extent that it comes to the right conclusion, not because it really proves anything. It does not take much scrutiny to discover that the conclusion is already built into the premise: if we grant that *"I* think," then we have already given the game away: "I am" follows as the night the day once we have granted that this "I" is there thinking. This is truth of the tautologous form, like "if A and B are so, then B is so."

Descartes' attempt to establish fundamental truths beyond doubt failed, but like many failures in bold experiments, it turned out to be importantly instructive. Important instruction number 1: even so elemental and indispensable a truth as your personal existence cannot be proved: it follows that if you find the failure of proofs of God either conclusive or demoralizing, you are simply being unrealistic. Important instruction number 2: what we mean by "I" is perhaps not as obvious as we had supposed.

The latter conclusion takes longer to incubate, but is now a subject of some fascination among psychologists. Freud's dramatic fracturing of the agent self into the ego, the id, and the superego was only a beginning.[128+] There is now serious discussion on quite different planes about the extent to which that which you call by your name is an identifiable unity. Investigation from the side of abnormal psychology, where the dramatic phenomena of split personality and fugue[129] are seen to modulate into less exaggerated forms in each of us, raises serious questions about personal unity. But normal psychology provides its own direct testimony that "the unity of consciousness is illusory."[130!] The overall weight of evidence suggests at the very least that "unity of personality is only a matter of degree, and we should avoid exaggerating it."[131]

As I write this sentence, I am simultaneously taking a rough inventory of what is present at the edges of my awareness of my inner goings-on. I find that I am still working with a discussion on Hellenistic religion in which I was just participating; the song "Juanita" is, for reasons unknown, bobbing through my mind, sometimes surfacing with bits of the lyrics but keeping the music going even when I am not attending to it; I am making vague plans about a book that I am planning to try to track down shortly in the library stacks upstairs; I am sorting out my geographical situation with respect to where I might snag a bit of lunch if time permits, and my schedule with respect to whether time will permit; I am noticing some of the comings and goings of people around me, and dipping into my memories of the ones I recognize; I am remembering my plans to meet with three of my closest friends later in the afternoon; I am considering what the writing of this book has to do with my meaning and my life. All of these tracks are running at once, and each time I glance more specifically at one of them, I note that it has developed—I am aware of further memories that have begun to make their presence felt, the tune is in a later phase, I have somehow decided against fettuccine, another relevant Hellenistic text has occurred to me, an additional warm cheerfulness has collected around the friends, I recall that I left the necessary book reference at home, I find myself concerned about whether the tone of my writing will adequately convey how I mean. And a few other things have come into mental view to remind me that my initial inventory was far from exhaustive. All of these things belong to my life, and it to them. But the life seems to require many names if it is to be adequately addressed.

The notion that I, publicly labeled John C. Meagher,[132] may despite my habitual illusions to the contrary be a collection of more or less simultaneous ongoing happenings, a parliament of possibilities—or a commune, a minor political party, a federation of trade unions—rather than a sharp sheer self, is initially unsettling. But that is because I am used to supposing otherwise, not because it would be genuinely inconvenient to change my suppositions. In fact, as I reconsider, I realize that my most elemental sense of wholeness and unity is a function of imaginatively constituted and coordinated bodily multiplicities. My eyes see things from slightly different angles, and although the left one apparently has more authority than the right, it seems to defer cooperatively to give me the helpfully truing illusion of three dimensions. My two ears sometimes take in significantly dissimilar environments, but manage in doing so to offer a coherent orientation from which I can act successfully. My experience of taste is quite different from my experience of temperature, and neither of them resembles my experience of texture, which in turn is unlike my experience of the kinesthetics of the cup at the lip, but the convergence of all these informs me persuasively, and usefully, that I have finished my coffee. The pluralism of my body's performances, constituted and coordinated in routine imagination, is decidedly convenient.

So is the pluralism of my personhood. By reflective stages, the notion of a parliament of self—or a mixed community, an improvisational acting company, an underdeveloped fourth-world country, a protest demonstration monitored by a grim riot squad and anxious representatives of the social order—makes increasing sense. Not only does it help to account for my multitrack and frequently divided mind, it also offers other consolations.

It means that I do not lose what I do not choose. I retain a member of parliament for traditional Christianity, who is presently outvoted but whose presence remains to remind me of a major part of my life's belonging. I have my father's voice, my mother's, my sister's, all mobilized to encourage me and to correct my behavior. I incarnate versions of my teachers, my heros, my friends and memorable events and places and failures.

It is a large parliament. Its voices buzz and throb as I try to go about my life. At times it strikes me that it might be better to silence all the voices except those I select with my majority vote—but I know that as a ten-year-old I cannot afford to deprive myself of the grace of second thoughts that may come from what my majority had once thought obsolete. Being a parliament is occasionally cumbersome, but is far better adapted to the truth of unfinishedness and to the work of progressive truing than the dictatorship of a singular ego—including, and perhaps especially, mine—is likely to be.

Still, it feels disordered and awkward—sometimes, ironically, even lonely, despite its virtue of peopling the psyche with companions—and we look for ways of dodging such a condition. There are several established ways of dodging. We can enlist in the fight to defend the ego against all that nibbles at its supremacy, in the false name of mental health.[133+] When that doesn't work, we can submerge ourselves in the exploration of altered states of consciousness through drugs and their metaphorical equivalents and wait for something else to take over the responsibility we would rather shirk. We can find cults, domineering spouses, enthusiasms,[134+] gurus, or comprehensive ideologies that will help us avoid admitting that we are stuck with being personal multiplicities that can be reduced to the culturally encouraged simple identity only by sustained evasion, psychic violence, or a long road of disciplined specialization that learns how to silence the competing voices one by one, thus losing their contributions along with their raucousness. That is false economy. The community of self, like the larger communities to which selves belong, must come to terms with pluralism and find a way to honor all the voices while keeping an apt stability. All the voices have their claims and their imaginings, and they are best honored by being federated Godwardly.

STORIES, AND THE MUSIC OF THE DANCE

There are clever strategies that offer themselves as, and may indeed be, alternatives to the awkwardness of facing oneself in the mental mirror and finding multiple images. There is a strong school of thought that recommends the mediating balance of entrusting oneself to living in a story, especially the Christian story. That is, to identify oneself not according to the categories and statistically significant measures appropriate to census bureaus and opinion polls, but in terms of the narrative that recounts where one has come from and the larger narratives that tell the stages of experience and self-understanding in the life of the nation or people or religious tradition to which one belongs.[135+]

One of the fundamental wisdoms of such a move, in my opinion, is that it offers a psychic escape from the provincialism of the scientifically described world that dominates the imagination of those who have undergone the mixed blessing of having been reared in our particular nook of time and culture. My earlier remarks demonstrate that my reflexes are as habitually provincial in this as almost anyone's, and I will say more later that will prove that I haven't gotten over them, even when being explicitly suspicious of them. I accept these reflexes of imagining, despite misgivings (and despite my awareness that I don't control them more than they control me), because this way of imagining the world is an important instrument of truth and of truing, making it more readily possible to identify and choose the illusions we use with a knowledge of their cost. But this way of thinking should not be the only matrix of imagining, though it should be employed frequently if we can do it with discretion: overused, it tends to reduce all happening to a low-energy-level (the vocabulary shows my indebtedness to it) pattern of causality, in which moments of delight and fallings in love and the steady formation of enduring and faithful friendships are only epiphenomena, random chances of convergence that have no better status than forest fires or the creation of habitable islands via volcanic eruption. It does better as the Loyal Opposition than as the Government.

An appeal to storifying sneaks around this cultural disability by recognizing that the more important meaning of sequences to *us* is not how they were caused but how they are perceived as appropriate. Story lore puts us back in the driver's seat: *we* are in charge, not some nameless and impersonal *it,* and we get to say what it all means. This is good, and it works. I have marveled, over recent years, about the effectiveness of starting deep-interchange meetings with each participant storifying her or his life: we recognize this way of locating each other, and we turn out to be wonderfully talented at grasping with sympathy the story of a life that has almost nothing at all to do with the major landmarks of our own personal experience.

This is amazing. It suggests important possibilities for breaking through the glass cage of our habitual devotion to scientific causality, and it leads inevitably to a reconsideration of the Greatest Story Ever Told, a formula that will be undoubtedly winced at by those old enough to have been embarrassed by Fulton Oursler's best-seller of that title. But I introduce that awkwardness deliberately, to make a point about story.

It is, I think, demonstrably true that we know one another most congenially through a sharing of stories. The blank wonder about "who are you?" that normally obtains on first meetings is not adequately resolved by a name, or the proffering of a business card, or a report of a history of formal education, or even a list of hobbies. What the computer matchmakers have not yet realized, or have tried to bypass on the grounds that their machines can handle data brilliantly but have not been taught how to represent their connections with proper style, is that people receive themselves, and therefore receive other people, not as bundles of statistics and preferences but characteristically as trajectories, both themselves and analogues of themselves being perceived as movement through life, trailing, like meteorites, clouds of what may be glory or dust or both but is more significantly the reminders of where they are coming from. One of the most important dimensions of our truth is that we appropriate, constitute, and coordinate our experience mainly in narrative forms.[136]

As you have probably noticed, I tend to be mercilessly historicist when attempting to get my mind around anything that I suppose to be of substantial and permanent importance, and also anything that strikes me as having a false authority and needs to be reduced to appropriately manageable size. I admit my bias, but I do not apologize for it. Historicizing well entails both the appreciation of story and the critical capacity not to be bamboozled by it. If we meet, I will gladly hear your story, and can guarantee that I will be moved and impressed by it. I admire story as I admire belief: a way of holding things together in a usable coherence, as a temporary stage of knowing who we are, which is always provisionally welcome.

But do not ask me to suppose that your story of you *really* tells me who you are. It tells me where you have been and how you have been there, which gives me a sense of the trajectory that has formed who you think you especially are now, but who you *altogether* are now requires a quite different mode of conversation to start discovering. Story is preliminary and provisional. It is a good protection against alternative follies, but contains its own. It selectively short-circuits your multiplicity by the selection of who you think you have arrived at being. I will want, if we are to become deeply acquainted, to learn about the other trajectories whose vectors tug against your present course, and to hear some of the voices that you have muted or smothered in the course of getting to where your story says you are.

I am—my parliament is—wary about the wisdom of investing in a story, either personally or globally. My parliament's objection is essentially that while to storify is to disclose important truth, it is also to falsify, to canonize an illusion that is benign as a way to understand a stage or a pattern of trajectory but potentially malignant if absolutized or fixed.

One of the difficulties with which we must contend is our consistent provinciality, which orates grandly in our parliaments that where we are now is the best or the right or the inevitable or at least the *accomplished* place, and the appropriate conclusion of where we have been. The imagination can storify any sequence whatever, given a certain right to edit, omit, emphasize. But to pretend that one's life, or even the life of the people to whom it especially belongs, can be described by a given story is to imperialize an interpretation over its complexities, arrogantly deciding what is important and what is not as if one were really in charge and in a position to judge. We do indeed perceive our lives in stories, and it is useful to report them as such; but it is only out of parochial ignorance that anyone would offer the provisional story of now's self-perception as the key to the real qualities of the life it purports to describe.

The same is true of the Christian story. If we suspend belief appropriately, we have only the slightest notion of how its last nineteen centuries should most appropriately be told (though we are negatively guided by examples of false tellings from Luke through Eusebius to the sermon you will hear next Sunday) and we have almost no idea whatever of how, or even whether, it will conclude. The chances are that Christianity would be better understood not as a story at all. Not in history, not in you, not in me.

Even the practice of classical apologetics has given up the attempt to capitalize on the history of Christianity as an argument for its rightness, now that the study of history is sufficiently independent not to be bullied by, or conscripted into the service of, theological needs. The same is true on grander levels: the traditional story of the Abrahamic covenant and its Christian transmutation is attractive to Christian sensibilities, but it leaves far too much out of its narrative grasp to be entertained as the greatest story ever told. What it does with Judaism, what it fails to do with Islam, what it neglects about the past and ignores about the present and presumes about the future disqualify its candidacy. It contains too much untruth and is too costly to keep on immodest display. It is an important chapter in a much larger tale that already surrounds it, with more to come.

But even the larger story in which it shares a part is not itself the reality. Why should we care so jealously about story as the mode of truth's playing-out? Beyond the vicissitudes of our works and days, ancient wisdom turned to the stars to imagine that the deepest ground is in a music, a dance. We know more about the stories of the stars than they did; but they knew more about the ultimacy of their dance and about the music of the spheres. That is what their seas and seasons were, their tribes and kingdoms, their epics and their epochs, their gardens and their gods. And that is what I am, and so are you. The Christian attention to prophecy in the Hebrew Scriptures has been a search for story, and its results are largely false history and false prophecy. The Christian neglect of the Wisdom books has been because they have nothing to do with story, with prophecy, with long-range developmental design in the constantly recurring story that links its characters in a dance that is grander than all plots. That is one of the marks of their wisdom.

It is a mark of wisdom in persons to acknowledge themselves by their stories, since that is in fact how they perceive themselves and can, at least initially, best communicate their self-perception to others. But it is a mark of deeper wisdom eventually to leave the story behind, acknowledging that it has only as much authority as the imagination accords it and that story is —at least for some types of central nervous systems—an inhibiting and retarding constraint on what we can mean and be.

Beyond our stories, and beyond all our words, we may find the music and dance where our deeper truth joins more intimately with the truth of others, and the truth of God, than stories and words can tell; and beyond the dance and music, there is perhaps only the embrace.

Music and dance lack some of the precisional advantages of grammar and plot, but they have their compensations, some of which are appropriate to the theological occasion. For one thing, they do not presume to define anything in relation to another thing: they merely enact pattern and rhythm, juxtaposing elements for the sake of that enactment rather than to fix them in arrested places, wisely (or, more accurately, with convenient inevitability) offering a rhythmic flow of overwhelmingly wonderful happening rather than reducing them to a merely whelming and catalogably orderable experience over which we are in charge. Where premature definition would falsify, this is a clear advantage.

It is an advantage in holding together the parliament of self, and it is a corresponding advantage in addressing God. The two must obviously be coordinated, and the God to whom I appeal in my more infantile moments, or my times of depression and abandonment, or my periods of fierce and silly independence, will necessarily be different from the God whom I seek out in elation, in gratitude, or in sheer longing. There is a measure of constancy in the John Meagher who runs this gamut, but it is tenuous, better understood in terms of dance than of substantial identity. Likewise, the God I pursue through these moods and changes must be imagined (or illusioned: the difference between the words is lost at this stage of experiment) selectively in order to true me to where my faith aspires. Sometimes she is Lalita, the cosmic mother who is the fecund source of all reality; sometimes he is JHVH, the enigmatic initiator and protector of covenants; sometimes it is the nameless Absolute into which my prayer offers to dissolve itself.[137+]

I play, occasionally imagining that God plays in response, assuming the many guises I project. Because it is play, I try not to take it too seriously; but because there is nothing more serious than this kind of play, I try to take it seriously enough, enough to play it thoroughly.

You may habitually suppose that play is by definition unserious. But whoever thinks that play is not earnest has never seen a soccer cup final, a performance of *King Lear,* a good poker game, the inner works of a political campaign, a wise employee dealing with an irascible superior, or a successful spouse. Play is in fact what we do almost all the time. We change our play according to the roles bestowed upon us by the situation at hand, or the roles we invent for ourselves; but play is our native habitat and calling. If you can find, in any one of your days, twenty minutes where you are not playing at all, I shall be startled; and I shall also be skeptical about any claim that these are among what deserve to be considered your better moments. You even play at being you, because there is no other way to do it. The challenge is not to quit playing at it, but to play it well.

Playing it well is playing for the truth. The truth is what trues, and this is often, provisionally, deliberate illusion. It allows untruth only as an instrument to pry ourselves to truth, never as a resting-place. What the imagination sees as untrue cannot, in the long run, true, though it may offer a bridge to the next sturdy place. That is why belief comes into question. It is an instrument for moving beyond into the larger reaches of faith. But it is to be outgrown, abandoned, dissolved, left behind as one moves more steadily into faith.

Faith is where beliefs should eventually vanish in the name of Godwardness. The beliefs may be revisited playfully, as one may desire, as long as it is understood, in the name of faith, that the revisitation is also a form of play, often a diminished form. We must sometimes come back to diminished play, because we are often diminished, and it would be foolish to expect ourselves to be constantly capable of the faith to which we ideally aspire.

But let us be clear about what we are doing. The storifying of reality ought to be accompanied by its dance—or, if you *must* be verbal (as I must), its poeticizing, which breaks the boundaries of story's plot and releases us to new and more musical configurations. Traditional Christianities may true us partially on the way, stabilizing our belonging to those who have preceded us, but the way is best served by whatever brings truth, which has more dance and poetry and hugging to it than the Christian tradition has yet absorbed. Christianities should cherish and belove what they have been, but they should also dance and sing and embrace who we are in order to become truer. And they should become truer in order to belong more to God. And what that might mean is the next question.

10

NAMING GOD TRULY

AND THE MANAGEMENT

OF ILLUSION

Suppose, then, that you are skeptical about the desirability of accepting the imaginative option of God as the best way to become trued in faith, or about the possibility of imagining God in a way that is not ultimately silly or incoherent or flimsily fantastic. Is there a way of entertaining this option that will stand in all critical weather without special protection and that might really make a helpful difference to your imaginative world and to the faith in which you address it? A way that genuinely trues the mind as well as the heart?

Or suppose that you have accepted this option and want to do it well in company with others. What then should we imagine together about God? Our private imaginings may differ as we differ, and fluctuate as we fluctuate. We can share them with one another to enhance the repertoire of our Godwardness. But can we also find a theological constant that will serve as a shared stability in these imaginings? A steady mutual understanding that will coordinate and discipline the selected illusions that we use to stay faithfully Godward? One that will constantly remind us of what we pursue beyond illusion and beyond belief?

I propose one where I think we may fruitfully start, whoever we may be: God is truing.

GOD AS ILLUSION TOWARD GOD AS TRUING

Please do not in any way suppose that I am making a claim for the truth-value of any of the specific imaginings through which I conduct my God-wardness. I disavow that entirely (or almost entirely, the qualification to follow later). My imaginings of God, including my beliefs about God, are not truth. They are illusions.

But they are illusions that are capable of bringing about truth, able to true. If that still sounds odd or contradictory, only a little further reflection is required to demonstrate that our truth, our proper functional alignment with reality, is often brought about through the instrumentality of illusions, some of them instinctive and some of them deliberately chosen. Here are a few more practical examples:

1. By any reasonable definition of humanity that you may wish to use, infants are not fully human except in the abstract sense that they are endowed with the potential of becoming so. At the time of their infancy, they are inferior to cocker spaniels in resourcefulness, independence, responsiveness, the understanding of language, and the capacity to do minor household chores. To give them human names is to project upon them an illusion of humanness that their actual behavior will not validate (high-born infants of Imperial Rome were often left nameless until they were more clearly qualified). To speak to them as if they understood is to spin out another illusion. However, to treat them strictly as they in fact are, not yet ready for either names or conversation, turns out to be retarding: if they are not spoken to, with some frequency and volubility, they will not make the first preparatory steps toward learning to speak, and if they are not treated as if they were already endowed with some genuine humanity they will not acquire it, but will become listless, dull minded, and sometimes death bound. (Analogous phenomena occur later. It is well known that children generally learn poorly from teachers who suppose them poor learners, whether the teachers are accurately informed in the matter or not, and adult workers at various tasks regularly bungle them if their superiors treat them as if they are bunglers. But established poor learners and bunglers seem to be able to rise above their habitual performances if they are dealt with as if they were known to be proficient.)

2. The first time one encounters a telephone answering machine, one is likely to be struck dumb, or at least somewhat stupid, by the realization that one is being asked to address a mechanical device. (The same thing

happens, of course, to those whose first direct telephone conversation happens to occur later in life than yours did.) If one cultivates the illusion that one is rather speaking directly to another person, the whole operation turns out to work successfully. A car, similarly, is an awkward, alien, and perilously dangerous piece of equipment during the learning period when it is experienced as the mechanism that it in fact is; but once it is "felt into," and experienced illusorily as an extension of the driver's body, it becomes much more congenial, controlled, and safe.

3. Thomas Kuhn's impressive and influential *The Structure of Scientific Revolutions* reminds us, among other things, that great advances in knowledge and technological control have been made through the use of scientific imaginings that are no longer taken seriously, and that the imaginings that are now taken seriously by scientists are quite normally regarded by them not as mirrors of the truth of things but merely as convenient illusions that effectively guide current research. The rise of the sociology of knowledge has amply confirmed and refined Francis Bacon's insight that our thinking is guided more by communally shared Idols of the Mind and Idols of the Tribe than by truths independent of social validation. Many of the universal truths that we think we've found turn out to be more local, but effectively true within the boundaries of communal imagining.

4. The perceptions that lovers have of the beauty, wittiness, exquisite taste, grace, and social winsomeness of their beloveds may stun and baffle unsmitten observers, and may later be a source of retrospective amusement to the lovers themselves. But few lovers would deny that these illusions worked as effective vehicles to bring them to genuine and permanently valuable personal relatedness, and the beloveds will regularly testify that despite the patent falsity of the surface of the relationship, they experienced through it an authentic being-known and being-loved of unusual depth and intimacy.

5. When trying to do delicate calligraphy, I move my fingertips with gentle precision. My mind, together with the habitual instincts that transcend its explicitness, puts me in direct touch with my fingertips, and it is *they,* and they alone, that I move. When I am not trying to do delicate calligraphy, I know perfectly well that I am not constructed in such a way as to be able to move my fingertips directly. I have to activate certain muscles in my forearm which pull tendons in my hand to bring about the desired effect. I might, after an assiduous imaginative self-retraining, be able to focus on the forearm muscles and hand tendons, but to do so now gums up the calligraphy. It is far more efficient, and more truing to the calli-

graphic results, to accept the illusion that I am moving my fingertips directly.

6. Self-knowledge is notoriously loaded with illusion, often a source of annoyance to others and not infrequently to oneself. But not less important, though less often considered, is the positive function of illusion in holding together in imagination the divergent aspects of the self so as to relate them effectually and sustain them as balancing resources, constantly on call if needed. The somewhat scattered diversity of our selves functions most effectively if we accept the convention that each of us needs and deserves to be identified by a single name rather than the directory that might be more technically correct. To overrate the singleness is to risk being domineered by a fascist ego whose rule may provoke disastrous revolution in the oppressed provinces, but unless we exaggerate the sense of unity at least somewhat, the coordination of one's personal federation may give way to the anarchic dissociation of personalities that seems, in known cases, to be an unsatisfactory condition for doing life effectively.[138] The role of illusion in developing an adequate sense of security, in training and sustaining a capacity to enter fruitfully into the worlds of others, and generally in "maintaining a healthy mental life,"[139] ought to be better appreciated.

I have no intention of calling into question the reality of infants, machines, the physical world, lovers, fingertips, or personal selves. I am merely registering that our sense of what *sorts* of realities they are is sometimes well askew, and that this askewness is not an insuperable impediment—on the contrary, it is often an indispensable condition—in the enterprise of relating to the realities in a stable, effective, and harmonized manner. Moreover, in the instances I have just sketched, the illusions *become true* by being faithfully pursued: the infants emerge into nameable and conversant human personalities, the retriever of the messages from the machine hears the familiar voice inhabited by the familiar friendly tone, refined microscopy shows that the molecule really *does* look like the model elaborated from experimental evidence, and my fingertips move just the way I intended. Illusions can true. They are not any the less illusions for all that, but they are nevertheless illusions that, like the benign bacteria of the digestive tract, it would be unwise, retarding, and harmful to attempt to do without.

GOD AS TRUING BEYOND ILLUSION

Is "God is truing" also an illusion?
Yes and no.

Yes, insofar as neither your imagination nor mine is likely to leave it open-ended. We will respond by supplying uninvited illusions to fill in the blanks left by the unspecified "God" and the highly ambiguous "truing." If I say "Kelly, who lives with my aunt, is extremely fond of blueberry ice cream," you will probably, if you listen attentively to my saying it, respond with vivid or shadowy projections of Kelly's approximate age, particular sex, relationships with my aunt, and maybe even probable attitudes toward butter pecan. But these are your illusions: I have said nothing inconsistent with Kelly's being a neutered beagle. So what you do to fill out "God is truing" at first, before I have said more, is your doing, not mine, and is illusory.

"God" and variations on "truth" have long, complex histories, and some of the notions attached to them are bound to seep randomly into my mind and yours, however unwelcomed, however inappropriate, when such a statement is made. In short, what happens in the mind in response to "God is truing" (as it would happen also in response to other combinations of complex terms, such as "persons are symbolic" or "health is wisdom") inevitably produces a considerable mixed bundle and blur of imaginings.

But no, on further reflection it emerges that "God is truing" is not an illusion, insofar as my intention is to mean this as a definition of an unspecified item, with the specifications still to be issued. Neither your blank-filling illusions nor mine are relevant. I am not saying that a known A is to be identified with a known B ("Modern Hissarlik is ancient Troy"; "Olivier is Hamlet in that film"), but rather to say that I define the term *God,* taking it as initially without content, as being identical with what I propose to mean by "truing." That is, I am putting deliberately out of bounds all previous meanings attached to *God,* and inviting the imagination's exploration of what would happen if we gave it, at least as a start, one meaning only.

"The origin of the universe was the Big Bang" might possibly be proved some day to be an illusory formulation. Only twenty-five years ago it was still in hot competition with the steady state theory, which denied that "the origin of the universe" was even an appropriate notion, let alone one that could be specified. But if you entertain the imaginative option of an origin to the universe, it is not an illusion to say that what you mean by that phrase is what you mean by the Big Bang, and then to define the latter so as to provide the most promising way of making the former successfully meaningful. I am assigning a sense of "truing" to the term *God,* as an initial step in imagining what we can most adequately mean in directing our faith toward God.

What I mean by *truing,* partially touched upon in Chapter 2's discussion of *true,* is essentially *the power that makes reality progressively more true.* It is at once the power that holds the real together in coherent, ordered, and intelligible relatedness, and the power that brings us into harmony and effective relationship with it.

These two are inextricably intertwined. We are not in a position to talk about "the real" except in terms of our relationship to it, since without that relationship it is not there for us at all, has no presence in our imaginations, and simply cannot—not may not, or should not, but absolutely *can not*—be considered. In being filtered through our individual and collective capacities, reality is shaped and colored to fit them—but it is useless to ask how much distortion is thus introduced, because we can ponder that question successfully only to the extent that we become true enough to remove the distortion. The night sky still looks like a dome, sounds of ascending pitch still seem to cease to exist after a certain point, and the eye distinguishes orange from blue in a way that it does not distinguish cold things from warm ones. We know now that the dome is an illusory perception of billions of stars at highly varying distances, that the sound becomes inaudible but does not disappear, and that infrared, though invisible to the eye, is a real color. But we can know and correct these distortions only by having found ways of overcoming them: our instruments have made our understandings truer, and our imaginations now encompass the enhanced truth. Receiving the truth of reality is therefore a function of our own truth and will doubtless shift and improve as we become more true. But we cannot think about what the next stages might be except in an imaginative void where speculation is numb. In the meantime, the reality apprehended (and admired, feared, loved, or merely scrutinized) by our truth is *the* reality, all that real can be for us. Whatever we may dream about future developments, the construction of our own reality must take place in conjunction with what is realized *already.*

The power that defines reality and holds it together is a power in which we participate. It is ultimately identical with the power that holds us together and makes us who we are, since the two are, as far as we can know, reflexes and reciprocals of one another. Further refinements, new dimensions, transformed realizations in the future must continue this reciprocity. I presume that things that are not ourselves will continue to happen in a coherent, ordered, and theoretically intelligible fashion even if our martial and aggressive folly should wipe us entirely out of the picture; but that presumption is inevitably based on a simple extension of the way it evidently works now, from the only viewpoint I can truly occupy. In the meantime, while we still participate, the truth of reality is as much the source of our truth as vice versa. The obviously personal distortions of ignorance and falsity and self-deception become recognizable and corrigible only as they lose their hold by being jostled by truth that we share in but do not control, and are replaced by truer self-awareness; and this change in self-truth is inevitably accompanied by change in what we grasp to be the truth of the less obviously personal reality that is not ourselves. The power in which and by which this truing is brought about is named God.

In tossing around the term "power," I am not trying to sneak in a mysterious Agent, a ghost in the universal machine, a raw energy that throbs in everything like a metaphysical vital pulse, or a force that exudes truth like some sort of cosmic sap. I mean something closer to a possibility that is constantly being realized, power not as in "powerful" (like nuclear weapons, or Victoria Falls) but as in "empowering" (like the power of attorney that you may confer upon your lawyer or your sister, or the power of living things to grow), an invested capacity that manifests itself in the evidence of even quiet happenings.

We clearly live in a reality where truth abounds. Even if it does not always seem to triumph, it is always on the march. Physics and chemistry and biology try to describe its workings in the physical universe; psychology and sociology and economics pursue it in the social order. And in our personal lives, at least in what we consider our best moments, we pledge allegiance to it. Ethics attempts to describe what this allegiance implies, and so do philosophy and, ideally, theology. We are in principle very fond of truth, and consider it significantly better than falsity. We are biased against delusion, and even against wholesome illusions that can be identified as such, so much so that we tend to mobilize an impressive degree of vigor in defending the truth-value of our favorite illusions.

You may wryly observe that this bias in favor of truth extends even to the point of some of us arguing in behalf of illusions if they result in more adequate truing—and if so, you are quite right. That is of course what I am doing. I confess to being a truth-bigot who does not scruple about embracing useful illusions in the cause of truing, on the grounds that the pursuit of eventual truth and of the overall trajectory of truth is more important than trying (unsuccessfully, perforce) to stay clean of all falsity. I am basically pledged to pursue this quirk wherever it takes me. This is what is metaphorically called being on the side of the angels, and was called so literally before angels were called into question precisely by those who were on their metaphorical rather than their literal side.

Here those who know me well may be heard to chuckle, aware that if there were an Olympic competition in self-deception, I would certainly be a contender and possibly a safe bet for at least a bronze. Some of them have seen me in breathtaking performances of resistance to truth. But those who know me *very* well are likely to testify that I am deeply chagrined at how indifferently successful I am at carrying through with my pledge of allegiance. They know that the pledge is there sincerely—not necessarily more sincerely than yours, but as sincerely as *I* can muster—and that I am probably at least as disappointed as they are that I am such a dull boy when it comes to carrying it out. And I think they will admit that I work at it as if genuinely discontent with my resistance.

We all have to struggle with a perverse resistance to truth, and we all regularly lose the fight. We tend to have an instinctive preference for who we think we already are, and what we think we have, even if we aren't especially fond of either: they make us feel substantial, and there is an unpleasant vertigo that comes with letting go. The problem is not so much one of self-love as it is one of self-clinging, submitting to the bullying of the ego to let it stay unchallenged and in charge: the ego's present form is no more eager to die than the rest of us, and is marvelously resourceful in avoiding mortal danger. Our sins, the Fourth Gospel appears to maintain, are much less important than Sin, capital *S* and singular. Sin is the protectiveness we instinctively have about our *personal* darkness, where we feel safe. Truth is threatening to that safety, and although we may concede that it is best, it is not what we want, even when we are pledged to it. We want what we cannot have. We want our darkness labeled *Truth*.

Wisdom and truth come with age only as silver comes with rock: the stuff is there, but it takes a lot of grinding and sifting and smelting to make it accessible. I wasn't claiming that we are good at bringing truth about. I merely alleged that it's what we know to be best, whether we want it or not—the contract we would sign if given an alternative option of settling for being happily and effectively deceived. I would undoubtedly wince, but I would sign. Not to be willing to sign is a self-consignment to falsity, and to prefer falsity is, in my opinion, a sign of a weakness of faith that is probably remediable, and should be remedied.

Faith, you will remember, is quite different from belief. Belief offers the way stations of faith, where those who have never thought it safe or possible to venture further—and unscrupulous touts who simply want to ply their trade—whisper about this being the end of the road. Faith can recognize no such terminus, being "an active receptivity and self-engagement, a responsive and responsible readiness to accept, affirm, value, and even love whatever is really given and whatever one invites into realization."[140]! Faith is the openness to and cherishing of truth, and is therefore, by the definition I am proposing, Godwardness.

Moreover, the truth that is active makes a palpable difference, and since the difference it makes is precisely what the most universally benevolent disposition would invite and foster, it is also an authentic—perhaps the ultimate—form of loving. Ultimate truing is also loving, and its name is God.

GETTING TRUED

I appreciate that there are persons committed to the truth who do not want to be mixed up with God. If you happen to be one of them, please indulge me for a moment while I offer an explanation. I am not calling into question the integrity of your bias for truth. I recognize that you may fulfill all the conditions of my definition of faith, without budging from your uninterest in God. I ask you only to notice that I have not yet asked you to be interested in any God you have not already accepted. I have defined God in a way that does not entail anything you do not already mean through other ways of describing your allegiance. Godwardness— even if you would rather be spared that particular term—is therefore, so far, nothing other than your own trajectory. I will, of course, go on from here to suggest further ways of filling out the implications of such a trajectory, but these will be invitations only. I am not building a trap to catch the decent unwary in a theistic bind which they may have taken considerable trouble to stay free of. I am trying only to build a sense of God, hospitable to Christianity even if not made in its traditional image, that will stand in all weather, including yours. You get to say whether imagining God as truing strikes you as worth your while. Others, who should ideally be chastened and disciplined by your judgment, get to say whether it speaks, and enhances, their truth.

Some of them will inevitably be impatient with this apparently trivial first step, either because it is not enough or because it seems falsifying to their habitual imaginings, another god of the philosophers when they want a better case for the God of Abraham, Isaac, and Jacob, or the one who laid down the law to Moses on Sinai.

Of course it isn't enough: first steps rarely are. But they must be taken if one is to go further. And of course it is not the God of the patriarchs. It is not the God against whose petulant wrath Abraham pleaded for mercy on Sodom, or the God who promised Moses on Sinai that he would wipe out the incumbent inhabitants of the Promised Land. It is a God that calls into question the adequacy of those ways of imagining, which in the long run look so little like truth and so unworthy of the faith to which we aspire, and therefore seem so little like God.

The constant Christian spiritual struggle to acquire a faith that is worthy of God has obscured and retarded the task of acquiring a God that is worthy of faith. The authors of the Scriptures have given wonderful hints and glimpses of such a God, but they did not tell the whole truth and what they told is not all true. For all his complaining, Pascal did not really worship the God of Abraham, Isaac, and Jacob either, at least not without a great deal of editing and reinterpretation. Christians are called to worship the God of Jesus, who is the God sought but not quite found by the patriarchs—nor by Christians, who do not yet love truth, and therefore God, enough.

We shall love the truth, and the truth will make us—though probably only by the slow and gradual stages by which we learn to embody it—free. That is what it is to be trued; that is how the power of truth works in human lives. That is how God loves us. For what could be a grander expression of love than to make us true? Consult your own best paradigm of love. Is it the way the good mother cares for her child? Friends caring for one another? Spouses embracing in the ecstacy of wonderment or in the steady routines of mutual devotion, losing their lives to one another only to find them received again transformed? Jesus on the cross? All these are images of being true, of giving truth, of truing. If God is truing, then God is loving. And if God is loving—not the parodies of loving that appear in possessiveness or the self-gratification of warm feelings or the showing off of generosity or the deferential admiration that often accompany and falsify love, but the untainted real thing of your perfect paradigm—then God is truing. To imagine God as truing is to find God as loving.

THE PERSONHOOD OF GOD, AND OF US

Is God also lover?

This is a potentially momentous question, since it touches on what makes all the difference for some religious people: the personhood of God. The failure to cross the boundary between impersonality and personality is undoubtedly what made the god of the philosophers intolerable to Pascal, and to those who quote his repudiation of it with approval and relish. The boundary? Perhaps the gulf. The history of religion and theology is deeply conditioned by the sense of how much may be at stake in this matter, and by the apparent unbridgeability of the gap experienced on each side of it.

The popular religion of ancient Greece was filled with personal deities and hostile to the impersonality of such philosophical forms of deity as Aristotle's "unmoved mover" and the Stoic Nature/Necessity/Destiny/Law/Logos; undiplomatic philosophers dismissed the personalities of the popular traditional gods and diplomatic philosophers cast a thin transparent veil of personality over a divinity that showed no face through it. Israelite theology began with a firmly personal God, but some Jewish philosophical movements at the time of Christian beginnings eroded the divine personhood in favor of more abstract characterizations that they found confirmed by certain ways of reading the Scriptures. Christian thinkers who brought a personal Jewish God to an encounter with the Greek philosophical tradition struggled with the apparent dilemma that they could not invest God with metaphysical ultimacy without surrendering personality, and vice versa—and later, Christian mystics reported, often to the dismay of religious authorities, that the divine personality tended to disappear at the farthest reaches of their prayer. In the mainstream of the Christian tradition, virtually no one wanted to imagine God as other than personal, or as other than ultimate, and virtually no one could claim to have done very well in making the two compatible.

The problem has always been essentially the same, and its modern edition is the conflict between theistic and scientific views of the universe. Much sophisticated thought has been spent on offering solutions to the conflict, and there are ways of thinking that can resolve it if certain concessions are made. But a traditional biblical personal God clashes still with a traditional scientific impersonal Nature. If the world works by regular scientific laws, then it is in no need of personal governance—hence Laplace's reply to Napoleon. If it works by a form of personal management that intervenes at apparent random, then there can be no regular scientific laws. Or, to put the matter less crudely, if the standard scientific vision is true but only because there is a personal God who voluntarily created it that way, then there is no way of distinguishing the divine will from impersonal laws, and thus no symptoms of personality in the putative divine will. God becomes as good as impersonal.

I am not going to propose a satisfactory solution to all this. But I am going to offer some brief suggestions about how to live with it.

First, I don't think that there is anything theologically decisive in our inability to move by rigorous argument from a definition of God as truing, and the corollary of God as loving, to a personal God. There is no way to move from the realization of the world as you know it in your imagination to a proof that the world also exists outside your imagination—an interesting gap, but one that does not often trouble anyone. I am postulating that we can think of truth in the way that I have proposed, and that it is a good move to define God in accordance with it—and that if it should somehow turn out that this way of imagining God is in fact accurate, this way of imagining God is in the meantime the only way we can arrive at the accuracy: we can't check it out some other way. If we can further imagine God as truer and lover, nothing may require us to do so, but nothing forbids it either. Does it true you to do so? If so, why not? If it is in fact the case, imagining it unprovably is the only way to get there: it can't be demonstrated.

Second, it is important for those who care about the matter to inspect what is really at stake for them. That specifically includes an inspection of what they can mean by personality in the case of God. Presumably, they will not suppose it true to imagine God as occasionally moody, or subject to lapses of memory, or beset by insecurities and changes of mind, or devoted to interesting hobbies, or susceptible to flattery. When you really remove from the imagining of the divine person all the limitations of ordinary, and then of extraordinary, human personalities, what is left? I do not argue that nothing is left, merely that it is likely to be less than we instinctively suppose. If you then decide that you prefer a more limited divine person, more like us, then you must also decide what to do about it. The resulting illusion may be temporarily truing, but should not be thought theologically respectable and would be better outgrown as soon as convenient.

Third, it is well to remember that, as I just implied, there are two personalities involved when I ponder the divine self: mine as well as God's.

Mine starts with that version of me that thinks about such things, but eventually has to own up to other versions, including some that take more account of you than I usually do. These other versions will form differing notions of God's self. When my parliament finally legislates the imagining of God's person that has the best chance of truing me for the next while, strengthening and energizing my faith toward truth, I need not be anxious about getting it wrong. If it is importantly wrong, I am likely to find out sooner or later if I keep at it—which is what faith requires of me. You can be very helpful in the process, if you are patient: important change is usually slow, and we must remember that our uniqueness is ultimately irreducible even if complementary. You get to decide how to imagine God's personhood, and how and when to revise your imagining as you assimilate others' views.

Our truths will differ from one another in this as in nearly all things. We are not put together in the same way, and what trues Molly and Mike may not true Kate or Sean and could turn out to be falsifying to Marg and Sarah. We differ in sex, temperament, culture, upbringing, and the fundamental peculiarities of style that neither should nor can be eradicated.

Such differences will show up in our instinctive responses to God as truing, even when the phrase is purged of projections that I have explicitly disinvited. There are some cool and clear persons for whom the truing to which I give the name God will appear relatively abstract, routinized, and self-effacing, like geometry or metabolism. Some such persons may never be able, or willing, to arrive at a God who is more than the theoretical underpinning of reality, not particularly interesting to contemplate and no more worthy of love or worship than time, space, matter, causality (though some people of this style will find, perhaps to the bafflement and consternation of other-styled people, both contemplative and worshipful interest in just such a God). Others, the children of Mother Nature and Father Time, will spontaneously think of Truth as warm and personal, and make the transition to gratitude and reverence with the ease of habitual reflex.

Each of us inhabits a slightly different reality and must work within it even while working to share in the reality of others. I know people who admit—not braggingly, as an accomplishment, but apologetically, as if reporting a deficiency—that they have no detectable interest in sex. What trues such persons must obviously be different from the truing of those who experience life with a constant erotic edge. The imagining with which they receive and enact reality will, perforce, be different in its texture and temperature. (Those who are caught in the unfortunate Christian prejudice against the erotic may consider this an objectionable example; they may substitute another pair, such as one who is spiritually mindful only because utterly uninterested in the condition of her body and one who feels whole only when she takes care to tone hers with athletics, exercise, yoga, and other disciplines.) The God who is truing will differ accordingly, at least in the provisional illusory-imagined but temporarily truing forms.

We entertain reality with whatever equipment we have, and while we can expand the imagination's capacity and correct its incoherences and maladaptations by borrowing from the insights of accomplished friends, electron microscopes, reliable historians, perspicacious psychotherapists, and intellectually innocent children, we always start from who we are, and we differ in that.

But we need not go even that far afield in order to find variables in personal truth. My truth is not uniform, because I am not. What trues me at this moment is of temporary authority and differs from what trues or trued me in other phases of myself that vary with age, setting, health, mood, and time of day. My imagination encompasses them all, more or less, but their variability has an important bearing on my address to God. Some of them can feel quite at home in conventional Christianity, just as it is or was—but most of them cannot, and they must be cared for. They presently dominate my parliament and steer me toward the quest for a reconstruction of my Christianity, and myself, that may accord better with my faith and my sense of truth.

I believe (provisionally, of course) that it is possible to develop an unconventional Christianity—and please note that I did not say an *untraditional* Christianity: the tradition is much more capacious than what has been made of it thus far—that would be able to answer better to our faith and truth, and bring us closer to imagining, and being, the image and likeness of God. Whatever your provisional belief about such a notion, it is at least worth exploring as both a theological and a personal question, and such exploration is the business of the next chapter and of the rest of this book.

SOLVING [Part IV]

THE PROBLEM:

SHALL CHRISTIANITIES

TRUE?

11

THE

THEOLOGICAL

TASK

As I remarked at the beginning of Chapter 2, there are two ways of knowing Christianity: in the piety of engaged Christian belonging, and in the more detached perspective of critical theorizing that is theology.[141+] The two are often kept aseptically apart, as if neither had any claim on the other's attention. The average-person-in-the-pew is frequently as indifferent to serious theological speculation as to what goes on in higher mathematics, and theologians often seem unconcerned about how people pray or feel saved or draw comfort from beliefs. But one premise of this book is that being true as a Christian ultimately includes coming to terms with the theological implications of one's way of doing it, and the book is addressed mainly to people who recognize that this ought to matter. Another premise is that good theology must come to terms with the ways in which people actually go about being Christian, and should attempt to embrace various manners of engaged Christian belonging.

The rest of the book will try to address both these ways and their interconnections. This chapter is concerned primarily with the theological side of the issue.

THE PRINCIPLE OF APPROPRIATENESS

The task of the theologian is to think out what has to do with God, as appropriately as possible.

Appropriately is here a carefully chosen word. It is meant to be importantly different from *accurately,* which is usually about fidelity to what can be observed, as in measuring tangible things and reporting witnessed events. Accuracy can't meaningfully be talked about unless we have an independent view of the target that a thought is trying to hit, so as to be able to evaluate the aim. But we do not have access to an independent view of God by which we can decide whether a given theological statement conforms to the reality. We are not in a position to say whether "God is Love" is accurate, simply because God, like the intrinsic value of *The Odyssey* and the simultaneous position and momentum of electrons, is not one of the matters that we can be accurate about.

Appropriately is also meant to be importantly different from *adequately,* which is concerned with sufficiency, comprehensiveness. The discussion of hidden happenings, which we cannot observe directly because they belong to an obscure past or an unarrived future or a present that is subtle and elusive (particle physics, market projections, the structure of prehistoric societies), requires some guesswork, and there is no way of deciding definitively between two guesses that both take account of everything relevant. To be adequate, a guess must be consistent with what is more firmly known —with what we can be accurate about—but it also must take enough of it into consideration. To describe Michelangelo's *David* as a piece of rock is accurate, but not entirely adequate—unless it is an answer to a highly simplified question. When the question is more ambitious, as theological questions tend to be, it is much easier to say what is inadequate than what is adequate. Theological statements aspire to adequacy, but theological imaginations tend to be too small to venture as far as the next level of adequacy beyond their own. Whether "Jesus is the answer" is adequate will depend on what the question is, and we don't all pose the same question. Adequacy is what satisfies the need. Inadequacy is what doesn't. The need differs from person to person, within a person from stage to stage, within a stage from time to time. "God is truing" is obviously inadequate as a final answer to the practicing Christian, however adequate it may be as an initial theological point of departure. A good beginning is important, but even good beginnings are no longer sufficient for the guidance of those who have already journeyed to the middle.

And what may be adequate for those who are already well on the way is also not the last word. If their Godwardness is still in progress, they will require what will foster their further steps rather than leaving them at the point where they have already arrived. A fully adequate theology must therefore anticipate what it would be like to be in a state of complete faith and what may be said about God that will lure an incomplete faith in that direction. Hence the criterion of appropriateness.

Appropriateness is still more ambitious than adequacy, and encompasses it. What is inadequate is not appropriate, but what is adequate to all present needs will still not be entirely appropriate if we can anticipate, and especially if we wish to encourage, a longing for more. The Christian tradition has consistently encouraged a longing for more thorough belonging to God, and theology has consistently pursued a longing for more understanding. That is as it should be, and the two should get together more often to compare notes on what is appropriate in the circumstances.

Theology deals with reality in terms of how it has presented itself in our appropriation of it, and how it fits together, and how we imaginatively form the whole context of all that. A theology that does this well may certainly be called adequate. But there is a further imaginative option: going beyond adequacy to touch upon what is beyond the reality we know, both the reality of ourselves and that which is not ourselves. To be fully appropriate in the light of that option's invitation, theology should take responsibility not only for reality as we know it already but for the imagination's most ambitious reach: what reality may best be.

We are unfinished and partially revisable. The reality in which our imaginations live is therefore unfinished and partially revisable. God is truing, and the most ambitious way of addressing truth is in the longing for what is best: most accurate, most adequate, most appropriate. Theology is the quest for the appropriate, Truth at its best.

Theology is not poetry,[142] nor is it history,[143] though it has sometimes been reduced to both. Neither is it law, despite the fact that it has often been conducted as if it were, with the statutory Scripture applied through decisions of the higher courts (creeds, Ecumenical Councils, Church Fathers, founding Reformers, major catechisms) which set precedents from which speculations of lesser constitutional authority are not allowed to deviate. (It is not irrelevant that the Greek word *dogma* originally meant— and basically still means, in its denizenized English presence—"the proclamation of a formal decree."[144]) Theology is, of course, unique, having to deal with a God who is truing, and therefore with everything that is; but its claim of uniqueness should not be used as a way of escaping accountability or intelligibility. Theologians have often taken refuge in unaccountable authority and unintelligible mystery, as if that were a respectful way of honoring the grandeur of the project. It isn't. It is a sly evasion of responsibility. Good theology must be accountable, intelligible, and responsible. Nothing less is appropriate to the quest for Truth; nothing less is appropriate to the quest for God.

Theology is not poetry or history or law, but it does have an interesting and underrated resemblance to politics. Politics is the regulation of public life, and has as its goal the vague ideal of regulating it *appropriately*. The modern political preoccupation with economics and defense (and/or aggression) is not to be scorned: it does make a notable difference in life's stability to have public officials in the back rooms juggling the international value of the national currency and playing chess with missiles in order to keep the black king in check and the black queen inhibited, however much one may wish that such things were entirely beside the point. But this preoccupation should not be allowed to obscure the deeper ideal of organizing the public sphere so as to optimize social values—not to protect the power of the powerful, or even to take care of those who are disadvantaged by The System, but to make The System itself better, more appropriate.

What is the proper sense of appropriateness for politics? What is the better System to which we may next practically aspire? That is where the fun starts in politics, although the customary obsessive attention to a merely adequate sustaining of the System already in place usually keeps us from the fun. Do not expect any bright answers from the likes of me: the best I can do is to call attention to the questions. The answers have to be created by a difficult and intricate communal process through which those who constitute society reflect on the possibilities and choose a goal and a way to proceed. But that is a distant dream, which we are far from realizing. Societies that constantly fuss about the pulse of the aptly named Gross National Product while their educational systems deteriorate and their disadvantaged members are increasingly demoralized, and that invest vastly more talent, ingenuity, and resources in sophisticating their armaments than in rendering them unnecessary, cannot be supposed to have got beyond the most rudimentary stages of genuine political realization. Such political inadequacy ironically distracts us from the pursuit of appropriateness, and we miss the real political fun.

We live in a primitive political environment. The theological situation is similar. Both theology and politics are faced with the nearly overwhelming task of imagining how to bring about greater truth, the truth of faith on the one hand and the truth of the social order on the other. Both are crippled by old habits that are thought too reverend to be freely reexamined, both suffer from a failure of imagination about potential alternatives, and both are accordingly inclined to spend too much energy in promoting pieties that obscure the retardation and remediability of our collective situation.

So I want to make some proposals about deconventionalizing and reconstructing theology. (*You* can do the book on politics.)

THE CONTEMPORARY THEOLOGICAL SCENE

There are various ways of distinguishing different types of Christian theology. The traditional way is denominational, and indeed there is still considerable theological work being done that bears the distinctive stamp of Catholic, or Lutheran, or Calvinist traditions; familiar characteristics can still be seen in the writings of Jehovah's Witnesses and Greek Orthodox, Southern Baptists and Anglicans. Or we may concentrate on another set of differences that can distinguish Pentecostals from Evangelicals and both from Neo-Orthodox and "Liberals," all cutting across denominational lines: many churches contain exemplars of all four styles. For the purposes of this book, I would like to use another set of distinctions to divide most (though not all) current Christian theology roughly (*very* roughly) into four camps, according to what especially characterizes their governing sense of appropriateness.

One is dedicated to the protection of traditional belief on traditional grounds. The sense of appropriateness that obtains here is bent to the shape of the received tradition, as if that were accurate and adequate. I have already said enough about why I do not think the tradition either adequate or accurate, and why accordingly I do not think that this kind of address to theology will suffice, and I will not belabor the matter further.

A second camp, presently commanding considerable attention because of its creative novelty, its occasional intellectual accomplishment, and its association with obviously important causes (in both major senses of the word), is occupied by the various theologies of liberation. Here, the sense of appropriateness is especially addressed to the conditions of human life, respectful of its dignity and keen to emphasize the Gospel's call to its release from oppressive power. It is refreshingly free of the objectionable ideology, long protected by previous theologies, that justifies things as they are on the grounds that God has willed them so,[145!] and is ready to justify in its place practical steps to make things more true. Its particular genius, the insistence that theology ought not to assume the propriety of the present political and social and economic order and should make an influential difference in correcting its systemic injustices, is also, at least at present, its major limitation: for good practical reasons, it tends to stay preoccupied with such themes at the expense of others. As a result, its long-range theological usefulness presently suffers from a tendency of its exponents to be uncritically zealous in pressing their main point, and to be naive or careless about other theological concerns, especially the treatment of systematic implications and of the present state of biblical investigations (few writers in this camp rise beyond cheap proof-texting, the irony of which I will touch on in the next footnote). Its specialization thus leaves its writings often inadequate to the task of forming a comprehensive or critically unimpeachable theological imagining.[146+]

A third major group, considerably more in tune with (though also showing the limitations of) the traditional dominant Western mode of theologizing, is attentive to the radical critical problems that beset the theological enterprise at large, and may be characterized by its ingenuities in defense of a traditional theological imagination, its sense of appropriateness disciplined simultaneously by a protectiveness about the tradition and an honest appraisal of the present reality of thought and world that the tradition did not anticipate. Most of its practitioners have accepted some version of the method especially associated with Paul Tillich, correlating the canonized Christian answers with the experienced existential questions of the contemporary world.[147] Its obvious limitation is the assumption that the adequate and appropriate answers are already given in the principal Christian symbols (which seems to me doubtful and at least deserving of more questioning scrutiny than it is normally given), and the parallel assumption that theology should mainly limit its attentions to the validation of those symbols (which I think is disappointing and inadequately imaginative).[148!]

A fourth style is process theology, which has the great virtue of investing its sense of appropriateness in trying to think cleanly about God with a loyalty to truth rather than to the main tradition. This strikes me as in many ways the most promising style presently available, and it is no accident that its proponents are also among the most open to the contributions of other religious traditions. Its present state, however, is still limited by an attempt to make it all come out loyal to traditional Christian suppositions (a task in which it has a metaphysical head start since its ultimate ground has more to do with Love than with Being), which I do not think to be where its best promise lies. Ironically, its creativeness, which inevitably puts it occasionally at odds with the classical tradition, is at once what makes it suspect and marginalized by those in charge of churchly doctrine and what makes it most potentially valuable to the eventual Christianity of my great-grandchildren. Presently, it straddles two ultimately incompatible jobs, and I wish its resources were deployed more in correcting the traditional understandings than in sustaining them.[149+]

TAKING STOCK TOWARD RECONSTRUCTING THEOLOGY

While these four styles of approach, and senses of appropriateness, do not exhaust the contemporary theological scene,[150] they characterize its mainstream.

In doing so, I think that they demonstrate the insufficiency of the mainstream.

The first is basically obsolete. It makes an honorable attempt to remain faithful to what it takes to be the roots of Christianity, but does so by excluding the growth of stem, stalk, and flower, and cutting them off when they begin to sprout. A sort of dandelion theology.

The second is still parochial, focused honorably on the needs of particular contexts but at the expense of an adequate integration of those needs with the full stuff of the Christian tradition—so far, mainly plucking from it what will serve special purposes and detaching this from the disciplines that belong to its full appropriation, and thus producing a banana theology.

The third and fourth try to be honorable about sound and systematic thought, and do make an effort to get in firm and respectful and conservative touch with the roots; but they mistake for the roots something merely adjacent to them, and build upon that tuberous error a potato theology.

I am fond of bananas, but I respect the whole bunch more. I enjoy potatoes (I *am* Irish, after all), but throughout my meat-and-potatoes history, I have always gone for the meat first. (Besides, potatoes let us down in the last century when blights on the crop drove millions of Irish to the New World, where one of their descendants tried—portentously?—to grow in his miserable little World War II Victory Garden not potatoes but good rooty carrots, which came up stunted despite his vigilance against the dandelions.) There is room for all four styles (though I would leave much less room for the first than for the other three), but they do not exhaust the possibilities. There is room also for a meatier, or at least more carroty, variety that can be reconstructed, and that is what I am proposing that we should concentrate on doing. But before embarking on it, we must think carefully about the genius of each of these theological projects and see what we can learn from them.

I won't try to do that here, but I would like to glance at something that is to be learned from looking at the four of them together. The three latter, less traditional modes, which have arisen precisely because of the inadequacy of the first one, display an instructive common tendency. They recognize that a fundamental criterion of theological appropriateness is a responsiveness to the human condition as it is experienced apart from traditional theological presuppositions, and an ability to make a helpful difference in that condition—in short, theology's capacity to true what we know of human life.

In traditional theology, correlation with human experience was neither necessary nor desirable. God held all the cards, and we were not allowed to peek at what had been dealt. In Shaw's *Saint Joan,* Bishop Cauchon asks Joan of Arc whether she supposes herself to be in the state of grace. This is not a concerned pastoral inquiry, but a trap. Joan evades it disarmingly with a modest noncommittal reply, out of her own simple honesty. We know that she would be condemning herself if she said no, and that she may not say yes without such presumption as amounts to another kind of self-condemnation. Traditionally, we're not supposed to know the answer to that question, ever. We are supposed to carry out with dutiful obedience what has been divinely commanded of us, but whether or not God has graciously deemed it sufficient is a matter reserved to his (I use the masculine pronoun because this form of the tradition always did) inscrutable judgment. Feeling good about oneself before the face of God (we have been told) is not a symptom of the state of grace, but a potentially dangerous condition. Human feelings and imaginings, like human projects and experiences, simply do not count.

Catholic liturgical revision has adjusted the solemn *tantum dic verbo et sanabitur anima mea*[151] to the more integrative but equally solemn "Only say the word, and I [rather than "my soul"] shall be healed," but the thought remains equally dizzy minded. The notion that we are sick with something that God can cure by ceasing to withhold the right word is theologically outrageous, and would be grounds for a suit on the charge of defamation of character.

No one with much experience in this world would be foolish enough to take the opposite stand, maintaining that we are always reliable witnesses on the subject of our spiritual condition. That would not merely be presumptuous with respect to what is reserved to God, it would be utterly unrealistic about human self-knowledge. Realism about self-knowledge is discouraging. As individuals, we constantly misrepresent our condition to ourselves: neither the standard "I'm all right, Jack" nor the standard "Lord, be merciful to me, a sinner," between which we do our secret pendulum swing, is on the mark.[152+] Even when we have the relief of emerging from the job of personal self-scrutiny and tackle the easier (because less immediately threatening) task of social spirituality, we are still at a rudimentary stage.

When we come to terms with that, there are two ways to go. One is the cherished fantasy that there *has* to be a revelation and an authority that takes care of what we lack: hence the devotion to the Bible, the Vedas, the Torah, the Qur'an, Papal Infallibility, the Rabbinic Council, the Imams, the Guru. The instinct is good, in that it expresses a longing to be true and an admission that we aren't there and need help; but the forms are childish, like letting mother make your decisions or studying the horoscopes in the morning paper (or the compact high-tech version of such abandonment of responsibility that is available in the Ginza district of Tokyo, where you can put your hand on a xerographic copier and get a computerized readout of your destiny). The alternative is scary, but right. We are at a rudimentary stage, childish, and there is no adequate role model for corporate maturity, not in the Bible, not in the Talmud, not in the Qur'an, however helpful their insightful hints may be: our task is to invent maturity, appropriately.

Appropriateness, as the measure of proper theology, depends upon the invention of maturity through the responsible imagining of truth. In effect, it depends upon the invention of truth.

Invention is not fantasy. It means, etymologically and still in some aspects of usage, *discovery,* and it accommodates the realization that revelation is not in this book or that, nor in a specific set of exercises, nor in a particular person, but utterly *everywhere.* Truth is hidden in reality not as the treasure is concealed in the secret cave, but as the gift is decorously obscured by the elegant wrapping paper that declares it a gift. It takes some work to open it, but no trouble whatever to find it in the first place. It is everywhere, everything. Revelation is simply the completion of a transaction that has already been proffered by the other party, who simply waits for us to sign and receive. God is Truing, and must be found through faith's embrace of all reality in order to be adequately sought.

And more: God must be sought through imagination's enhancement of all reality in order to be appropriately found.

Let me elaborate on this latter point, since it is less obvious than the one preceding it, and seems to me *at least* as important.

I am not speaking of rose-colored glasses, or getting a slight buzz on, in order to take the drab out of a banal world. The enhancement I point to is not cosmetic or falsifying, but rather the condition of getting a truer relationship with the real, which requires rising beyond the soggy and unambitious perceiving to which we, despite the guidance of poets and painters, ordinarily sentence and confine our reality.

The romanticism about children's wonder is almost always accompanied by an escapist and sappy tone, and with good reason. Children start small. When you're that small, almost everything that isn't downright dreary seems—in the parlance of contemporary children—"awesome." That is not because a child sees with profoundly intuitive unjaded innocence. It's because they're little and dumb. Shakespeare spoofs the standard myth when his Miranda in *The Tempest* sees the first human beings she has ever laid eyes on apart from her father, Prospero, and her recently acquired fiancé, Ferdinand. "O brave new world!," she exclaims, "that hath such creatures in't!" Prospero replies, " 'Tis new to thee." Miranda doesn't answer, and perhaps doesn't hear him: she is busy gazing upon grief-stricken Alonso, doddery Gonzalo, villainous Sebastian, and his corrupted sidekick Antonio, all of whom are dazed and disoriented under a magic spell. Miranda is charming, as she stands bedazzled by the novelty. But she doesn't see much beyond it.

Shakespeare's work, in fact, provides a good metaphor for what I am trying to say. I don't mean that he wrote one down, or that the aforementioned scene is it, though it is analogous. I mean that the reading of Shakespeare's work is rather like the reading of the world: we start out engaging with it inadequately, perhaps impressed but missing a huge proportion of what is offered, and will stay there unless our faith is strong and persistent and unless we work, and get help, to reform our imaginations so that they demand, and thus can get, much more than we normally settle for. The much more is authentically there, built into the basic stuff and available for the taking. But it's not there merely for the *asking*. We have to get ambitious, and demanding, and ready to reach well beyond our accustomed habits in both scope and precision before our imaginations can be in a position to bring the whole thing and all its contributory parts to vigorous life in our reenactment of it.

To the extent that we succeed in rising to the occasion with the richer Shakespearean plays, which may take some years of practice, we can come to inhabit them intimately and make them work in us, whole and part. Inhabiting and enacting all of reality, ambitiously and invitingly, is a much more demanding project. To the extent that we succeed in outgrowing childish limitations, we are vulnerable to the adult limitations that succeed them. We stop only a couple of steps beyond, feeling mature and ready to retire because ten *is* much older than six, and how far can you go, anyway? If we don't discern the twelve-year-olds and see them beckoning, we're likely to think that there isn't any more.

But there is—twelve is attested, and there may be fifteen attainable beyond, still unexplored—and it's a lifetime's work to pursue it well, with steady faith and an imagination that keeps the pace, continuously discarding the obsolete realizations in order to make room for advances. And what we are doing as we keep at it is realizing with increasing adequacy our condition as the image and likeness of God—the God who offers reality in truth and love, holding it together in a rich and varied and ultimately coherent world, allowing all its moments and minutiae to belong so excellently and exactly that all their possible flavor is there for the tasting, all their dance and song is released for those who have eyes to see and ears to hear. The imagination's vocation is to imitate God, following in the divine footsteps to reenact what is already given but not yet realized.

Imagining in God, becoming trued to ourselves and to reality, is how we get closer to revelation. We don't get the voice directly from heaven, but we do get that echo of the voice which the rabbis called the *bath qol,* "daughter of the voice," as authentic an echo of the voice itself as we are authentic echoes of the ultimate speaker. And how authentically do we echo God? Let us not fuss for an answer. It is enough to continue to become truer and to do truth more amply. The rest will be added.

How we are trued should condition—perhaps determine—our theologizing and our religion, and they should condition (and perhaps determine) our further truing. There is not much more that we can know about it. We have never liked realizing this: we have taken sanctuary in some of the most improbable archaic shrines rather than face the task of inventing further truth. But the shrines crumble in time, leaving us naked to the task, the quest for our truth, the quest for God, in which there are no shortcuts or premixed quick-serve ways of doing it. This is an arduous and uncharted journey, tasty nourishment that is built by the slow and careful cooking of the market's unpredictable best ingredients. There is no revelation except everything. There is no authority except us, together, pursuing the authority of God, which is found only through our pursuing it together.

If imagination can take on the job of seeking God inventively, and realizing all of reality in God, our theology can move on to do its share in the invention of the appropriate. Inventing new standards of appropriateness, enlivening the imagination with greater ambition, enlarging the scope and the command of faith, is the only way that we six- and ten-year-olds can become twelve, and twelve-year-olds can advance in age and grace, in their attempts to realize God. And realizing God who is truth is probably the only adequately interesting, and surely the only appropriately ambitious, realization we can pursue, either theologically or personally. The next chapter will touch on some of the personal preliminaries.

12

INVENTING

GODWARDNESS

Theology can instruct personal religion. When we register our individual and communal efforts to find a truth that will stand in all weather, theology can refine and coordinate the results so that we can share them in common, in a thinking that is unified and unifying, free of individual quirks of imagining and special answers to peculiar individual needs. But personal religion can instruct theology as well, since it is there that theology gets its initial impetus and it is often there that valuable shared truths are pioneered as private imaginative experiments. Being both stable and on the move in personal faith and imagining is a complex act, and there are many things to keep in mind in order to do it well. I want to concentrate initially on two of them that are not routinely remembered.

THE ONE AND THE MANY

The first is self-caring. We have been so deluged by tickets to guilt and invitations to selfishness that we have virtually no cultural instinct for real, genuinely considerate, compassionate caring about and for ourselves, buffeted as we are between the extremes of self-contempt and self-indulgence (I can speak both languages fluently). Where self-caring is not instinctive, it must be invented, because it is indispensable for the journey. To love your neighbor as yourself is easy if you are habituated to treating yourself unlovingly. We must begin with the honoring of who we really are, which is often different from who we try to be in order to please parents, bosses, spouses, childhood ideals, personal ambitions, and social expectations. It is not easy for me to keep my imagination aware that I am, even in the midst of my frustratingly disordered and disordering ways, acceptable just as I am, notwithstanding that a great deal of improvement is devoutly to be wished. It is not easy, but it is necessary. If you have similar difficulties (i.e., with yourself, not with me), it probably means that you do not sufficiently and appropriately remember that your essential truth participates in God, and is validated and loved by God—no matter how you or your spouse may feel about it at present.

The second thing to remember is the other side of the first: you do not belong to yourself. You are to be respected just as you are, quite aside from what you pretend or aspire to be, but who you are is not yours. It is a product of your language, your culture, and all the rest of your equipment for dealing with life, along with the experience appropriated through it that bears its stamp, almost all of which you did not invent but only received. But beyond your belonging to others who came before and who sustain you now and who will come after, you belong to the Truth and truing: you belong to God.

Many people fancy that they are self-made, self-educated, and suppose that they owe nothing to anyone and are alone in the project of their lives. Nothing could be more starkly false. You are mainly the gift of others, owe everything to everyone, and are utterly unalone. Your personality carries in its parliament all that you have been part of. Much of it was unconsciously assimilated and is now consciously unrealized only because it has been so thoroughly realized in the habitual structure of your imagination. You are a gathering of possibilities that are, happily, beyond your creation, beyond your control, even beyond your imagination. Until we are released from the illusion of self-belonging, there will be a deep flaw in our sense of the reality in which we live and move, because everything will be falsified by the failure of adequate self-imagining. We are not what we have been trained and acculturated to suppose we are. That can sound like bad news insofar as it asks us to let go of what we have learned to hoard as if it insured survival. But it is good news insofar as it helps to disabuse us of the illusion that such hoarding works, and insofar as it invites us to see ourselves as sharers and belongers in something far grander and better than two small fists can clutch.

THE BETTERING OF OUR BELONGING

Belonging to God the truer, knowing that one is already there and needs only to continue to arrive more appropriately, is the most exciting of possible adventures. It is open to everyone. It is costly in the expenditure of belief, including belief about oneself, but that payment buys an enlargement of faith, and there is scarcely a better way to spend one's savings.

The adventure of arriving well begins with faith. It is indispensable not to confuse this faith with belief. We have beliefs, some of them effective in bringing truth about, some of them regretted but hard to shake (like the residual beliefs of inherited prejudice and bigotry), and some of them cherished but crumbling. But we do not have faith. Faith has us. When we let go of the common impeding illusions, we know this clearly, experiencing faith not as a technique or a faculty or a notion that we can employ, not even as an openness that originates in us, but as a truth that flows through us: God seeking God via you and me and you with me.

In case that strikes you as too romantic, let me back up a bit. The task is truing, which is, by my definition, God. We are to become more true, which is, again by definition, more Godward and Godlike. But if you feel uncomfortable with such talk about God, you are welcome to skip it for the time being, and concentrate simply on the project of becoming more true. Some of what that means in your peculiar case is already launched and en route, and only you can know its shape and texture; but to carry on further involves the management of illusions, both the muzzling of those that distort and impede and the taming of those that may be helpful. Knowing which is which, and how to deal with them, is close to the heart of the matter, and is a job of such complexity and scope as to require the help of all the accumulated resources there are. What I am about to offer is accordingly a ludicrously inadequate sketch of the terrain, but it will at least point out a direction in which I am proposing that it be traversed.

Truing does not require any explicit attention to God, but it will be constantly preoccupied with values. How they work in the political self-organization of your parliament is certainly impossible for me to say, and probably for you. But some rudimentary choices are predictable. You prefer to avoid receiving or giving unnecessary pain; you do not like being unhealthy; you don't approve of willful self-deception; you would rather see other people hopeful and happy than powerlessly miserable. Rudimentary, but not a bad start.

Of course, one does not always behave in good accord with even the most fundamental principles, and it is often not easy to discover why. But that takes us to another level of truing. How do you deal with yourself when you blow it? When you violate values that are so elemental as to be beyond suspicion? Your parliament will undoubtedly offer various options: pretend it didn't happen, justify it by special self-excusing explanation, blame your mother, cite yourself for (and with) contempt, melt with shame, select a punishment, drink until your perspective changes, find people to confess to or to impress, forgive yourself and undertake to undo the damage. The unwelcome voices cannot be silenced, but they can be outvoted; implementing your choice may be difficult, but is rarely impossible. You may have to resort to steamrollering over ineradicable sillinesses and bribing a few bad habits, but you can probably get the job done. It will be obvious which of the sample options I am minded to elect, but I know how to yield to all of them. Only one trues well, but to get at it I may have to lean on some of the others. If I do so, approximating truth through compromises with untruth, how should I regard myself? And here the process begins again, selecting diplomatically and realistically among the possibilities so as to steady my course as truly as I can while steering my way through self-indulgence, delusion, and rank stupidity.

Blessed are they who *do not* hunger and thirst after righteousness, for they shall have a better chance of keeping their sense of humor and avoiding fast-food imitations to quench the longing. It is enough to have a healthy appetite for righteousness. Truing is slow work, always very unfinished. One has to get used to that. It is cripplingly untrue to pretend otherwise. Small wonder that Christianities have been so obsessed with theological strategies for resolving the starkness of our untruth.

On the other hand, as the late Theodore Wedel observed, Total Depravity is an edifying doctrine but very hard to live up to. We are not helpless or hopeless, and however you may imagine your sin or your ignorance or your clumsiness, you will know that you are not without adequate resources if you are sufficiently self-caring and keep your belonging straight.

But we must take account of our limitations. Whether or not the name of God comes into the picture, we must all deal with the problem of situating ourselves and our attitudes within our unsuccesses in the project of truing, and must find some way of coming to terms with them. And we must come to terms with the marshaling of our resources as well. How much should we care about this? How urgent is it? What is the range and nature of the responsibilities we will and can take on in its behalf? How do we assess our performance, get our bearings from our blunders, manage our disabilities, compensate for our limitations, make our next choices?

We invent ourselves together, through the common pool of possibilities, and also apart, because each project is unique. The styles are different and should never be imposed. The way in which faith engages with, shapes, and realizes reality through you is bound to be interestingly different from the way it happens through me. But since this is the most important matter there is, it should be done with care; and proper care involves taking account of the experiments that have already taken place and those that are still in progress.

We can learn something of what has been attempted in the lives of others, and how it is done; we can see around us, in the remains of the past and in the living present, indications of what has worked, and not worked, in the invention of varieties of human persons. And in the midst of what we learn, we become more understanding not only of the range of possibilities, but also of what is congenial, what best fits our talents and disciplines our deficiencies, what will nourish our truth and bring us home.

It is easy to know that patience is better than impatience, that trustworthiness is worth acquiring and protecting, and that ruthlessness is not as satisfactory as ruth. But we must eventually get to the finer tunings in the construction and truing of awareness and moral selfhood. Which shall we then prefer to cultivate, the detached indifference of Stoic ataraxy or the self-engagement of fervent love? Aspiration or resignation? Serenity or joy? Activity or contemplation? Independence or mutuality? The exploration of the new or fidelity to the traditional? The imagination of a reality that is finally empty or one that is filled with God? I do not suppose that these alternatives are necessarily mutually exclusive, and I am sure that they can be entertained simultaneously within the needs of our parliaments and lived out in a stabilizing rhythm, but most of us cannot handle quite so much at once and must focus our styles in order to build well and truly.

It would not be much to the point for me to promote or even mention my own leanings, or how I try to pursue them, since much of what I do *not* attempt is just as viable as what I do and may suit you better (and may eventually suit me better too, if we stay in touch). The celibate may wish to acquire a sympathetic understanding of the happinesses of the wife and mother, and the political activist may be genuinely interested in knowing how the reclusive scholar spends and enjoys her days, but each must dance to a different tune. Still, I do want to make one exception: now is the time to make a further case for naming truth God, and for beginning to follow through with the implications of doing so.

YOU BET YOUR LIFE

To begin with, I acknowledge that this is optional. There are probably some people who simply cannot avoid finding that reality requires God (just as there appear to be some people who see auras and others who hear with absolute pitch) and I see no reason not to suppose that still others may belong to reality in a way that leaves them constitutionally unable or at least deeply disinclined to imagine finding room for God. I presume that you are in between—or at least accommodate within your parliament some important modes of yourself that are in between—or you would probably long since have lost patience with this book and would not have read this far. So here is an in-between question:

What are the grounds for making God a preferential option?

On the default side, there is no compelling reason not to do so. Some editions of God-imagining finally fall apart: not only the bearded old man in the sky (in whom nobody ever believed anyway, despite the popularity of the caricature) but also the God of selective intervention, the God who is miffed by a lack of admiring attention, the God who is male, the God who forbids the erotic. The imagination may play with these temporarily for special purposes, but I do not think that any of them can be permanently sustained. I can find nothing incoherent, however, in the God who is truing and loving. Maybe if I get smarter and clearer I might develop difficulties with that, but at present I find it thinkable, even experienceable, and I know that in this I have plenty of reassuring company among those wiser than I am.

On the positive side, it seems to work effectively. The evidence suggests not only that some people successfully imagine God's reality, but that the quality of their lives is decidedly enhanced by doing so. Survey your experience: if the most wonderful people you know include some who are obviously configured to God, you will know what I am talking about— and if not, you should enlarge your acquaintance. You will also recall people whose truth profited by being liberated from obsolete Gods, but that is *not* what I am talking about. If you know anyone who stopped revering a genuinely revereable imagining of God and was noticeably improved as a result, drop me a postcard.

You can recognize the smell of good life when you come across it, whatever your criteria for spotting the symptoms. Perhaps you are struck when you find freedom from irritability, a steady brightness of the eyes, the easy physical grace that expresses mindfulness, attitudes of capacious generosity, laconic simplicity of expression, remarkable poise in the midst of adversity, a gracious readiness to endure real hurts without resentment— whatever your checklist may be, you have your ways of identifying those, both the living and the long gone, who have realized some of the public secrets that are clearly worth knowing and embodying. The strong tendency of such lives to be associated with God is a matter of public record. If the state of your faith is skeptical or insecure about the desirability of Godwardness, check the evidence.

You may suspect that I am about to invoke Pascal's wager argument[153] for embracing a way of God. Not quite. The trouble with Pascal's wager— choosing between the risk of missing out on eternal beatitude if the traditional Christian claims are true but rejected, and the risk of living a harmless lie (whose austerities are compensated for at least by the acquisition of desirable virtues through its discipline) if they are false but accepted—is threefold.

One, it is too parochial: it assumes that to choose God is to choose Catholicism. Muslim claims, for example, are not obviously less worthy of attention, though for historical reasons they did not get much of Pascal's. The dilemma of decision is insoluably complicated if one takes into account the number of options presented as definitive revelation, or definitive interpretations of it. Several of these, not just one, threaten us with damnation if we choose to live elsewhere. To bet on God is thus, on Pascalian terms, to have then to make still another wager with much higher apparent stakes and no adequate guidelines to protect one from the risk of losing hugely. The Real Revelation does not stand up when asked to do so.

Two, the wager is made at the ticket counter, before the trip begins, making it a *Reise in der Blaue,* a journey into the unknown, a leap into a gnostic dark that is lit only by others' convictions that the beginner does not share and must try to affect with blind trust. Only under unusual conditions is such a venture reasonable. Whether or not those conditions obtained in the world of Pascal's imaginative understanding, they do not obtain in mine, nor I daresay (if you are still with me after nearly a dozen chapters) in yours.

Three, there is too much to lose. Though Pascal quite reasonably trivializes the finite potential loss by comparison with the infinite potential gain, he puts at risk the integrity of faith, substituting the beliefs and habits of others for whatever sense of truth one may have already, and asking one to talk and train oneself out of being who one is and into being what they are. If, as Pascal seems to assume about his imaginary interlocutor, one already wants to change and especially admires the model of the devout Port-Royal Jansenist Catholic and sees no viable alternative, something may be said for the proposal, even though it is still extremely expensive; but if that is not the case, then the cost is disproportionate and the wager as irresponsible as betting one's life's savings always is. This is too much to ask, if another way is possible.

Another way is possible. What frightened Pascal's interlocutor, despite his predisposition to be reasonable and to change his life reasonably even within the parochial boundaries of immediate possibility, was that Pascal pulled out his imagination's description of God and presented it as a bill. I think that this was a major mistake. It is an invoice only. The God who is truing requires nothing of you that you do not demand of yourself, and you have nothing to lose except what you voluntarily surrender. If you are respectful of the reality you have received and are progressively receiving, and elect to respond with gratitude, it is appropriate; but it is not required. To respond with love and reverence is not necessary, it is only better, truer. Worship is optional—but there are ways of doing it that assist truing.

Nothing of any importance is set at risk in deciding to belong to God. It is not a toll road but a freeway, more wage than wager: a form of gamboling. It is rooted in the fundamental issue of whether your faith prefers truth to falsity, and what comes beyond this, if invited, comes largely of its own accord. One does not have to wait for it to come in order to see that it is worth inviting. A reality pervaded by holiness is as clearly better than one without it as, in an Arctic winter, a room with a stove betters one that is without. To be able to understand that you are blessed, and can bless, must be worth the trouble it may take to get there.

It is not difficult to find people who are much more proficient in these matters than I am. I am aware that I am talking about baby steps, five-finger exercises. I wish merely to say that if you are embarked on some such way, then I think you have made the right choice—and if you are not, having abandoned it or left it unconsidered or preferred a way that is incompatible, then I think you should reconsider.

Actively seeking God, deliberately shaping the imagination to find and belong to God, seems to me to make everything better and more appropriate; but it is an option which we are free to decline. Either way, we will want, if we are realistic, to honor who we really are and what we best decide to do with it, and to keep close to the realization that we do not belong to ourselves. That is an option that no one should feel comfortable in refusing. I have reason to suspect that if anyone stays true to these principles, the rest, whatever the rest may be, will be added unto her in the right ripe times and the appropriate seasons, perhaps slowly, but truly. And I think it extremely probable that when the rest comes, it will finally be recognized, however surprisingly, as coming in the name of God, who lovingly gives life and truth.

13

TURNING THE CORNER:

RECONSTRUCTING CHRISTIAN BELONGING

Within my lifetime, we have begun to make important changes in the way we imagine our world and how we relate to it, and the changes are none too soon.

Nearly everyone now knows the basic sobering facts about the damage we have done to lakes and rivers and oceans, and that we devastate land more swiftly than we reclaim it. Resources that once seemed inexhaustible are being exhausted; the expanding population strains our capacity to produce and distribute food, the poor are increasingly with us, and weaponry of almost ungraspably destructive power is poised for quick release.

We are not especially good at changing our imaginations, especially on such a scale, and even less skilled at arranging the appropriate changes in our behavior. But we have begun to realize that "The results of the world's present profligacy are rapidly closing the options for future generations."[154] We have begun to know that we are in trouble, that we are all in it together, and that we must change our lives as well as our minds if we are to face the truth of what we have brought about and arrest and reverse its cost to my great-grandchildren and yours. The traditional imaginings are no longer sufficient to equip us for what must be done. The provinciality is no longer tolerable, the ambitions no longer possible, the confidences no longer justifiable.

The religious condition is parallel. Much of what our forebears relied on will not work any more in their way, and although the riches of the tradition are still great and underdeveloped, they must be budgeted and spent in a different fashion. A more modest standard of religious living is in order. Not poorer: only more modest, less lavish, and less dependent on overextended credit (especially credit that is left for our descendants to pay off). There are things we need to give up, but they are things that we can afford to do without, even if doing without requires some disciplined adjustment.

CERTAINLY NOT

One of the things to give up is certitude. Well-founded certitude can be extremely convenient: to be quite sure what time it is, that there is food in the cupboard, and where you put your shoes, allows you to invest your attention in matters other than getting the day started. Certitude is also satisfying in an aesthetic and psychological way, as everyone knows who has done mathematics without classroom anxieties. The reliable steadiness of the stars communicates a responding steadiness in observers, the beginning astronomer with her pleasure at the unfolding of the cosmic map, the Kantian philosopher who sees in them the image of the outer and the metaphor of the inner order of the universe, the navigator who finds in them a way to guide the ship confidently homeward.

But we have a tendency to crave certitude, and to try to wrest it from situations that do not offer it, and to become distressed when apparent certitudes crumble. Improvements in the telescope in the sixteenth century resulted in new discoveries among the stars, upsetting not only some traditional confident assumptions about them but also many people who had taken their metaphysical and spiritual bearings partly from the supposed eternal invariability of the physical heaven—which we now know to be full of change and surprise, its stars not only mutable but unfixed, bursting and collapsing and rushing away at dazzling speeds. A longing to penetrate the great uncertainty of the unrealized future and what is still undisclosed within persons supports the practice of astrology, where secrets are extorted from the stars by tortuous and unfair modes of questioning, until they tell us what we think we want to hear. The craving for certitude can easily become addictive, leading to substitutions of the closest equivalents when the real stuff is unavailable, and withdrawal symptoms when the substitutes fail to work.

The craving shows itself especially, as one would expect, in cases where much is at stake and certitude does not seem to be conveniently available. Ancient texts record requests to oracular gods to advise the petitioner whether his contemplated business deal will in fact pay off; modern advertisements in marginal magazines offer special devices for selecting winning lottery tickets and access to varieties of fortune-tellers who can tell you whether to marry her or move to another country or bet your savings on a particular horse. But it is in matters of more comprehensive religion that the most is at stake.

Religion deals with the largest questions: who we are, what powers govern the reality in which we are embedded, what our best possibilities may be, how to arrive at them without mishap. It is clear that offers of certitude about these things were importantly influential in the spread of early Christianity among the Gentiles (and also influential in its relative failure among the Jews, who had their own sources of certitude already). It is the knowledge received that is especially celebrated in the earliest surviving Christian eucharistic prayer,[155] and it is to assure Theophilus of the certainty of the things he had been taught that Luke ostensibly wrote his Gospel (Lk 1:3–4). *Gnosis,* privileged confident knowledge, is a theme in Paul's characterization of his gospel message, and formed the basis of the movements that most threatened to replace early Catholic Orthodox Christianity. When Paulinus evangelized the court of King Edwin, one of the trusted advisors opined to the king that life was like the brief flight of a sparrow through the mead hall, out of the darkness for a moment and then back into it—and if this new lore can tell us where we come from and where we are going, it is worthy of embrace. We want to know. We are not ready to settle for congenial myths that orient us helpfully as we play with them, while putting the craving to rest. We want certitude: an infallible Bible, an infallible Church, an infallible Pope, an infallible inspiration by an infallible Holy Spirit.

It is possible to imagine a reality in which these things are available. But it does not seem to me that the evidence invites us to suppose that the one we inhabit is like that, and each of the various of ways of pretending otherwise creates virtually insoluble problems for its own viability. In my judgment, a political meeting in which representatives of six (or three, or twenty) different programmatic views each try to persuade the audience that *there can be no possible doubt* that his position is *the* right and true one should eventually leave the audience not in a state of anxiety about how to discern the one that really *is* infallibly right, but with the conviction that they are all mistaken about the nature of political reality. Things don't work that way, and it has often, in accumulated history, proved enormously destructive to act as if they did. Political imagining is much better served by refusing, right from the start, to be hospitable to claims about leaders who make no mistakes or systems in which injustice cannot happen. The dream of certitude in politics is pleasant, if not scrutinized too closely; the practical reality of enacting certitude is usually some degree of nightmare. I do not think the record of experimentation with certitude in religion significantly better. One thinks of the comfort and confidence and gratitude it inspires, but one should also consider the smugness, tyranny, bigotry, division, persecution, pain, anxiety, confusion, despair.

And, after all, comfort and confidence and gratitude are not exclusively the by-products of certitude, even though certitude is often defended as if that were the case. They are available with a different flavoring through possible alternative imaginings that do not exact so high a price. Ambiguity is not frightening, even if it increases the workload of sifting and choosing as it multiplies the possibilities. It also increases the opportunities for life and grace to abound, and that is a much greater gift than certitude.

To live with the realized imagining that what we have is provisional and may be taken away does not mean that we are sentenced to pale skepticism. We make deep friendships, marry with conviction, and usher children hopefully and zealously into the world without having to overstrain the illusion that any of us is safe from being taken away at any time: we love the dying and the dead in full view of their mortality. No canon of truth forbids the love of beliefs that are dead or dying; we are asked only, when we find them so, not to pretend that it is otherwise. The surrender of certitude is not a form of euthanasia for Christianity—any variety of euthanasia would be genocide in thin disguise—but part of a cure for an ideological Alzheimer's disease: it is not too late for the arteries to be unhardened, the memories clarified, the recognition of present reality to be restored. I am not remotely suggesting that Christianity is obsolete, only that the bases of its life and wisdom have been misconstrued, and that the misconstrual need not be considered an indispensable part of the gift that has been bestowed through it.

The loss of certitude leaves several other options. I have touched on one important instance earlier: Christians are those who choose to define themselves in terms of fidelity to the classic tradition. I do not now question the integrity of this way of imagining. I question only its adequacy. While it takes thoughtful care of a holding operation that needs to be cared for, its scope is deliberately limited to that task. It does not leave sufficient room for the tradition to turn a corner *now,* into new places that require a revision of what it has been. And that protectiveness is the second major thing that I think should be given up.

CHRISTIAN ADAPTABILITY, THEN AND NOW

The Catholic Church has the longest continuous survival of any major empire in world history. That is impressive, and I pause a moment to let the fact sink into my mind as well as yours.

That record of survival owes something to adaptability, which included the baptizing of pagan festivals[156!] and texts[157] and shrines[158] and artistic images[159] and rites[160] and modes of prayer[161] and styles of living[162] and philosophical underpinnings for theology[163] and adjustments in official thought,[164!] and it is now assisted, however belatedly, by a capacity to accommodate cultural traditions beyond the Mediterranean/European ones in which it was formed for its first 1900 years.[165] It owes more to isolation and stubbornness and sheer power, which permitted it not only to survive but to dominate as well in the homeland in which it succeeded—sometimes quite self-consciously—the Roman Empire that disintegrated along with the Church's advance. After some centuries of attempted imperialistic expansion, some of the attempts (especially in Latin America) basically successful, the Church has begun to recover its tradition of adaptability.

But its adaptability is currently under close and stingy surveillance. Those in highest Vatican authority, like their counterparts in many other Christianities, inherit an official and dogged view that there have never been corners turned, no matter at how wide an angle, and they are apparently not about to reconsider whether or not parking is critically permitted on the premises of their logic or whether the handwritten Dead End sign on the roadway just ahead is in fact based on competent inspection of the probable consequences of driving on.

But if the leaders do not entertain the possibility of turning the corner, then the followers should remember that they are not really passengers after all, at the mercy of drivers' decisions. The metaphor offered by the tradition is wiser: they are, together, a flock, and the Lord alone is their shepherd. If the God who is truing inspires the flock to turn the corner, then the flock is free to do so, even if some of its crozier-carrying members want to discourage the turn. They are conscientious enough to catch up with the rest of the flock eventually.

I am not trying to persuade the hierarchy of my own church or of comparable Christianities, though I would be glad—and very surprised—if I could do so. That is not where the Church's vitality is located and, for good reason, not where its creativity originates. I am offering thoughts to those who have experienced the limitations and failures of church governance (Roman Catholic or otherwise) with respect and disappointment. Anger is usually inappropriate: we must recognize that the governors are pledged to the same loyalties but in a different pattern and have responsibilities that range beyond those of us who feel the need to shift our patterns of loyalty if we are to get on with our lives, and with the preparation for the lives of our great-grandchildren.

"Let the dead bury their dead" includes all of us, in both roles, but does not exhaust our calling. The burden of taking responsibility for keeping all the peoples of the world within the discipline of inherited tradition is, I am sure, far greater than I can presently imagine. It is for me to compassionate, not to belittle. I think it is a burden that should be lifted, and can be lifted only from below, by those whose faith realizes that Christianities, in their present forms, do not true, and who insist, for the sake of the tradition, on the struggle to find a form that does. We want to pass on the life we were given, without the varieties of death that came with it. We need to turn the corner, with or without the help of those officially in charge.

TURNING THE TRADITION

How do we turn? And in which direction?

We turn by turning. If what I have said so far speaks to your condition, turn, if you have not already done so, in the direction that you are actually facing. Or if not facing, your head loyally oriented to where it used to be, you turn to where the rest of you faces: true yourself. You probably know the direction. I will make more suggestions later on, but now I want to say something restraining.

Those of us who grew up in old-fashioned ways and lived through the lively changes of mind and lifestyle that took place roughly in the 1960s witnessed an interesting and instructive set of happenings. One was the failure of flower power: a wholesome attitude was not enough to derail the powerful engines already in motion. Another was the eventual accomplishment of the antiwar movement in the United States, but this ran parallel to the unsuccess of the war and was only a parochial success: twenty years later, we can count perhaps fifty wars, not all of them less outrageous, on the planet. We saw other happenings, many of them quite promising but turning out to be fads that faded rapidly (also instructive), but what especially sticks in my mind now, as a wet blanket sticks to those upon whom it is thrown, is the realization that so many of us were supportive, sometimes unequivocally, of the claims for freedom bannered by the young who had no idea what to do with it, despite the vision and efforts of some of the most generous of them who gave their minds and lives to the cause. The generation gap was sloganed about, and some of us wanted to close it. Many of us tried. We were mainly unsuccessful, not because we couldn't ingratiate ourselves with the would-be revolutionaries, but because we failed to take adequate account of just what the gap was.

Those whom I knew most closely in those days, including me, blundered totally in not realizing that it is one thing to be released from severe disciplines that you have lived through into adulthood and quite another thing to shortcut the process into undisciplined liberties that cannot possibly be understood in the same perspective that postdisciplined liberty brings. Those who are the beneficiaries of a routine freedom of the press may easily entertain smart suggestions about the reform of its practices through restriction, but tend to be slow to realize that proposals that mean to eliminate its openness in favor of correct thought are demonic.

There is no correct thought in the principles of politics or of theology or of religion. Correctness, which is a form of accuracy, simply does not operate at such levels of discourse, just as it does not obtain in the theoretical reaches of physics, astronomy, psychology, or any of the forms of policy from the Department of Foreign Affairs to the editorial offices of newspapers. These deal with adequacy and appropriateness, but are out of the reach of correctness. Even the realm of Emily Post and Amy Vanderbilt, who have long presided over the game of socializing, is really about what is customary and conventional rather than what is genuinely "correct," as Miss Manners' self-ironizing witty solemnity offers to remind us as she steadily passes the same tradition onward. The illusion of theoretical and behavioral correctness may yet, like smallpox, be cornered and eliminated. Or at least quarantined to the needs of pretentious social events, diplomatic decorum, and boistrous legislative meetings. It will remain useful to insist on correctness in bank balances, the measurement of javelin throws, and the calculation of rocket trajectories, but correctness has no real meaning in either behavior or theoretical thought, including religious doctrine, convenient as the notion may be to those who offer to preside over it. Conventions, customs, norms, yes; correctness, no. It is inappropriate.

A great deal of harm could come out of a turn in Christianity that neglected conventions, customs, usual norms. A great deal of harm could come out of sustaining the customary assumption that certain ways of thinking and acting are correct Christianity. The question is rather whether they are adequate and appropriate. If they are not, then we ought to turn from them to something that is. It is now time to take a major turn and therefore to explore the best wisdom available about where and how to turn, but it would be something of a disaster to stop remembering that the inherited Christian conventions, customs, and usual norms are part of our best wisdom, and are to be consulted constantly and reverently even by those who think their truth, and their capacity for truing, defective.

Some of the best wisdom in the Christian tradition escaped us in our Christian acculturation, and has been long neglected but is not yet obsolete. John Main, whom I have cited previously, was evidently reassured when he found that his technique of meditation, learned in the non-Christian Orient, had analogous roots in the Christian tradition. I want to make two simple points about this. One is that the tradition is far more rich than we habitually suppose: we live in a time of Christian spiritual impoverishment[166] and are out of touch with what has already been offered through and within the belonging that we have gratefully espoused. The other point is that Christians are not the only ones aspiring Godwardly. It would be stupid, in the present circumstances, to worry about whether other peoples' Godwardness had Christian precedent or not. The market is not cornered. The project is importantly unfinished. We are all in this together. Whoever has something to offer about how to pursue it should be welcomed, with or without a search for legalizing Christian precedents. We need a turn. We can use all the help we can get, from our own tradition first but then from the traditions of others, to which this book now turns.

14

CHRISTIANITIES AND OTHER RELIGIONS

The changes that have taken place within Christianity with respect to mutual understanding between different specific theological and worshipping traditions have been spectacular in my lifetime. Members of the various Christianities have in times past produced bales of polemical literature explaining how and why their positions were true and others' false. When I was a child, informed members of competing denominations rarely investigated these things together, and were accordingly able to preserve childish caricatures of one another to be used, as caricatures usually are, to justify at least satisfied complacency and often to fortify it with smugness and scorn.

The ecumenical movement in Christianity made deep changes in all that. At first, it seemed to offer a chance to allow the other fellow to see the light: the critical scorn was set aside in favor of earnest thoughtfulness, in the hope that those who professed distorted or immature forms of Christianity would, upon discovering the pristine and mature form, see the error of their ways and convert. What inevitably happened was that with closer investigation, the sense of the other's distortion and immaturity faded, but along with it faded the sense of the compelling perfection of one's own way. Knowing and being known brought self-knowledge. In Roman Catholic circles, the favorite kindly explanation of why people did not all become Roman Catholics used to be that they were victims of "invincible ignorance." Now, the explanation is more often that they are the beneficiaries of invincible knowledge.

Genuine interchange has a habit of bringing people to a more realistic and stable resting place that lies approximately midway between two false images—i.e., the caricature that each group forms of the other's way, in ignorance of the reality, and the grand portrait that each paints of its own way, ignoring the warts that familiarity overlooks. Once one arrives at that place, one experiences a permanent corrective change in posture.

This has now come to pass in the experience of Christians who have explored the reality of other religions' traditions with honesty and openness, looking not for their points of vulnerability and possible inferiority but for their integrity and capacity to true those within their embrace. What these Christians are doing is not, alas, very traditional.

THE BACKGROUND: IMPERIALIST CHRISTIANITY

Christianity was characterized from the beginning by an intolerant triumphalism that was founded on exclusive claims to definitive truth and treated the faith and beliefs of others as falsities from which they should be converted. If Justin Martyr could be generous enough at the beginning of the second Christian century to embrace Heraclitus and Socrates among those entitled to be called Christians,[167] he nevertheless followed Paul in characterizing other religions as demonic distortions of the true Christian way.[168] The so-called First Epistle of Clement, evidently written from the church at Rome ca. 90, has moments in which the author is fairly liberal in his attitudes toward non-Christian religions,[169] but the unusual character of this is highlighted by the fairly unremitting hostility of the Fathers of the Church to all forms of non-Christian religious life, Judaism not least.

The plea for religious toleration lodged on behalf of the faith of his fathers by Quintus Aurelius Symmachus as post-Constantinian Imperial Rome began to close down the temples and privileges of its pagan heritage[170] was simply rebuffed, and the program for restoring traditional Roman religion attempted by the Emperor Julian was vanquished along with him. Christian thought thereafter sustained an animosity toward other religions that was rarely qualified, let alone suspended. The first important suspension that is extantly recorded (probably prepared by a few generations of quiet advice at home, which is the deep good work that doesn't surface in the history books) is that Cardinal Nicolas of Cusa wrote, ca.

1453, "there is but one religion in the variety of religious rites."[171] But it seems that hardly anyone paid much attention (though we must always allow the possibility that streams flow underground, and erupt with apparent spontaneity as springs). After Nicolas, despite occasional exceptions such as Erasmus[172] and Zwingli,[173] the case remained basically the same for the next few centuries. Pioneers of a different attitude, who had learned firsthand in the midst of other religious cultures (e.g., Matteo Ricci in China, Roberto de Nobili in India), were subjected to discipline by the European religious authorities; that non-Christian religions are true, and that non-Christians are saved in their own religions, are propositions explicitly condemned by the Synod of Diamper at the end of the sixteenth century.[174]

This starkly negative attitude, which persisted and prevailed into very recent times among Protestant and Catholic Christians alike,[175] even found its way into one of the most solemn moments of the Roman Catholic liturgy. On Good Friday, the liturgy prescribes a series of special prayers for various sectors of the Church and of the secular world, and in the course of doing so it turns attention to the Jews in one passage and to other non-Christians in another. The texts of these prayers as they were prayed until the early 1960s, translated fairly literally from the original Latin, are as follows:

> Let us pray for the perfidious Jews, that our God and Lord may remove the veil from their hearts that they also may acknowledge our Lord Jesus Christ . . . Almighty and everlasting God, you drive not even the perfidious Jews away from your mercy; hear our prayers, which we offer for the blindness of that people, that, acknowledging the light of your truth, which is Christ, they may be rescued from their darkness.

> Let us pray also for the pagans, that almighty God may remove iniquity from their hearts, that, putting aside their idols, they may be converted to the true and living God . . . Deliver them from the worship of idols, and join them to your holy Church.[176]

Was it that these prayers suddenly became intolerably embarrassing when the veil of Latin was lifted from them? At any rate, with the vernacularization of the liturgy, first "perfidious" was dropped, and then a wholesale recasting of both prayers brought about a most dramatic change. Last Good Friday, this is what was prayed instead:

Let us pray for the Jewish people, the first to hear the word of God, that they may continue to grow in the love of his name and in faithfulness to his covenant . . . Almighty and eternal God, long ago you gave your promise to Abraham and his posterity. Listen to your Church as we pray that the people you first made your own may arrive at the fullness of redemption.

Let us pray for those who do not believe in Christ, that the light of the Holy Spirit may show them the way to salvation . . . Almighty and eternal God, enable those who do not acknowledge Christ to find the truth as they walk before you in sincerity of heart. Help us to grow in love for one another, to grasp more fully the mystery of your Godhead, and to become more perfect witnesses of your love in the sight of men.[177]

Note that there is no reference to even the desirability of conversion, let alone to perfidy or blindness or iniquity. The new versions of the prayers allow one to suppose that "the fullness of redemption" and "the way to salvation" are specifically Christian, but they do not say so: they express hope for the fidelity of the Jews and the sincerity of other non-Christians, and apparently trust that this will be sufficient. Their governing spirit is in harmony with this succinct pronouncement by a Tamil Jesuit who has been deeply involved in such questions: "The older subtle distinctions that non-Christians are saved in their own religions becomes irrelevant. They are saved in and through their religions."[178]

The shift is little short of astonishing: the most outrageous moment of bigotry in the entire liturgy has been canceled in favor of what is now the most generous-minded of its glances at non-Christians and the most thorough of its fulfillments of the new look in, and at, interreligious dialogue codified by the Second Vatican Council in its document *Gaudium et spes,* which announced that

We turn our thoughts to all who acknowledge God, and who preserve in their traditions precious elements of religion and humanity. We want open dialogue to compel us all to receive the inspirations of the Spirit faithfully and to measure up to them energetically. For our part, the desire for such dialogue, which can lead to truth through love alone, excludes no one . . . (92)

Even in the official prayer of Catholicism, hoary and long-persistent tradition does not always win the day and lose the faith. Even in the conciliar gathering of bishops, an occasion which has tended historically to bring out their most tradition-oriented conservatism, they don't always decide to do it the way we've always done it. Even Pope John Paul II, in the midst of the solemn formality of his encylical *Redemptor hominis,* has advocated "coming closer together with the representatives of the non-Christian religions, an activity expressed through dialogue, contacts, prayer in common, investigation of the treasures of human spirituality, in which, as we know well, the members of these religions are not lacking." The leaders are not always reluctant to turn important and untraditional corners or to intervene appropriately in what is to be handed on.

Vatican II did not of course create this change in Catholic attitudes. It reflected and endorsed changes that had already taken place and had been brought to the council by the Bishops and their *periti* advisors. Once the door had been officially opened, a new breeze blew across the lands. I offer one further striking example, from India. After a series of three All-India Liturgical Meetings, the CBCI Commission for Liturgy approved a new rite in which readings from the Indian scriptures regularly precede readings from the Bible, and in which—not just on Good Friday, but daily—the following prayer is offered:

God of the nations,
You are the desire and hope
of all who search for you with a sincere heart.
You are the Power almighty
adored as Presence hidden in nature.
You reveal yourself
to the seekers in their quest for knowledge,
to the devout who seek you through sacrifice and detachment,
to every man approaching you by the path of love.
You enlighten the hearts that long for release
by conquest of desire and universal kindness.
You show mercy to those who submit
to your inscrutable decrees.

Seven appended footnotes, referring to the Vatican II Declaration on Non-Christian Religions, the Rig Veda, Isaiah, the Chandogya Upanishad, and the Bhagavad Gita, make it clear that these are deliberate references to animistic religions, the Three Paths of the Hindu scriptures, Buddhism, Jainism, and Islam.[179] It took fourteen centuries to arrive at the publication of the views of Cardinal Nicolas of Cusa, and another five for them to prevail; but the time has evidently come at last among many Christianities. (Final approval of the Indian anaphora, however, is at this writing still being stalled in Rome: the leaders are not always hospitable to even the most obvious improvements in the tradition.)[180]+

We have yet to digest theologically what all this means.[181] But if there is no turning back from this achievement (and it is difficult to imagine that it either would or could be successfully repudiated), then it seems to me clear that we have to deal with a new model of interreligious relationships.

INTERRELIGIOUS DIALOGUE

Over the last few decades, writings that bear on interreligious discussion have tended to fall into three main groupings with respect to how a given religious perspective relates to others. (1) The triumphalist: "my religion is true and theirs are false." This is the traditional and prevailing Christian position, until recently. (It is also traditional in Judaism and in Islam, though Jewish commentators have tended more toward "my religion is true, and I do not much care about the status of theirs.") (2) The hegemonist: "my religion is true and theirs share in its truth." This is the position expounded most notably by Karl Rahner in his notion of the anonymous Christian, according to which the uniqueness and superiority of Christianity are preserved but the salvific grace released by Christ is understood to be available to all earnest persons of whatever religion, whether they are ignorant of Christianity or have cordially declined its invitation. (Some Muslim writers are generally of this mind, seeing in Judaism and Christianity a rudimentarily adequate version of what the Qur'an offers in perfected form.) (3) The egalitarian/pluralist: "my religion is true, and theirs may well be true too." After Nicolas of Cusa, this position was taken by some thinkers of the European Enlightenment, and more recently by representatives of "liberal" Christianity, but it has been relatively rare among Christians. (This is a traditional Hindu view, and is found regularly among Buddhists as well, though both are sometimes compromised by sectarianisms that are more skeptical about, and sometimes extremely intolerant of, the possible rightness of other religious positions.)

What is happening now within Christianities, and to some extent within other religious traditions, is a drift toward the third position. It is true that there is also a strong "fundamentalist" movement in the Christian world and in other religions that leads back toward the first position, but it appears that the more informed and experienced a religious thinker is in these matters, the less likely it is that she will move toward position one and the more likely she will tend toward position three. The reasons for this include the erosion of confident belief that arises from attending respectfully to critical thought, but derive much more from the effects of a genuine understanding of another religion and of the personal presence of those who profess it truly.

As in the case of Christian ecumenism, interreligious discussion used to begin with the Christian participants feeling that the non-Christians were in a childish state of religion, benighted and superstitious, and they accordingly took the stance of the old-style proselytizing missionary, there to convert the others from the backwardness of their ways. Later, the Christians came to see that the piety and thoughtfulness of other religions was authentic and fairly mature, not obviously inferior to their Christian equivalents even if somewhat more distant from the definitively revealed truth, and the stance shifted to something more akin to that of the medical missionary, there to give example of the goodness of the way to which he belongs. This is where much of Christianities' mission-oriented dialogue has arrived. But there is a new stage that has come about where mission is not in question, such as in exchanges in an academic setting or in community-relations meetings in the multireligious communities that have suddenly become widespread in the West: the Christian participants frequently succeed in shedding virtually all patronizing attitudes, accepting that each of the participating religious views is in fact fully mature, requiring not to be changed or improved but only understood, in a spirit akin to that of the ambassador, representing her nation with faithful dignity, but in a posture of sincere respect.

A new humility is making its way into Christian understanding, in the face of the chastening negative experience of lost confidence in the underpinnings of traditional apologetics and the enlightening positive experience of the evident richness and maturity of other religious paths. This may seem at first like the bad news of an embarrassing demotion at the banquet table, "Friend, go down lower." But I think that closer scrutiny turns it to the good news of an invitation to come up higher. We are all in this together. Christianity can make good use of the resources disclosed in the other religious traditions, which are not less wise or less authoritative or less revealed. Only false pride can disguise the historical truth that the Christian tradition has always borrowed from its neighbors to improve its standard of living. Now is a good time to fill the cupboards with what will be gladly given.

IMMATURITY AND MATURING

But there is one important change of attitude still to be accomplished. For although the progressive recognition of the maturity of other religions is a decided improvement over earlier attitudes and judgments, the most recent stage still misses the mark. I suggest that the more appropriate disposition would be to acknowledge *not that all the major religions are fully mature, but that none of them is.* The religions of the world, Christianity included, are at best at a stage of adolescence, and this new situation is a clear invitation to advance toward maturity, and a novel opportunity to do so.

There is no role model for this kind of maturity. Genuine religious maturity has to be imaginatively invented, and self-criticism's contribution can now be supplemented by a cooperative effort of interreligious dialogue, in which the eyes of the beholders can assist one another in the detection and removal of the various motes that trouble the vision and beams that, though unfelt, disfigure. Although used to thinking of themselves as finished and complete, Christianities should revise their self-images in order to take advantage of a ripe and almost utterly unprecedented[182!] chance to find a still better way of honoring the faith to which they are pledged by using the opportunity to reach more adequately toward the God in whose name it has been, however clumsily, preserved.

But this is not an invitation to a new mindless enthusiasm. However interesting, the new situation must be absorbed with restraint. The swiping of helpful attitudes, styles, techniques, images, and goals from other religions must be done cautiously. We are ten- and twelve-year-olds swapping on the playground, and it is important to remember that we come from, and return to, different homes. Her joke may not sound funny at his house; his trick with a matchbook could get her in serious trouble; my stunt with my sister took a lot of practice and would be dangerous if you tried it with yours. The assumption of Nicolas of Cusa that all religions are ultimately one (nicely supplemented by a remark attributed to Disraeli, that "sensible men are all of the same religion"; and what that is, "sensible men never tell"), turns out to be false.

Different religions get different provisional answers not because they grow in different climates, but because they ask different basic questions.[183] Islam is especially concerned about how God wants us to perform our lives, while Hinduism is more preoccupied with getting in touch with God, with an ambition that few good Muslims (apart from Sufis) would countenance. Tendai Buddhism longs for the dispelling of all illusion, including its own fundamental principles; Pure Land Buddhism aspires to a salvific grace that carries us where we otherwise cannot go. The meeting-point that has long been presumed to lie in mysticism is now under deep question: mystics of all styles seem to be unable to get out of the place from which they start, and at the farthest reaches of their experience see the images of their own religions as in a mirror, however darkly.[184+] Jewish mystics do not have visions of the Virgin Mary at the summit of their climbing; their Christian counterparts do not report disclosures of Krishna or Kali, even in their most exalted aspects. We never leave home, and must adjust to this limitation. Truth is bound up with where we started to love it. There is no reason for regretting that, unless one is impatient or unrealistically ambitious. Realistic ambition will suffice for now: with patience, it may become bolder at a later stage of tradition.

All the same, the playground offers possibilities of good swapping. Without leaving home, Christians can—and must—pick up some alternatives to supplement their provinciality and correct their distortions. We still have a rather primitive notion of divine power, protective of a solemn God who holds all the good cards, close to his chest, and whose favor, like a despotic king's, may perhaps be softened by flattery. We are still too protective of Bible and beliefs. We retain a distorting emphasis on sin, inadequately counterbalanced by our imaginings of grace. We have allowed our tradition of spirituality to be arrested, and even to decay. It would be immeasurably good for us to spread out a little, picking up accomplishments and hints from other religious experience—cautiously, but ambitiously after the caution. God as love is happily part of our tradition, but we are too bullied by our imaginings of God as power and will and judgment to be able easily to entertain other imaginings of God that could be useful and truing.

The early stages of the inspection of other people's resources are disappointing. Representatives of other religions are, on the whole, as protective and provincial as their Christian counterparts (though in interestingly and instructively different ways), narrowly loyal, constrained in their imagining, and often less candid than Westerners can afford to be. Orthodox Jewish and Muslim thought about revelation is on the whole even more conservative than the Christian equivalent and much less discussed; Hindu thought and practice are edifying and illuminating but still cluttered with unsifted myths and bizarre formulas and inordinate dispositions to revere and obey religious teachers unquestioningly; Buddhists are skilled about ritual and solitary meditation at the expense of community and social concern. But they all have interesting goodies up their sleeves, even if, like us, they are often unaware of what the sleeve contains; and especially when they are old and have stopped caring so much about being loyal to their religion, preferring loyalty to the truth of God, they have fine things to offer.

What we have to offer in return is for them to decide, but is also for us to discover. I guess that G. K. Chesterton's celebrated remark, that Christianity hasn't failed but simply hasn't been tried, is more true than he intended. I think he meant it in terms of behavior and attitude, and there he is surely right. But it may also be said of the larger reaches of imagination. Christians have never really managed to believe in their own central doctrine of the Incarnation, which fascinates reflective members of other religions; we have invented a thousand strategies for avoiding the imagining that Jesus could burp and get confused and have erections in his dreaming at night,[185] and some Christianities have then flipped to the other extreme of evacuating his divinity because our paltry imaginations can't combine the inherited God of Abraham, Isaac, Jacob, and the Philosophers with the crude stuff of human flesh. Some non-Christians seem to have less trouble with this,[186] and can be of good help in getting Christian self-understanding to the places it aspires to occupy. Christians have rarely managed to believe that they are *really* forgiven, even though this is the pivotal point of traditional belief. We cultivate guilt as if it were a commodity that can be presented for the mysterious infinite pleasure of a God who prefers us to be dependently miserable. We don't even do our own stuff well. There are other religious traditions, less inhibited in places where we lack courage (though beset with their own inhibitions), that can help us become more true.

Again, what we offer in return is for us to discover and for them to decide. In the interim, it is appropriate for Christians to be humble—*not* humiliated, but humble, a distinction that we are not good at—about our condition. We are amateurs, professing a religion that is still amateurish. There is no religion out there that is obviously better, but there is potential help. We are all in this together, and we all can use all the help we can get.

Well-digested precedents are to be preferred, but sheer invention may have to step in from time to time; adolescence isn't easy to weather on the basis of what is already available, especially if there is no one around who can say what it is to be mature. I certainly cannot say what maturity would be, but I think I know something about what will be maturing: the realizing of ourselves in the realizing of God. If that sounds at all foolish, please read on. If it sounds right, please read on anyway.

15

HOMEWARD
AND
GODWARD

However you may name those members of your parliament of self who have brought you to read this far, I hope that you will be adequately attentive to their well-being, which may require some unconventional versatility on your part, and that you will not underestimate their potential contributions to the well-being of my—our—great-grandchildren. I speak to them now, as well as to you (and to myself, for the admissions and reminders and suggestions that follow require rehearsal and practice), in the hope that we can collude in doing what must be done, however dimly we may understand its outlines at present. For, as Socrates says shortly before his death, "the prize is beautiful and the hope great."[187] Socrates was speaking of the pursuit of goodness and wisdom; so am I. Their name is God.

ON FOOLISHNESS AND HOME

Imagining and pursuing God is admittedly foolish, even if it eventuates in wisdom, but so is everything else we do. We are fools who live foolishly in a life that offers no rescue from folly. The task is to be *appropriately* foolish: not successfully, or triumphantly, or admirably, or efficiently, or even effectively, only appropriately. "Appropriately" may or may not encompass the adverbs I have just pushed aside; but it is important not to care about them. Being appropriate, which is the same as being ambitiously true, is the creative use of our foolishness to steer ourselves, or to let ourselves be steered, homeward.

Home is almost the deepest word of all. We have all left what it once meant, when we first learned the word. We all ache to find its equivalent in larger life, knowing instinctively that the glorious fidelity of Odysseus to Penelope and Penelope to Odysseus is ultimately a metaphor for a homing that casts a far wider net and captures nothing but the realization that the home we are bound for will be recognizable as we arrive. I think that it may be found at the center and at the outer limit of imagination and that it may be called, conventionally, God.

God is home: the two deepest words we can speak mean the same thing. God is truth, and God is love: these flow through us and can be recognized when we are at our best, but the name of their source and resting place is *home*. It is foolish to think this way. But it is even more foolish not to. We must accept our foolishness and be appropriate.

If you sift through your best experiences of home, and ask yourself if all of you is willing to settle for what has already been given, I suppose that you will find that the necessary answer is "no," or a more modest "not quite." If your faith is as large as your imagination can handle, then you will honor your friends and lovers and parents and favorite memories and dearest places as hints of home, but you will have a dream beyond them, a grander glory of homeness for which all the best is metaphor. It is a foolish dream. I think it the best dream there is, and that it would be foolish not to pursue it. All dreams are foolish, because we who dream them are fools, but it is in conjunction with our dreams that we have our closest brush with wisdom.

Fools make spectacular money and fools have universal fame and fools are malnourished and fools die young of preventable diseases. You may be none of the above, but you live in a unique foolishness of your own, never before experimented with in quite your way. You get to choose how to use and define the foolishness of your life through your own sense of appropriateness.

You will use it doing your job well, cleaning the toilet, telling stories to the children, figuring out your taxes, eating lunch. Each of these has its appropriate time and manner. But in all of this, you should always be heading home. That is what we were meant to mean, or at least what we are allowed to mean best, which is the same thing: being appropriate. What our lives mean is their enacted sense of appropriateness. The meaning of life is not bestowed *upon* us but *by* us, and if we do not make our lives mean something, they don't. It is possible, and I think highly desirable, to make life mean, among and beyond other things and flavoring them all, homewardness, Godwardness.

REALIZING GOD AS HOME

Life means Godwardness as homewardness only to one who has *realized* that this is what it means.

I italicize the word not just to draw attention to it but to give it the full range of its meaning. I use it not in the ordinary casual fashion, where it is a sort of recognition, as when I realize that it's already after six o'clock. That form of realization is only a first dimension of a three-dimensional full sense.

The second dimension of realizing is more creative and more transforming, as when I began to realize the power and splendor of the Hebrew Scriptures: I had known them before as obsolete and partially benighted anticipations of the Christian gospel, but now my imagination embraced them differently by starting to enact and make real for me a quality of reverend profundity in them that inspired a new quality of reverent and respectful response. I realized (sense 1) that these were the same texts I had read before—but now I realized (sense 2) them to be significantly and pervasively different from what they had been. I made that change real, accorded them a depth that they had offered before but I had not made real in my act of imaginative reception.

The third dimension occurs in living out the implications of the second: making it real beyond the boundaries of my imagination by enacting it in the world that is not myself, as when we say that my hopes were realized— not that I recognized that I had them, or that I became aware of their importance to me and their implications for my behavior, but that what I had hoped for came to pass, entered the world of shared reality.

Realizing that life has meaning as Godwardness and homewardness starts as accepting that it is appropriate to think of it this way (sense 1), transforming the imagining of oneself and one's world so as to make that recognition the main principle for determining what is appropriate in the course of living life out (sense 2), and enacting life in all its aspects under the governance of that sense of appropriateness (sense 3). Three-dimensional realization sets us on course, Godward and homeward.

SOME SUGGESTIONS FOR THE JOURNEY

The practical suggestions that follow are to be understood as foolish. I make no claim to wisdom, and those who know me best will confirm that I make no claim and shouldn't. This is simply the best I have to offer at present, offered in case some of it will be useful or will stimulate you to useful responses. The order of presentation is not systematic, but neither is it entirely random: it starts with items that seem pertinent even to those who are still unsure whether Godward is where they want to go (1–5), and tries to arrive at a place where it would appear that this is indeed if not the logical conclusion of being devoted to the true and the real at least not a terribly dramatic further step (6). Then a few words about what may come after taking that step (7–9), why you should be patient with the difficulties inherent in my, or your, or anyone's talking about it (10), and some final remarks on how the voyage may be best stabilized and enhanced (11–13). And 14 will probably not be a surprise to anyone who has read attentively this far.

1. It is helpful to relax into foolishness. We are acculturated to avoid foolishness, but in fact we can't; to pretend that we are not foolish is merely a compounding of the folly, and to admit it is no virtue but at least offers a clean start. To know oneself as foolish is liberating, freeing the parliament of self to open discussion and a better chance of truth. Earnestness and seriousness are not excluded by the admission of folly: on the contrary, they are made possible. They are the focused steadying of appropriately selected foolishnesses. When they are attempted otherwise, they are only brittle and stuffy parodies of the real thing. Foolishness is to be embraced and cherished, because it is part of our deepest truth and a needful dimension of self-caring, especially as it assists our not taking ourselves too seriously and thus frees us to take ourselves seriously enough.

2. It is indispensable to love oneself. If your self-love is qualified or compromised or defective, start over: you obviously don't know who you are, and your faith will suffer from that ignorance. You are a unique experiment in a totally precedented but unfinished world. Admire the precedents first, since they are easily admirable; the uniqueness of your project may be put on hold while you consider the persons who especially inspire and empower it. After that, admiring your own dignity may be relatively easy, even if you're shy: appreciate yourself as a new contribution to a great tradition. If it still seems difficult, a useful practical trick is to use

your parliamentary versatility to regard yourself as if you were someone else, which is basically true. Since you are better habituated to respecting other people than yourself, use your skill that way. Slightly sneaky, but often effective. Sneakiness is often required, given who we are, to creep up into increased truth.

3. Because stability is so attractive, we are likely to create it in a dysfunctional way, locating it in some satisfying constellation of imaginings, places, persons, patterns. It is sometimes difficult to remember that all specific imaginings are provisional, and all general states of imagining are stages in the process, which is necessarily inexhaustible. The true stability is in fidelity to the process, and the process is a *tradition of personhood,* which will of its own accord, as we hand ourselves on to ourselves stage by stage, identify the persons and places and thoughts and loyalties that appropriately belong to our permanence and give us our best definition, our clearest truth. But these are more often given by the process than taken from it. We do not belong to ourselves; what and whom we particularly belong to will be chosen sometimes because of who we aspire to be, but more often because who we are has become further disclosed.

4. Keep the faith—or rather, abide in faith's keeping. That is, locate yourself especially in the flow of truth, rather than in its by-products, including yourself. We must stay as ironic about the beliefs we use as is necessary to keep caring for truth. To do so steals nothing from whom or what you love. At most, it merely repositions them in the stream of truing time rather than artificially and inaccurately pretending that they should or can be arrested. And at best, it gives you grounds for patient hope even in the midst of loss and pain and anxiety and the eviscerating bleakness of depression, where it is clear that you can no longer have faith. Let it be clear that you never did: it was not yours even when it brooded most fruitfully over your waters. Let it brood even over your wastes and voids until it sends your dry roots rain. Make your imagination remember who and where you are, and that what you sometimes become, however ill or well, is only a passage in your becoming more true. It is also a passage for those with whom you are interconnected, and to whom your life inevitably belongs, like it or not. We are affected by you; you make a difference to us in ways neither you nor we can imagine. Stay true to and in faith even when it is barely possible: especially then.

5. It is good to allow the imagination to be bold and grand in its work of realizing our world and situating us within it. We are instinctively greedy, and the instinct is given for the health of bold and grand imagining.

We distort its purposes, shifting our wholesome greed to acquisitiveness and the search for power and status, which must be at the expense of other people. Misplaced greed empoverishes everyone. But proper greed, appropriately set free in imagining, is generous and enriches us and those around us. It reaches to the farthest limits of what reality may be, and is the only way of finding what it can offer. We know only what we realize, and realization is a creative act. There is no call to be stingy about it. Let Aaron keep his beard, and be decked in magnificent robes.

6. Full imagining, the complete release of faith, includes imagining God. I obviously don't mean forming an image of God: I mean grasping all of reality as being pervaded by God—or, more appropriately, *releasing* all of reality to its Godfulness. Depending on your style, it is probably the same thing to love the real and the true as intensely as possible: what your imagination sees out of the corner of its eye when you do so is the shadow of God, but glimpsing the shadow is enough to allow us to get our bearings and receive the invitation to go further. The invitation is to embolden faith and enhance imagining accordingly. Good faith is literally an imaginative exploration beyond belief, *realizing* reality in and toward the truth and love of God.

7. The shadow of God is all most of us get. It is appropriate to ask for more, but not to demand it: getting more than the shadow is a function of our capacity to receive, and of the scope and strength of our faith and imagination. Faith and imagination will often register that more is offered long before they are capable of receiving it, and receptivity will often precede the faithful imaginings that might fulfill it. In the meantime, we must be patient. We may guess about the shadowed from the shadow, but we should not take our guesses too seriously. We should, however, take them seriously enough. The beliefs that spill out on the way are to be cherished and cared for, but they must be understood as landmarks of where and who we recently used to be, already obsolete and pointing beyond themselves.

8. You can imagine God without experiencing God, and that is enough to provide the appropriate orientation. But it is not necessary to settle for that: if your imagining is apt, you can get in touch. What you touch is of course for your imagination to realize, but if you are not timid you will incorporate it into what you mean by God, and you will be right.[188] But it is important not to take it too seriously. Any getting in touch is a sample only, and it is a mistake to suppose that it is a normative sample or that to begin is to arrive. It is thrilling to get in touch, and one must be wary of

the bedazzlement that comes from thrill, because it is like falling abruptly in love, which tends to make people giddy, a temporarily pleasant condition to the recipient but rapidly boring to his associates. To get in touch is not to be unusually blessed, and in no way constitutes credentials. It is a routine fact of life, and should be treated so. Beauty is not in the eye of the beholder; it is in the *thou*.

9. Getting in touch takes various forms, and only your personal style can determine what works. Some form of deliberate attention is probably necessary in most cases, though evidently not in all. If what you know of praying works, continue. In any event, it is good to augment traditional forms of prayer by regular meditation,[189] emptying the busy mind to make room for the reminding that should be named God, or at least God's shadow—you get to say what it is, and if you find that it is an emanation of yourself, you should not on that account disqualify it: if your self-love and self-knowledge are up to par, you will know that the name of God may still apply, since God is how you are animated and is never far from your pulse. It is also good to remember the versatility of your parliament, with all its talents and insubordinations and discontents and delightednesses and capacities for play. Our accustomed spiritual diet is not as impoverished as the dinners of the poor, but is as restricted as our breakfasts, whose conventionality arbitrarily excludes salads, ice cream, spaghetti, pickled peppers, and port. These are available, and convention should not be allowed to bar you from what would be good for your present needs and longings.

10. Don't be bothered, or contemptuous, if you find that all this sounds fuzzy in my version of it, or even in your own. Mine could not possibly be otherwise, given my limitations, and I have reason to think that fuzziness persists in the whole journey and in all reports of it even among the competent. Clarity is desirable, and should be cultivated both for self-communication and for communication with others; but the appropriate degree of clarity depends on what one is trying to be clear about.[190+] If you try to tell me about the person you most love or the experience that most changed your route, I can hardly expect you to deliver the news in a form that will really let me in on it. I guess you had to be there, and only you were there; you can't give me more than a peek. Trying to be clear makes the peeks better for others, but clarity in such matters is difficult and usually requires the standard equipment of the poet, transformations of language that have different rules of responsibility from those of scrupulous description. But it is easy to get lost in poetry, and even easier to get lost in

poeticizing. If you want to talk to yourself or to others about what is most important, try not to get lost or to lose. If someone else is talking to you, it is not impolite to admit when you are getting lost, and may be helpful to the stability or the insight of the one who is reporting. If it's you who's talking, be ready to be found unclear, and patient when it happens, and try again. The attempt will probably be beneficial to both of you.

11. It is dangerous to travel alone. No one can come entirely with you, but experienced others can accompany you in a neighboring compartment. Find them: they will usually be glad to come along well enough to give the stabilizing presence of the reality from which one gets easily distracted when the going gets heady. Never underestimate the human capacity for self-deception and craziness; never underestimate the importance of staying in touch with representatives of the larger human reality to which your life belongs. It is admittedly often difficult for anyone to know a unique movement of truing from a bizarre deviation from reality, but even—especially? —such private matters as this are best known in company rather than on one's own.

12. Although the adventure is beyond belief, that is so in the sense that it is not bounded by beliefs or limited to their implications. It does not mean that you should not feel free to believe, to play seriously with myths and rituals and symbols you inherited or others that you borrow and even to *realize* them, as long as they don't get in the way of your faith or your truth. Relaxed and comfortable visits back to the metaphorical smalltown former home are within the boundaries of integrity, and may sometimes be indispensable to its sustaining. Faith can be nourished by the hospitable entertainment of visiting beliefs and rites, both old or new. When entertaining such guests, it is good to range widely and not be stingy, just as it is good to be loyal to what one is more used to. The serious imagining of unfamiliar beliefs or practicing of unaccustomed rituals may bring new insight; the serious reappropriation of familiar ones may bring helpful stability. Beliefs once beloved may stay beloved; even if their authority is diminished, their capacity to bring about your truth is not necessarily lost and may indeed be enhanced by their being differently, but still loyally, entertained. The same is true of values, practices, rituals, liturgies, music, prayers, and so on. The stuff of the Christian tradition, however much it may be in need of critical readjustment, is still, even in its unadjusted condition, one of the best resources we have, if appropriately entertained. And besides, your way of reappropriating it may offer a significant improvement to the tradition itself.

13. "The tradition itself," I emphasize once more, is not a museum or a library or a Halloweenish complex of special customs and costumes. The tradition itself is primarily the handing-on, and only secondarily the what and the how of it, the stuff and the way it's taught. When tradition is recognized to be more an *action* than a *content,* its moral dimensions can be more adequately appreciated. That means that there is no excuse for handing anything on as important without being able to make a case for its importance, or for failing to hand on something that may well be needed for the journey of later generations. It also means that the content—the stuff, the truths of the past—is rescued from being a set of limitations and constraints, and is liberated to take its proper place as a kit of resources or a repertoire of skills and options. And of course it further means that we cannot escape the responsibility of evaluating and deciding about what is to be handed on and how. I think it means, moreover, that every Christian is by definition constantly engaged in the act of tradition, and ought ideally to behave as if all actions are a way homeward and Godward, truing, important in ways beyond reckoning, and rather exciting.

14. And some further development of these latter thoughts is the business of the next chapter.

16

RESTORING

CHRISTIAN

TRADITION

In our heart of hearts—that first inner core that stays hiddenly alive within the rings of growth that surround it—we all want to go home, whether or not what was home is still the shelter and warmth that it once was. Eventually, it is not: the people who made it home have vanished, and the rooms where we lived are eerily vacant without them, and also without much of us, whose homing presence cannot be quite adequately summoned without them. Going back home, or wanting to, is a rite of passage that is good to pass through, if you are ready. Readiness is the ability to realize that this is no longer home. Home has moved. Its skeleton may be still there, rooms and hallways that once were resonant with who you were, but now remind you that this is no longer where you live. You bless the vacancy with the grateful memory of what it was, and realize that what it was gave you the metaphor for where you are going. You are going home, a place that you have not yet known but will recognize bit by bit as you approach it.

It is best approached through the familiar rooms, which tell us yes even as they say no. The no is heard in the odd echoey sound that comes from the absence of protective drapes and comfortable chairs, and your clothes no longer being strewn on the floor; it is felt in that sense of not quite, no longer, that is the echo of having learned to live elsewhere. But the first home is never outgrown, even if no one is waiting for you there any more other than the shadow of who you used to be.

We still are who we used to be, even if not entirely. We have changed, but we haven't really forgotten or ceased to belong. What is conventionally called the unconscious is mainly just an attic of mislaid memories and unthematized imaginings that still have claims on us. Our truth must accordingly include a reappropriation of who we used to be and the grandeur of the Christianity that gave us life then. I think it was mistaken about many things, frustratingly misleading in many respects, but, like well-meaning parents of quite ordinary talent, it did the main job successfully. It made life seem important and linked with other lives, communicated an awareness of the centrality of love, aroused a sense of the holy together with a reverence for its ubiquitous presence, encouraged a large and daring hope, fostered a mind-stretching boldness of imagination, and inspired a dedication to truth with a conviction about how much it matters.

The tradition reared us pretty well, and is capable of doing still better with our great-grandchildren. Not ready, but capable. For however much it is pretended that the classical tradition is as unchanged and unchanging as a museum's reassembled dinosaur, the full unclassicized tradition is in fact capacious and hospitable and adaptable, and the process of handing-on is not only alive and versatile but crafty in survival techniques. The tradition's official voices would be likely to rebuff most of what I have to say about the inadequacy and inappropriateness of its present underdeveloped pseudoclassical state, but its own vitality is certainly capable of absorbing whatever in these pages may turn out to be worthy of consideration. If, as I suppose, it is time to turn a corner, I guess that the corner will be turned, perhaps not in the direction that I promote, but if not, perhaps better than I can envision. I no longer think that those who formally guide the tradition are unusually wise, but I increasingly find wisdom in the tradition itself, both in its noun sense, where there are wonderful precedents hidden away in various ancient and modern pockets, and in its verb sense, where I see some new things quietly and appropriately added, and some old things quietly and appropriately withheld, in the course of the handing-on.

Much of what it has to offer is obscured and neglected. We have recently been witnesses to the efforts of the hungry offspring of a debilitated Christian tradition to embezzle exotic Oriental spiritualities, indiscriminately importing astrology and palmistry and ganja along with incense and yoga and meditation, largely (and ironically) because we have left so much of our Christian spiritual tradition unexplored and unavailable. Clarity begins at home. If there is much to be learned from the accomplishments of other religions' traditions, there is still more to be gathered from our own. The modern breakdown of belief is something of a blessing, in that it releases us to better faith, but it is not to our credit: it has been occasioned sooner than we were ready, partly by our collective failure to stay true enough to our tradition to sustain its adequacy by feeding on what it still offers rather than getting impatiently hungry.

But now that this has taken place, we are released to be truer to our tradition than has ever before been possible. Because it has been irresponsibly neglected, we get to rediscover it. Because it has been inappropriately classicized, we may reconsider and reappropriate elements that were once repudiated for historical reasons that no longer obtain. I would like to make some suggestions about rediscovery.

REDISCOVERING THE INHERITANCE: BELOVING HOW IT WAS

First, the tradition is initially to be honored on its own terms. I will shortly make some further comments about changing those terms, but that is a secondary matter. The first principle is to grasp as well as possible what Godwardness was to those who preceded us in the ancestral home. There are two irrefutable reasons for this.

One is that truth cannot be appropriately, or even adequately, served without some understanding of how our inheritance was thought and lived and actualized by those who made it possible for us to receive it. If we can borrow usefully from other religious traditions, and invent imaginatively to take care of the remaining deficiencies, we can hardly do better for a grounding start than to appreciate how the shapes of the home from which the journey begins were once filled with life and meaning by those who built and maintained it.

The other reason for reappropriating the tradition on its own terms is the same reason that motivated Chapter 14's exploration of other religious traditions: deprovincializing our spiritual journey is a sensible way of providing for its needs. And deprovincializing includes not only attending to what others are doing beyond the Christian boundaries, but also getting past the naive supposition that the body of the tradition to which we may lay claim is identical with the face by which it was presented to us. That face, and the faces that did the presenting, should be understood as having dignity and authority, even wisdom, but must not be thought to define the tradition. It is larger and grander and more complex than they, even if they pretended otherwise. By its essential nature, a live tradition is a sequence of creative reunderstandings, not the mere shuffling of sealed and bonded goods from warehouse to warehouse. It is therefore self-releasing; no matter how much its temporary custodians may plead, cajole, or threaten, insisting that no word of the book may be altered and no gesture of the ritual may be changed and no deviation from the proper way of thinking may be countenanced, the tradition does not belong to them. They are at best important instances of it, but it is bigger and more permanent than they; no matter how bullying their attempts to arrest it, it moves on beyond them, and comes into the temporary care of others. But those others should not assume that what they receive defines what is available.

The transmission process is sloppy, despite its built-in wisdom, and as a result important resources are left behind. Those who now fuss about the importance of keeping things just as we have received them are fighting not only in futility but in quaint uniforms, habits that more or less replicate the habits of an earlier century but totally misrepresent the nature of tradition in their pretense at being classical.

TRADITION AND CLASSICISM

There is no classic that has a legitimate claim to being thoroughly normative. Every attempt to identify and become subdued to a pattern of classicism has ended up sterile, as hybrids usually are, when it succeeds. When a notion of classicism is leavened in practice by the vitality and creativity of its recipients, it has usually begotten something quite new, so firmly stamped with the authenticity of its own time that even clever attempts at forging texts or artifacts from the classical era have often fooled their contemporaries but been easily spotted and historically located by later observers.[191] This is not because the later observers are more clever, but merely because the fakes incorporate ideas and presuppositions commonly shared in the taste of the faker's time—and undoubtedly projected into their perceptions of older admired works, whose discipline they do not thoroughly undergo—but no longer sustaining the necessary blind spots when the taste-fashions subsequently shift once more.

Styles inexorably change, and possibilities change with them. Tradition cannot be expected to hand on the whole history of accomplishment directly, but the process of transmission should at least admit that its filtering judgment is not final, and should offer the key to the archives as part of the heritage rather than adding new locks so as to limit access to the alternatives that might be mobilized to overthrow the provisional government.

The process of reappropriating the heritage can learn important lessons from watching how language works. The behavior of English, unregulated (in many ways, unfortunately) by the sort of academy that presides over French and Spanish, is a model of untrammeled tradition. Those familiar with medieval art but not with medieval English may be initially surprised to come upon texts that describe the Blessed Virgin Mary as "buxom." The word then meant "docile," "obedient," quite fitting in the context—but that is no longer what it means. No use claiming that it still should, or that it really *does,* mean docile and obedient, on the grounds that this is closer to its etymology,[192] because the language has moved on, and what tradition does with it outmodes what scholars can rediscover about where it once was.

The tradition of language is not contained in its etymologies. They mark only the traceable starting places, which are themselves the result of untraceable previous shifts in meaning. The Christian tradition is not bounded by fourth-century creeds or first-century witnessings; the notion that authentic new contributions to it ended with the death of the last Apostle is a fiction as desperate and outrageous as a demand that English meanings must be restricted to their earliest traceable etymologies, so that schoolchildren may be scolded for using *sophisticated* as if it were a desirable condition, and *buxom* as if it had anything to do with the body, and *glamor* as if it meant anything other than "grammar," from which it is derived.

The language is ever new, and ever deteriorating even as it advances to new meanings. The deterioration is to be lamented: *disinterested,* despite its useful distinction from *uninterested,* is about to lose its power to communicate what it used to say, and there will be no ready replacement in its traditional job; *velleity* is now usually recognizable only by snobs, and normally left unused even by us snobs, even though it has potential moral, as well as semantic, importance; *awful* is wrecked beyond recognition of what it once said. Still, in addition to technologically necessary inventions like *interface,* we have spontaneous enrichments such as *hang-up* (no one has been able to tell me how this used to be said, or even whether it was capable of being said before this word isolated a useful set of coordinated notions), *humongous* (I resent it, but it witnesses to the vitality of the language to mint new currency as a compensation for debasing the coinage in circulation). It retools meanings according to need: *decimate* meant 10 percent destruction and has now shifted to something like 10 percent survival (we evidently more often need the new sense than the old one, and presumably when the old need resurfaces strongly enough, another word will be conscripted or invented to do the job), and the relatively new twist in the flavor of *Establishment,* which has now come to invite wariness rather than complacency, strikes me as a decided advance.

The tradition of a religion is very like the tradition of a language. It lets useful things go; and it produces other useful things, not always in the place of what was abandoned, but in new places that need to be taken care of. Neither a religion nor a language is capable of addressing well all that needs to be addressed. Both contain neglected nooks that are worth reviving, and messinesses that ought to be better sorted out, and novelties that come to be because the inherited equipment won't do what needs to be done, and blank places that are hardly noticed because of their blankness but offer chances of discovery and enrichment.[193+]

And the traditions move on, because that is what tradition is. It is up to those who participate in them to retrieve what they lose and reintegrate it into what is handed on. Lots of the participants don't care. Those who do should make an additional effort, and be accountable for what they promote. But they must look forward as well as backward, tradition being what it is. In the specifically Christian case, we must honor what it was, for the sake of appropriateness and sanity; but we must care more about what it will be when our great-grandchildren arrive to inspect its hospitality or its ruins.

BELONGING TO THE PAST, BELONGING TO THE FUTURE

Nostalgia is an important fact of life, but it is a lopsided fact. Although literally and etymologically it means "distance sickness," the underlying thought aptly zeros in on "sickness for home." That touches a deep truth, but it refers only to the home we left, not the home toward which we aspire, for which we have no comparable word. It is always easier to recall the vivid comforts of what was than to press onward to what comes next, but that too deserves our longing.

We are only temporarily in charge of the tradition, but we are indeed in charge. The responsibility is huge, but untransferable. Dietrich Bonhoeffer's remark that the world has come of age must be taken cautiously: it is of age in the sense that it gets to make its own decisions without requiring permission. But the metaphor should not be pushed very far. The child come of age has the advantage of being able to fall back on elders, living and dead, who can supply to a neophyte whatever wisdom comes from long and reflective life. With respect to the tradition of which we are temporary custodians, we are in a situation where there are no adequate elders: we have reached the legal age where we are allowed to do as we will, and are held responsible for what we do, and have a charge that we cannot fob off on others, but there are no elders to fall back on if we don't know how to do it or get in trouble trying.

There are presences from of old, but they are predecessors, not elders: Thomas Aquinas and Luther and Calvin are not hundreds of years old, though they often get respectfully but carelessly imagined that way—they all stopped, before they were sixty-five, making new contributions to what we now struggle with, and what they knew when they made those contributions, breathtaking as they still are, lacked some of what we now know that makes a difference. We can't rely on them, or on anyone else: they can be enlisted as consultants, or co-opted into the committee, but they have no veto and can cast their votes only by cooperative proxy. We have to do the work, having come of age, of learning how to make the next move and how to prepare the next stage toward growing up.

The opportunity is unique in a way that resembles how raising a family is unique: we cannot find a way to thank those who have made us possible except by doing our best version of what they did for us, passing the inheritance on with both a reverent remembrance of how we experienced it and a deliberate care about how we make adjustments as we transmit it. I am occasionally asked if I am a practicing Catholic. I reply politely to the real drift of the question, but what I long to say is that *of course* I am practicing! It is only by long rehearsal that we learn to perform as we should. I suspect that my practice will never eventuate in a proper performance. I regret that. I intend to keep practicing.

This book is practice, a trial stab at what I would like to be able to say. I hope that you are being patient with its insufficiencies in the same benevolent spirit in which we should be patient with the inadequacies of past contributions to the tradition, trying to sift out what is worth appropriating rather than dismissing wholesale what does not altogether work. Good tradition requires sympathetic discrimination, and one may learn helpfully from what predecessors were trying to do even when the results fall short.

READJUSTING THE TRADITION

I will try to be as lucid as I can in the following rather random suggestions for the adjustment of our collective and individual practice. The suggestions bear on both personal and theological practice, and I make them as a gesture toward the project of growing up individually and collectively, a project that has no normative achievement-model but already provides a chronicle of suggestive, however inadequate, good tries. The matters they touch on are delicate, and I ask you to appreciate the diffidence with which I proffer them.

1. Although assisted recently by much good work and appropriate pressure, our tradition is still primitive about the status of women. This is a subject on which I am bound to offend many readers, not because my views are unwholesome but because I will not say enough and am too ignorant to do so even if there were room in this book to do it. I do not know the experience of women adequately, and realize that observation, reading, listening intently, and all the compassion I can summon up will not be enough to turn the balance of my deficiency. So I might as well go ahead and offend further by saying that I do not perceive the feminist cause as a uniquely urgent case, but see it rather as an important instance of a generally institutionalized self-brutalizing and self-deformation that barricades the mind of the Establishment self-protectively and smugly against sharing power, against any compromise in its own self-satisfaction, and against the provision of justice for *any* of the disadvantaged. The feminist movement, like every other attempt at massive reform, offers varieties of selfishness and silliness to replace the old ones, and its opponents and resisters take unfair advantage of these inevitable concomitants in their attempts to discredit the brilliant critical accomplishments of the movement's best voices. But I distrust the mythologies of both sides. The problem does not seem to me to be the shrillness of uppity women who have forgotten their place, but neither do I think it to be a specifically patriarchal regime that resists a salvation that belongs to a matriarchal kingdom. The problem lies, I think, in deeper, and more pervasive, darkness and untruth that cripple both the disadvantaged and the advantaged, in multiple ways. If the culture is bigoted against a recognition of the dignity and rights of women, it is also significantly blind to the dignity and rights of children, of the poor and the ignorant, of the oppressed in other parts of the world than one's own (which is usually a small neighborhood of privilege, even if sometimes an

international small neighborhood), of the ugly and the deformed and the disabled and the mentally disturbed, of the people who speak with accents because they grew up in unfashionable places or know more than one language, of the obese and the unborn and the mentally retarded and those who are confused by loneliness and pain and all of the otherwise inconvenient or odd people who don't manage to pass muster according to some unarticulated but established pseudometaphysical dress code that determines who is allowed to be respected and adjusted to. Our general condition is bad, and rots the sensibilities of almost everyone. The elderly, whom our forebears once knew more or less how to revere and care for and honor in ways that we have substantially forgotten, have also been driven too far toward believing that they are obsolete: they are systematically demeaned and patronized, which seems to prove the point if they can be made sufficiently demoralized. The solution is not a redistribution of power, or an honoring of the best-articulated special claims (though that would surely be a helpful start). The solution lies in a total and systematic change of mind and heart. *Metanoia,* the call to reform that Matthew, for example, attributes to both John the Baptist and Jesus (Mt 3:2 and 4:17 has the two of them saying the same thing, word for word), is usually translated as "repentance" and reduced in imagination to a change that might appropriately be accompanied by an apologetic promise that it will be better done next time. That is unfortunate. *Metanoia* at the level in question really means a total transformation that is well beyond what an apology can reach. The changes we need are probably much broader and deeper than we can presently imagine: no known society has ever realized them, no known religious tradition has ever envisioned them adequately, and it will take much longer than we have at our immediate disposal—through the time of my great-grandchildren, and the time of theirs, at least—to invent and pursue them together, even if we can gather together uncommon vigilance, unhabitual discernment, and tireless fidelity to the cause. We have moved beyond dedicating special days of remembrance to needed reconsiderations, and have recently established special years. The Year of the Child came and went, without making many ripples of serious difference. Now (1988–1998) we are embarked on a decade internationally and ecumenically dedicated to Churches in Solidarity with Women. This is a good and hopeful step, but when the decade is over there will still be vast work to be done. Repairing the known damage in this cause and in coordinate causes will take generations. Learning and undoing the still-unknown damage will take even longer.

2. We are backward about the accommodation of the erotic. Christianity is perhaps the most deprived of religious traditions in this respect, but the others aren't significantly better: even the Hindus have almost totally forgotten this dimension of their heritage, despite its being publicly registered in many of their major religious monuments, and will sometimes bristle at the mere mention of Tantra. The major traditions all seem to overvalue self-denying and self-abasing solemnity, and only here and there can we get glimpses of what it would be like to imagine God as transcendent cheerfulness, eternally playful, infinite fun. None of them is even particularly clever about the appreciation of good food, which, like fun in general, is anomalously left outside the religious purview, a potentially dangerous piece of neglect. All traditions appropriately register that most of what brings ready joy routinely brings self-indulgence along with it; but the denigration of delight as a protection from self-indulgence is not a satisfactory solution. Hasidic Judaism is one of the best resources for discriminating between the truing and the falsifying uses of this kind of spontaneity, but its ways are deeply disciplined by means that may be impossible for others to emulate. Overcoming delight has been proved spiritually possible in most traditions, and appears to be importantly edifying, but arduous and costly. *Harnessing* delight in the meantime has evidently proved to be difficult, but not as much energy and imagination have been invested in learning to do so as in expunging it. Overcoming is not necessarily the only, or even the best, solution. This needs further consideration, universally.

3. We have so impoverished our tradition of prayer that it scarcely has strength to beg even at the church door. Many are uneasy about prayer altogether, possibly out of an appropriate embarrassment about the inevitable failure of pleas for divine intervention. Ritual and liturgy are indispensable, and will force their way in: if not into the church, then perhaps into the lesser aspects of civic and social life—pledging allegiance to flags, giving toasts at testimonial dinners for crass bosses, fancy coming-out ceremonies, political convention nomination speeches—where they may seduce us into a disproportionate and distorting seriousness. The appreciation of the stabilizing and orienting value of liturgy and ritual has been, in my judgment, diminished in recent years, and has probably not been adequately received by the newer generations. But they may have a better instinct than their elders for the realization that even the largest solemnities of public worship do not substitute for unformulated prayer, either collectively or individually. Both our tradition and the traditions of others are rich with experienced technique for prayerful invention, and we should learn better

how to exploit them, both individually and collectively. Versatility and balance in prayer are at least as important to the cultivation of faith as nourishment and good cooking are to other dimensions of well-being.

4. Liberation theologies have awakened us to unfinished agendas of justice, and it is now religiously inexcusable, except for extreme contemplatives, not to participate in their realization in some practical way. But we need a liberation deeper than usually envisaged if the agenda is to be taken care of.[194] We have all but forgotten the tradition of ascetic theology, which once taught us how to do without, or else have relegated it to clerics aspiring to mysticism. There is an urgent need for its reappropriation. We have systematically forgotten, so systematically that the forgetting is built into the structure of our cities as well as the structure of our habits, how little and few and simple are our actual needs. Possibly the old dogs can't relearn the traditional trick, but they should at least take care to try to retrieve it for the new dogs yet to come. Not only is it edifying, it is likely to become indispensable for a just survival, and quite possibly for just surviving.

5. We are far too obsessed with power, control, dramatic doing; we project this on God, and worship our fantasy of power, control, dramatic doing. This is built into the tradition and ought to be expunged except where carefully controlled as a playful fantasy: its standard forms are unworthy of God, and untrue. Divine omnipotence means that God is doing and has done and will do all that is possible. Not that God can do whatever we may fancy, but that God does all that is possible in this reality, including our empowerment to deal with it. We are not very good at dealing with it, but that is not an excuse for pretending that God reserves (and now withholds) a solution utterly beyond our empowerment. We need not rescue but shaping up, and the desirable shape is the shape of God, whose omnipotence is expressed in what has already been given.

6. We must—repeat, *must*—shed our acculturated and perversely uncircumspect assumption that we live in a smart world. We are victims of its dumbest recorded state. Once we realize that we are the crippled products of an extraordinarily stupid, insensitive, selfish, blind, and self-deceived moment in history, we can get on with what needs to be done about it; but until then, we are likely to compound its dizzying insanity. If you have managed to reach ten, for God's sake don't accept the constant invitation to slip back to five, which is nowhere, or six, which is comfortable collusion with collective atrocities.

7. We should protect the solemnity of our tradition, but we ought to

augment it with more amusement. Unfortunately, human beings do not seem to have an instinctive mechanism that protects them from taking themselves too seriously. Those who specialized in jolliness probably perished in the course of evolution, leaving us the heirs of the earnest strivers. The inheritance is a blessing, but we can now afford to replace what got diminished in more environmentally merciless times, and perhaps can't afford not to. "You do look, my son, in a moved sort,/ As if you were dismay'd: be cheerful, sir," says Prospero to the less-experienced Ferdinand in *The Tempest* (IV.i.146–47). It is, like many of the toss-offs of Shakespearian characters, good advice. Be cheerful, sir, or madam, or child. The situation, adequately scrutinized, is dismal and somewhat scary, enough to inspire a "moved sort" that should lead to deeply serious changes—but that is not a legitimate excuse for withholding good humor. I am not recommending the cynical and desperate "Ridi, Pagliaccio" that asks the clown to appreciate the supreme irony that the amusement of others is carved from his own pain and he might as well ironically share the joke. I am claiming that reality is delicious and God is, among other attributes, fun, and that it would be supremely silly not to respond appropriately to this wonderful combination. It is not unrealistic to whistle while we work. Our religious tradition is a bit short on relaxed hopefulness and good cheer, and offers few invitations to sheer merriment. It leaves lots of work to be done before it is entirely safe for human consumption, but as the work proceeds, it is good to remember that the gaps in the labor, and much of the labor itself, deserve to be treated as apt occasions for the mirth that a robust faith knows to be a grateful response to grace.

17

RECONSTRUCTING
THEOLOGY

I have occasionally, in the course of this book, neglected to distinguish what I take to be implications for religion (both personal and communal) and what I take to be implications for theological practice. I consider the two closely related, of course, but they are not the same. Religion is the way faith is lived out; theology is the way it is thought about. The thought is ideally in the service of the life: theology is the handmaid of religion—or perhaps more precisely the valet, in the way that Jeeves is valet to Bertie Wooster, dedicated to keeping foolishness in check while assisting its vitality. The next two chapters are accordingly given to these two topics, in ascending order of importance. This chapter concentrates on the theological implications of what I have been attempting to say.

THE TASK OF THEOLOGY REVISITED

There are two basic positions on the question of theology's field and scope.

One is that it begins in allegiance only to the canon of appropriateness, finding a way of imagining God through the use of any resources available, refining and organizing that imagining in the way that simply makes best and most fruitful sense, and returning to the imaginings of a specific tradition only at a later stage, correlating them with the first stage's results where possible and critiquing them accordingly: "The task of theology, as I understand it, is to think through and make explicit the criteria for an adequate understanding of God and then to reconstruct traditional images and ideas on the basis of these criteria, so that God will be grasped in faith and life as in significant creative relationship to our actual experience."[195]

The alternative, sometimes differing from the first position mainly in accent and emphasis, is to give priority, and thus the first phase of the theological enterprise, to what constitutes a particular tradition's way of imagining God and its relationship to God, and then, only after appreciating its style, to offer interpretations and adjustments that might make its content more coherent and appropriate as a way of appropriating the vision that is assimilated otherwise by other traditions: "this vision is expressed in and through the symbols (exodus, election, people, messiah; creation, incarnation, church, eschatology, etc.) that make up the ideational content of that religion; when formulated, this cluster of symbols becomes its 'truths,' its teachings, its doctrine. This content can be delineated by those within and without the community; reflection on it, and construction or reconstruction of it is the task, I would take it, of theology."[196]

It is obvious that these are both legitimate conceptions of the task, each with its own integrity. But they differ. Proponents of the former often prefer that the work of those in the latter camp be adjectivally specified: they are not doing theology as such, but *Christian* theology, or *Catholic* theology, or *Eastern Catholic* theology. Proponents of the latter approach frequently suggest that the former are engaged in a kind of philosophy of religion that is not sufficiently concretized in a tradition to be called theology at all (or at best, with a touch of disdain, allowed to be called "philosophical" theology). I vote with the former way of defining theology, as being more efficient, lucid, and historically sound.[197]+

Reconstructive theology then becomes a dialogue between what has been and what may better be—the critical reevaluation of the symbols and dogmas and notions and thoughts of a specific tradition, not with the aim of validating them by apologetical defense or reinterpretive finesse, but as an attempt at housecleaning, shining up the items that will still take a shine, arranging them in an appropriate and coherent way, and scuttling things that are broken beyond repair or have become too shabby to be presentable.

This is perhaps the point at which the difference between the two addresses to theology becomes most crucial. From the perspective of tradition-specific theology, a reconstructive theology such as I am advocating may be thought a disloyalty to—even a betrayal of—the tradition, ironically undermining just what they wish to strengthen; from the perspective of the more universalistic theological style, defensiveness about the content of the tradition may be perceived as a disloyalty to—even a betrayal of—traditional truing, and therefore an infidelity to God precisely in the very acts of resistance in which the advocates of the traditionalistic mode understand themselves to be most specifically faithful.

It is possible that there is no solution to this dilemma, and that the situation is irremediably painful. You may have noticed in the matched quotations above that both spokemen talk about reconstruction: I am appropriating the word in a sense that more closely resembles that of view number 1 (though not identical with it), because I think it more appropriate to use it in that sense: the analogous activity in the other camp is often referred to as constructive theology, which seems to me to be both adequately respectful and adequately descriptive. At any rate, those who hold view number 2 are likely to judge that what I am calling reconstructive theology threatens to invade and desecrate the intellectual shrines of the tradition. Such a thought is unsettling even to a reconstructive theologian, not to mention those to whom such a theologian is an enemy of an especially pernicious kind. That is not the intent of the project, but it would be unrealistic not to face the fact that some such consequences may ensue. The collision is full of shock waves, and of shock. There is no way to make it comfortable, as far as I can see, no way to create the conditions of a congenially cooperative enterprise when the stakes are so starkly different. But there is at least a consolation.

The consolation is this: the reconstructive theology I am advocating defines God, by its very ground rules, as truing. That means that even if those who pursue it had power to impose, condemn, anathematize, or excommunicate (which they don't), they could not use such power without betraying what they stand for. Reconstructive theology means to offer to the tradition reconsideration which the tradition may accept or reject, according to its best lights. Nothing is compelled, through any means whatsoever. The handers-on (who are everyone) are free to accept, free to decline. In the meantime, it strikes me as also appropriate for the official guardians of the tradition to resist novelty. That is one of their jobs as guardians. I do not think it appropriate for the official guardians to anathematize or excommunicate, since that is not only an unfair use of power but a demonstrably dysfunctional way of trying to shut up ideas; such power plays seem to inspire more protectiveness than shunning among the faithful who are most likely to make a long-range difference to what eventually is to happen. But resistance is appropriate to the office and the duty of official guardians, even from a reconstructive viewpoint, because that establishes the conditions under which the tradition can best be served by both sides.

Reconstructive theology trusts in the tradition as it is alive, even if it manifests some detachment from some of the fossils and quaint implements in the museum that memorializes where the tradition used to be. And the tradition as it is alive is located where people live, not just in where its official guardians tell them they ought to (though the latter also deserves respectful consideration). The contest for the minds and hearts of the faithful is organized fairly, in my opinion: on the one hand, the organized authority of the official guardians, including the custodians of the world's oldest and longest reigning empire, full of dignity and power and intelligent understanding of what has been handed down; and on the other hand, the reconstructive unauthorized amateurish would-be reformers, who either manage to make good sense or don't, and must stand or fall on that basis. That's fair. Let us proceed.

RECONSTRUCTION AND TRADITION

Reconstructive theology arrogates to itself the right to call anything whatever into question. It values, however warily, all attempts to search for God, all reports of the experience of God, all writings and rites and myths and icons that seem to have been found helpful in the Godwardness of any tradition. That is what its form of faith requires. But it pledges no allegiance to any of them, assuming a universal religious immaturity that makes all approaches interesting and none definitive. Its only unqualified allegiance is to the God who presides over Truth, and while it assumes that all that is necessary has already been revealed, it also assumes that the unpacking of the revelation is a long and difficult communal task, and that what is *necessary* is not the only point of interest.

The task begins by redefining the meaning of "we," thoroughly and irrevocably. "We" in the vocabulary of reconstructive theology is not counterpoised by "they"; it is everyone, without exception. *We* are in pursuit of God.[198+] *We* should collude in examining how to do it well, discovering what works and what doesn't, to which aspirations various texts and techniques help to true us, what is spent and what is bought when we do it this way or that way, what resources are available—both the well explored and the still unexploited—for making the venture in various ways.

Reconstructive theology does not dream of finding One Way to prescribe as our common solution. It aspires to locate and argue the inappropriateness of deforming spiritual exercises, theological surds, and other pieces of bad business that deserve to be purged from our traditions; and it is especially eager to identify successful imaginings and doings that can enhance the repertoire of our Godwardness. But it tries to remain aware that one man's meat is another man's poison, and that flexibility and versatility in the strategies for belonging to God are not only indispensable for offering nourishment to various styles of personhood,[199+] but highly desirable for supplying the needs of any individual parliament's efforts to get through a given crisis, a given situation, a given day.

Reconstructive theology, because it is pledged to appreciate the potential contributions of whatever is available, tries in its sifting of any given tradition to be careful to respect what is life-giving and truing within it. It is conservative of what works successfully before it is progressive about impugning what doesn't or tinkering with what is good to make it better. It attempts to stay aware that to hand on one's own tradition by reconstructing it (rather than simply preserving it or subtly reinterpreting what has become awkward) is to acknowledge one's personal indebtedness to what it has been. Proper reconstruction neither ignores nor patronizes the voices that protest its meddling, since it appreciates that unassisted self-criticism is not enough to keep the project honest, and that zeal about traditional motes is no protection against acquiring novel beams. (All the same, that too is a two-way street, and when reconstruction is accused of throwing out the baby with the bathwater, it must be allowed to observe that its opponents may be victims of a misperception, and may themselves be guilty of keeping the hambone while they throw out the soup.)

DISCERNING MYTHS AND CONVENTIONS

The Christian tradition, like other religious traditions, has gathered to its bosom a variety of customs, suppositions, beliefs, legends, and myths, of varying degrees of claim, truing-value, and capacity to mislead. There is no simple calculus for evaluating them. It is surely not appropriate to assess them simply on the basis of the soundness of their historical or philosophical foundations.

To identify something as a myth is not to accuse it of falsity, though the term is commonly used to do just that: more technically and appropriately, *myth* means the imagining of happenings in an invisible order, past or transcendent, that show the pattern of, and perhaps bring about in some way, parallel happenings that (it is supposed) did, do, or will take place in the arena where we enact our lives. The myth may in itself be bizarre, silly, absurd, and simply unthinkable according to the canons of decent thought, but that does not mean that it loses its capacity to true. If taken seriously— not necessarily by being *believed,* but by being accepted as a guide to the appropriate patterning of life and understanding—it may perform a service to truth that perhaps cannot be accomplished in any other way.

Plato, though devotedly keen in the pursuit of true and sound under-standing through direct and explicit thinking, is usefully instructive in his employment of myths in the course of his philosophizing—not just in that he used them, which is helpfully instructive in itself, but in how he used them. I appeal to two examples, representative of how not to do it and how best to do it.

In the *Republic,* Plato, in the course of spinning out an extensive allegori-cal approach to the meaning of justice, sketches a utopian state that is strictly ordered and sharply divided into classes with different kinds of power and responsibility. The educational system that prepares and sustains this organization includes the indoctrination of the young with a myth of their origin that will account for and justify their eventual placement in specific classes and duties. The myth explains that human beings originate from a common source but are composed of different kinds of material, and those who happen to be made of iron must be satisfied that they are well served by being allowed to take care of the things that iron people can do; they must not dream of trying to fit into the work of the silver, nor may the gold people dream of taking on the less demanding life and responsibili-ties of the brass. Everyone thus sees the inevitability and appropriateness of the station to which he is appointed. Plato calls this myth a lie, and it is generally understood to be a "noble lie," on the grounds that it is effective in reconciling everyone to what must be done, making the state more true as a result.[200]

In the *Phaedo,* Plato develops a myth of the True Earth, the place above and beyond the ordinary Earth to which souls pass into their afterlife, as a way of providing a guiding perspective on who we are and how we should live.[201] If we consider where we came from and where we are heading, we can see more clearly and satisfactorily what we really are, what is at stake in what we do about it, and what we can aspire to. But in this case, after elaborating the myth, Plato concludes in a very different fashion:

> Now, it would not do for a sensible man to maintain that these things are just as I have described them: but that either this or something like it is the case concerning our souls and their homes— . . . this seems to me quite apt and worth daring to suppose, for the risk is a noble one. And one ought to, as it were, *enchant* oneself with such things . . .[202]

The notion of a noble lie is not intrinsically absurd. A noble lie can bring comfort, steadiness, hope, wholesome motivation. The lie told by Marlow to Kurtz's fiancée at the end of Joseph Conrad's *The Heart of Darkness* may, as Marlow suspects, be sentimental, but it is unquestionably noble, sparing the idealistic woman a devastating shock and reaffirming her sense of dedication to noble values. The doctors' dilemma when reporting to patients who have been diagnosed as terminally ill is not a struggle with sentimentality or cowardice but a tough ethical decision involving assessments of the patients' capacities to digest the truth, the reliability of the patients' and others' judgments about those capacities, and a share in the responsibility for consequences; many a noble lie has been prudentially told in consulting rooms, to good effect.

But a programmatic lie, I would argue, must forfeit the claim to nobility. If we assume—as I do, the assumption being a necessary consequence of the fundamental axioms of my theologizing—that faith is in principle capable of absorbing any truth whatever (even though particular embodied instances of faith may be less capacious), then there is no justification for the systematic imposition of false belief in order to bring about a useful result. Even if the whole system substantially depends for its stability and the stability of its members on shared misapprehensions and misplaced confidences (which I think true of religious systems, social systems, and cultural systems generally), the proper task is to restructure the systems to accommodate truth more hospitably, not to perpetuate false stability. What we deliberately and voluntarily charm ourselves into as a way of getting closer to truth, through the entertainment of illusions as instruments of approximation, is for us to decide according to who we understand ourselves to be and where we judge to be right to go with it. A measure of strategic self-deception is not inimical to good faith; the programmatic deception of others is.

The Christian tradition harbors a good deal of deception of others, and it is the assumption of reconstructive theology that this may be dispensed with—and that a careful examination of the tradition will support this assumption. Let me offer a few examples.

We are culturally fussy about anniversaries, and can get into considerable personal trouble when we overlook those that loved ones take seriously. A day late may cost heavy penalties, and it's no use appealing to the Julian calendar against the Gregorian in order to beg a grace period. But in spite of this, Easter—the major traditional Christian anniversary—is a movable feast, with more than a month's worth of variability as to where it may fall in a specific year. Nobody seems to care when the "real" anniversary is. This is possibly a cultural incoherence, but it is at least suggestive about how we have already learned to live with imprecision and shrug it off as unproblematic. It is socially convenient for the British to invest their reverence about the monarch's birthday on a fixed day that does not vary from reign to reign. The convention of celebrating other people's birthdays on their anniversaries is also rather arbitrary, and there is no compelling reason why the event of one's birth should not be celebrated regularly every twenty-three days, if one can get by with it. If you *can* get by with it, don't try to pretend that the regular interval is significant; even your children can be conned only for a while. Just make the parties good, and all is forgiven —even the lack of certitude.[203]!

The preoccupation with certitude, and its concomitant defensiveness of an ultimately untenable view of the Bible, has strewn the Christian tradition with blunderings about the nature of the inheritance. Much of it is convention, which is useful, decorative, and unmisleading when accepted as such, but distorting when mistaken for truth. The Christmas tree is a pleasant convention that no one mistakes for anything else. The stories of the angels' annunciation to the shepherds and the visitation of the Magi are pleasant conventions that are still often mistaken for something else, and should not be. Few critical biblical scholars will any longer argue that these things actually happened in history, but the more reflective of them will acknowledge that as conventions, they have dignity and meaning that deserve to be cherished and handed on, a part of Aaron's beard that needs only a little shampoo, not a shave.[204]

Reconstructive theology accepts all the elements of the tradition as conventions. Its subsequent work identifies some of them as being also something more, but this is the starting place for the work of inventorying what we have received.

In taking its preliminary inventory of the tradition, reconstructive theology should attend to determining what is there (i.e., creeds, dogmas, beliefs, customs, habits). It must also inquire about what kind of allegiance is invested in these items, either officially or unofficially (e.g., "light from light" is solemnly enshrined in the Nicene Creed, but I don't think I have ever met anyone who is jealously protective of its high status, or even pretends to know what it means; on the other hand, St. Jude, normally neglected by theologians and ecumenical councils, commands pious imaginations rather powerfully in some quarters, and must eventually be reconsidered).

Reconstructive theology must also notice carefully how these items are connected with one another. Limbo, though presently fallen into limbo, is not an isolated odd habit of old thought but the logical conclusion of thinking through a cluster of related ideas about original sin, redemption, grace, beatitude, etc. Creation, sometimes treated as a mere logical necessity to get the ball rolling and subsequently inconsequential, is, when scrutinized more closely, a doctrine that turns out to be pervasively involved in almost everything else that can be theologically considered. But the assignment of guardian angels to baptized Christians and the question of whether Jesus' birth took place in the physically usual way or miraculously bypassed it, both of them matters that have sometimes engaged thoughtful theological attention, do not seem to me in the long run to have anything useful to do with anything else in the catalogue.

Once we know what the conventions are, how they are conventionally founded and conventionally connected with one another, and how they are conventionally related to by the Christian faithful, the critical work can begin.

EVALUATING CONVENTIONS

The next step is the evaluation of the conventions, in two ways. The first is to discover what value is attached to them by those within the embrace of the tradition. The New Testament apocryphal books have faded almost out of sight and are rarely read outside universities; they have given us the ox and ass of the nativity, firmly ensconced in our carols and crèches, and the image of the child Jesus making clay birds and breathing life into them, but virtually no one attaches any importance to either, and the rest is forgotten.[205]+ On the other hand, the New Testament itself retains a powerful presence, and important work remains to be done in assessing how it is selectively read and selectively valued—which books and passages are (and which have been in the past) thought most important and which are relatively neglected, and just whose valuations are in question (contemplative nuns, priests trained in East African seminaries, Mexican migrant workers, process theologians, admirers of Kierkegaard, charismatics, medieval mystics, the imprisoned, political activists, the dying). How and why were indulgences, confession, relics, churching, holy water, Dionysius the Areopagite, St. Christopher, and the rosary held once in such high esteem and why and how has the esteem faded? Just who is the Son of Man thought to be *now,* in seminary textbooks, in the imaginations of Filipino children, in Bolivian prayer meetings, in European liturgical art?

There are official positions on most of these matters, and the voice of the Magisterium (or its equivalent in non-Catholic Christianities) is one that must be assiduously attended to. But tradition is what is handed on by everyone, not by the Vatican or the Elders alone; the latter must compete with new vitalities and creativities that erode the magisterial conventions and sometimes leave them lifeless, museum pieces that tell us at most what the tradition used to think.[206!]

There is a useful Japanese word, *teisetsu,*[207] that denotes (among other things) the received conventional opinion on any given topic. On an examination, a Japanese student is expected to deliver not her creative insights into the matter, or a critique of others' opinions (both of which will weaken her grade rather than strengthen it), but precisely the appropriate *teisetsu.* This is not because Japanese students are assumed to have no original thoughts, nor because Japanese examination-readers are incapable of understanding and evaluating originality, nor because Japanese culture disapproves of creativity. It is because Japanese examinations have a specific function: to determine whether students are in adequate command of the *teisetsu* that ought to be fundamentally mastered before one starts correcting or improving upon it.

Magisterial teachings, be they pronounced from Vatican City, Geneva, Canterbury, Grand Rapids, Wheaton, or Brooklyn, are *teisetsu,* the central conventions. Members of the relevant churches ought to know them. Members of the relevant churches ought to revere them and belove them. But it does not follow that they ought to believe them.

Magisterial teachings form a central point of reference, and therefore a central point of departure; but they should not be considered to form the point at which the imaginations of the faithful are obliged to arrive and settle down. Their intellectual function in a seriously thinking Christianity is more liturgical than critical: these are the traditional and conventional answers to the perennial questions, and deserve to be absorbed in a sort of doctrinal *anamnesis,* a solemn calling-to-mind that these are the traditional and conventional answers. But for an intellectually responsible theologian, they are the first word rather than the last. The provisional last word is what the theologian, in full view of the traditional and conventional answers, judges to be the best answers to put forward as candidates for the next official reformulation of the ecclesiastical *teisetsu,* and the best understandings to pass on in the meantime, as a supplement to official doctrine, through the unsolemn and nonliturgical teaching and learning that takes place in the practical magisterium exercised in schools and parish study groups.

The first evaluative job of reconstructive theology accordingly starts with a respectful and reverent reappropriation of the magisterial *teisetsu,* but then turns to examine how they are in fact valued by those who are not directly responsible for their promulgation and defense, and finally moves on to see how they, and those valuations, stand up under critical scrutiny.

The second phase of evaluation takes us back to the calculus I proposed in Chapter 1. Step 1 is included in the first phase of evaluating: discovering what values and implications we customarily attach to the various conventional elements of tradition (beliefs, rituals, rules, remembrances). Step 2 is the analysis of how much the given element actually implies those values and implications, and the extent to which they are merely conventionally associated with one another. Step 3 examines whether those values and implications are available through another route, and offers alternative routes when they can be found. Step 4 asks how much of value would be lost if the convention were ironized or taken purely as a convention (and no more), or even abandoned altogether. And step 5 evaluates the price of taking a given convention as more than merely conventional—as a truth or a fact or a required belief or an authoritative command—and takes a steady look at what must be supposed or ignored or accepted or excluded in order to stay where we were.

RECONSTRUCTION

The two evaluative phases are concurrent, because they influence one another, and they lead, as they go, to the specifically reconstructive dimension of the enterprise. Once we have become more candidly clear about how elements of the tradition are or have been valued, how—and with what degree of soundness—the interpretations on which they are based have come about, and how they are (as well as how they are mistakenly thought to be) structurally interconnected, the job of reconstruction can begin on a stable footing to undertake such tasks as these:

1. Proposed Revaluations.

Some of the disused aspects of tradition have a good claim to being more appropriate than what eventually displaced them. Recent emphasis on the humanity of Jesus, for instance, has recovered that half of incarnational theology that had long been overwhelmed, almost to the point of Docetism, by disproportionate attention to his divinity, and certainly makes Christian thought more faithful to its inheritance from the Council of Chalcedon than it has been for several centuries.

But there is no unimpeachable privilege to be extended to the Council of Chalcedon, which was rejected from the start by the Monophysite branch of Christianity, which is still carrying on its own un-Chalcedonian tradition. The total complex of tradition offers precedent for the whole range of Christological views from Docetist and Monophysite through Chalcedonian compromise to varieties of attempts to understand Jesus as a human being empowered by God to make more than an ordinary difference (this latter view being represented by extremely early tradition as well as more modern revisionism). The official view of the Catholic Church, like that of the World Council of Churches, is a convention whose value-implications need to be scrutinized and compared with alternatives.

Reconstructive theology does not rule out any traditional view that is not demonstrably pernicious, and therefore although not necessarily committed to the Chalcedonian formula, "true God and true man," is willing to entertain it as one of the viable ways of thinking if it can be shown to be coherent. Much that has been relegated to the trash heap of heresy (e.g., the work of Origen early in the third century, which is now being interestingly reconsidered in some circles) deserves reconsideration and ought to be reactivated as part of the legitimate repertoire of theologizing, which must necessarily be a pluralistic activity if we are to be honest about it. On the other hand, the notion that non-Christians cannot be saved through their own religions appears to be demonstrably pernicious (it is also ill founded, but that is another question) and should be deeply suspect on account of its implications alone, despite its having been kept sturdily in place by many generations of Christian theologians.

2. *Proposed Reinterpretations.*

What goes into creeds, catechisms, dogmatic decrees, and conciliar pronouncements, as well as what goes into popular piety, Christian folklore, and random enthusiastic movements, is ultimately grounded on what is taken to be a sufficient authority—be it the authority the Bible or the Fathers of the Church or Thomas Aquinas or Luther or the Westminster Confession or Our Lady of Fatima or just The Way We've Always Done It —and confirmed by an authority of another kind (pope, council, congregation of sacred doctrine, custom, *vox populi)*. The revaluation process mentioned in the previous paragraph calls into question both types of authority to the extent that they claim divine privilege, since reconstructive theology supposes divine privilege not to be so localized.

What is to be interpreted is therefore to be understood as disciplined by revelation in general, which is everywhere and everything. The appropriate way of interpreting the Christian tradition is accordingly guided by the evaluation of that tradition, and inevitably results in readjusting the sense of what counts importantly and unimportantly in determining how best to understand what has been given.

It is best to stay within the tradition where possible, as in our century's revival of the ancient but long-neglected doctrine of *apokatastasis,* eventual universal salvation, as an alternative to the eternal hell that has been losing its grip on the imagination of thoughtful Christians over the last few centuries.[208] But sometimes interpretations must be newly constructed where the tradition is insufficient, as in the modern proposals to reinterpret the Catholic understanding of eucharistic consecration as *transignification* (the transformation of the *meaning* of the eucharistic elements, a wonderful notion sponsored by recent Dutch theologians and patronizingly rebuffed by the Vatican) to make up for what *transubstantiation* (the transformation of the elements' metaphysical reality, sponsored by Thomas Aquinas and endorsed heavily by central Catholic authority ever since) lost its capacity to accomplish once the Scholastic philosophical/theological framework could no longer be assumed as the matrix of imagining.

3. *Proposed Restructurings.*

There is a need to reorganize the theological imagination to grasp and order a theological vision that thus revalues, reinterprets, demotes, ironizes, and athetizes elements of tradition, acknowledges their conventionality, and revalues what they have attempted to purchase. Such restructurings may be borrowed from the achievements of other religious traditions; some progressive Christian theologians are currently exploring ways of appropriating the Buddhist *sunyata,* emptiness, as a way of compensating for deficiencies in the inherited doctrines of God. Or they may be imitated from the imaginings of science[209] or philosophy[210] or sociology[211] or art.[212] Or they may be simply imaginatively invented according to what will meet the needs that emerge in the course of reconstructing (I have attempted to offer some sketchy examples in the course of this book).

The whole of the reconstructive project should be guided by a preference for what makes a difference to the lives of those for whom it is designed, including my great-grandchildren. Its practitioners might well conclude that we don't really know whether the Holy Spirit proceeds from the Father and the Son or from the Father alone, and that we cannot tell which is preferable to imagine, and that we can think both of them alternately, just as we can think of light as waves or as particles, and that it doesn't really matter when evaluated according to the canon that governs the reconstruction of our imagining of God: discerning what leads to spiritual health and vitality and to a vigorous and active compassion—what fosters faith and truth and love.

As the work proceeds, and even as it is begun, it becomes progressively more possible to answer with greater clarity and conviction the four questions posed in Chapter 2. Is Christianity true, free of important falsities? Are we keeping Christianity true, faithful to a realized and realizable Christianity? Are we true as Christians, true to ourselves when attempting to be most loyally conformed to the Christian tradition? Do Christianities true? You may decide for yourself what the appropriate answers are likely to be. But if, as I suspect, responsible and honest investigation and reflection result in answering each of these questions somewhere between "not really" and "no," then I suggest that there is one other alternative possibility for an answer, one that is still more truing in its effect and that motivates and sets the agenda for reconstructive theology. That answer is "not yet." It should be pronounced firmly, but with a twinkle that reassuringly suggests that a better answer is on the way.

18

RECONSTRUCTING

AFTERLIFE AND

RECONSTRUCTING TRADITION

The last chapter was given over to the public, communal side of Christian thought, and specifically to the form of thinking that attempts to be most responsible about what can be claimed as Christian truth: theology. I tried, in the course of it, to indicate how I think sound theology should be responsive to the lived experience of Christians—not accommodatingly imitative or inventively reassuring, but at least responsive. This time, I turn to the other side of the coin: the lived experience of Christian life in its concern for personal truth, along with how that concern should ideally be responsive to what theology can and cannot say about what may preoccupy the faithful. I want to illustrate the practical application of a reconstructionist program by offering a few reflections on a subject that has traditionally occupied a large and throbbing place in Christian imaginations: the afterlife.

Christianities have been propelled and steered by their doctrines of the afterlife as by no other element of the tradition taken singly, and perhaps even more than all the rest taken in combination. The promise of immortality and beatitude was undoubtedly a major factor in the conversion of Gentiles in the earliest days,[213+] and seems clearly to be the most important consideration throughout the history of Christian adherence, especially when backed by the promise of unspeakable eternal torment for those who don't do life right, morally and religiously. Authorized to interpret the rules for salvation and damnation, Christian leaders have generally not scrupled about availing themselves of this most powerful of ideological weapons to keep the faithful disarmed and docile. But it may be questioned whether they really knew what they were talking about.

ORIGINAL CHRISTIAN AFTERLIFE LORE

What is the original Christian doctrine of the afterlife, and what are the bases of its authority?

I will bypass, for the moment, what the various Christianities have to say about how one becomes eligible for heaven; these rules are highly variable and changeable. I will also bracket the consideration of hell, and concentrate on what Christianities say about reaching the pearly gates and passing through, and where they get their information.

The surviving evidences for earliest Christian suppositions are easily available in hotels as well as libraries, for they are virtually all in the New Testament. They show considerable variation. For example:

1. When does afterlife begin?

One school of thought, still sustained in nearly all Christianities' official doctrine, maintained that it begins with the general resurrection—though there are variations on that too, since while a general resurrection has been the dominant expectation in subsequent Christian tradition, it is supported by surprisingly little New Testament evidence,[214+] while Paul[215] and John[216] and some of the Synoptic texts[217] envision a resurrection of the righteous only.

Another school of thought supposed that it began shortly or immediately after death: Luke's Jesus tells the "Good Thief" that the two of them will be in paradise together *today* (Lk 23:43), and Paul tells the Thessalonians not that the righteous dead will come out of their graves when Jesus returns in judgment, but apparently that those who sleep in Jesus will *accompany* him when he descends to greet his still-living followers.[218] Most Christianities have also held on to this version of afterlife, usually without noticing (or at least without publicly examining) its incoherence with the first school's views.

A third school is found in one of the major strata of the Fourth Gospel, according to which afterlife has *already begun:* judgment has taken place through one's acceptance or rejection of Jesus, and the accepting have already been raised to eternal life while the rejecting remain stuck in the death they were born to.[219] Such a doctrine is at least partially present in Paul's writings,[220] though rebuffed as false by 2 Tm 2:18, and it appears to have been countered by a later stage of the Fourth Gospel's composition[221] —the various schools did not always accommodate one another—and it subsequently had only a wispy place in the Christian tradition, but it clearly was present in early Christian afterlife lore.

2. What is our condition in afterlife?

One school was literal and virtually unqualified about "the resurrection of the body," and prevailed in the work of Luke, who establishes the reality of Jesus' resurrection by having the witnesses invited to feel his flesh and bones, note his wounded hands and feet, and watch him eat (Lk 24, Acts 1:10); these motifs also appear, if less clearly, in the resurrection accounts of the Fourth Gospel (20:20, 25, 27; 21:12–13).[222]+ There is not much said specifically about the restoration of the flesh and bones of the resurrected faithful, but I think it fair to guess that Jesus' risen condition was taken as a model for what we can expect for ourselves, and that at least some early Christians took literally the promise that they would drink wine with him in the Kingdom (Mt 26:29).

Another school insisted that flesh and blood would not inherit the Kingdom of God: Paul pointedly instructs the Corinthians that the risen body will be not fleshly but spiritual (1 Cor 15), the Synoptists' Jesus says that marriage in the resurrection is not an issue since its members will be like angels (Mt 22:30, Mk 12:25, Lk 20:35), and the Fourth Gospel's risen Jesus appears in the midst of a room whose doors are firmly locked.

Most of the remaining evidence is indecisive, given the possible ambiguity of "body" insisted on by Paul: the holy men resurrected at the time of Jesus' crucifixion in Mt 27:52–53 may have had flesh or may have been spirit bodied (even though the latter would evidently not have been a real resurrection in the opinion of Luke's Jesus), and evidently either one can be said to rise from a grave. It is also unclear whether the Fourth Gospel's resurrection-already doctrine constitutes a third school of nonbodily afterlife (to which Luke's Good Thief would very likely belong); but Christian tradition at any rate has generally supposed that the righteous dead live quite satisfactorily and happily in heaven without bodies, and appear to have a warrant for this in Paul's presumption, recorded in Phil 1, that he would live with Jesus directly upon leaving this world (which is of course inconsistent with 1 Cor 15, but even Apostles may be allowed to change their minds).

3. What will it be like?

This is still harder to track down, since it is difficult to tell when descriptions and hints of descriptions are offered (with a confidence that they would be taken) as symbolic or metaphorical and when they aim at something more direct. We are told that we will see God (Mt 5:8), that "paradise" (i.e., something like Eden) is an appropriate word (Lk 23:43), that we will drink with Jesus (Mt 26:29, Lk 22:30), that the Father and the Son will dwell in us and we in them, where they are (Jn 14:3, 17:23), that it will be a new and very much improved Jerusalem with a great deal of ongoing ceremony (Rv 4ff.).

But, fortunately perhaps, no consensus was established, and probably none was seriously attempted: the last word belongs with Paul, quoting from a lost and probably pre-Christian text: eye has not seen and ear has not heard and it has not come upon the heart of man what things God has prepared for those who love him (1 Cor 2:9).

The tradition, left rather unguided by the sources, has generally (if half-heartedly) located afterlife in the sky but has been properly indecisive about how to characterize it, apart from the confidence that it will be even better than our most daring dreams. It is possibly this lack of guidelines that has allowed this subject to become one of the few aspects of belief about which Christians have allowed themselves to be playful (spinning out a wonderful variety of amusing fantasies about wings and harps and clouds and interviews with St. Peter and problems in administration) and also somewhat creative—the boundaries of the tradition have been elaborated by detailed speculation on the nature of the Beatific Vision and of disembodied existence, and spontaneously enlarged by a redirection of emphasis from the tradition's focus on the ultimate encounter with God and Christ to a concentration on reunion with the lost beloved ones[223] and even by a fairly widespread adoption of a notion of reincarnation among Christians who certainly were not encouraged in this direction by the Bible or Sunday school.[224]

• • •

So what is the *real* Christian view of afterlife? What should good loyal traditional Christians believe?

Obviously, we have hardly the faintest idea. The tradition is equipped with various conflicting precedents from earliest times, and various additional alternatives acquired along the way. The proposals for belief are incoherent with one another, and it is plain that if any one of them had divine revelational authorization, it would be impossible for us to divine which. Christians who dedicate their imaginations to a given version, on the assumption that it is what God has promised to those who love him in an appropriate way, are quite possibly on the right track to personal truth but are certainly deluded about the auspices under which they received what they have chosen. Clearly, the tradition, from the very beginning, has mainly been guessing into the dark, at first swiping leads from the variety of Jewish speculations on the matter (which started from an assumption of virtual extinction at death—Midrash *Mekhilta* is fudging when it tries to foist afterlife expectations on Moses—and then ranged from the reconstitution of flesh and bone in a sumptuous setting to the Book of Wisdom's disembodied fellowship with God [2:23–3:3])[225+] and then borrowing from Greek philosophical and religious traditions as the spirit seemed to move. If we look for sturdy authenticity in any of the results, we are looking in the wrong place.

THE TRUTH ABOUT AFTERLIFE

So what is the real *truth* about afterlife?

Evidently, no reliable answer can be given. The Christian tradition has been making imaginative guesses from the beginning, and your guess is very likely to be as good as any of the others that went into the mix we inherit. Outside the tradition, there is no reason to suppose that we can find anything more authoritative than what is found within. All is imaginative guesswork, from the minimalist assumption that there is none to the ambivalent snuffing-out of the Theravada Buddhist Nirvana, and the Pure Land of a popular Buddhist alternative, and the Muslim paradise, and the varieties of metempsychoses, and the Vedantic reabsorption into the eternal *atman. Nobody knows.*

But it is too important a question to shrug off merely because nobody knows. Nobody knows what her pre-afterlife situation will be a week from now, but the idiom "wait and see" does not describe the human condition. Merely to wait obviously changes the possibilities and evacuates one's chance of making a difference in what they are. The correct idiom is "wait to see," i.e., recognize that the situation will be created by what happens in the intervening week, and thus can be known only when the time has elapsed; in the meantime, don't wait otherwise—get on with what you're about, knowing that you're heading into a week that is not entirely subject to your management but can be partially shaped according to your preferences, and in any event will probably not benumb your capacities to be ready, when the seven days have transpired, to plunge into the next week with the same aplomb. With respect to afterlife, we are even more in the dark. It is difficult, and I think imprudent, to suppress the questions that spontaneously arise in most people: Is there one? If so, who and what will we be, and what will it be like? And how do we get ready?

Such questions are essentially a recycled version of the standard What are you going to be when you grow up? This is normally addressed to people with a spectacular degree of incompetence to answer. (My earliest response was reportedly to project a career as a cowboy who spent much of his time fishing: this has not come to pass, and I have shifted to a reply supplied by a wise friend: "Very old.") Here is another, perhaps more important, question that I am incompetent to answer other than guessingly: Which is the better condition for a child, to be in a position to reply with some version of "Obviously, I have no idea: there are far too many unpredictable contingencies," or to be ready to come up with some dopey notion inspired by parental ambitions or TV glamour or his current crush? My guess is the latter is to be preferred, whatever its content. Having a sense that the future is real, even if nonexistent, is, I suppose, better for a child than having a sense that life is the job of contending uncertainly with the present, and I have the suspicion that even the limpest imagining of a future self-image is good for the development of a child's sense of ongoing trajectory in a way that clean agnosticism is not, and I think that a sense of trajectory is a useful acquisition.

To the extent that one eventually attenuates the childish condition, I also opine that it is useful to acquire agnosticism about the future. Such agnosticism, that is, as supplements trajectory rather than canceling it, enabling one to say realistically to oneself: "This is what I plan for the indefinite future, this is what I will prepare over the next three years, here is what I'll do this week, and now I'll spend the next hour at *that*—of course I can't count on a thing, since there are variables beyond my control and imagining, and the few that I have prepared myself to meet may not be the decisive ones, and besides, I might be carried off at any moment by the sort of utterly unpredictable embolism that caught brilliant and beloved Stephen Rogers in the midst of his routine to keep fit—but in the meantime I will pursue the trajectory with the verve that will have served it best if it chances to be given room to be pursued into the distant indefinite future."

The illusion of a reliable future may be counterbalanced by a realism about the unreliability of any future projection at all, so as to prepare one's stability to handle whatever happens. I think that worth doing. But I guess that such a balance should—and perhaps must—be built in that order, the motivating illusion first and the modifying realism after, in good time. The projected self-image, after all, may turn out to be realized; the illusion is not the forming of it and the aspiring to it but only the *counting on* its realizability. Those who can pursue it with undiminished vigor without somehow imagining that they can certainly get there have, I guess, become very unchildish indeed. But that is too much to ask of most of us, who need to be indulged in our entertainment of the still-childish imagining that this is where we are *surely* going to arrive some day.

INVENTING AFTERLIFE

So what are you going to be when you blow up?

The same rules, I think, obtain. The *very* indefinite future is better imagined as a carefully selected possibility than as an utter blank. Those who can accept a blank without losing heart or hope are of course free to do so, and will undoubtedly at least not be disappointed. Those who decide that the answer is "nothing" have selected one of the available choices, and if that makes their systems work best, I pick no quarrel.

But the option of annihilation has no more authority than any of the others, and those whose self-knowledge and self-governance lead them to select another of the alternatives are not to be faulted. There is nothing irresponsible in picking a goal for an afterlife beyond death, any more than in choosing one for an afterlife beyond Wednesday. In both cases, it is best to make the selection carefully, according to one's best knowledge of what it would mean to pursue such a goal, what effect it would have on life in the course of the pursuit, and whether one really has the necessary equipment.

It is to my mind entirely reasonable to form one's vocational plans in the light of a realistic assessment of one's talents (Are my synapses really wired in a way adequate to astonish the world with a violin, or hold down second base for the Cardinals? Am I temperamentally fit to be happy through the exhausting pace of the international currency exchange or the slow unsuccesses of teaching mentally defective adults? Do I have the physique necessary for a jockey or a model or a Sumo wrestler, the tough smarts to start a new computer company?) and of one's willingness to do what is required to get there from here (six hours' practice a day, *every* day? move to the slums? give up sex? shave my carefully groomed beard? wear that embarrassing uniform? raise seven million dollars? *nine more years* of school?!).

The same may be said of selecting the vocation of ultimate aspiration. The field is open, but one should pick something that fits.

What is fitting is not necessarily what is in direct continuity with how you deal with your life now, since closer inspection may reveal that you are in some respects radically dissatisfied with the way you do it now (you consider yourself far too domineering, or passive, or self-centered); or that you have good reason to think that it would be better to enlarge it to encompass more vitality (or restfulness), more gregariousness (or solitude), more trust (or less credulity), more self-confidence (or greater tolerance for ambiguity); or you may even conclude that despite the sham of pretending to yourself and the world that you are veryvery happy, your present life is actually not good for you at all.

Then comes the great temptation, and yielding to it has been a terrible mistake in the Christian tradition: one can pick an afterlife image that will *compensate*. Then one can relax, bear the present burden quietly, carry on as usual, enduring unhappiness, defeatedness, boredom—and also one's own deficiencies, faults, and vices—more easily by imagining that next time it will be different.

It is not good to imagine that there is a next time. Any afterlife, be it day after tomorrow or day after death, must be imagined as a continuity of *this* time, a continuity toward a goal to which one aspires as a life-project, constantly practicing to be adept at it, and therefore the choice of an afterlife must not be the choice of a compensating alternative to this one, but an appropriate continuation of the trajectory that must be followed to arrive there. The selection of an afterlife to strive toward is the choice of a life to follow in the meantime, made in its image and likeness, and the image chosen is false if it is not one that you are prepared to imitate from now on, until the time comes when your training simply ushers you into its perfected continuity.

With this realization comes the second great temptation: self-serving. Religious traditions that have not been constantly censored and edited by governing authorities (which obviously excludes most Christianities) have a tendency to project into their afterlife imaginings what their members like, what they want, what they especially crave for their satisfaction. These usually wind up sounding like a good time: banquets, lounging, orgies, submissive servants, strength and beauty, adulation. When this is outgrown, it can readily be replaced by something built out of higher, but still routinely provincial, values: permanent glowing health, respectability, vast knowledge, grand music, brilliant light, total security, fellowship with saints and heroes. None of these is contemptible, but I think they all fall a bit short of being inexhaustibly inspiring and presently preparable. To propose what eye, ear, and mind can't guess gets around the problem of limitation, but it's difficult to figure out how to practice for it.

The best way I can think of to locate an appropriate vision of afterlife is to keep pressing the question, What would be best? Not What do I want? or even What do I *really* want? since the truth of what we want, though it is not always easy to discover, only takes us part way to the truth of who we are. It might be useful to find out the wanting first, both for self-knowledge and to keep it from sneaking in disguised as what is best. But the answer to build on is the answer to What is best?—and not the first answer, either.

The first answer should probably not be taken very seriously. It may not be yours at all, but rather that of a voice of habit or loyalty, echoing what your church or your mother or your most admired mentor would have you say. Ask again. This time you may get the voice that routinely speaks in your behalf to say "Yes, I think it is time to break off this relationship," and "No, I am not going to do what he demands," and "Tomorrow, on my way home, I will stop in and buy it." Ask again. You will hear the voice that speaks *to* you as if you were another person, perhaps calling you by name or nickname or just saying "you," depending on the etiquette that obtains in this level of your self-familiarity. But ask again. There is a decent chance that if you keep at it, you will eventually wear out the voice of former authority and the voice of taking charge and the voice of self-instruction and the voice of self-management and the voice of self-indulgence and the voice of self-punishment and the voice of self-encouragement (or at least you may get to the point where their reiterations start sounding hollow) and arrive at a voice that is recognizable as speaking your truth, though you may never have heard or listened for it before. When that voice tells you what is best, be attentive; keep asking, and stay attentive; and if it stays recognizable as speaking your truth, take it from there.

The best afterlife-image for you to construct and entrust yourself to is accordingly the projection, anywhere up to the vanishing point, of what you are convinced is best. You may come up with more than one answer about what is best; you may construct more than one afterlife. You may find it helpful to supplement the terminal vision with additional imaginings of processes that would be of concrete assistance in getting you there— reincarnations,[226+] metamorphoses, a long sequence of dreams within dreams through which you ascend through stages of waking, an intervening period of possession by alien spirits whose failure to defeat you frees you of fears forever: whatever you need to be cured of or lured to should find a reflection in your afterlife, but it should be a fairly practical reflection that you can relate to now, so that you can begin practicing for it.

Inventing an afterlife may feel more foolish than adventurous, but it actually shouldn't (and of course if it were that would hardly disqualify it). It is as practical an undertaking as supporting an adopted diet or routine of exercise by imagining how fit you will feel and how good you will look and how much healthier that unrealized future self will be; it is no more unrealistic than for a weary student to whip up the stamina to keep at it by envisioning the satisfaction of commencement.

But these are demonstrated possibilities, you may say, and therefore quite unlike a fantasy that someone builds for his own habitation about a world that may not even exist and is not, at any rate, likely to resemble the fantasy. The difference is not as great as that natural reaction instinctively presumes. The thinner and fitter self doesn't exist either, and the one who aspires to it cannot be sure that she will get there, since the fact that others have done so—even if she herself has done it before—does not mean that this unique never-tried-before time will work; the student may fail in resolve and in courses, or the university may collapse and offer no more degrees. Their projects are not significantly more secure than the one I am recommending, which is at least as practical an adventure as those undertaken by Columbus on the perilous seas, and Caesar crossing the Rubicon, and Ben Franklin unlocking lightning with a kite. And as for the specifics of the fantasy, if you insist on calling it that, what can you propose as a better way of divining the nature of the afterlife than imagining the fulfillment of your truth? Take a poll? Ask your pastor, your father, your lawyer, your dentist?

Of *course* the other side of death will not be as you or I imagine. Neither will commencement, or slender fitness. The image is a carefully selected illusion, and only an approximation of the unknowable truth beyond it—and is of course only an approximation of your truth as well. After working toward it for a couple of years, or three months, or five days, you may need to change your imagining or add another, in order to accommodate what you have learned about your truth in the meantime, or having discovered another image that fits it more precisely. Eventually, you may experience a new image being *given* to you, rather than being confected by you, that will seem truer than all its predecessors. But it is not fair to call any of them mere fantasy, for two reasons.

The first reason is best expressed by Socrates, in the passage from Plato's *Phaedo* that I quoted in the last chapter, moments before his planned and certain death and immediately after he has described *his* afterlife imagining:

> Now, it would not do for a sensible man to maintain that these things are just as I have described them: but that either this or something like it is the case concerning our souls and their homes— . . . this seems to me quite apt and worth daring to suppose, for the risk is a noble one. And one ought to, as it were, *enchant* oneself with such things . . .

Admittedly, no one pays any practical attention anymore to the myth of the True Earth that Socrates had just recounted. But the fault in his summary lies not in its basic advice, but in his use of the plural. If his vision of the True Earth was an appropriate projection of his truth, then it was quite apt and worth daring to suppose—but as something like the case concerning *his* soul and *its* home. Anyone who is not Socrates must be left to her own construction of "such things" and should stay aware that the result is not generalizable as an appropriate imagining until it has in fact been proposed to and accepted by others as an apt supposition of what they find to be best. Your afterlife, tailored to your truth and to your various quirks that have to be dealt with in order to get there, may not fit anyone else at all; but all that matters is that it should fit you. It cannot be expected to be received as more than an analogue of or a metaphor for someone else's truth. On the other hand, you may come up with something that, when discreetly shared, clearly strikes others as truer, more truing, than any other they have encountered. At that point, it begins to become *theologically* interesting, because its original private appropriateness is revealed to have a more general capacity to confirm and inspire faith. That is what reconstructive theology is looking for. Please bear that in mind.

The second reason for not dismissing a private home-baked image of afterlife as fantasy is that if you do it properly, with care to concoct an imagining that really corresponds to what you find best, that lies at the end of a practical trajectory, and that you can and will play out seriously, then it becomes certifiably unfantastic as soon as you start living toward it. Afterlife does not begin after death; it begins after *now*. Please do not dismiss that statement as trivial wordplay or suppose that it is meant to be cute. The intended point is as serious as, and analogous to, Paul's repeated insistence that Christians have already received a down payment on what is promised, tasted the firstfruits of an abundant harvest, and have already begun to share in the great completeness that is still to come. Your practice for and pursuit of your afterlife, if it is sincerely and effectively designed, sets you en route to its progressive realization: you already start to share in what it will be when completed, get a taste of what its full realization would be like, and begin to incarnate and *realize* its ultimate promise.

Who made the promise? According to the axioms of reconstructive theology, God is truing, working in and through us; and if you succeeded in finding your trajectory of truing and expressing it in your projected afterlife in such a way as to guide you toward a still truer version of your present life, then I think it may fairly be argued that your promise to yourself is more surely the promise of God than what Paul proclaimed. It is home baked not only in the sense that it begins where you really are, but that it leads toward your truest home. The way, the truth, and the life are one.

What can be expected at the end of the trail? What is the final truth of this way of life? We don't know where the trail ends. It may, for all we really know, end with death (though there are intriguing evidences to the contrary),[227] and death may end your trail at any time at all. If it does, what you can expect is that you will be closer to your ultimate afterlife (if you continue to pursue it through the continuous afters that occur on this side of death) than you are now, and it will have turned out that this *better* is the closest you could get to what is best. That may fall well short of your imagining, but if your imagining was the authentic expression of your truth, it is vindicated by your approximation of it, and you by your fidelity to it. God will have been well served.

And if, on the other hand, death is a gateway to what eye has not seen nor ear heard nor the human mind and heart entertained, then what better way can there be to approach the gate? Although we get this thrillingly grand assurance from Paul, he got it from elsewhere[228] and was considerate enough not to bend it to the peculiarities of his own theology. It ends, you will probably remember, by saying that this unthinkable glory is what God has prepared for those who love him. Not those who belong to the right church, or profess the right creed, or who have taken Jesus as their personal savior, or who have a correct understanding of afterlife, but those who love God. God is the giver of truth; to love God is to love, and do, truth.

19

RECONSTRUCTING

CHRISTIAN

REMEMBERING

Through most of this book, I have been alternating between remarks about recon-
structing Christian theology and remarks about reconstructing Christian
life. Sometimes I have intermingled them indiscriminately, partly to emphasize the interconnectedness of the two. But I have usually tried to keep
them apart, partly to emphasize that they are sufficiently distinct to make it
possible for a saintly Christian to be entirely uninterested in theology and
for theology to be done competently by one who has no concern about
living a Christian life. Chapter 17 accordingly concentrated on theology as
the public and communal search for an appropriately comprehensive and
critically sound mode of thinking out a shared understanding of Christianity; and while that chapter cast glances at implications for living, I tried to
remain aware while writing it that a well-informed Muslim could participate effectively in the invention and refinement of good Christian thought.
Chapter 18, on the other hand, was given over to matters of personal
religion with the recognition that some aspects of religious imagining may
be privately truing and yet have no usefulness at all to the public theological enterprise.

I consider it helpful to keep that distinction between the task of critically
appropriate thinking and the task of living faithfully. The Coptic church

apparently went through a long passage of history when its clergy were innocent of serious theology without losing their dedication to Christian living or their capacity to inspire it in others; Pope Alexander VI absorbed an ample theological training without its having cramped an imaginatively profligate lifestyle. Such examples should be neither incredible nor surprising, however regrettable one may find them. There have, after all, been effective politicians who never paused in their practical work to develop even a rationale for what they were doing, let alone a theory of political principles, and the notorious ivory tower image of academics recognizes that one may know the theory with marvelous thoroughness without being able to implement it in practice.

But having acknowledged that the two are genuinely distinct, let us be done with insistences on the distinction. What is far more interesting is their integration, and if you have made your way through the first eighteen chapters, I owe you one that offers a clearer picture of what a reconstructed Christianity might be like if its participants took responsibility for bringing good theology into the reordering of their piety and reflected on what the results may provide for making theology better. I will give you two, this chapter and the next, in the hope that between them they may pay the debt.

Some readers will doubtless consider the notions I have proposed too radical to be taken seriously; I register my apologetic regrets to them and hope that someone else may catch their imaginations more successfully. If I haven't persuaded them by now that the overall argument of this book is sound, appropriate, and promising, I won't try to pull that off in the final pages. I have reserved no argumentative tricks up my sleeve by which I could seduce them against their better, or at least their decisive, judgment. Others will find this book much too conservative. I differ from them in who I am and in what I think best, and if they are not convinced that what I think is at least better, I have no new strategies that are likely to win them over. I have already given it my best shot. This is as far as I can jump, even with a tail wind. If you fall into either of these groups, you are welcome to read to the end but I ask you to be aware that I am no longer keeping you much in mind. The rest is for those who want a provisional glimpse of how it all might work.

ON REFORMING REFORMATION

I presume that my critiques, proposals, arguments, and ideas may be faulted in ways that I haven't thought of, though I have taken advice from various people in the hope of finding out some of the faults, and at least have managed to make successive drafts better through the help of my friends. What I have offered is therefore necessarily provisional, and I welcome further improvements in it. But it is too late to change this version, and before I leave you to your final decisions about how and whether you might make use of these or analogous ideas about how to reconstruct a Christianity for all seasons, I want to try to locate the project generally, so as to suggest how it may best be imagined.

There have been reform movements in Christianity from the beginning. The New Testament records attempts to detach it from its inherited observance of Jewish Law,[229] followed by counterattempts to bring the resulting freedom back into closer conformity with conservative Jewish practice.[230] There were proposed revisions of early Christian doctrine that made it conform better to Gentile imaginations[231] or to the observed facts of life.[232] There was even a movement to question the central role of Jesus as proposed by the early tradition.[233] What we somewhat naively call "The Reformation" was a set of happenings with deeply traditional precedents that ranged well beyond the elusive pristine and unspoiled Christianity that it attempted to restore: reforming, both the tightening and the loosening of the imagination's belt, was a traditional Christian pastime from the start.

I of course have my own opinions about the value of various attempts to reform Christianity, and it is pointless to mention them. It is pointless not only because you are bright enough to guess what they must be if I am to be faithful to the last eighteen chapters, but also because I don't think that there is any point in picking quarrels with the reformers. They are all part of the tradition. I am on their side, all of them. I disagree with many of them, perhaps most of them, but I approve enthusiastically of their motives and wish to belong to their tradition. They were trying to make Christianity true.

And that is very different from two false reformative extremes that are sometimes confused with genuine reform. I *will* pick a quarrel with these extremes, and insist on dissociating myself, and this book, from both of them.

The first extreme is not, as you may have suspected, the back-to-the-basics type of reform that inspired Fundamentalism and analogous movements. They too were attempting to make Christianity true, and while I think that they contributed more to making some Christianities more false, I honor their intent. No, the first example is rather the type of revisionism that completely jettisons all the traditionally important elements of Christianity, or reinterprets them into vacuous notions like Ethical Monotheism or Becoming More Human, in order to adapt Christianity to the temper of a skeptical time. They are usually based on a concern for truth, and eager to weed out falsity, and to that extent I approve of them too. But what is left after they have pulled what they take to be weeds offers little nourishment, and is certainly not Christianity.

The second extreme sometimes arrives at similar results, but is discernibly different. It is the attempt to make Christianity more *convenient,* by a liberal relaxation of personal morality or an interpretive justification of an unsavory status quo or an adaptive apologetics for some other individual or collective piece of self-serving. Such movements often hang on to a traditional package of Christian symbols, because that makes it easier for its participants to persuade themselves that they are still presenting a Christianity. And they are: but it's a vapid one. Such a reform may preserve Christianity for future generations, but it has no real interest in making it true.

A reformed reformation derives a good deal of its integrity from staying aware that both extremes miss the appropriate mark. A specifically Christian faith need not entail a replication of traditional beliefs, but it must embrace them at least as having been important just as they were, still worth singing with seriously playful verve even if one can no longer literally subscribe. It requires belonging to the tradition, not just recalling that it is traditional and swiping its labels so that it may be dispensed with. Reformed reformation is all in the family and learns how to live with cranky parents and infirm grandparents and strident cousins and bigoted aunts and utterly wrongheaded brothers, not merely in the prudent realization that one's own turn may come next but because that is what families should do. It is appropriate. Swindling those who are gullible, threatening the weak into complicity, or "putting away" the burdensome into a comfortable oblivion is not appropriate. That is not belonging, and it is neither Christian nor true.

Belonging truly and Christianly does not require that one agree with everyone in the extended and still extending family—Augustine, the Council of Chalcedon, the Iconoclasts, the Oxford movement, Millenarianism, the neo-Pelagians—or pretend to do their bidding in order to keep a precarious peace. There is plenty of room for squabbles and confrontations and disappointments and unresolved disapproval. There is not room for what are usually euphemistically called "clean" breaks if they can be avoided. Breaks in a family are never clean. They are at best tidy, and such tidiness is decidedly not next to Godliness.

Reformed reformation learns how to belong forgivingly to the Inquisition and the execution of Michael Servetus even when appalled by them, takes the Jehovah's Witnesses seriously despite their sillinesses, remembers sobering and embarrassing family lore like the Crusades and the Great Schism, and comes to terms with eccentricity rather than rebuffing it as self-disqualifying heresy that cannot be Christian. No one in the family has the right to take refuge in the pretense that some of the other relatives have lost their claim to inclusion in the comprehensive *we,* or to be possessive about its most congenial members. And thus we belong to one another, like it or not, and might as well let the experience be chastening and instructive, helpful rather than retarding in the reformational effort to keep Christianity Christian while making it true.

ANAMNESIS AND INVENTIVENESS

One of the most important forms of traditional Christian thought, evidently from the initial stages of Christian life, is *anamnesis,* the ritual remembering of the significant past. Antecedent Jewish tradition had been a good training ground, for while the Jews of Jesus' time loyally continued to follow the Law's ancient injunction to offer animal sacrifices in the Temple, they also continued to observe the annual ritualized recollections of the events that were especially formative of their religious imaginations: at the feast of Pentecost, the giving of the Law on Mount Sinai; at Channukah, the rededication of the Temple after its rescue from the defilement it had suffered in Maccabean times; and especially, at the feast of Passover, the Exodus from Egypt that had been their dramatic religious new start after some five centuries of silence.[234] The traditional animal sacrifices were to disappear shortly thereafter, with the destruction of the Temple in A.D. 70, and are missed by few; but Jewish anamnesis is still alive and well in the celebration of those feasts, and it would be difficult—perhaps impossible—to conceive of Jewish religious identity without it.

The same is true of Christians. One of the earliest surviving Christian texts, Paul's first letter to the Corinthians, reproaches the addressees for their casualness about the "Lord's supper" by recounting solemnly what Paul had himself received and passed on to them, the remembrance of the founding event on the night that Jesus was betrayed, concluding that the eucharistic reenactment shows forth *(katangellô)* the Lord's death until he comes and may not be entered into lightly (1 Cor 11:23–27). The anamnesis accompanying the Eucharist as it was celebrated in the early Christian community of the *Didache* is of different content, remembering the new knowledge that Jesus had made available rather than his last supper or his death,[235!] but it is equally solemn and equally foundational for the Christianity of that community.[236+] But of course anamnesis need not be explicitly sacramental. The solemn recitation of the Lord's Prayer[237+] is fully anamnetic if it is mindful of being a participation in the way Jesus taught us to pray.

Seven points about such Christian anemnesis seem to me especially in order:

1. The practice of solemn remembrance happens to be part of the Christian and Jewish inheritance, and was an element of the tradition from earliest times, but these historically contingent facts are less important than the abiding appropriateness of anemnesis as both a symptom and a cause of Christian belonging. It is especially in anamnetic forms of ritual that a Christian community recalls, enacts, and reinforces its collective self-engagement in the specifically Christian tradition and transforms its shared imagining from a mere recollection into a grounded self-definition. Anamnesis is the continuing reinvention of Christian identity, much like the renewing of a vow.

2. While it might be edifying to treat *all* Christian recollection anamnetically, reinventing our kinship with Christian failures as well as with the tradition's most positive landmarks, the nature of the situation requires severe selectiveness. It would be appropriate to reaffirm from time to time in a general way our belonging to everything that Christianity has been (and will be), but a program of communal anamnesis hardly has time to go through the whole catalogue of known possibilities. That makes it obviously important to choose the key items with thoughtful care as the shortlist is continuously reinvented by successive Christian generations. The elements of it should ideally be traditional, but the list itself need not be. It is not inappropriate for a Christian community to invent a new anamnetic creed that reflects its most careful discernment of what is essential; it is probably inappropriate to give a place of great privilege to a creed that can no longer adequately reflect that discernment.

3. The choices are not only about *what* is anamnetically reaffirmed, but also about *how*. That involves a further element of inventiveness, since anamnesis is not about inescapable implications (which are normally few and often trivial) but about meanings that may be appropriately attached to what is being remembered. Paul chose to associate the Eucharist especially with the specific event of the Last Supper and the death of Jesus, which followed directly after. That is not inappropriate, but neither is it inevita-

ble: the *Didache* reminds us that eucharistic anamnesis may legitimately ignore the events that were initiated on that occasion and concentrate rather on what had gone before and has been handed on ever since in the form of the knowledge that has come to us through Jesus. Paul chose to exegete[238] the Eucharist's special meaning according to an Easter theology; the *Didache* chose to use an Epiphany theology instead. They are both legitimate interpretations, both ancient precedents. We get to choose which we prefer to pass on toward the anamnesis of our great-grandchildren.

4. Anamnesis and inventiveness are both indispensable. Without some inventiveness, there is nothing adequate to remember anamnetically, even at the starting point. Anamnetic slogans like Remember the Alamo! or Remember the *Maine!* or Remember the Holocaust: Never Again! are anamnetically empty if they evoke only the recollection of a fortress in Texas, a former battleship, and a complicated program that it would be good not to repeat. They call rather for a sense of further invented meaning with which they have been deliberately endowed, and to which the slogan calls us to dedicate ourselves. And so it is with the elements for Christian anamnesis: the remembrances are endowed with sufficient meaning not simply by having happened but by our—that is, Paul's, the *Didache*'s, Melanchthon's, Schillebeeckx's, my, your—creative interpretation of what we can most appropriately take them to mean. But the invention of those meanings is not sufficient by itself. If we are to be Christian, it is not enough to remember such meanings or to be aware of them. Any interested Buddhist can do that. We must belong to them.

5. Anamnesis is the act of renewed belonging. So whatever it is that we may be remembering, it is not adequately meaningful without inventiveness (either inherited or creatively contributed by ourselves); and without anamnesis, the meanings are not enfleshed and *realized* in us and in how we live. Without carefully critical inventiveness, the meanings are not true; without anamnesis, they are not truing. Without anamnesis, there is no tradition of Christianity; without inventiveness, Christianity cannot be made true.

6. The point of anamnesis is to make Christianity true, primarily in the sense of the special allegiance that the act of anamnesis manifests and helps to re-create and by which Christianity is sustained as a living reality. But the verb sense of *true* is at least equally relevant: what is anamnetically reaffirmed is not just the Eucharist or the Lord's Prayer, nor is it these taken in conjunction with their historical initiation by Jesus (which the *Didache* does not mention in its eucharistic anamnesis), but rather includes also the

effect of the anamnesis itself, the solemn retransforming of the imagination toward making the participants more truly Christian (renewing their belonging, reestablishing the priority of Christianity in their self-definition) and more truly themselves (resettling and reinventing themselves in an integrity that is sounder, better, more appropriate than it would be without Christian belonging).

7. Anamnesis can help make Christianity true in all these ways only if what is being solemnly reappropriated is interpreted in a fashion that is genuinely true and truing. No use trying to reaffirm a creed as if one believed its claims if one does not; but it may be positively helpful to recall solemnly[239] that these claims have been supremely important in the beliefs and Christian belonging of our predecessors, as a way of remembering and rededicating ourselves to a way of life that has traditionally intended to play for the highest possible stakes, and that once found a provisionally apt manner of expressing this, and renewing its reality, through what was meant in the creeds. But it would be still more helpful to redesign the anamnesis we enact and hand on so that its content and interpretation correspond more directly to what we can affirm with appropriate integrity and appropriate ambition, free of the accommodating qualifications that usually have to be made with other people's creeds. The tradition offers enough material that is still unqualifiedly true and truing to permit it to be tailored to a better fit (and I mean a *better* fit, an anamnesis that calls and dedicates us to becoming better, more true, in addition to providing room for who we are, support where it is needed, and enough elasticity to accommodate desirable growth) without compromising the tradition itself. This first phase of Christian history—i.e., the one we are still in—has not yet exhausted the possible styles of being authentically Christian. There are responsible ways of re-forming our interpretations of the tradition without evacuating it or reducing it to what is merely convenient. Those who try to do so will of course be accused of deforming Christianity rather than reforming it, and will be told that they are no longer Christian if they make such a move. But the accusers do not hold the patent. (They may, if they are in duly constituted authority, withdraw the privilege of belonging to their church, but they cannot withdraw the privilege of being Christian.)

I think that the current phase of Christianity can, and should, be made more true, and that the next phase will do better at making Christianity true if we can provide it with a more appropriate starting point. I care whether others think my proposals Christian and truing, but I wait to be persuaded by those who think they are not. In the meantime, I offer them as both Christian and Catholic (though I think them compatible with non-Catholic Christianities as well) and leave it to Catholics and other Christians whether such a reformed reformation is worth their undertaking. If they think not, I hope I will learn why.

RECONSTRUCTING AN ANAMNETIC CREED

Those who wish to participate in a reformed reformation of the Christian tradition would do well to begin with an inventive anamnesis for themselves, defining themselves in accordance with a dedication to a solemn interpretive remembering of what there is in the tradition that seems most true and truing. That is what they will want to pass on to their children. Your private and personalized style of belonging may well include an anamnesis of your grandfather as a model Christian, and if you are convinced that he was truly a worthy model of the Christianity you especially embrace, then by all means put him in your personal and even, provisionally, your family creed.

But you can't expect your friends to adopt him as well. There is a personal anamnesis for personal self-definition, personal realizing; that is where you settle how *you* are Christian, in a way that fits best. And there is a communal anamnesis for the rededication of the community as such, defining the Christianity its members share and rededicating them to it together. If one wishes to make one's reconstructed Christianity more public, inviting others to share in it, one must be ready to compromise. Others will find blind spots, theologically inadequate or inappropriate features, needed additions or subtractions. The community gets to decide what its corporate belonging is. My style or yours will probably require some readjustments before we can agree on how much of it is *ours*.

My own personal Christian anamnesis is beside the point, as yours is. Not that yours is none of my business and vice versa—though that too may be true—but that being Christian *together,* as distinguished from being Christian simultaneously, has to do with what we can share anamnetically. I would like to find that out. The obvious way of doing so is to propose an anamnetic creed, or Christian pledge of allegiance, explaining what it is intended to mean, and wait for your corrections and suggestions. If it is too far off your mark, send me yours and I can try starting from there. But even then, it would undoubtedly be helpful to my truing if you would let me know how and why my offering was unsatisfactory. In the meantime, think this one through and keep a close eye on whether it speaks to—and for, and about—your own belonging.

1. *My faith is in God,* . . . I prefer starting with faith rather than belief, for reasons elaborated in Chapter 1. I'm not sure that I would mind saying "believe" here, but I would rather put it this way in order to make two points. (a) While what I believe is only what I imagine and is only provisional (it may prove wrong or inadequate with further critical inspection), my faith is the way I engage with all reality and puts all provisional imaginings under judgment. Any given *state* of faith is of course also provisional—always aspiring to become more comprehensive, accepting, dynamic—but faith as a *project* is not provisional, because the project is to aspire always to become more comprehensive, etc. Faith reaches out to the reality of God in the recognition that any beliefs about God are only way stations, temporarily the best I can do but easily surrenderable if I find an alternative that is more truing. What I believe is only leased, and I don't want to declare more than a provisional loyalty to it. But my faith is how I shall always address all that is true, whatever the intervening beliefs may be, and I want to dedicate myself to directing it toward God as the most ambitious and encompassing fashion of engaging with reality. (b) Part of the meaning of the initial phrase is that my faith is not simply in me, but is in God: it is the way that God the Truer works through me. It is in God the way all reality is in God, but it is also the dynamic operation of God in and through me by which I am made more true and therefore more in tune with God. This opening phrase thus means to recognize God as the source of my faith and rededicate me to *realize* the appropriate directing of that faith toward God.

2. . . . *the giver of all that is true.* I discussed in Chapter 10 my identification of God with truing as a preliminary definition. But I don't want to put it the same way here, for four reasons. First, I would like to distinguish God from the process of truing: the intimacy with which God is involved in truing tends to blur the distinction, but on solemn occasions it is appropriate to remove the blur for a moment. Second, I would like to leave room for God to be understood as Creator (whatever one understands that to mean) of heaven and earth, things visible and invisible, all reality, whatever is true, without putting the creed out of reach for people who have trouble affirming any of the notions of creation they imagine. This phrase allows one to think in terms of creation but does not require anyone to do so, and has the further advantage of encouraging the realization that the creative work of God is not confined to some sort of initiation in a mythic

or temporal Beginning but is still going on, linking new realities with those that have already come to be and linking both with our grasp of them as true. Third, I want here not to appear to be giving a final definition of God (the one in Chapter 10 was of course only a beginning to build on, but temporarily appeared to be final) but rather to be selecting an attribute with which we may appropriately begin: putting it this way does not exclude the appropriateness of understanding God as Love, or Value, or Beauty. In traditional creeds, calling God the Creator of Heaven and Earth does not mislead anyone into supposing that God is not also Forgiver of Sins or Providential Protector. I want to leave similar options open without implying that they are less important ways of imagining God. Fourth, I want to open the question of the personalization of God without closing it too. This phrase allows the opening sentence to be available to anyone at all, including those who understand God as a personal giver and those who refuse, or are unable, to do so. Just as a committed atheist is not over-strained by saying that Nature (understood as a system of happenings that work according to scientific laws) is the giver of material reality, so the same atheist might affirm this opening sentence, meaning by it that God (by definition, just another name for the capacity of things to become and be real) is that by which reality is produced. At that level, of course, it is a trivial truth and Christians will normally take it to mean much more. But Christians will mean *at least* this, and it is good to begin at a place where *everyone* can theoretically plug in, even if some of them are only affirming a trivial truth. (It may be worth noting that the two Tibetan Buddhist monks to whom I submitted parts of Chapters 8–10 as a conference paper were happy with the definition of God in terms of Truth in the sense I gave it. I was much the happier with it as a result.)

3. *I entrust myself to God's love, which saves and abides, . . .* Whether Tibetan Buddhists and committed atheists can affirm this too, I don't know. I see no reason why not, at least in the sense of "love" offered in Chapter 10, but it is enough to have a first sentence that respects where they're coming from. The second one invites them along further, but it doesn't matter if they drop out now: the point was not to persuade them that they're Christians but only to make it clear that Christians start at the same place they do before taking further steps that they may or may not be willing to follow. (On the other hand, it would be delightful if they find no impediment to following all the way through this creed: being Christian need not exclude being something else too. But from this point on, I am no longer concerned with explaining why I think that the creed remains

within the reach of their integrity: I would be glad to do so on request, but henceforth I leave the matter to their own critical reflection and concentrate on its specifically Christian applicability.) Since this is an unconventional creed, not a catalogue of beliefs but an anamnesis of basic principles, it is appropriate for it to be explicit about self-entrustment whether or not one takes the conventional "I believe" to mean that too. No Christian should have any trouble recognizing that love, at least in the sense of Chapter 10, is appropriate to affirm as an attribute of God or in realizing the appropriateness of giving oneself over to it committedly. "Saves" is deliberately left ambiguous. You get to say what you think God saves us from. If you want to imagine Satan, sin, hell, evil, permanent oblivion, or anything else desirable to be saved from, you may infer them here. If you are content to think of falsity, unreality, fear, loneliness, cynicism, hatred, nihilism, or purposelessness, and feel uneasy about going further, you are not required to add more. God as giver of all that is true obviously saves in some important ways, even if not exactly when or how we may prefer. That saving evidently deserves to be named love. As for abiding, that should be indisputable: the giver of all that is true can hardly be withdrawn from reality, and even if one takes that to be a logical implication, it is worth recalling and affirming explicitly. We don't always stay adequately aware of even logical implications.

4. . . . *and give thanks for its generous mercy in all that I do.* Gratitude is, as I admitted much earlier, optional; but it is appropriate. But we need to remind and rededicate ourselves in this too. "Its" is meant to be inclusive, both in the sense that God's love is not a subdivision attribute with smaller scope than God's truth-giving but rather another way of looking at God's total activity, and in the sense that it permits me to avoid saying "his" or "his-or-her" or repeating "God's" (which would be stylistically awkward). It is plainly not depersonalizing to refer to my mother's love as "it," and it is potentially important to keep the phrasing such that a personalized sense of God is readily allowed but not required. "Generous mercy" may not be as evidently appropriate, but I think it belongs. It fits, in that giving all that is true is hardly stingy, and it is unquestionably merciful to save and to bring about truth at all. This invites a reimagining of reality as the product of God's love, recognizing that love accordingly as generous and merciful in its tendency to true, and thus identifies something to be hugely, totally, grateful for, thus suggesting how much is to be meant by the pledged thanksgiving. "In all that I do" is intentionally equivocal, meaning that I acknowledge that God's generous mercy is at work in all that I do (which

goes without saying, but is better said), while also able to mean that I am mindful, in all that I do, of God's generous mercy, and am trying to be incessantly grateful for it. The former is easy to acknowledge; the latter is scarcely something I can claim, or even muster adequately on my best days, but it is a condition to which I aspire, even though I will fall extremely short of realizing it. Good to have that sense available as a rededication to pursuing it. The first sense is enough to make the statement true; the second is a chance to make it at least more truing.

5. *I honor all those who have shown me the pathways to God, . . .* The specific weight of "honor" is left indeterminate. It can be as little as basic respect, or as much as worship of an incarnate deity. Fill in the appropriate sense. The phrase at large may be taken to include those who tried to be good pathfinders or pathkeepers but showed ways that I cannot, or will not, follow. Their attempts deserve honoring, and I learn something useful from them about what will not do for me, without being forced to say that they are intrinsically mistaken. (I think some of them are pernicious, but this is no time to be saying so: such a judgment does not preclude being respectful of their ultimate intent or grateful for the chance to decide that they should not be followed. The statement allows one to feel invited to reappropriate all Christian and non-Christian attempts, each in its own way, while also allowing one to have multiple reservations about the value of some or all of them.) The present-perfect tense, "have shown," does not exclude present showing: the experience of being shown is always subsequent to the act of the shower and therefore present perfect even if it is right now that you are seeing the light. A present tense would not be improper, since it's what I see now that matters to my honoring now, but present perfect is better as a recognition that I may well return to ways that I have temporarily set aside as not for me. The self-centeredness of "me" may seem objectionable but merits a considerate hearing. (It is my self-dedication that this trial pledge is provisionally about, after all, even if yours turns out to be identical and communal with it, and we have been shown—in the sense of being brought to consciousness of—what we have been shown in differing ways even if all the showers are theoretically available, directly or indirectly, to both of us equally.) I would not protest the substitution of "us" for "me," but I prefer the concrete specificity of the latter for its ability to remind me who is supposed to be taking responsibility for having been shown: this way of putting it doesn't get me off the hook if I have failed to notice some of the proposed ways (though admittedly, "us" would probably make that point more clearly). The reasons for the plural "pathways" should be evident

enough, and the word itself has an honorable place in various religious traditions, including the Christian. "Pathways to God" covers the spectrum all the way from getting inklings to understanding profoundly, and the spectrum from groping in the dark with modest success to becoming an ideal role model. It is also unprejudicial about the relative importance of being a good preacher (or theologian) or a good example of Godlikeness: it encourages theological seriousness, since that is one of the relevant pathways, but does not demand it in either the honored shower or in me. The spirituality implied is versatile and quite democratic.

6. . . . *and give myself faithfully into the life they have shown.* "Give" is a good self-dedication word, and "faithfully" should pick up the resonances both of "in full faith" (which is in turn "in God") and "steadfastly, truly." I like the dynamic and purposeful overtones of "into," and "the life they have shown" permits appropriate selectivity from what has been shown while (a) acknowledging that Godwardness is a manner of life and a source of life, (b) allowing that it may be lived out in various authentic styles, and (c) staying noncommittal about how the showing has taken place and thus reaffirming solidarity with all the showers without inspiring invidious comparisons.

7. *I give glory in faith, as God gave it and gives it today, to Jesus of Nazareth,* . . . This ups the ante on honoring, as a preparation for the first decidedly Christian statement. Giving glory is a familiar synonym for praising, but here it is under contextual controls that makes it mean more than that. "In faith" is both the old mild oath ("assuredly, definitely") and the more loaded theological meaning. "As God gave it" means both "since, because" it was given and "in the way that" it was given, i.e., trying to follow in God's footsteps imitatively. Just how did God give him glory? That's your side of the meaning: you are free to understand that it was as the Only-begotten of the Ultimate or as a prophet or as a stellar religious example. The creed only binds you to celebrate Jesus as God did, to see in him an epiphany *(the* epiphany is possible but optional) of divine glory and to pledge yourself to respond with a condign and equivalent glorification of Jesus when you imagine him. "And gives it today" is a reminder of the steady continuity from then until now, affirms that glorifying Jesus is still appropriate and under divine sanction, and summons the speaker to a recognition that it is happening again, renewed right now, and to a realization that the very act of reciting such a creed is a glorification of Jesus and one of God's ways of giving him glory. "Jesus of Nazareth" merely adopts the traditional way of naming him, concretizing him in history without preju-

dice to your freedom to think of him as Messiah, divine, Lord, Pantocrator, whatever you please. The singling out of Jesus is intended to highlight a specifically Christian loyalty and devotion, but does not imply exclusivity and does not necessarily entail anything beyond what the Qur'an enjoins upon a devout Muslim. But it clearly, and purposely, invites more.

8. . . . *leading the way to God's reign,* . . . Beyond the fact that we've already had enough about showing, *leading* has some happy additional qualities and recognizes that Jesus was far more than an example. You can make it mean that he founded a church if you like, but you don't have to; you can hear in this word the firstborn from the dead, the "Lord working with" his followers in the last verse of Mark's Gospel and promising to be with them always to the end of the world in the last verse of Matthew's, the Johannine Jesus who goes to the Father to prepare a place for those who believe in him. But if you can't, or won't, say more than that Jesus was a leader who directed people to seek the Kingdom of God, that is unquestionably true and the words do not exact more. "God's reign" is of course what "the Kingdom of God" means, and does not seem to me anything to balk at: we can talk of peace or prosperity reigning without getting into awkward notions of kings and subjects; and if you really want to imagine a community of resurrected Catholics in the sky, it is not forbidden by the wording (though not particularly encouraged). The bottom line is that Jesus, by word and example, pointed out how to live Godwardly. No one could possibly deny that. You don't have to suppose that he was the first ever to do such a thing, or that he made all other versions obsolete, or even that you're obliged to go about it in exactly the way you think he was promoting. All of that is open possibility, but not imposed. The definite article should not be a problem: most Christians will perhaps instinctively read it as "leading *the* way to God's reign," and find that reading congenial; but if it isn't congenial, it can be construed as "leading the way/to God's reign"—i.e., showing and pursuing a path that leads to a complete responsive givenness to God. A by-product of this phrasing is the possibility of adding the sense that glorifying Jesus leads to the Kingdom of God, another option. The shift to the present participle "leading" allows this last phrase to be understood in the present tense, "who is now (or still) leading," but it does not compel any notion of present direct action.

9. . . . *and celebrate him in the blessing conferred on us all,* . . . "Celebrate" is both a slightly stuffy synonym for "praise" and a very ordinary word for having a party on some specific occasion. The former is appropriate, but has already been established (though not yet with reference to the

rest of what this passage evokes). The latter is now made explicit: the solemn recollection of Jesus, and what he stands for, is an occasion of personal and communal joy, a religious feast. The rest of this text is vague, but I think that appropriate. The vagueness—some sort of blessing that we all get in some sort of association with Jesus (derived from him in some way, maybe?) is the context of the celebration—is useful, since it allows a desirable range of relevant interpretations, from the fundamental capacity to recognize that what we mean by God is indeed manifest in the career and person of Jesus, to the Fundamentalist conviction that through him a chance of being saved from hell was given to anyone who accepts him as his or her personal savior. "Blessing" is meant to be a weighty and spirit-lightening word—a reminder that there is a glory already built into the fabric of life even if we don't habitually notice it, and an invitation to notice it more consistently. "Conferred" seems to me better than, e.g., "bestowed" in that it sounds a touch more belonging and unwithdrawable; "us all" might be ambiguous if this were recited communally, but carries in any event an open-ended invitation to think beyond the local community to all Christians and beyond them to all persons, living and dead and to come. Taken all together, this is intended to imply that a Christian life well lived is a lifelong religious feast; but it does not say that Jesus must be central to it, only that it is appropriate to remember him gratefully as we are in the midst of it and in the midst of celebrating God for it.

10. . . . *with our hope that we all will soon share it in spirit and truth.* "Hope" is meant to carry its customary religious intensity, not a benign velleity or wishfulness but a realizable possibility that inspires dedicated action in its direction; "with" is accordingly not just "accompanying" but also "by means of"—with our hearts, with our minds, with our hope. The "we" picks up from the recent "us all," and conditions the meaning of "share" by making it clear that this is a big order, not just what three people reciting this creed together may already share but an eschatological universalization of sharing, the "soon" being intended to add to the sense of dedicated responsibility and the "will" (not a weaker "may") being not just future tense but a part of the verb "to will." "Share" carries both a static and stable sense (as in sharing a common friend or conviction) and a dynamic active one (as I am sharing my thoughts with you and inviting you to reciprocate). The implication that the crucial blessing may be imparted from person to person in addition to already being there upon both of them is advisedly courted: this is not a subjunctive well-wishing ("may the peace of the Lord be with you") but a bolder recognition that we have

been empowered to give such blessing to one another effectually. "In spirit and truth" is intended to raise the standards beyond what already obtains, so as to obviate any illusion that I, with some others, have already arrived where we ought to be and need only to enlarge the circle of participants. It deliberately evokes the Fourth Gospel's use of such language, for similar purposes, and introduces whatever sense of "spirit" one may wish, including a Pentecostal one if necessary. By now, I need hardly gloss what is intended by "truth."

11. *Amen.* This isn't necessary, but there's nothing quite like it as a cachet of religious solemnity, and it has the additional virtue of linking the English text with a language that was there long before English existed, one that is of supreme importance to the matrix from which Christianity emerged, and one that is shared by all Christianities and plainly transcends both their internal and external boundaries. That, I daresay, is argument enough in its favor.

Other clauses could be added, but I'll stop here. This seems to me to get at the essentials I want in the anamnesis I would like to share with other Christians. Try it on your sensibility, as well as your faith and belief, and see how well, or ill, it fits. Here it is, uninterrupted by commentary:

My faith is in God, the giver of all that is true. I entrust myself to God's love, which saves and abides, and give thanks for its generous mercy in all that I do. I honor all those who have shown me the pathways to God, and give myself faithfully into the life they have shown. I give glory in faith, as God gave it and gives it today, to Jesus of Nazareth, leading the way to God's reign, and celebrate him in the blessing conferred on us all, with our hope that we all will soon share it in spirit and truth. Amen.

It is a pledge of allegiance, a self-definition, a solemn remembering of where I am and where I want to be and what I am to do about it—and an invitation to a communal affirmation that others share this with me. Do you? Can we build together on such an anamnesis? If this one is too defective, let us not scrap the idea, but rather try to find one that will do. One that will do not only to limn the Christianity in which we are held together, but also to introduce our great-grandchildren and set them on their way toward being Christian and true—on which subject there is one more chapter to consider.

20

GETTING IT

TOGETHER

This is the last chapter, and I intend to go light on the expressly theological in order to attend to some of the concrete practicalities of Christian life—for however theologians may behave, they really *do* know that Christianity is not theology. Christianity causes theology (or perpetrates[240] it), and ideally should be instructed and disciplined by theology, but the last word belongs to the living out of what good theology should be preoccupied with: the truing of lives in God's name.

I have not said much hitherto, and will not say much in this chapter, about the works of justice and mercy by which Christians should make a visible and vigorous difference in the world, both singularly and in concert with one another. That would be another book, one that I did not intend to write this time and do not threaten to write at some later date. The subject is of extreme importance, but I am more confident of my inability to handle it well than I am of my inability to deal adequately with the subject at hand. I will accordingly settle for acknowledging that not treating it leaves an especially conspicuous blank place in my overall treatment of Christianity, and with that will turn my attention to some points bearing on that central and privileged set of activities in which Christians are most thoroughly and explicitly Christians: worship.

By "worship" I do not mean only what goes on in church (though that will be the main preoccupation of this chapter): I mean what goes on in the life of a Christian in moments in which Godwardness is not only an accompanying intention, as it should be in all conscious actions, but the central focus of what is being done. Some of what belongs to worship is not altogether obvious, and can be incorporated only with a bit of imaginative effort. But some of it is very obvious indeed, and I will begin with some of what is supremely obvious: prayer.

I. PRAYER

You may have been wondering how one can pray within the reconstructed Christianity I have been advocating. The answer is: very traditionally.

Traditional Christian prayer—that is, the prayer of the earliest known tradition—was always addressed to God. The standard formula was *to* God, *through* Jesus, *in* the Holy Spirit. That is as it should be.

Let me comment on them in reverse order.

A. Earliest Christianity did not develop a very clear idea about who or what the Holy Spirit is. Sometimes it is a form of emanation from God, as it evidently is in the accounts of Jesus' baptism, coming down upon him and designating him God's chosen Son. As such, it is an inspiring communication of God's providential intent: after the baptism, the Spirit leads (Mt 4:1, Lk 4:1) or drives (Mk 1:12) Jesus into the wilderness, and thereafter Luke has Jesus returning to Galilee in the power of the Spirit (4:14) and announcing in Nazareth that the Isaian prophecy of one preaching the good news with the Spirit of the Lord upon him is now fulfilled (4:18). On the other hand, Paul modulates from the phrase "the Spirit of God" to "the Spirit of Christ" as if they are the same thing (Rom 8:9), and then refers to Christ being in Christians as if he intends this to be another synonym (Rom 8:10), concluding with further remarks about God's Spirit as the indwelling and life-giving force by which they are led and self-disciplined and adopted as God's sons (Rom 8:11, 13–16). The Fourth Gospel sometimes treats the Spirit as quite distinct from Jesus, a spirit of truth that proceeds from the Father and will be sent by Jesus (e.g., Jn 15:26), and at other times simply identifies the Spirit with the postresurrection Jesus as loved by the Father (e.g., Jn 17:26).[241] Further early variations could easily be cited, but the point is that the tradition warrants various ways of saying that the raising of the Christian consciousness to God is in itself that approximation of human spirit to coincidence with God's presence that merits being called the Holy Spirit. We pray in the Holy Spirit. It is especially when we are in this mindful state that God's mark is made upon our minds and hearts.

B. Praying through Jesus is traditionally praying in his name (e.g., Jn 16:23). That seems sometimes to have been understood as a bit like using a password to get through, and sometimes to have taken a more mystical turn, as if the name of Jesus is really Jesus' identity as Son of God and the faithful followers have been transformed into it by belonging to him (e.g., Rom 8:15–16). I see no theological difficulty in concluding that it is appropriate for Christians to continue to pray through Jesus in the sense that they recognize that he is the special inspiration of their shared, and usually their individual, Godwardness, and that their prayer explicitly aspires to be animated by the faith with which he himself prayed, a faith that was—as ours longs to be—God working well through him.

As for praying *to* Jesus, there are fairly early examples of this, including the next-to-last sentence of the New Testament. But the basic tradition addressed prayer to God, as Jesus did, and the text just mentioned is probably an example of a reinterpretation of a prayer to God. *Maranatha,* an Aramaic expression meaning "Come, Lord!," appears in almost exactly the same immediate context at the end of 1 Cor (16:22) and in the *Didache* (10.6). It was undoubtedly a traditional Jewish invitation to a visitation of God—and, once Jesus was given the title *Lord,* was (like many other texts addressing God as Lord) susceptible of being misinterpreted or reinterpreted as an address to Jesus. Hence it is probable that Rv 22:20 represents another instance of *maranatha,* but this time presented in Greek rather than Aramaic, and explicitly applied to Jesus. How shall we assess the appropriateness of such rendering unto Jesus the things that are God's?

The matter does not turn simply on the question of Jesus' divinity. On the one hand, the Apocalypse does not seem to suppose Jesus divine but prays to him all the same; and on the other hand, after Jesus' divinity was firmly established as unimpeachable dogma, the Latin church prayed in its most formal liturgy in the second person singular, to God through Jesus in the Holy Spirit. The plural would hardly have been objectionable: God was officially and popularly understood to be three persons in a unity of divine nature, and might well have been addressed *always* in the plural. But that is not how it was done. Prayer was understood to be appropriately addressed to the First Person of the Trinity, through the Second and in the Third. There were even arguments about whether appropriateness could be pushed further, and John Milton, for instance, concluded that it was not right to pray to the Holy Spirit.

Still, when Milton wrote *Paradise Lost,* he started with an invocation to the Holy Spirit, no matter what he may have said elsewhere against such a practice, and the Church in the meantime had countenanced prayers not only to Jesus and the Holy Spirit but also to Mary and the saints. Theologically, this is defensible as long as some distinctions are made. Medieval theologians discriminated three kinds of reverence, *latria* (worship in the full sense of the word, reserved for God alone, though with all three trinitarian persons eligible), *dulia* (veneration, proper to saints), and *hyperdulia* (the highest veneration, restricted to the mother of Jesus). Worshipful prayer might accordingly be directed to any of the three persons of God, and *intercessory* prayer—i.e., through, rather than to, a heavenly mediator, asking her or him to pray to God on one's behalf—could be directed to anyone in heaven. But there is a catch, according to strict traditional theology.

The catch is in what we mean by *anyone.* Mary was thought entitled to a veneration beyond what could be given to other saints (but not of course worship, which belongs to God alone) because of her special status as interpreted by the titles and attributes bestowed upon her through the centuries: Mother of God, *Theotokos,* Mediatrix of All Grace, *Full* of Grace, Queen of Heaven, Immaculate Conception, and so on. As a potential mediator, she had an additional edge over other saints. It was long believed in both the Eastern and Western church (though not formally promulgated by the Vatican until the middle of this century) that Mary was taken bodily into heaven at the end of her earthly life. Therefore she could be thought fully and personally on call for mediatorial work, free of the ambiguity that surrounded saints whose *souls* were understood to be with God but whose *bodies* would not be available until the general resurrection. Is a soul without a body a real person? Careful opinion was generally negative. Other saints were thus at best personesque. Heaven held only two indisputably qualified human beings. One, in heaven since her aptly named Assumption, was Mary; the other, there since his resurrection (or shortly thereafter) was her son.

Jesus had got there first and perhaps with infinitely higher status. He was accordingly thought, even by early Christians who had not come around to attributing divinity to him, the ideal mediator—in 1 Jn 2:1 he is the Paraclete who presses the cases of Christians with the Father, like a powerful and influential defense attorney. And mediation was crucially important:

given human unworthiness and the majesty of God, Jewish tradition had long since developed an elaborate angelology to explain, among other things, how human prayers come into the presence of the Transcendent One. They are delivered by mediating angels, said the rabbis (one of them playfully arguing for using traditional Hebrew for prayer, on the grounds that the angels don't understand Aramaic). Christians had mediating angels too, inherited from Judaism—but they also had Jesus, and the early Christian interpretation of Jesus maximized his mediatorial functions, nearly making angels obsolete. He had brought God's message to us; he had paid the sacrificial price to redeem us; he had taken our cause to his Father at his ascension and left his name behind as a calling card that God would not rebuff; and eventually he was understood as having closed the gap between God and man by being both at once.

I suggest that there is wisdom in the traditional theological distinctions, fussy though they may seem to be at first, and that the wisdom is the same as that embedded in traditional liturgy. One prays through Jesus rather than to him; one prays in his name, in his spirit, in his honor, in his wake, in his solemn and grateful remembrance, but one prays *to* God rather than Jesus. The sound reason is that Jesus is, no matter how high your Christology may be, a human being. If you also hold that he is the Second Person of the Trinity, you will nevertheless probably acknowledge that he is not identical with the Son as from eternity, before mortal flesh, or even immortalizable bodies, were invented.

Jesus evidently ate and drank, slept, walked, and was nailed to a cross. In a less public way, his deepest reality may have been coequal with the Father whom he proclaimed—but specifically as *Jesus,* he should be thought of in terms of flesh, even if divinely inhabited flesh; and as incarnate, he is a mediator. Not only was mediation the constant implicit theme of his God-centered preaching and teaching (for preachers and teachers are essentially mediators of the subjects of their discourse), it has been the constant explicit theme of Christian thought. The appropriate way for Christians to pray in formal circumstances (whatever they may do in private with saints or worthy ancestors or deceased infants, as a provisional supplement to the stricter truing of liturgical prayer) is to God, through and in and with Jesus as mediator and the Holy Spirit as mediation itself. Such a role does not demean Jesus. It honors him by accepting him as what he so devotedly tried, and proved himself, to be: one who leads the way to God's reign.

C. Praying to God needs little further comment as a principle, once one has overcome the natural diffidence about rushing in where disbelievers in God's loving mercy fear to tread. But it warrants a few asides as a strategy.

It does not seem to me theologically sound to pray as if God can and might change the course of events if adequately persuaded. I have already given my reasons for saying so, and will not rehash them now. But I have already also argued that it is not necessarily illegitimate to play with fantasies of such a God temporarily, for special tailor-made purposes. What should the guiding principles be for doing so?

The key principle is whether it is truing. It is decidedly not truing if it strengthens one's sense that God is presently withholding something that could be released if there were a divine change of mind. That way of imagining God is not spiritually healthy and is not to be encouraged. But if one is adequately clearheaded about that, it strikes me as wholesome enough to address one's specific longings prayerfully to God as a sort of admission that they are there, they feel important, and it is in and through the constant empowerment of reality by God that the outcome will in fact be decided.

Does such prayer make a difference? Not, I suppose, to God, whose care and support are universally unconditional and cannot be enhanced. But it makes a difference to the one who prays, in at least two substantial ways.

The first is that it lays the matter on the proper line, submitting events to the empowerer by whom (or, if you prefer, by which) they are brought about. Addressed with suitable mindfulness, such prayer can help us rediscover and realize how God reigns undespotically over us and over the universe. The second is that earnest prayer for something particular, performed solemnly in a reach for the presence of God—that is, in the Holy Spirit and through Jesus—is bound to clarify our sincerity and with it our motivation, and readjust our imaginations so as to set us more fervently afoot to do what is appropriate toward bringing it about. Prayer that proves enlightening about our responsibility is surely spiritually edifying and theologically appropriate. The old slogan is not paradoxical: pray as if everything depended upon God (it does, but not upon God's whims) and work as if everything depended upon us (it does, but it should be remembered that the *us* is very large and the crucial difference-making activities may or may not be within the scope of one's own powers to do or to influence, and that one's powers to influence are undetectably larger and subtler than one's powers to do).

If one can get such principles incorporated into the habits of imagination, prayer can make all the difference. In monitoring one's own degree of success in picking up the proper habits, there is a simple rule of thumb. Good prayer of this kind—good prayer of nearly every kind—ideally produces both an energizing and a relaxation of tension. If the relaxation comes in the form of a feeling that one has successfully passed the buck, mailed the dunning letter, got the matter off one's chest, that is not so good. If, on the other hand, it comes in the form of a realization that the outcome, whichever way it goes, is bound to be an occasion of grace for oneself and for others, that is not so bad. If the energizing is in a strengthening of desire for what one is asking without a corresponding strengthening of purposefulness in pursuing it without clinging to it, one should regroup and try again. But if it comes as an enspiriting sense that God is with us and we with God, and that we are accordingly empowered and embraced, and that realizing this convinces us that we can afford to lose anything else whatever, then one may fairly conclude that the energy comes in the name of the Lord.

Some brief thoughts on the manner of prayer:

1. In principle, almost anything can work satisfactorily, even if it appears inappropriate at first blush, so long as it is framed within the serious playfulness that defines the occasion. Imitations of Moses' frustrated and testy reproofs of God on Mount Sinai[242] can be effectively truing if conducted with proper irony, and we should never stray far from the remembrance of the "Jongleur de Nôtre Dame," who put on his best performance before the altar of Mary in the dark of night, alone, and collapsed in weeping exhaustion "because he knew no better prayer than tears, no better worship than his art."[243]

2. But I recommend the deliberate avoidance of two common tendencies that seem to me to diminish the truing power of prayer. One is archaism. "Thou dost" does less to dignify what is said than to distance it from the contemporary mind and heart—an ironic reversal of what was probably the intent of using the second-person singular in days when it was a live expressive option for intimacy within families and friends. Archaism in rhetorical and thematic manner—imitating the courtly flattery of the Psalmist, for instance—is also probably dysfunctional. Prayer works best when speaking out of who we are, and should only occasionally don the august and somewhat uncomfortable robes of another era. The other tendency to be avoided is subjunctivity. "May the Lord bless you," etc., is timid wishful thinking with no more punch than "Have a good day." "The Lord blesses you," etc., is direct, calls us to attention, and is more theologi-

cally sound. Never use a subjunctive when a stronger indicative lies ready to hand.

3. Speaking of stronger indicatives, let me pause to modify what I said a moment ago about imitating Moses with proper irony. You probably took that to mean that we should, when complaining to God, stay aware that we have no right to complain, and do it only to release frustrated feelings. Sometimes that will be true—e.g., in a prayer that I used quite a lot for a while and should probably use more often now, "Why do you let me be such a fool!!"—but there is a deeper sense in which I intend this.

Humble submission is not always appropriate. We have a right to justice, and we have a right to clamor for it demandingly before the face of God. Justice is among the things we are entitled to, and it should not be treated as if we have no idea what it is, or as if outrageous injustice is really justice in disguise, or as if God doesn't owe it to us. It is a potentially damaging mistake to treat what belongs to mercy and grace as if it belonged to justice, since that can lead to pernicious envy (the most underrated of the Seven Deadly Sins) and sulkiness (the most self-excused of the Seven Sickly Faults). But it is perhaps worse to treat what belongs to justice as if it were a matter of optional mercy (for a considerable while, this error totally gummed up the capacity of Catholic moral theology to say anything sensible about the obligations of the rich to the poor[244]). Forget for a moment that it is not always easy to identify injustice: remember cleanly that there is sometimes no question about it whatever. And get ready to assert your rights: God owes us justice.

The foundation of this claim is what I have called elsewhere[245] the Primal Covenant—i.e., Genesis' characterization of the creation of humankind as in the image and likeness of God combined with its assurance that God pronounced the rest of creation good once it was inspected. The Primal Covenant, whether or not one thinks Genesis reliable on such matters, is a reflex of sound theology—without recognizing and insisting on its terms, no serious critical theology is possible—and, more to the point, is indispensable to the underpinnings of sound spirituality. If God is the giver of all that is true, then God is the giver of justice; and if reality is fundamentally good, then it ought to be made better as it is trued. And if we are made, and work at making ourselves, in the image and likeness of God, then the eradication of unquestionable injustice is something that we have a right to demand. We should be careful about discriminating between what is really just and what we just happen to want, but if the discrimination is made prayerfully, the voice that cries within you for justice is the *bath qol* I mentioned in Chapter 11, the "daughter of the voice," the echo of the authentic voice of God—not the thing itself, but at least the next of kin. The resulting demand may thus be made on the basis of nearly unimpeachable authority.

Demands addressed to God need, I think, a touch of irony to keep them from being absurd. The ironizing that is proper in a demand for justice is not an undermining of the demand itself, nor an apologetic qualification of our sense of right. It is in two aspects only. One is the realization that the Primal Covenant includes our being in the image and likeness of God, therefore striving to become more so, therefore becoming more true and more just, therefore required to be energized and purposeful in bringing justice about and eradicating injustice where we can. A good prayerful demand for justice should therefore result in a greater clarity about what we can, and should, do about causing it. The other aspect is the realization that reality has been authentically pronounced fundamentally good, therefore already endowed and empowered with the capacity to become better, therefore already charged with the grandeur of God and ready to flame out —or at least start to smolder noticeably—with truth and justice. On both counts, God has kept the divine side of the covenant, and the ball is in our court. But the name of the game is justice, not mercy only, and prayer should remember that it is hardball.

4. The form of good prayer is highly versatile. The versatility should be exploited. Private meditation, which I touched on in earlier chapters, I will bypass here (with one more commendatory salute) in order to concentrate on communal and shared prayer-forms. One underdeveloped communal near-equivalent of private meditation is shared silence, which deserves more attention than it gets. The Quakers have a wonderful tradition of making rich use of silence, but most congregations I have known behave as if silence were terrifying, boring, or rude. Most of us are extremely awkward at sharing silences that spontaneously occur in the course of interpersonal conversation as well, and it would probably be a good thing to practice allowing and enjoying such silences with understanding friends: it's good training for friendship as well as for praying. It helps us remember how much unproductive silence there is in our lives, underneath the surface noise, and also how little we are really in control. It also, of course, helps us get in touch with the deep quiet ground of truing. Breaking that pervasive silence may be prayerful too: there are times when a mere moan or a shout of joy (a good Appalachian tradition) are right as prayers, but one should be cautious about the social and religious readiness of other participants

before letting loose where it is not customary, and cautious about conventionalizing and routinizing such expressiveness where it is. The homely conventional prayers deserve respect also. No one need feel childish about continuing to cherish "Now I lay me down to sleep . . ." or stuffy about giving thanks before eating. Grace at meals is graceful, and offers a comfortable small-community occasion for spontaneously sharing with intimates a grateful sense of God's presence, or even for a reminder to non-Christians, through a traditional grace or a formulaic prayer of your own composition, that God may be acknowledged with unembarrassed and unembarrassing dignity.

5. Having dropped deliberately provocative remarks about the erotic here and there since the early pages, I feel duty bound to address the matter more frontally before we're through—and what better place than in a context that is devoted to the versatility of good prayer?

I will not bother you with a makeshift history of Christian denial, which has run consistently from the initial inheritance of Jewish uneasiness about sex (especially as practiced promiscuously by Gentiles: note that the Jewish-Christian leaders of Acts 15 make some remarkable concessions to Gentile Christians, but the shortlist of requirements in verse 29 includes abstaining from fornication), through Augustine's suggestion that it is sinful even within marriage, to the current Catholic insistence on celibacy in Latin Rite priests[246+] and the common (though, happily, not altogether universal) Protestant squeamishness or indignation about even highly regularized (and a fortiori, irregular) sexual behavior. Suffice it to say that a religious tradition that has reserved special honor for virgins (with or without martyrdom) from the beginning, and has been especially preoccupied with and excited about elaborations of the commandment on adultery while relatively casual about most of the others (have you read about any public scandals over covetousness recently? and have you ever noticed that the Mount Rushmore memorial, your favorite picture of Jesus, your holiday snapshots, and Mickey Mouse sweatshirts are all forbidden by God's orders to Moses on Sinai, while fornication isn't?—check out Ex 20, especially verses 4 and 14) may possibly carry a somewhat distorted view of some fundamental human realities.

But my topic here is not sex, but rather the erotic. Let me treat the general subject first, and then return to the more particular department in that light.

The erotic is about love, erōs. The Christian tradition is in favor of love, and its founder is reported to have endorsed that principle with considerable emphasis. It is of course true that the Greek version of his words (we have no record of the Aramaic alternatives, but it is not intrinsically unlikely that he spoke both languages on varying occasions) does not use *erōs* or the corresponding verb, but rather uses *agapē* and its verb, *agapaō*. Some Christian commentators have attempted to argue that this difference is highly significant, and have explained at length what they take it to imply,[247] which is (in a very small nutshell) that erotic love is worldly and insufficient for true spirituality, while agapic love—"charity" in the Latinate tradition—is the sort of love God has and the kind Christians should cultivate.

I do not wish to badmouth *agapē*, but I want to defend *erōs*. The main problem with the attempts to make a big point of their difference is that the words did not have modern theologians' careful distinctions when they were used in the biblical texts. The Hebrew Scriptures command the love of God and neighbor—enjoined, as you will remember, in the two greatest commandments as posed in Dt 6:5 and Lv 19:18, and endorsed by Jesus in Mt 22:37–39—using the verb *ahb,* which is precisely the same root word used in the Song of Songs for a love so sexy that Rabbi Aqiba, shortly after Christianity got started, suggested that although that book definitely belongs in a place of honor in the canon of inspired writings, it perhaps should not be read by people under thirty.[248+]

The New Testament never uses *erōs* at all, nor the corresponding verb. The custodians of the Old Testament were almost as stingy with the same words: the pre-Christian Greek translation of the Hebrew Scriptures renders *ahb* by *agapaō,* never by *eraō,* and contains only two trivial instances of *erōs* —and a glance at the facts (e.g., Song of Songs 2:4–7, which contains three instances of *ahbh* in Hebrew, rendered as three instances of *agapē* in Greek) should disabuse anyone of the notion that those prevailing words are unerotic. In short, the Hebrew and Greek that formed the biblical books did not keep the distinction that later commentators took pains to force upon us, and texts dealing with love should be treated as having the same ambiguity as they get in English translation, where only the overall drift can disclose to us what sort of love is meant. And anyone who supposes that *erotic* love of all kinds is excluded for Christians by the persistent use of *agapē* in the New Testament might add to the foregoing remarks on historical philology a rereading of Eph 5:25–33, where the verb is indeed *agapaō* but the message is that husbands should love their wives in a way appropriate to being one flesh with them, and that this is how Christ loves the church.[249]

The heart of the matter, as it applies to Christian spirituality now and in the future, is that (a) Christians are supposed to try to love as God does, and (b) nothing in the revered Scriptures indicates that God's love is unerotic, and (c) there are clear hints to the contrary (if you can't remember the opening chapters of Hosea, reread them), and (d) despite such leads as are offered by the Song of Songs, the *Didache,* and the Epistle to the Ephesians, Christians have been chary of entertaining the thought that Christian love may be properly erotic, and (e) we obviously need to reconsider what is appropriate.

Sex aside, the Christian wariness about erotic love has a great deal to do with the ideal of detachment. We are not supposed to love the things of this world in a way that interferes, or might interfere, with the love of God. Erotic love intensifies our relatedness to that which, or those whom, we love. It sometimes creates attachments, clingings to a world that is passing away, dependencies that distract and impede us from more important self-givings. Ergo, it is to be eschewed, and if possible ascetically expunged. Systematically and thoroughly expunged, that is: a nun should not develop "particular friendships," a monk should not enjoy his food (and is invited to sprinkle something distasteful on it if that will help), and anything that is beautiful is therefore dangerous.

The premises of this argument, up to the "ergo," are sound. The love of God is our paramount vocation and should be carefully fostered and protected; and sometimes the manner in which we love other things and people gets in the way of who we are called, and want, to be. But the stuff after the "ergo" simply doesn't follow.

As James and 1 John and Jesus' words about the penitent harlot in Lk 7:47 especially remind us, indifference to others—whether spontaneous or cultivated—is an impediment to the love of God more damaging than loving others undiscriminatingly or uncircumspectly. And as Bernini's celebrated statue of Teresa of Ávila[250] reminds us, with its clearly orgasmic representation of her mystical intensity (and if you don't trust Bernini, feast on Teresa's own description of the depicted event for more of the same—and throw in the poems of John of the Cross for a tasty dessert), loving God with erotic passion is not necessarily indecorous or spiritually retarding. Nor is loving what God loves, which is everything.

Erotic love is not religiously inappropriate, if it is disciplined and unpossessive. Well-aimed eroticism energizes and trues. The appropriate way to imagine God's love of reality is not *detached* but *utterly intense*—"passionate" is potentially misleading if it renders the imagined God full of throbbing emotion, but otherwise it's dead on, the best metaphor we have for what intense love is. Let me take you back to the paradigm cases I suggested in Chapter 10, and to your own ideal image of love, the love you would like to be able to direct from your heart of hearts to God and to the world God loves. Or better still, let me take you back further, to Chapter 1 and the ideal condition of faith. I stopped short there, and now want to complete the thought. Faith at its best is not merely *robust,* as I claimed there: it is the *passionate love* of all that is real and true, especially God. Erotic love, redolent with the smell and taste of the good fertile earth we are made of, is not to be thought of as the source of temptation and sin unless we also know it to be the source of our deepest spirituality and prayer, an imitation of God that trues when the imitation is a good one.

That once said, I return to the specifically sexual dimensions of the erotic, and their relation to prayer. Never mind the daunting example of big-leaguers like Teresa of Ávila and John of the Cross. This is not reserved for adepts and special mystics; it has a rightful place in the spiritual life of ordinary bread-and-butter Christians too. And that includes its physical expression, though I want immediately to turn to the inevitable cautionary qualifications.

We are not culturally in a very good position to integrate the explicitly sexual with our spirituality. Our culture is quite gummed up about sex, and the Victorians are not to blame (though most of them, with rare exceptions like Havelock Ellis, didn't help much, and even Ellis didn't do terribly well at helping himself). Our deformation derives from a much longer and deeper tradition. And deformation it is, manifesting itself in caricatured distortions in language that show our preoccupation with, and our uneasiness about accepting, our sexuality. If someone is accused of telling a "dirty" story, it probably wasn't the one about Br'er Rabbit and the Tarbaby or an account of a mud-wrestling melee. The vice squad does not occupy itself with battling Sloth or Envy; when a young lady is said to have lost her virtue, it is unlikely that this indicates that she was caught cheating at bridge; "living in sin" does not normally mean "unbaptized." Even my beloved *Oxford English Dictionary,* which undertook to record all "the words that have formed the English vocabulary from the time of the earliest records down to the present day,"[251] balked at two of them that every schoolboy has known for at least hundreds of years—and this was not only because their printing was prohibited by English law.[252]+

Language symptoms are of course only the tip of the iceberg, or perhaps the hair of the dog. We are deeply messed up on this subject, and constantly subject to further messing up from all sides: reinforcements of our prudery, disguised as decorum, compete with tasteless exploitations of our more recent legal liberations from it to put us into a tangle of unwholesome attitudes, complexes of ludicrous denial, espionage-level self-deception, and nearly total moral confusion. So let us have no glib talk of liberated (usually a euphemism for self-indulgent) sexuality, or facile notions of developing a general Christian Tantra, or even modest campaigns for reintroducing the ancient, and unsuccessful, experiments with *virgines subintroductae*.

But let us at least think, for starters, of beginning in a relatively safe and uncomplicating place, transforming marital sexual love at least occasionally into a mutual form of prayer. That would be challenging enough, and likely to have (if taken slowly, and carefully thought out, and genuinely mutual) a decent chance of being successful—and if successful, a stunningly profound prayerful experience that could at least begin the slow, generations-long, restoration and redemption of the malformed sexual eroticism that now seems so alien to the spiritual life. By the time my great-grand-children arrive, it would be wonderful if it did not seem shocking or stupid to acknowledge that God is sexy. In the meantime, we have enough work to do just rehabilitating the awareness that faith, and truth, and the love of God ought to be as passionate as one's personal style permits.

Having discharged that duty, I will drop the subject—except to invite you now to think of it again when I talk about sacramentality a few pages further along—and turn to one final and entirely uncontroversial form of prayer: the use of formulated texts.

6. Formulaic prayer tends to be underrated, possibly because it also tends to be recited drearily, or with odd and alienating features such as stilted accents or sixteenth-century grammar or words that show up only in such prayers (e.g., *lovingkindness, vouchsafe,* and the *O* of obsolete apostrophic rhetoric). It should be better, and perhaps more often, used, but with good texts and as much communal awareness as can be induced that this is a place where we meet God together on mutually familiar ground and that we're used to doing so. Trying to recite the Lord's Prayer with pretended spontaneity, as if one were making it up as one goes along, or melodramatically, as if in a high school drama-club tryout, is a mistake and is bound to sound like showing off. It is not appropriate to sing a hymn with the vocal technique typical of nightclubs.

And that is the next subject, once I underline again the importance of good texts. Admittedly, some people may not particularly notice how things are said, as long as they are generally churchly. But those who do include an appreciable number—me, for instance: one is enough to be appreciable—whose prayerfulness is not well served by blowsy rhetoric, inane theology, sentimental maundering, self-conscious cuteness, or creaky and pointless affectation. Examples are not hard to find, especially when we look into hymnody, which we are about to do.

2. SONG

I came up in a tradition of two hymnodic tendencies. One, which smote me with awe as a child and still claims, and inspires, my reverence, is the classic liturgical side of Catholicism, where the standards were strict and high. Dies Irae, Veni Creator Spiritus, Salve Regina, Pange Lingua, Stabat Mater, O Filii et Filiae—admitted occasional theological infelicities were partially covered by the required Latin and the equally required doctrinal docility, and at any rate adequately compensated for by the grandeur of the melodic line and the disciplined monody of the singing. The Gregorian Commons (Kyrie eleison, Credo, Sanctus, Agnus Dei) and at least some of the Propers (Vidi Aquam was to me the most notable if I'm not allowed to count the once-a-year Exultet), were equally arresting and inspiring—and if many of the latter were overfussy and overfancy, they still had an identifiable liturgical dignity, enough to sponsor the conclusion that the difference between what was liturgically admissible and what was not, like the Schubert "Ave Maria," was essentially the difference between worship and self-conscious performance, and sometimes seemed as different as love and lust.[253+]

And then there were the vernacular hymns, which were mainly (with a few exceptions) appalling: the syrupy "Jesus, Jesus, Come to Me," and the "Immaculate Mary," which combined sappy theology with the bounciness of a Bavarian drinking song, and one that intoned "O Sacred Heart of Jesus, I implore / That I may ever love thee more and more" to a melody that would have been more at home if sponsoring further reflections about Galway Bay—and others that I have happily forgotten. Catholic songs were as bad as Catholic sermons. Almost, anyway. In both, dogma was substituted for thought, grimness or dullness for solemnity, and clichés of every available kind abounded in a welter of sentimentality, artificial earnestness, and empty phrases. We weren't allowed to sing Protestant hymns (or hear Protestant preachers, for that matter, even though one of them was my grandfather), perhaps for fear of raising our standards to a pitch that would make the home-grown equivalents seem as impoverished as they were.

Since then, there have been dramatic changes. Basically, we lost both musical traditions, or at least set them aside, unused; and with the loosening of Catholic rules, we had access to Protestant hymns and even churches where Protestants sang them (in rich harmonies, unlike Catholics); and a flood of new music came rolling in, some of it borrowed from the Hit Parade but most of it written for liturgical purposes; and I took on some musical responsibilities in a small worshipping community, making some selections and accompanying them on the now-canonical guitar and attempting to belt them out with enough gusto to raise other voices. It is out of that more recent experience, against the background of remembering the earlier phase, that I make the following remarks.

The condition of liturgical music is very like the condition of dogmatics and traditional theology: occasionally grand and inspiring, often embarrassingly limp or silly, and on the whole suggestive of a need for reform. Listening to congregations of various denominations at prayerful song, I come to the conclusion that perhaps it's a good thing after all that liturgical dancing was systematically expunged long ago. Most of the texts are somewhere between regrettable and dreadful, the latter including

> Lord, what a thoughtless wretch was I,
> To mourn, and murmur, and repine,
> To see the wicked placed on high,
> In pride and robes of honour shine.
> But oh, their end, their dreadful end,
> Thy sanctuary taught me so,
> On slip'ry rocks I see them stand,
> And fiery billows roll below.[254]

For illustrations of the former, one may choose from thousands of instances of sentimental thoughtlessness, but my intended point is perhaps better indicated by an example of what can be done with unsentimental thoughtfulness:

> Firmly I believe and truly
> God is Three and God is One;
> And I next acknowledge duly
> Manhood taken by the Son.

I can understand why such lyrics might bring about the tentative timidity with which hymns are, more frequently than not, sung, but I should have thought that they would tend to correct the languid and wearying pace that seems to be spontaneously customary: surely these are texts to rush through as quickly as possible.

My biases on this subject are, as you see, verging on outrageous, but that does not make them all wrong. So let me lay some of them candidly on the table, and then say a word or two about biases and community worship.

I like singing. I like singing good liturgical songs very much indeed, and when I bite into one that takes my fancy I invariably get carried away into singing too loudly and with what must appear to be an indecorous verve. I am aware that decorum in church implicitly prescribes that one must sing in a manner that does not betray conviction, animation, or delight, just as I am aware that dinner party decorum forbids the discussion of religion. But these are customs more honored in the breach than the observance, and my sense of decorum bids me to honor them accordingly, by breaking them. I do not dodge the charge of being selfish and insensitive in this, which is true, by the excuse that I am also trying to be principled and pedagogical, which is also true. But the point I am trying to make when singing thus, and in writing this, is that hymns should be treated with the kind of serious playfulness that ought to be typical of being Christian, entered into as sacramental opportunities in which we are being reconsecrated to the extent that we can rise to the occasion and help others do so too. That means that we need good texts, worthily expressive music as a vehicle of meaning the texts more exaltedly, and a manner of singing that means them firmly.

Good texts are not a nickel a gross, but one doesn't need lots of them. Most of the hymns in an average hymnal go unsung by an average congregation anyway. In these textually reformational days, when everything is being scrutinized and readjusted to gender-inclusive language, a little theological rewriting might well also be invested in some hymns that almost make it, hymns that are musically effective (the sort you spontaneously sing when feeling especially good, for instance: if you don't do this, your hymnodic repertoire is probably impoverished) but limp remediably as prayers or as poems. There is ample good stuff available beyond the conventional favorites (some of which should be retired or relegated to the everyday equivalent of carol-sings). And there is probably much that is inadequately noticed within the old favorites, especially by those who (like me) tend to wait for the fourth or fifth singing of a good tune before concentrating on the words. As example of the former, I sang for the first time last Sunday (at this writing) a hymn by Carey Landry, to music of gentle stateliness—sang most of it anyway: I was so choked by the stunningly good theology of the opening verses that I had to bypass a couple of the later ones:

The love we have for You, O Lord,
Is only a shadow of Your love for us,
Only a shadow of Your love for us,
Your deep abiding love.

Our own belief in You, O Lord,
Is only a shadow of Your faith in us,
Only a shadow of Your faith in us,
Your deep and lasting faith.*

As for the old favorites, I admit that I had loved, and often sung (churches, showers, highways), this eighteenth-century Quaker hymn over a period of years before I ever got around to studying how profound it is, even beyond the level that raised my eyebrows when I first met it and admired the dignity and joy of its melody:

My life goes on in endless song above earth's lamentation;
I hear the real though far-off hymn that hails a new creation.
Through all the tumult and the strife I hear that music ringing;
It finds an echo in my soul—how can I keep from singing?

I pledged a couple of remarks on biases and community worship. My bias about biases is this: within a Christian community, one should be both generous and true. That means that (a) someone with biases should attempt to alleviate them through the exercise of sympathetic imagination, and should be candid about what remains, and (b) the others should be tolerant and accommodating, and equally frank. In practical terms, that means not that we sort out one common-denominator level of agreement and stick to it, but that we take turns. You get to tell me that it bugs you when I sock it to "Amazing Grace," especially when I change some of the words, and in return I accept you by doing it only every other time, and you accept me by being graciously understanding on the alternate occasions. If you have a favorite hymn that I can't stand, and vice versa, that means not that we

*From "Only A Shadow" by Carey Landry. For further information see copyright page.

agree to trade off by excluding them both (that would be an anemic solution) but that we share by accepting each, every once in a while. Communities are not homogeneous, and are not honored by attending exclusively to what their members agree on (though it is good to aim for this standard in their central moments of mutual solemnity): they are highly pluralistic, and should find ways of knowing and accommodating the quirks of each of the members, not by according them vetoes but by giving each a turn.

That's enough on the subject for now. The overall message is essentially the one that a few friends have tried diplomatically to get through to me for years: it is imprudent and careless and lazy to eat junk and compensate with vitamin pills when a little effort can arrange a diet that is natural, nourishing, and tasty. But that once done, a little occasional junk, with or without a supplementary pill, doesn't hurt, especially if it's in a good cause.

3. HOMILIES

At a conference last spring, a friend who was participating in the same discussion group with me mentioned that he thought that one of the other participants, a vigorous and interesting man from Sierra Leone, was probably a Catholic priest. I was temporarily chagrined, fancying that this was the sort of thing I ought to have picked up sooner than he. But when, back in my room, I returned to the putative priest's precirculated paper and thought about his contributions to the discussion, I realized that my friend had to be wrong. An hour later, I found the two of them together, and we established that he was a Methodist minister. I told them that I had at least excluded my friend's hypothesis, on the grounds that the paper cited one of the Tyndale Bible commentaries, and the even more conclusive grounds that he was obviously far too good a preacher.

The homily, or sermon, has always been something of an interlude in the mainstream of Catholic worship, not infrequently dispensed with altogether in the course of weekday masses. The burden of worshipfulness has traditionally been carried by the liturgy itself, and the congregation ordinarily expected little from the preacher and usually got it. Things are remarkably better now, but few Catholics are likely to invite Protestant friends to their parish churches for the purpose of homiletic edification. By contrast, the centrality of the preaching of the Word in the Protestant mainstream has resulted in a varied and powerful tradition of sermonizing from which Catholic preachers still have much to learn. I want to make the simple point that the Protestant traditions are superior in their awareness that a sermon is neither a lecture nor a mere exegesis, and add the additional simple point that there is an important place for good lectures and exegeses in the development of reconstructed Christian culture (every worshipping community should have some), and then pass on to the problem of the unreconstructed preachment.

One can more easily work out the accommodation of pluralism and the editing of texts with hymns than with preachers. A given parish will have two or three preachers, two or three of whom are likely to give dull or pedantic or theologically objectionable sermons from time to time. They are also likely to be touchy about criticism and lack of deference to their magisterial authority or their clerical dignity. One must be accordingly diplomatic, but candor is still in order. Those who are prepared to take a stand on inadequate theological thought, especially if they are prepared to offer better alternatives, should try to find a way to open a discussion about it with the preacher in question—in private at first, in a group if that seems to be a reasonable next step.

Tensions will arise. They should. Christian harmony is built out of a capacity to face and relativize such tensions within the unifying blessing the community celebrates, not based on the avoidance of acknowledged disagreement. Even if nothing is satisfactorily resolved, it is better to have such disagreements in the open. They need not, and should not, be confrontational: no preacher deliberately inflicts on a congregation thoughts she or he considers unworthy of serious Christianity, and it may be useful to start with discovering why and how the offending sermon seemed appropriate to its inventor, followed by how and why it failed to negotiate its intent with the objectors. But one should set aside anger, indignation, and all patronizing poses, and treat the matter as what it is, an interesting, and potentially problematic, difference of perceptions and imaginations.

Some Christianities allow greater access to the pulpit than others. Those that do not insist on ordination as a qualification to preach may do well to take advantage of the opportunity to give a chance—maybe only one—to any member of the congregation who wishes to try. There should be good preparation for this, so that the listening congregation is mobilized to listen for what the preacher is trying to say rather than to evaluate the style. Among the results is likely to be an easing of pressure on the regular preachers, not only in giving them a break in sermon preparation but also in reminding the congregation that their offerings are usually not so bad after all, or if not usually good at least deserving of similar generous forbearance.

In all preaching, the congregation should be trained to realize that a sermon is not a performance. (So should the preacher, but that is sometimes a more difficult pedagogical task.) Nor is it an isolated and specifically individualized act. It is a form of liturgy, in which the speaker, though ordinarily not using a borrowed or familiar text, is primarily to be thought of as a temporary vehicle of the whole tradition's celebration and reflectiveness, anticipated and received more in the manner of the "how have you been?" exchanges at family get-togethers than in the way you are perhaps reading this book. That way, what is tedious or shallow or benighted may be largely overlooked in the light of the occasion and the inescapable awkwardness that often accompanies it and the communal ties that invite uncritical benevolence. Unsolicited complaints are better suppressed, except those directed to regular preachers who fail to solicit even suggestions for improvement. What is excellent may be overtly appreciated, but mainly as a gift of the tradition rather than as a personal accomplishment: good preaching should be complimented out of gratitude rather than admiration, and the gratitude should extend beyond the sermon itself to embrace what the preacher reminds us of rather than originates. Preachers are as hungry for approval as the rest of us, but (like the rest of us) are best approved as effective agents of their task, which does not happen to be impressing people with their eloquence. There is always hope even for sermons, if both those who give them and those who hear them can be brought to take them seriously and unseriously in a mindfully Christian way.

4. SACRAMENTALITY

I embark on the subject of sacramentality with a little uneasiness, since what I have to say will undoubtedly strike Catholics as too Protestant and Protestants as too Catholic. But this will not be the first time that has happened in this book.

I do not intend to say anything about how many sacraments Jesus inaugurated, or whether foot-washing should count as a sacrament (as it does in several modest-sized Christianities, on better scriptural grounds—Jn 13:14–15—than can be claimed for matrimony), or what conditions must be met for a sacrament to be authentic. In fact, I do not intend to say anything about sacraments at all: the heading of this section is a deliberate evasion, chosen to allow me to concentrate on what the Catholic tradition calls *sacramentals,* i.e., happenings that may be occasions of grace even though not theologically or ritually formalized as such.

Alert readers will probably have anticipated that I am virtually bound to acknowledge that anything at all may be a sacramental. God is at work in everything; nothing whatever is empty of grace. The trick is in being aware and receptive. Grace will have its effects even when one isn't (we would be in sorry shape if we didn't constantly, at least in some ways, get truer in spite of ourselves), but it improves the situation considerably if one cultivates a habitual readiness and attunement to the mediated presence of God in all happenings. Those are of course relative terms: if the lore is correct that we use only 10 per cent of our brainpower, we surely fall far short of that margin when it comes to our sacramental power, both in giving and receiving.

The foundation of sacramentality is another dimension of what I have called the Primal Covenant: the happy truth that reality is basically *congenial* to the well-trained and faith-filled imagination, not merely inescapable. Of course, the Primal Defect—a.k.a. Original Sin—always gets in the way of our *realizing* this adequately, but that compromises only our capacity to take advantage of the Primal Covenant, not its trustworthiness.

As a result of the Primal Covenant, grace abounds. Whatever you habitually imagine (or carefully judge) grace to be, it is bound to be some form of unmerited blessing. And there is no experience in conscious life that does not offer unmerited blessing. Received wisdom counsels us, unsuccessfully, not only to look for it but to assume that it is available even when our looking produces discouraging results. As a routine example, I acknowledge that when an earlier draft of this book was rejected by two companies with whom I had published earlier books, I was too sulky to appreciate that I had thus been presented with a splendid opportunity and motivation to improve it—and whatever you may think of it now, it is certainly better than it was and I am improved in mood and understanding as a result. Perhaps you will be too; and if so, the adjustment in you, as you filter and perhaps significantly improve upon what I say, is likely to have an effect on others; and the things you stimulate in them will be similarly filtered, and passed on, and the chain of happening may wind up benefiting my great-grandchildren's faith, so that it could turn out, ironically, that they profit more from the effects of my discouraging rejection slips than from their reading of what I have written.

I would naturally prefer them to be edified by my carefully chosen words rather than by the adventitious by-products of my insufficiencies as filtered through the revised version along the fruitful grapevine, but that is because I am egocentric. It is not because I want the best for my great-grandchildren. I *do,* of course, want the best for them; but that is a fatuous wanting if I fail to recognize that they, like me (and you), will be presented with a thousand chances per minute for becoming more true and more Godward, and that it is finally a matter of supreme indifference whether any of the chances has my name on it. Nothing matters all that much, because everything matters a lot. If we move beyond trivial setbacks like rejected manuscripts and tackle the big stuff, like pain and death and destructiveness and disease and whatever you think comes closest to sheer evil, I venture to say that the Primal Covenant still holds.

I vote with Ivan Karamazov when it comes to approving of a universe that can work effectively only at the cost of the suffering of a child, but it does not appear to me that this describes the one we live in. Children suffer, and that remains one of the most evident symptoms of the limitations of the cosmos, quite enough to stifle the glibness of "it's all for the best" or "whatever is, is right," or "look on the bright side" when used in contexts that offer almost nothing but shadow and darkness. But however monstrous it would be for the suffering of children to be *required* in order to keep things going, it is decidedly another thing for it to be *not excluded,* especially when a clean and careful imagination cannot conceive of a way of excluding such things without subjecting the cosmos to a massive and detailed overhaul that would render it literally unimaginable.

God's omnipotence, *pace* Ivan (and conventional theology), means not that God can do whatever we may carelessly and unsystematically fantasize, but only that God can do whatever can be done. Eliminating all suffering is apparently not one of the possibilities. In the meantime, while it would be grotesque to attempt to *justify* pain and devastation on the grounds that truing results are sometimes drawn from them by the resourceful and the fortunate, there is nothing dishonorable in admitting that people actually do this, or in attempting to participate in it when the occasion arises rather than spending one's responses exclusively on indignation and outraged denial. To paraphrase a splendid remark by C. S. Lewis in *The Problem of Pain,* I am merely trying to suggest that the potential sacramentality of even evident and undeniable evils is not an incredible notion: to prove it palatable is not part of my plan.

But let me return to the less troubled side of the question. If Christianity has always recognized that pain and bleakness and terror roam about like hungry lions, it has aptly spent more energy on toasting our usual success in evading them. Days of fasting were part of the Christian tradition from the beginning, but were always grandly overshadowed—or overshone—by the feast days.[255]+ Paul's gruff and disappointed criticism of the Galatians' observance of special days and months and seasons and years (Gal 4:10) was technically appropriate at one level of theory, but popular Christianity, backed by official Christianity, has more appropriately overridden his objections.

In Christ, it is true, as Paul avers, that no particular time has an ineluctable claim on one's mind and heart. But that does not mean that no moment merits special treatment: it means that any moment whatever may be singled out for celebration because every moment belongs to the time of salvation, belongs to the process of becoming true, belongs to God. The proper Christian response is feasting.

I speak metaphorically, of course—though more literalism would be in order here too. I speak specifically of the general principle of sacramentality, which empowers us to carve out not only feast days (and the roasted fowls that traditionally accompany them) for the glory of God, but any happening at all. I submit one representative example, one that hovers between the explicitly solemn and the casually ordinary, and illustrates how both can be transformed by sacramental awareness:

In the traditional Mass, there is a moment between the recitation of the Lord's Prayer and the distribution of the Eucharist in which the celebrant says to the congregation (with regrettable subjunctivity) "The peace of the Lord be always with you," and then invites or asks them to show one another a sign of peace. In the masses of my childhood, this invitation did not exist. The subjunctive was followed by no imperative; at most, in especially solemn masses with multiple celebrants, there was a stylized bowing and touching among those in the sanctuary, euphemistically referred to as "the kiss of peace," whose manner was rubrically prescribed and of uncompromisable formality. The relatively recent extending of the gesture to the congregation at large did not include extending the formal style. There are indeed some recommendations about what sign of peace might be shown, and presumptions about decorous reserve in showing it, but people are technically left on their own to do as they see fit.

For more than twenty years I have worshipped with a group that sees fit to cut loose at this signal. When we had our own space (the "Basil's Basement" of my dedication of *The Gathering of the Ungifted*) it was generally known as "the Sandbox Mass," on account of the liberty accorded to small children of permissive parents to crawl or scamper or play around as the spirit moved them, a deliberate policy that was sustained (to the occasional consternation of visitors and the regretted annoyance of the more traditionally decorous members[256+]) for the purpose of making the children feel more at home in worship than the local parishes seemed to encourage. Having scrapped the confining pews during the early stages, the Sandbox adults responded to the call of the Pax by milling about, shaking hands, hugging, chatting briefly, wandering onward to locate others— sometimes *all* the others—to greet. They took a long time at it. When I led music, it was one of my unpleasant duties to begin the singing of the Agnus Dei after a reasonable interval (reason usually being dictated by the schedule of the next Mass or the limitations of the celebrant's patience), as a signal that the "kiss of peace" (often quite literally bestowed) was to be considered over. After a few last encounters, the congregation collected itself into silence and stationary attentiveness to await the Communion.

I learned especially two things from this tradition, both of them applicable to any other practical aspect of sacramentality. One was that sacramentals can upstage sacraments, no matter how solemnly the latter may be presented. My children were not alone in spontaneously concluding that there was far more efficacious communion in the melee of the Pax than in the subsequent Eucharist, which ironically returned the participants to their old habits of isolation and privacy, without any contact of either eyes or hands. For them, and for many others, the Pax was the most intensely Christian happening in the entire hour. Note that I do not say "seemed to be": it *was*.

The other lesson was that an explicitly and intensely Christian context makes it possible not only to give and to receive more through friendly greetings and expressions of concern and welcoming smiles than is normally possible on sidewalks and in buses and across crowded rooms elsewhere, but even makes it possible to give what we do not have. We offered one another the peace of the Lord. Most of the participants did so with the traditional subjunctive, or an ambiguous plain "Peace," but some could be heard saying outright "I give you the Lord's peace." We were authorized to do so. It was not ours to give, but it was God's to allow us to give; and the giving was profoundly real even when the giver was hard pressed to keep a lid on grief or depression or anxiety or pain. As the title character in Georges Bernanos' *The Diary of a Country Priest* realizes that he has been a vehicle rather than a source and that God may make effective use of one person's emptiness for the gracing of another, he marvels in his diary: "O wonder! that one can thus make a gift of what one does not possess for oneself. O sweet miracle of our empty hands!"[257] Such gracing, such bless-ing, is at the heart of Christian Godwardness, and the moral of the story is that sacramentality means that not even desolation can have the last word when one is truly in the presence of those who are in the presence of God.

5. MORALITY

Having just mentioned the moral of the story, a brief reflection on the story of the moral is in order. I introduce the topic as a subsection of the subject of worship, rather on its own, as a recognition that living truly is, in our tradition, one of the deepest and most sincere forms of worship—and even more pointedly, as a recognition that morality is a communal matter only to the extent that it impinges on worship. The basic acceptance of pluralism means that you are not obliged to comport yourself in accordance with my conscience, and if what you do, or fail to do, bothers me enough to spur me to inquire how you find it consistent with your ostensibly dedicated Christian belonging, it is more likely that I will come away with my horizons enlarged than that you will be enlightened about the error of your ways.

But the principle of fraternal correction advanced by Matthew's Jesus (Mt 18:15), especially when supplemented by the advice about what to do when you know that your brother has a grievance against you (Mt 5:23–24 —note that the text is explicit about relating this to worship) and the warning about judging and about motes and beams (Mt 7:1–5), is not obsolete. I think that what Matthew does with it in 18:16–17 *is* largely obsolete and is probably not derived from Jesus, who otherwise is not so smug about being right in moral judgments and not so unforgiving about differences of moral opinion. Still, the differences are real and can become nettling. If they get in the way of communal worship, they should be aired. If you are convinced that I am wrecking my life, or even worse, the lives of others, it is hardly polite or responsible for you to refrain from saying so. I would expect you to hear me out, and if all you hear strikes you as self-serving rationalization I would not think it out of line for you to say so. If we part with you disapproving of me even more than before, that is a discomfort I should live with—a member of my parliament that may unexpectedly swing the vote months or years later. In the meantime, for-giveness is one of the primary Christian callings.

I incline to think that forgiveness is the supreme, and most difficult, act of responsible and creative imagining, as well as the toughest and most exalted virtue. If there is no greater love than that expressed by laying down one's life for one's friends, there is at least no more appropriate love than forgiving—and although, as one who has not yet laid down his life for anyone, I am not in a position to question the pronouncement of Jn 15:13, I admit that it sometimes strikes me as easier to die generously than to forgive genuinely. No wonder that Christianity has been so obsessed with forgiveness, and so incapable, from the very days of Jesus' preaching to the present, of believing in Jesus' assurance that God forgives and has forgiven and will forgive because that is who God is.

We cherish hurts, and we cherish guilts. If one wants to find an argument for the meaningfulness of the doctrine of Original Sin, there is probably no better place to look than this. Righteous indignation seems to infuse us with a sense of dignity that we don't want to tamper with, even if we were capable of peeling off the layer after layer of unsympathetic self-clinging from which it is built in order to find that it is not a peach with a good hard stone at the core but an onion, with nothing at all in the center. We handle guilt as if it's the ticket of admission to a cosmic muffler shop where we are finally Somebodys, who have done Something Significant. Mistaking ourselves too for peaches, we suppose in our stony hearts that praise, commendation, gratitude, even love, are all empty: it is through others' resentment, disapproval, rebuke, disgust, and, if we're really playing for keeps, *hatred* that we learn and feel our truth.

There's no use in my speculating amateurishly about why this is. The specific etiology of the disease is relatively unimportant if we have access to a cure, and the wisdom of the tradition that traces back to Jesus carries the remedy still, despite the traditional refusal to take its demands seriously enough. We must forgive.

We must forgive. We must forgive ourselves and forgive our friends. We are summoned to health in the midst of our perverse enjoyment of illness, just as we are summoned to light after having accustomed our tender pupils to the darkness. We are called to the arduous moral task of infiltrating our imaginings of self and others with a reimagining that does not blame, and *realizing* the new imagining, in the full force of the word, thoroughly enough to dismantle its predecessor.

Forgive me if I make it sound too manageable. Huge forgiving *is* like dying, laying down what sincerely seems to be one's life, or at least what feels to be an indispensable organ. It is spiritually exhausting, and in all the long dark night's wrestlings with our angels and demons, it is hard to credit the promise that we will rise again on the other side of that grave trial, embodied in the spirit of truth. But Jesus has called us to take responsibility for being in the image and likeness of his unqualifiedly forgiving God. He never promised a rose garden. His own garden was Gethsemane, and I guess, in not altogether unfounded speculation, that if he sweated blood there it was not out of a fear of death, nor a longing to have a wife and kids, but in order to be ready to pray truly, from within the desolation of his shattered mission to spread the acceptance of God's true reign, for the forgiveness of those who had so disastrously misunderstood.

We must forgive our enemies. We must forgive God for not being what we think we would prefer. We must forgive ourselves for needing to forgive and being unable simply to accept God's reality as it is. We must forgive those who seem blind and destructive in their active stands on homosexuality and abortion, those who crazily abuse children and themselves, those who use power like a stiletto and those who refuse to take responsibility because they do not know who they are and what it is that they are called to, or who is calling. We must make Christianity even this true, however arduous and constant the exertion may be—and forgive also those who sneer at us for deliberately undergoing, for the sake of truth, what they take at their distance to be the cozy comforts of illusory religion.

This is the most demanding side of what I remarked, with apparent casualness, in the last words of Chapter 18. I repeat them now, with a different emphasis.

God is the giver of truth; to love God is to love, and do, truth. Nothing more should be asked of anyone—and perhaps nothing more *can* be asked of anyone—except possibly to love and do truth with all your mind and heart and strength. And anyone who manages to approximate that will surely discover that it must follow as the night the day, without the need of a separate injunction, that thou canst not then fail to love thy neighbor as thyself.

CONSTRUCTION, RECONSTRUCTION, AND TRADITION

This last turn to Jesus' best-known quotations from the Hebrew Scriptures,[258]! presented in a mingling of the language of King James' most memorable poet with that of his most memorable project, is meant as a reminder of tradition, from which much of what I have been saying in this book may have seemed to have deliberately and pointedly strayed. If you acquired that impression, please reconsider before we part. The main argument of this book has not been that our tradition is importantly false and ought to be correctively changed. That is a subsidiary argument, but is so rude that it is likely to have overshadowed the primary argument that our tradition is importantly home and ought to be creatively belonged to, and passed on with confidence and gratitude. I therefore wish to close by putting the emphasis in the proper place.

This book has offered a variety of suggestions that clash resoundingly with the New Testament and with classical Christian tradition. I am not aware that it has made any proposals that cannot be readily harmonized with the good news proclaimed by Jesus, as I understand it.[259] I grew up Christian, am grateful for having had the privilege of doing so, and am not remotely interested in resigning or retiring. If I am fired by anyone who claims the right to preside over Christian credentials, I will try to accept my discharge with good grace; but I will remain a pupil of Jesus and will continue to invite other people to consider whether it would not be appropriate to make substantial adjustments in what we received before we pass it on, in order to bring it into more satisfactory conformity with truth, with God, and with Jesus, and in order to make it something better than it has been, to which our great-grandchildren may be both thrilled and grateful to belong. If you have taken offense, I apologize for being the occasion, and ask you not to quit thinking about it too early. If this has struck a resonant chord in you—spoken to your condition, as the lovely Quaker phrase puts it—then I hope you will do something about it. And one of the things I hope you will do is to be thoughtful about the intended continuity between the critical revisionism and inventiveness of reconstructive theology and reconstructed Christianity, and the tradition that it is intended to protect and prolong as well as correct and augment.

Those who have been alienated from the tradition, or from its embodiment in a particular church, are often conscientious objectors to doctrines that are neither true nor truing. We are surrounded, in our huckstering world, by claims that are not true, coming from every quarter, and it is a matter of individual temperament and judgment to determine which may be humored and tolerated, which should be opposed and refuted, and which simply cannot be endured and call for a clean break. As I suggested in the last chapter, one should think of clean breaks as a last resort, and think of the human capacity for complex accommodation as one of our most important resources. Those who feel alienated by the insistent falsities of significant others should remember that there are at least good grounds for handling conscientious objection in a way that keeps in touch.

Those who have stayed within the tradition (especially if within one of its particular churches) because their misgivings and botherments about false or exaggerated claims are not sufficient to overwhelm the nourishment of life and faith that they experience there have undoubtedly been making quiet adjustments for years—mental reservations when dutifully reciting creeds, metaphorical and symbolic receptions of notions proffered literally by the liturgy or the preacher, gentle skepticism in the reading of certain passages of the Bible, private interpretations of some of the moral rules of the relevant church, resigned but discreet doubts about some of the official beliefs. Such a person is therefore well equipped to make further adjustments along any of the lines I have proposed, should she be so inclined, without disturbance to her allegiance to the tradition, even in its present state, and without disturbing anyone else.

If he wishes to avoid disturbance, I hope that his own share in the work of passing on the tradition will include the preparation of undisturbance for those who follow, seeing to it that Veronica is given her proper place with the demoted and legendary St. Christopher (which would make it quite unnecessary to expel her, as long as it is made clear), and that the traditional conventions are appropriately respected (i.e., as especially dignified and solemn conventions), and that the mediating word is justly appreciated without being mistaken for the final word. If she feels called upon to disturb, and decides in her reflective and meditative judgment that the feeling impels her in the right direction, then I hope that she will disturb thoughtfully and effectively, and patiently.

Living as we do in a world where one may be startled to see a fifty-eight-story building downtown in a place where last week there was only a parking lot and a few derelict houses, we have to pause to imagine how the great medieval cathedrals were put together. The original architects knew that they would be long dead before their efforts were fully realized, and that the plans may have been changed in the meantime. The masons and sculptors of the next generation knew that they too would be long gone before their contributions were embraced and graced and completed by the final result. The great-grandchildren who continued the project, and *their* great-grandchildren who finished it, knew nothing of those who started it except perhaps the names and a few bits of family lore to go with them. All of those who participated did so in the realization that they were building a place of worship that would honor the religious tradition they had received through the fidelity and labor of people whose names had been long forgotten, and in the expectation that the cathedral would stand, for the glory and glorification of God, well beyond the time that they themselves had ceased to be remembered.

I admire the great facades they built, with their imaginative depictions of the Last Judgment and the Assumption of Mary and the New Jerusalem; I admire the crowned saints and martyrs in the chapels within, and the crafted images of two bearded men and a bird, representing the mystery of God, and the stained-glass windows that show beautifully an implausible sense of redemption and a doubtful understanding of Jesus' origins and how to read the Hebrew Scriptures misleadingly. I disagree with the builders' sense of the tradition's content, but I empathize with their sense of its overarching grandeur, and do not consider their visible statements alien to me even though I interpret differently and see as reverable conventions what they saw as truth. I see their work as an honorable stage of passing on a tradition that had changed between the beginning and their generations, and was to change further after they were gone. I am glad that they built well, so that I can participate, albeit not exactly in their way, in their vision of the inheritance.

I am trying to do similar work. Having carved this particular rock into the shape of a gargoyle, I leave it to the ongoing builders to accept or reject or modify it. If it gets installed somewhere, I hope that it will carry its proper share of water off the roof, helping to make the structure more true and enduring, and that it will eventually seem at least a quaint bit of what is still recognizable as home to the great-grandchildren for whom this book is, as I told you at the start and now faithfully remind you at the end, a welcome, and an invitation to join in Christianity's glorious and joyful and transforming and perpetually renewed feast of epiphany.

And Moses slept. And the voice of the Lord came to him and said, "Moses: make your people my people." And Moses answered, "If we keep your commandments and be your people, shall we then prosper in peace, and grow in strength, and rule the world, and bring all the nations under your dominion?" And the Lord said, "That is not how it shall be." And Moses asked, "What then shall be changed?" And the Lord replied, *"You* shall be changed." And Moses asked, "Is that all?" And the Lord said, "That is all and everything."

And Moses awakened and descended the mountain and stood before his people, and wondered how to say what he had heard. And Moses said, "My people have come out of Egypt in fear and in hope, and have learned to dream dreams of glory. These are good dreams." And again he said, "My people are a hungry people, and the Lord is a great provider." And he said, "The Lord is testing me. If I accept this offer for my people, he will know me as a man of little faith in his power and in his love and in his faithfulness." And Moses broke the tablets of the Law and returned to the mountain.

And Moses said to the Lord, "I have come back for more." And the Lord replied, saying, "There is no more." And Moses said, "Give what you are withholding. Give it for your glory, and for your love, and for your faithfulness." And the Lord said, "I have given." And Moses answered, "Give again." And the Lord said, "I have given, and I give again, and the gift is the same, then and now and always." And Moses asked, "Will there be no change?" And the Lord said, "There will be change always: that is part of the gift." And Moses asked, "Will the change be for the better now?" And the Lord replied, "The change will be for the better and the worse, for the richer and for the poorer, just as it was then and is now and will be, for I give and have given and will give in power and in love and in faithfulness." And Moses said, "My people have learned to dream dreams of glory, and they learned their dreams from you." And the Lord said, "Let them dream dreams of glory. But teach them that these are dreams of me, not of themselves." And Moses said, "Dreams are not enough." And the Lord replied, "Then be awake, and awaken your people. Taste with your tongue and feel with your hands and see with your eyes and hold in the embrace of your arms and love with all your heart and mind and strength, in my name, what I have given and give and will give always."

And Moses was abashed, saying, "That is all and everything."

And the Lord said, "Now you are awake. Go now, and awaken your people. Then they will be my people not only in dreams."

And Moses asked, "Will the dreams stop?"

And the Lord replied, "Only if you stop them. Dream. Dream in song and in story and in dancing and in the sweetness of man with woman alone. If you do not dream well, you will not know who I am and what I have given. If you dream only, you will not know who I am and what I have given. Learn this, and teach your people to dream and to be awake, and then they will be my people and will offer me the glory that is mine, the glory that because they too are mine is also theirs."

And Moses was awake and went forth to awaken.

—Midrash *Shemoth Dallah*

NOTES

1. I would like to say something about where this book came from, not because its origin will necessarily be of any interest to you whatsoever, but because I would prefer that it be read with at least something of its genealogy in mind. Since it is now published, it is of course no longer *my* book, but public though it may be, its author may be allowed an attempt to coax readers into considering his own historical perspective on it.

   When I wrote *The Gathering of the Ungifted* some fifteen years ago, pursuing especially the problem of Christians who do not believe what they are told they should believe and yet wish to belong authentically to Christianity, I decided that it would be the first study in a four-part sequence.

   The next was to be a study of how earliest Christians understood the way their Christian understanding was constituted. I did not suppose that later Christians were obliged to think in the same way that earliest Christians thought, but since traditional theology tends to suppose that they should, it was worth finding out—and I considered the current scholarship on the matter importantly misleading and in need of correction. This was published as *The Way of the Word*.

   Part three was to be a study of how it really happened, how the Christian message was founded and shifted and gradually built into the gospel we have received. That book is called *Five Gospels,* and it is (among other things) intended to show that the stuff on which Christian belief and Christian theology are founded is significantly more problematic than the modern Christians or the ancient Christians generally realized.

   The fourth part was to be a return to the territory scouted in *The Gathering of the Ungifted,* only this time in the light of the critical considerations, deliberately neglected in that book, that would surface in the intervening stages. I built an IOU into the closing pages of *Five Gospels,* acknowledging that I had stirred up theological problems and begging off from dealing with them until next time. This book is next time, stage four. It is meant, for your sake, to be quite independent of its three predecessors; but for my sake, it is meant to pay off the IOU of *Five Gospels,* offer a reinterpretation of the foundation for theology I discerned among early Christians in *The Way of the Word,* and propose a more radical and appropriate answer to the plight of Christian unbelievers than appears in *The Gathering of the Ungifted.*

   (P.S. If the exclamation point after the superscripted endnote number puzzled you, see the end of the Foreword for an explanation of the [n!] and [n+] signals that you will find throughout this book.)

2. Paul's Epistle to the Galatians is the primary locus for the Christian case. I think it extremely likely that this was rooted in a pre-Christian contention between Helle-

nist Jews and Hebrew Jews about whether the righteousness of, and Jews' sonship to, Abraham was keyed to his belief/faith (as in Gn 15) or his doing the works commanded by God, especially circumcision (as in Gn 17). See *Five Gospels,* pp. 172–79.

3. For the background and use of *pistis* and related words, see Rudolf Bultmann's article on the subject in Kittel's *Theological Dictionary of the New Testament,* ed. Gerhard Friedrich, trans. Geoffrey W. Bromiley, vol. 6 (Grand Rapids: Wm. B. Eerdmans, 1968), pp. 174–228. (This is the English translation of the monumental dictionary conventionally referred to as Kittel, or *TWNT.)*

4. This is of course paralleled in other languages as well, since the verbal dissociation had already taken place in the Latin of the Western church before the vernacular tongues took it over.

5. A representative brief example: in a scholarly review, published since I wrote the previous statement, the reviewer notes that in the major theological book under scrutiny "it is left unclear whether the object of these studies would be *belief,* i.e., faith itself, or *a* belief, i.e., an article of faith" *(Religious Studies Review* 13 [1987], p. 120). The casual *i.e.*'s are symptomatic of the general rootedness of the assumptions I am calling into question and wish to deracinate.

6. Ten different ways of discriminating between belief and faith are analyzed incisively by Donald Evans in "Faith and Belief," *Religious Studies* 10 (1974), pp. 1–19, 199–212. Since my treatment is skewed to the valorization of faith in contradistinction—and sometimes in opposition—to belief, I recommend this article to anyone who wants a more integrative approach. I have no quarrel with Evans' analysis, which seems to me quite penetrating, and I will occasionally return to the subject of belief to indicate how I see its best compatibility with faith: but for the time being, a counteremphasis is in order, both in general and as my personal qualification of the complementary half-truth implied by my acceptance of the common identification of the two terms in the argument of *The Gathering of the Ungifted.* For the distinction between faith and belief in earlier Christian history—and in Buddhist, Islamic, and Hindu traditions—see Wilfred Cantwell Smith, *Faith and Belief* (Princeton: Princeton University Press, 1979), a well-documented study that is already a classic on the subject, in which the author establishes the claim that "faith is not belief, and with the partial exception of a brief aberrant moment in recent Church history, no serious and careful religious thinker has ever held that it was" (p. 127).

7. Those who are opposed to religion may resent the way I define my terms. I do not mean to offend them, or to belittle the integrity of their position, or to drag them into places they prefer to avoid; but I can find no specific difference by which to distinguish religious faith from a faith that is not religious, so I feel bound to extend the terms. (Conscientious objectors may consider being opposed to "organized religion" or "religion as usually so-called" rather than to religion as I am using the term.) The faith in accordance with which a despondent and embittered atheist goes about her life may be the foundation of an impoverished religion, but it does not seem to me to be helpful to reserve the term *religion* until other conditions are met.

8. I will return to the discussion of imagination later. At the moment, I wish merely to

emphasize that despite the relative trivialization of the term in many quarters—psychologists still tend to restrict it to mental "image-making" and popular usage normally relegates it to fantasy, to playing with the imaginary, and to occasional instances of unconventional creativity—imagination is being rehabilitated as the comprehensive capacity that I will use the word to designate. A survey of philosophical reflections on imagination may be found in Mary Warnock, *Imagination* (Berkeley: University of California Press, 1976); its relation to science is treated in A. M. Taylor, *Imagination and the Growth of Science* (New York: Schocken Books, 1970) and Gerald Holton, *The Scientific Imagination: Case Studies* (New York: Cambridge University Press, 1978). As for my own ways of understanding what the term should mean, the most satisfactorily congenial exposition I can think of is Chapter 4, "Insight-Imagination," in Douglas Sloan, *Insight-Imagination: The Emancipation of Thought and the Modern World* (Westport: Greenwood Press, 1983), pp. 139–90 (cf. Chapter 5, "Living Thinking, Living World: Toward an Education of Insight-Imagination," pp. 191–246). This is a book that I shall commend again in later contexts for some of its other virtues.

9. See Louis P. Pojman, "Belief and Will," *Religious Studies* 14 (1978) pp. 1–14, and the same author's *Religious Belief and the Will* (London: Routledge & K. Paul, 1986).

10. Robert P. Abelson explores relevant features of more secular beliefs in "Beliefs Are Like Possessions," *Journal for the Theory of Social Behavior* 16 (1986), pp. 223–50.

11. Its basic presentation is in Leon Festinger, *A Theory of Cognitive Dissonance* (Evanston: Row, Peterson, 1957).

12. The fascinating account of all this is presented in Leon Festinger (with Henry W. Riecken and Stanley Schacter), *When Prophecy Fails* (Minneapolis: University of Minnesota Press, 1956).

13. Robert Browning's "Soliloquy of the Spanish Cloister" gives a neat cameo of such a happening in its earliest seedling stage, as the monk who speaks makes an invidious interpretive comparison in the fifth stanza between his own table practice and that of his evidently saintly confrere, whom he hates: he himself lays down his knife and fork in a deliberate cross and drinks in three sips in honor of the Trinity, while his rival does no corresponding symbol-making. I have long wondered why no one seems to have objected to a potential heretical scandal in the way the Catholic Mass is routinely celebrated. The traditional prayer at the Offertory, when the priest prepares the chalice for consecration, used to read ". . . give us, through the mystery of this water and wine, to be sharers in the divinity of him who deigned to be made a sharer of our humanity, Jesus Christ your Son . . ." The ancient routine dilution of table wine with water, still common among Italians, was in proportions of 50–50 or overbalanced in favor of water: it is not difficult to see how someone might get the bright idea of glossing the Offertory preparation with a little allegory that was comfortably consonant with orthodox doctrine on the Incarnation, even in its Chalcedonian form. (Cyprian makes an analogous point about the symbolic meaning of this dilution in *Ep. 63 ad Caetulium,* and Luther's scoffing at it was rebuffed by the Council of Trent, which reaffirmed its symbolic value in Sess. 22,

cap. 7 [Denziger 945].) But the masses of my childhood were performed by priests who were accustomed to the practice (which ancient Greeks sneered at as barbaric) of taking table wine straight, as you probably do (and as modern Greeks do). Hence it was customary for them to take the wine cruet and pour a couple of mouthfuls, glug-glug-glug, into the chalice as they said the first half of the prayer, and then to take the water cruet as they recited the second half and drip in a requisite minimum couple of drops, blip!—and to the best of my knowledge, no one ever denounced any of them for such a blatant reenactment of the Eutychian heresy, despite the virulence with which it was attacked both before and after its condemnation in 449 and 451, and despite their having been taught in their seminaries how outrageous it was for Eutyches to have claimed that the humanity of Christ was swallowed up in his divinity like a drop of honey in the ocean. (For details and evidence about wine-dilution in antiquity, see Everett Ferguson, "Wine as a Table-Drink in the Ancient World," *Restoration Quarterly* 13 [1970], pp. 141–53. Details on Eutyches can be found in standard reference books but it is poignant to note that he did not sponsor the views for which he was most often reviled in seminary textbooks: the drop of honey bit really comes from a Monophysite character in a dialogue by Theodoret [*PG* 83, col. 153], though it was widely thought that the author had Eutyches in mind and many assumed that he had said such a thing. After his condemnation by the Council of Chalcedon, Eutyches was exiled and, traduced and ruined, disappeared from history; Antimonophysites could therefore attribute almost anything to him without being effectively corrected. Which is too bad: he probably had some more useful things to contribute. Who knows? With gentler treatment, he might have talked the Armenians into keeping the practice of mixing water with the sacramental wine, which they had ceased to do by 632.)

14. All this, and more, may be found in J. N. D. Kelly, *Early Christian Creeds,* 3d ed. (New York: Longman, 1972), pp. 378–83.

15. This supposition was evidently in place quite early in Christian tradition, along with other—and equally vulnerable—criteria for deciding what belonged to Christian understanding (e.g., a certain style of scriptural interpretation and a discernment of the "mind of Christ")—see *The Way of the Word* and chapter 3 of *Five Gospels.*

16. There is an old tradition of assuming that the apostolic teachings are necessarily derived from Jesus himself, but it has disintegrated under critical inspection. There is also a relatively recent but strong tradition of treating apostolic interpretations as being especially privileged and authoritative because inspired by a more immediate response to Jesus than is possible for later generations. This tradition has remarkable staying power, considering how fallacious its assumptions are, and also disintegrates under critical inspection. No theory can validate all apostolic teachings wholesale without cheating; they all beg the question in one way or another. To decide which apostolic beliefs are sound, one must consider more than the mere fact that they are apostolic.

17. Herman A. Witkin and Donald R. Goodenough, *Cognitive Styles: Essence and Origins. Field Dependence and Field Independence* (New York: International Universi-

ties Press, 1981). The authors are among the leaders in this field of research and offer in this book both a survey of its current state and an extensive bibliography of previous work.

18. Martin F. Davies, "Cognitive-Style Differences in Belief Persistence After Evidential Discrediting, *Personality and Individual Differences* 6 (1985), pp. 341–46.

19. One of the few permanently valuable items I managed to glean from the Erhard Seminar Training (est) was a description of perseveration in laboratory rats that ran something like this: "They put the rat in a cage with five tunnels at the end, one of them with cheese in it. The rat sniffs around, dips down into tunnel 2, comes out, tries tunnel 5, sniffs some more, goes into tunnel 3 and finds the cheese. Next time, he hits tunnel 4, comes out, sniffs, checks out tunnel 1, comes out, goes back to tunnel 5, returns, sniffs, tries tunnel 3 and gets the cheese. Next time, he tries out tunnel 2, comes out, goes to tunnel 3 and gets the cheese. Next time he goes straight to tunnel 3 and gets cheese. After he takes a couple more straight trips to the cheese, they take the cheese out. Next time, the rat goes directly to tunnel 3 and finds it's empty. He comes out, sniffs, and dives back into tunnel 3: no cheese. Out again, back to 3, out, back, out, back. He keeps at it. Why? By this time, he knows there's no cheese, but *he knows it's the right tunnel!* And what's the difference between rats and people? The rats eventually learn that it isn't the right tunnel anymore!"

20. And that is actually what Ehret says: see Arnold Ehret, *Mucusless Diet Healing System* (New York: Benedict Lust Publications, 1979), p. 29.

21. *Faith and Belief* (Princeton: Princeton University Press, 1979) and what he describes as "its supplement, *Belief and History* (Charlottesville: University Press of Virginia, 1977). Smith disapproves of the terms "religion" and "religions," preferring "religions tradition" or "religious traditions" for good and well-argued reasons. I have used the former terms for convenience, but I commend Smith's thoughtful discussions of the subject to anyone who is unfamiliar with them.

22. Wilfred Cantwell Smith, "Belief: A Reply to a Response," *Numen* 27 (1980), p. 248. I think that this conclusion is too extreme for the case of earliest Christian belief, which Smith does not treat: a new and struggling minority inevitably has a stance different from what can be assumed once its cause has largely prevailed. (I have attempted to register the stance of the earliest known Christian cases in *The Way of the Word.)* But Smith clearly establishes that the usual ancient and medieval sense of belief was in some respects significantly different from the modern one, and the shift in understanding that would result from appropriating his well-documented discoveries is entirely congenial to the views presented in this book.

23. Of course, if one wishes to *make* it an issue, there are instructive discoveries available. But there's no good reason to confine ourselves to piecing together the little that can be known about the postconciliar Arians. The fourth century is already at quite a distance from Christianity's most authentic roots—as much of the New Testament is, in fact—and does not provide a significantly better role model than more recent examples of the same phenomenon. Consider the First Vatican Council (1869–1870), whose most celebrated piece of business was the question of

Papal Infallibility. A phalanx of French bishops was mobilized to prevent the passing of the decree that was finally issued. Having thought it a bad idea, did they subsequently, after the decree was promulgated, see the light and realize that they had been wrong? Surely you know more about Frenchmen than *that!* For the real story, see Margaret O'Gara, *Triumph in Defeat: Infallibility, Vatican I, and the French Minority Bishops* (Washington: The Catholic University of America Press, 1988), especially chapters 7 and 8.

24. Or *leubh*— or *loubh*—. (The asterisk also belongs with the *lubh*— variant cited in the main text, but I omitted it there in order not to inspire a search at the bottom of the page on the part of those who are unfamiliar with the linguistic convention of thus indicating that the word is not found in any surviving texts but is a necessary hypothesis for explaining the forms of words that are.)

25. John Main, *The Present Christ: Further Steps in Meditation* (London: Darton, Longman and Todd, 1985), p. 43.

26. Ibid., p. 44. I acknowledge that I am using the sound principles of this writer, whom Fr. Bede Griffiths has called "the best spiritual guide in the church today," to draw conclusions of which he would perhaps not have approved.

27. Documentation will be offered as I proceed, but I pause to acknowledge that in my most recent reading and conversation, I have been surprised both by the extent to which misgivings about basic Christian premises have settled into mainstream theological circles, and by the extent to which this is still unknown to many educated and intelligent Christians, both clerics and laypersons. For a brusque sample of the former, from two quite different backgrounds and viewpoints, I suggest Gordon D. Kaufman, *The Theological Imagination: Constructing the Concept of God* (Philadelphia: The Westminster Press, 1981) and Charles Davis, *What Is Living, What Is Dead in Christianity Today?* (San Francisco: Harper & Row, 1986).

28. The classicized contemporary treatments of the topic of truth are J. L. Austin, P. F. Strawson, and D. R. Cousin, "Symposium: Truth," *Proceedings of the Aristotelian Society,* Supplementary Volume 24 (London: Harrison and Sons, 1950), pp. 111–72; J. L. Austin, "Truth," *Philosophical Papers* (Oxford: Clarendon Press, 1961), pp. 85–101 (Austin's contribution to the preceding); and J. L. Austin, *How to Do Things With Words* 2d ed., (Oxford: Clarendon Press, 1975), especially pp. 140–49. A more recent candidate is Donald Davidson, *Inquiries into Truth and Interpretation* (Oxford: Clarendon Press, 1984). My exposition has been schooled by these and other works, but attempts to be more comprehensive of what belongs to the problem at hand.

29. It first shows up as an interpolation at the Third Council of Toledo in 589. Its background and history are succinctly discussed by J. N. D. Kelly, *Early Christian Creeds,* 3d ed. (New York: Longman, 1972), pp. 358–67.

30. See Donald D. Evans, *The Logic of Self-Involvement* (London: SCM Press, 1963) for a searching, albeit somewhat Barthian, exploration of these matters.

31. Some years later, "under God" was added to the text. But it was not there in my childhood. That strikes me as interestingly suggestive about the nature of tradition. If some of my great-grandchildren grow up in the same country and with the

present text, they will meet no one who ever recited the pledge the way we did, and unless they have recourse to historical scholarship they will understand that "under God" was there from time immemorial. They will be technically right, unless living memory is supplemented by historical investigation.

32. Also, I gather, as "the War of Northern Aggression" and sometimes as "the War for Southern Independence." Another morsel of food for thought about tradition, with its pluralisms and its inventivenesses.

33. This verse appears between Lk 6:5 and 6:6 in the *Codex Bezae* (named after Calvin's colleague Theodore Beza, who presented this extremely important manuscript to Cambridge University, where it may still be found, in 1581). The date of the manuscript itself is usually assessed at either the fifth or the sixth century. No one knows where this particular text came from, or what claim it has to authenticity. Its uniqueness makes it doubtful; but its theology certainly sounds consistent with what seem to have been the views of Jesus, especially in its combining a respect for the authority of the Law with a suggestion that a true knowledge would entail a realization that God does not forbid this activity.

34. The quotations are from Polonius' parting injunctions to his son Laertes in Shakespeare's *Hamlet* I.iii.78–80. Some commentators, impressed by the fact that Polonius is portrayed mainly as a bumbling dotard, have assumed that Shakespeare has set these lines in an ironic context that trivializes their meaning, and this gross misunderstanding seems to have been broadly disseminated. To think so is to misunderstand how Shakespeare worked and to ignore both the culture in which he was embedded and the subsequent cultures in which these lines have resonated as nuggets of wisdom. Lest that seem irrelevant, as well as petulant, please note that this issue of misinterpretation has a great deal to do with the origination and transmission of a tradition and with the distortions that ensue when the tradition's basic character is ignored. Such matters will arise in other concrete forms intermittently in this book, especially in what Christianity has done with Jesus so far.

35. Please note that "truly" is meant to have as much weight as you are willing to accord it. I am *not* suggesting that some sort of warm personal satisfaction is an adequate index of the truth of Christianity; but I *am* implying that Christianities that require us to believe what we understand to be untrue, or make other demands that seem by our best lights to be unwholesome, deserve to be considered at least as much on trial as we are when the two collide. And note that I say "on trial," not "condemned."

36. One of the most thoughtfully mission-minded of modern church historians has observed that despite the efforts invested up through the nineteenth century, Christian missionaries "had made relatively few converts from Islam, Hinduism, and Buddhism" (Kenneth Scott Latourette, *Advance Through Storm* [New York: Harper and Brothers, 1945], pp. 479–80). And probably, it may be added, fewer from Judaism. Conversions from the so-called "pagan" religions were of course rarely founded on religious grounds alone, and usually carried much of the previous religious allegiance into a Christian framework rather than dispelling it.

341

37. I learned this from a friend who had read more of Augustine, and more recently, than I had; but she could not recall just where the text appears, and my subsequent inquiries of other students of Augustine have produced some vague recognitions but no citation. Frankly, I don't really care whether he said it or not: it's a good maxim with or without him.

38. Flavius Philostratus' *Life of Apollonius of Tyana* is available in various editions and translations, including the widely distributed Loeb Classical Library edition in two volumes, ed. F. C. Conybeare (London: W. Heinemann, 1912 and reprints) and C. P. Jones' abridged translation (Harmondsworth: Penguin Books, 1970).

39. My references to Socrates are to his representation in the dialogues of Plato, with a glance at Xenophon's *Memorabilia* and Diogenes Laërtius' *Vitae Philosophorum,* which I take to be accurate enough to support my generalizations, though they are obviously not to be held to account in detail.

40. *Church Dogmatics,* I/2 (Edinburgh: Clark, 1956), p. 350.

41. For an excellent survey of apologetics from its beginnings to recent times, see Avery Dulles, *A History of Apologetics* (New York: Corpus, 1971).

42. R. C. Sproul, John Gerstner, and Arthur Lindsley, *Classical Apologetics* (Grand Rapids: Zondervan 1984), p. 141. The book is written especially from and especially to the Christian Reformed Evangelical tradition, but it is aptly titled: it replicates the basic forms of classical apologetics in both the Catholic and the wider Protestant traditions. (See Dulles' history of apologetics, cited in previous note.)

43. Mt 12:38–39, 16:1–4; Lk 11:29–cf. Mk 8:11–12.

44. There was in fact considerable bickering between early Christians and their pagan contemporaries over who was performing miracles and who was merely doing magic: that *both* worked wonders was readily taken for granted by almost everyone. (Cf. the analogous dispute reported in Mt 12:22–28 and Lk 11:14–19, where Jesus is accused of deriving his power to exorcize demons from the Enemy and retorts that if this were so it would bring the exorcistic powers of his accusers' sons into question; it is obviously assumed on both sides that both sides perform successful exorcisms.) For good recent examinations of this early controversy, see Harold Remus, *Pagan-Christian Conflict Over Miracle in the Second Century* (Cambridge, Mass.: Philadelphia Patristic Foundation, 1983) and Eugene V. Gallagher, *Divine Man or Magician? Celsus and Origen on Jesus* (Chico, Calif.: Scholars Press, 1982).

45. This is the meaning usually understood, but it may be noted that there is another legitimate way of reading the text as saying that all inspired and variously profitable scriptures are for the purpose of fitting us for good works—i.e., leaving entirely open the question of which scriptures are in fact inspired.

46. Verse 14 of the Epistle of Jude shows that the author and his community evidently accepted as scriptural some version of the Book of Enoch, the surviving instances of which are now relegated to the category of Old Testament Pseudepigrapha. Translations of the texts are collected in the two volumes of *The Old Testament Pseudepigrapha,* ed. James H. Charlesworth (Garden City, N.Y.: Doubleday, 1983 and 1985).

47. R. C. Sproul, John Gerstner, and Arthur Lindsley, *Classical Apologetics* (Grand Rapids: Zondervan, 1984), p. 7.

48. Not always, of course: the original Christian apologists were certainly attempting to defend Christianity to non-Christian officialdom (Paul before Agrippa in Acts 26 is a nice near-paradigm), and Thomas Aquinas' *Summa contra Gentiles* was apparently designed to equip Dominican preachers for encounters with Muslim philosophers, and missionaries, ancient and modern, are routinely armed with arguments for proving the truth of their Christianities to outsiders. But few exercises in apologetics have in fact been drawn up for full-scale confrontations with intellectually sophisticated unbelievers, or pulled out of circulation when found unpersuasive to them.

49. The quotation is approximate, dredged out of a forty-year-old recollection of my father's commendation of apologetics as taught at the University of Notre Dame. I thought the description thrilling, and could hardly wait. I eventually took the course, using as a textbook Joseph H. Cavanaugh's *Evidence for Our Faith,* 2d ed. (Notre Dame: University of Notre Dame Press, 1952), where I have just rediscovered the following prefatory remarks on p. 16: "In Apologetics we follow a simple, logical pattern of reasoning. First of all, we prove the existence of God without the aid of any religion. Then we consider the possibility and necessity of divine revelation (God speaking to us). Next we turn to history and discover that God evidently did speak to us through his Son, Jesus Christ. From historical documents, we likewise learn that the Son of God founded a visible teaching institution to which he entrusted his message. That institution can be no other than the Catholic Church. Once we realize that the Church speaks in the name of Christ and with his divine authority, we will be prepared to study Theology." This movement from revelation to Christ to Church, with somewhat less emphasis on the Bible as such, is a characteristic Catholic apologetic accent (cf. Joseph C. Wurzer, *A Course in Apologetics* [Chicago: Excelsior, 1931]; Austin G. Schmidt and Joseph A. Perkins, *Faith and Reason: A First Course in Apologetics* [Chicago: Loyola University Press, 1937]; Joseph H. Fichter, *Textbook in Apologetics* [Milwaukee: Bruce, 1947]; and Paul J. Glenn, *Apologetics: A Class Manual* [St. Louis: Herder, 1931], which relegates the treatment of the Bible to an appendix), but the basic pattern is the same in all varieties of classical apologetics. These books are, I presume it is needless to say, at least as critically vulnerable as the one I have just dealt with. That is surely inevitable in any attempt to deliver on such a naive promise as Cavanaugh's "In fact, there is no excuse for doubts after this class" (p. 14). It is worth noting that apologetics is not always so naive—Alan Richardson's *Christian Apologetics* (London: SCM, 1947) does not pretend that Kant's work has not changed the rules about what we can get by with, and acknowledges that scientific method is the norm for serious investigations of this kind (thereby disallowing such a move as Cavanaugh's acknowledging on p. 111 that the description of Jesus in the Slavonic version of Josephus' *Jewish War* is generally held to be an inauthentic interpolation, and then quoting it as Josephus' own testimony in support of an argument on p. 141). It is even more worth noting that there has been a shift away from apologetics since the 1940s to the

more plausible enterprise of fundamental theology, which starts candidly with Christian belief and tries to make good satisfying sense of it, rather than attempting to prove that it is the only route that a rational person can go (e.g., Gerald O'Collins, *Fundamental Theology* [London: Darton, Longman & Todd, 1981]). For still further advances in responsible sophistication, again in the Catholic tradition, see Francis Schüssler Fiorenza, *Foundational Theology* (New York: Crossroad, 1984).

50. Since the Reformation, there has been strident contention between Protestant and Catholic polemicists about the former's tendency to maximize the importance of Bible at the expense of Church and the latter's tendency to maximize Church at the expense of Bible. One of the happy, and amusing, side effects of more dispassionate twentieth-century critical investigations is that Catholic thinkers have tended to drift away from relying on church tradition for the rigorous reconstruction of Christian origins, and have put more weight on biblical evidence—while simultaneously (though without much consultation in either direction), Protestant thinkers have come to value tradition more, recognizing that from a historical perspective the Bible itself is a product of the Christian church as such. It is now much harder than it was even as recently as thirty years ago to discover, when observing an informed discussion of the nature of earliest Christianity by unlabeled participants, who is Catholic and who is Protestant. I glanced in the previous note at the shift, which took place during the same period, away from apologetics toward fundamental theology. It may be added that there has also been a shift within fundamental theology itself toward a greater emphasis on the natural-theology component as distinguished from authoritative pronouncement. On p. 268 of the last book cited in the previous note is a crisp distinction between the resulting new type of quasi-apologetics and the traditional Roman-style form of fundamental theology: "If the apologetical task focuses on the existence of God as a preamble of faith and the theological task is to interpret reality and faith in relation to God, then a certain continuum exists between the apologetical and the theological task. If, however, the fundamental theological task is considered to be the rational and historical demonstration of the external signs of the credibility of a supernatural and gratuitous revelation, and the theological task is primarily the exposition of the teachings of the magisterium to which this revelation has been entrusted, than a strong discontinuity exists between foundational theology as a natural theology and systematic theology as a natural theology." To the extent that the book you are now reading is a form of apologetics—which is a very considerable extent indeed—it differs radically from Schüssler Fiorenza's project (with which I am however sympathetic, and which I think he executes admirably) through my adamant and dogmatic insistence on thinking of *faith* not, as he does, as the inheritance of beliefs but rather in the ways I set forth in Chapter 1. That difference, however slight it may appear in Chapter 1, will broaden considerably by the time Chapter 20 is done sorting out what I think to be its implications.

51. The book with which I have been dealing over the last few pages, *Classical Apologetics,* spends about a third of its bulk rebutting one of the major forms of this

alternative approach in order to show that it is not an adequate substitute for classical rational apologetics.

52. See Dulles' *A History of Apologetics,* chapter 2.

53. *"Credibilis quia ineptum, certe quia impossibile," De Carne Christi* 5. The formula often attributed to Tertullian, *"Credo quia absurdum est,"* does not appear in his writings: it is simply a deformed version of this text (cf. "Money is the root of all evil," "Blood, sweat, and tears," "Play it again, Sam," etc.).

54. *Pensées,* Section IV, 277.

55. Literature on the ontological argument may be found under that heading in a special section of William J. Wainwright, *Philosophy of Religion: An Annotated Bibliography of Twentieth-Century Writings in English.* (New York: Garland, 1978). The foremost contemporary proponent of the ontological argument is probably Charles Hartshorne, who has produced at least eight different formulations of it (see *Process Studies* 15 [1986], p. 210). For sample critiques, see random articles in the *International Journal of Philosophy and Religion,* especially vols. 7 (1976) and 9 (1978).

56. See the literature listed in the section on proofs of God in Wainwright's bibliography, cited in the previous note, pp. 148–96, and the overview offered by Frank B. Dilley, "Foolproof proofs of God?" *International Journal of Philosophy and Religion* 8 (1977), pp. 18–35. A recent book, whose author is obviously very much in favor of the enterprise of proving God's existence, draws the sobering conclusion that "The theist can agree with the critic that none of the arguments for the existence of God, when taken individually, justify theism" (Donald Wayne Viney, *Charles Hartshorne and the Existence of God* [Albany: State University of New York Press, 1985], p. 6). John Hick, after writing about the question in (with Arthur McGill) *The Many-Faced Argument* (New York: Macmillan Co., 1967), and (alone) in *Arguments for the Existence of God* (New York: Herder & Herder, 1971), recently wrote that "the 'bottom line' can, I believe, only be that none of the traditional theistic arguments finally succeeds" *(God Has Many Names* [Philadelphia: The Westminster Press, 1982], p. 23). Louis Dupré, always careful, follows his inspection of the arguments with the conclusion that they "do not *prove* God's existence, since they do not pass beyond the point where the nature of the transcendent becomes a real problem and where the religious answer (including the existence of God) must be envisaged as a *possible* solution" *(A Dubious Heritage: Studies in the Philosophy of Religion after Kant* [New York: Paulist Press, 1977], p. 175).

57. There is apparently still some chance that a philosophically realistic argument from causation may work, and on the testimony of knowledgeable others I report that Hegel made what some find a convincing case for the biblical God. But even if so, that does not yet seem to have advanced the discussion very far toward the ideal of a universally persuasive demonstration.

58. F. Gerald Downing, *Has Christianity a Revelation?* (London: SCM Press, 1964), argues his title question in the negative, pointing out that notions of God's self-disclosure are not really even biblical but are rather theological inventions with little

to warrant them. Neither classical apologetics nor dialectical theology fares very well in the course of his discussion.

59. Bruce L. McCormack, "Divine Revelation and Human Imagination: Must We Choose Between the Two?" *Scottish Journal of Theology* 37 (1984), p. 455.

60. Id.; see also Werner E. Lemke, "Revelation through History in Recent Biblical Theology: A Critical Appraisal," *Interpretation* 36 (1982), pp. 34–46.

61. There is an extensive literature on the question of miracles, a good deal of which can be found through the section under that heading in William J. Wainwright, *Philosophy of Religion: An Annotated Bibliography of Twentieth-Century Writings in English* (New York: Garland, 1978), pp. 438–65 and, with succinct summarizing commentary, in David and Randall Basinger, *Philosophy and Miracle* (Lewiston: The Edwin Mellen Press, 1986). The bottom line is that arguments in their defense are almost entirely overwhelmed by contrary arguments.

62. This tripartite division is already given in the preface to the Greek translation of Sirach (Ecclesiasticus), well over a century before the beginnings of Christianity. The term "Bible," i.e., the Book, was a relatively late and indirect development.

63. It is perhaps worth noting that "Bible" was originally a plural, the Latin *biblia* being merely a transliteration of the Greek word for "books." This neuter plural came gradually, for theological reasons more than grammatical, to be perceived as a feminine singular, and was rendered accordingly into European vernaculars.

64. See "The Origin of the Canon of the New Testament" in *Introduction to the New Testament,* 14th ed., ed. Werner Georg Kümmel, trans. A. J. Mattill, Jr. (Nashville: Abingdon Press, 1966), pp. 334–58; any other edition will do. Or, for more thorough treatment, see Bruce M. Metzger, *The Canon of the New Testament: Its Origin, Development, and Significance* (New York: Oxford University Press, 1987).

65. An interesting parallel in history is the relegation of Edward Irving to rather inferior status by the Catholic Apostolic Church of which he had been the principal founder. (The details may be found in standard reference books, such as *The Oxford Dictionary of the Christian Church.)* The custodians of tradition often appear to have considerable power and authority independent not only of the original happenings but even of the tradition through which they inherit it. How they choose to exercise such authority and power is a matter of vast moral and cognitive importance.

66. See Hans Dieter Betz, "The Delphic Maxim ΓΝΩΘΙ ΣΑΥΤΟΝ in Hermetic Interpretation," *Harvard Theological Review* 63 (1970), pp. 465–84. The maxim is more often given as *gnôthi seauton,* in accordance with later standard Greek, but the original inscription was apparently *sauton.*

67. See Walter Wink, "The Bankruptcy of the Biblical Critical Paradigm" in his book *The Bible in Human Transformation* (Philadelphia: Fortress Press, 1973), pp. 1–15.

68. A good survey of the earlier interpretive movements, climaxed by an appreciation of this more recent phase, may be found in Sandra M. Schneiders, "From Exegesis to Hermeneutics: The Problem of the Contemporary Meaning of Scripture," *Horizon* 8 (1981), pp. 23–39.

69. For a somewhat fuller treatment of these thoughts, see John C. Meagher, "Pictures at an Exhibition: Reflections on Exegesis and Theology," *Journal of the American Academy of Religion* 47 (1978), pp. 3–20.

70. Bruce Vawter's *Biblical Inspiration* (Philadelphia: The Westminster Press, 1972) is a thoughtful and judicious survey of the history and present state of the matter. But it clearly describes a trajectory of retreat, ending in contemporary attempts to save the appearances of a doctrine that now has virtually no practical implications, and no claim to credibility other than its having been formerly believed and formally affirmed. This foundation is no longer sufficient, and the version of inspiration it now supports is of little genuine consequence. (See also James Tunstead Burtchaell, *Catholic Theories of Biblical Inspiration since 1810* London: Cambridge University Press, 1969 for historical perspective on how this has come about.)

71. Avery Dulles, "Ecumenism and Theological Method," *Journal of Ecumenical Studies* 17 (1980), p. 41.

72. Just which scriptural texts were used to arrive at these conclusions—or for that matter, just which texts were thought to predict Jesus' third-day resurrection—is not reported by Paul or by anyone else. For the former, the obvious candidate is the Suffering Servant in Deutero-Isaiah. There is no really good candidate for the latter: the closest we seem to be able to get is Hosea's "in the third day he will raise us" (6:2), which is obviously not much to lean on, especially when the original context shows that it meant that God will restore Israel soon, after severe punishment. If this was in fact the scriptural peg on which the third-day resurrection was hung, it may help to explain why the repeated motif of "in accordance with the scriptures" comes to us fortified with so little concrete citation: the specific correlations probably came under critical non-Christian attack for their feebleness, and began to be prudently withheld, leaving only the general assurance that the blueprint that has been fulfilled is there in Scripture *somewhere*.

73. In addition to such ingenious and ultimately untenable eisegeses as I have sampled in this chapter and in the previous one, there were apparently some instances of sheer forgery. In Justin Martyr's "Dialogue with Trypho the Jew" (chapters 71–73), Justin accuses the Jews of deleting certain passages from Scripture in order to deprive Christians of some of their best proof-texts; his Jewish interlocutor quite rightly observes that the passages in question appear only in Christian copies of Scripture not because the Jews had erased them but because the Christians had added them. The claims of the Ebionites that parts of Matthew were forgeries, and the parallel claim of Marcion about parts of Luke, were probably inspired by a knowledge of such goings-on at least in Christian writings (2 Thes 3:17 is clearly a protection against them), and it was probably notorious in Palestine that Jews and Samaritans accused one another of falsifying the text of the Torah.

74. Ignatius' word is *archeia,* and my translation follows Kirsopp Lake both in his felicitous choice of "charters" and in his acknowledgment that the word's meaning is at any rate apparently a reference to the Hebrew Scriptures as foundational.

75. I.e., in the Scriptures: cf. the conventional formula, "It is written" for "It is said in the authoritative writings."

76. Epistle to Philadelphia 8:2. The passage is difficult—my translation attempts to reproduce in English the awkwardness of the Greek original—but the basic drift seems clear enough.

77. 1 Jn 4:1–3 and 2 Jn 7 (and cf. Jude 8) refer to this. See *Five Gospels,* pp. 201–28, where I argue that 3 Jn derives from the movement in question.

78. It is well known that the date 25 December is entirely artificial, invented in order to provide a powerful Christian competitor to the pagan festivals that occurred around the winter solstice. It is much less well known that the year is impossible to determine. The conventional date of 6 B.C.(!) is derived from Matthew's account of the Massacre of the Innocents: if Herod, who died in 4 B.C., was gunning for boys of two years and under after hearing the testimony of the Magi, that would suggest a birthdate of approximately 6 B.C. if this was one of his final acts, which seems to be implied by Joseph's apparently brief sojourn in Egypt before Herod's death. But no other evidence has been forthcoming to put this outrage on the historical map at all, let alone to place it specifically at the end of Herod's reign. It would not have been uncharacteristic of him, but there is so much that is implausible in Matthew's story, none of which is reported by any other early Christian writer despite its impressive dramatics, that it does not inspire belief on historical grounds but only for reasons of uncritical piety. Another ancient witness, deriving from Victorinus of Pettau, sets the birth date at A.D. 9. The conventionally accepted age of Jesus at the time of his crucifixion is thirty-three, but that is based merely on Luke's testimony that he was "about thirty years of age" (3:23) when he began his public ministry, conflated with the Fourth Gospel's treatment of that ministry as apparently lasting about three years. But a curiously neglected early tradition puts Jesus past forty at the time of his death, and perhaps closer to fifty: Irenaeus' *Adversus Omnes Haereses* II.33.1–4 bears witness to this tradition along with a few other ancient texts—including, perhaps, the Fourth Gospel, for Jn 8:57 seems to hint this, especially when compared with 2:20–21. (See W. Bauer on "Jesus' Earthly Appearance and Character" in E. Hennecke, *New Testament Apocrypha,* ed. W. Schneemelcher, vol. 1 [London: Lutterworth Press, 1963], pp. 433–34).

79. The date of the crucifixion is also uncertain. Gerd Luedemann puts it at either 27 or 30; using a different weighting of evidences, Robert Jewett proposes 33 as an alternative possibility. But some early texts place the event under the reign of Claudius rather than Tiberius, and as late as A.D. 59. (See the piece by W. Bauer cited in the previous note.) For a good example of how such matters are discussed, see Jewett, Luedemann, and others in action in the "Seminar on Pauline Chronology" in *Colloquy on New Testament Studies: A Time for Reappraisal and Fresh Approaches,* ed. Bruce Corley (Macon, Ga.: Mercer University Press, 1983), pp. 263–337. As for the charges, neither the evidence of Jesus' career nor the reports of his trial before the Sanhedrin provide grounds for convicting him of a capital offense under Jewish law. It does not matter whether he dodged the question about being

Messiah or not (Matthew and Luke indicate that he did, the usually reliable manuscripts of Mark say that he didn't), since, for obvious reasons, being or claiming to be the Messiah was not against the law: even if Pharisees and Sadducees differed in their interpretations of Torah, and disagreed about whether it had anything to say about a Messiah, nothing in Torah forbids a messianic claim—and those who hoped for a Messiah would not be likely to support an interpretation that would automatically make the real one guilty of a capital offense if he admitted who he was. The likelihood is that the Sanhedrin either railroaded him on an illegitimate charge (if so, we don't know what it was) or found no way of convicting him; but in either event, it was perhaps not difficult to take advantage of the assumption of some of his followers that he was the Messiah in order to persuade the Roman authorities that it was in their best interests to get rid of someone whose supposed mission was to overthrow their regime.

80. See Sigmund Mowinckel, *He That Cometh* (Oxford: Blackwell, 1956) and Joachim Becker, *Messianic Expectation in the Old Testament* (Philadelphia: Fortress Press, 1980).

81. There were various nonmessianic theologies available among the Jews, including that of John the Baptist, with whom Jesus is consistently seen in ideological continuity, and while it is clear that early Christians insisted on applying the messianic title to Jesus, there is good reason to suppose that they did it without any encouragement from what he had said. (These points are argued in greater detail in *Five Gospels,* chapters 1 and 2.)

82. David H. Kelsey, "The Bible and Christian Theology," *Journal of the American Academy of Religion* 48 (1980), p. 386.

83. Kelsey's definition is not timid, only tactfully descriptive—as one might say that Muslims are those for whom the Qur'an is the definitive revelation. The substitution of "resurrection appearances" for the expected "resurrection" sustains the descriptive neutrality: the convenient ambiguity of "appearances" makes it possible for it to be understood as referring merely to experiences that gave the appearance of a resurrection, leaving it evasive enough to be assented to by someone who thinks that Peter et al. were hallucinating. Once again, this cautious wording does not impose such a minimalist interpretation, but merely accommodates one; it is equally hospitable to a completely literal and objective version of Jesus' resurrection.

84. Neither Holy Trinity (tenth century) nor Corpus Christi (thirteenth century, dedicated to the Blessed Sacrament of the Eucharist) is really dedicated to an event, and could be placed rather arbitrarily within the liturgical calendar. The difference between these and the more ancient feasts is not necessarily important for purposes of worship, but marks them as different from the historical-landmark feasts, much as artificial (though appropriate) holidays such as Labor Day and August Bank Holiday may be distinguished from such commemorative holidays as Independence Day and the now largely secularized Thanksgiving.

85. I am dealing only with the Roman (i.e., Western Catholic) tradition, and the details may be found in any Roman Catholic (Latin rite) breviaries, missals, and

Libri Usualis published before 1960. Further commentary may be found in Fernand Cabrol, *The Year's Liturgy,* vol. 1 (London: Burns, Oates & Washbourne, 1938), pp. 211–19 and in J. A. Jungmann, *Pastoral Liturgy* (New York: Herder and Herder, 1962), pp. 238–51.

86. Details readily perceivable through a careful reading of Jn 14–17; or see *The Way of the Word,* pp. 124–26.

87. More detailed argument and supporting evidence may be found in *Five Gospels,* chapter 3.

88. But I do not think that this is the original state of the text or a deliberately constructed emphasis on the Incarnation. In "John 1.14 and the New Temple" (*Journal of Biblical Literature* 88 [1969], pp. 57–68), I argued that the original reading was "the word became spirit, and dwelt in us"—a difference of only one word in the Greek text, and precisely a word *(pneuma,* spirit) that controversies of the time made particularly susceptible of being changed into the word in the received text *(sarx,* flesh). The article seems to have had virtually no influence whatever, but I am now more convinced of the rightness of its argument and conclusions than I was when I wrote it—which is hardly a persuasive argument, but is at least more than I can say for anything else I turned out twenty years ago.

89. I don't see that it should, for reasons already advanced and others to be presented shortly. But I pause to acknowledge that followers of Hegelian thought make a more persuasive case for a difference made by Jesus' divinity than most others. My present limited sense of Hegel's views on the subject leave me unconvinced that they are incompatible with my own, which seem to me coherent with the drift of Hegel as expressed in James Yerkes, *The Christology of Hegel* (Albany: State University of New York Press, 1983). A Hegelian view does not seem to me to require that the incarnational dimension be expressed through a unique instance, and I don't see that the rest of this book need be thought to conflict with what Hegel's system proposes, even though it be a different way of going about it.

90. I here mean to include nonphysical survival as one of the possible options. Some early Christians apparently believed that Jesus had been exalted to the Father after his death without becoming visible to the eye or recovering a physical form. I see no reason to consider that an illegitimate, or even an inferior, alternative to the standard physical versions with empty tombs.

91. Easter and Pentecost were liturgically classified as doubles of the first class, with privileged octaves of the first order; Christmas had a privileged octave of the third order, Epiphany of the second (Corpus Christi was given the same rank as Epiphany, but was a thousand years younger).

92. In the last stages of revising this chapter, I stumbled upon a congenial and more authoritative description of the Feast of the Epiphany by an eminent historian of liturgy: "the Epiphany-thought in the Roman liturgical year takes on a much more distinct character when seen in terms of its extension understood in its original light. It is concerned not with a certain appearance of Christ; but, in contrast to Christmas and to the original Eastern feast of Epiphany, both of which have for their subject,

the Incarnation or the coming of the Redeemer, with the manifestation of divinity in Him who has come to us in the form of a man. The power and the Wisdom of God have appeared in Christ. For this reason most of the records of the older Roman liturgy favour the expression *theophania*. It is therefore, not a particular event which is being celebrated, but a concept of faith; at any rate, a concept which is visibly expressed in a whole series of events and which never appears in abstract isolation" (J. A. Jungmann, *Pastoral Liturgy* [New York: Herder and Herder, 1962], p. 222).

93. Not, however, as *carelessly* chosen as may appear. There are historical grounds for supposing that the feast originated in Egypt, the date of 6 January being elected to compete with a feast of Isis celebrated on that day, and that the inclusion of the Cana miracle was motivated less by the reference to the disciples' glimpse of Jesus' glory than by competition with a water-wine miracle celebrated in the Isis feast, which dealt with the virgin birth of Aion—and that the water-wine miracle was interpreted by Christians with reference to baptism. (See Gertrud Schiller, *Iconography of Christian Art*, vol. 1 [Greenwich, Conn.: New York Graphic Society, 1971], p. 95.)

94. It is the original inspiration at least in the sense that the religious impact of Jesus does not seem to have been made at all before his emergence as an adult (once we have pared away what is historically doubtful in the infancy material, there is essentially nothing left but the names of Mary and Joseph, and the identification of Nazareth as their hometown) and was firmly in place long before his arrest in Jerusalem, and well before any Christmas/Incarnation or Easter/Redemption notions had been attached to him. But it might be said to be original in more literal evidential terms too: it is entirely possible that the oldest Christian evidence that still survives is the hypothetical document Q, reconstructed from its presence as incorporated into the Gospels of Matthew and Luke, which presents Jesus in epiphanic terms without any attention to his birth, death, or resurrection.

95. I use the term "gospel" here, of course, not to refer to a written record but to a preaching of good news—i.e., in the same sense in which I use it in *Five Gospels,* to whose second chapter I refer any reader who is curious about how I go about reconstructing what Jesus preached.

96. I admit, however, that I could be cajoled into writing a systematic theology based on this book's principles, if I had decent grounds for thinking that it would be not only published but read as well.

97. *Wovon man nicht sprechen kann, darüber mu*β man schreiben . . .

98. A concise Jewish example lies ready to hand: "it would be the theories and procedures of the archaeologists and historians that would require re-evaluation, and not the Torah teaching with which they clashed" (Chaim Dov Keller, "Modern Orthodoxy: An Analysis and a Response," Reuven P. Bulka, ed., *Dimensions of Orthodox Judaism* [New York: KTAV, 1983], p. 266). You have read, or heard, parallel Christian statements. But for something perhaps more typical and more poignant, consider the report of Father Adam Otterbein, head of the Holy Shroud

Guild (based in Esopus, New York), on the subject of the early news leaks concerning the dating of the Turin Shroud to the Middle Ages: "We've always claimed that there should not be a contradiction between science and faith. This seemed to be the case here until this carbon-dating." (Quoted from the *Toronto Globe and Mail*, October 1, 1988, p. D8.)

99. An especially thoughtful articulation of this stance may be found in an article from which I quoted in Chapter 6: David H. Kelsey, "The Bible and Christian Theology," *Journal of the American Academy of Religion* 48 (1980), pp. 385–402.

100. A fine critique of this mentality, together with suggested cures, may be found in the opening chapters of Douglas Sloan's *Insight-Imagination* (Westport: Greenwood Press, 1983).

101. A few random samples: "Chemistry is actively involved in the reconceptualization of science. We are probably only at the beginning of new directions of research" (Ilya Prigogine and Isabelle Stengers, *Order Out of Chaos: Man's New Dialogue with Nature* [London: Heinemann, 1984], p. 179); "in order to deal with the phenomenon of life, the laws of physics will have to be changed, not only reinterpreted" (Eugene P. Wigner, "Are We Machines?" *Proceedings of the American Philosophical Society* 113, 95–101); "The human brain is a vastly complex instrument; its operating principles with respect to language and indeed, to behavior in general, are practically unknown" (Oscar S. M. Marin, Eleanor M. Saffran, and Myrna F. Schwartz, "Dissociation of Language in Aphasia: Implications for Normal Function," in Stevan R. Harnad, Horst D. Steklis, and Jane Lancaster, eds., *Origins and Evolution of Language and Speech* [New York: New York Academy of Sciences, 1976], pp. 868–69); "We can be overwhelmed by the immensity of high level investigation on the visual system of primates in the last two decades . . . but it must be emphasized that the great achievements in vision research can be regarded as only the first steps in providing an explanation of how the image on the retina that is encoded in neuronal discharges is eventually reconstituted as an observed picture" (Karl R. Popper and John C. Eccles, *The Self and Its Brain* [Berlin: Springer, 1977, 1985], pp. 270–71).

102. "The Second Coming," *The Collected Poems of W. B. Yeats* (London: Macmillan & Co., 1955), p. 211.

103. In general retrospect, it strikes me as not just curious but downright startling that so many contemporary intellectuals have bought the view, promoted by Heidegger among others, that the fact of death makes all the difference and requires a systematic redisciplining of all our thought. What is curious about it is that this implicitly acknowledges that we tend to start thinking as if death didn't make all that much difference to how we go about thinking of and living life. What is startling is that instead of drawing the obvious conclusion that the fairly well-known fact of death therefore need not cramp our style much even when we attend to it explicitly, this program urges that we develop an artificial grimness about it even in the midst of life. Fancy a philosopher cautioning you that your comportment at a great party

should be deeply tempered by the constant realization that you have to go home when it's over.

104. If you are old enough, you will perhaps recall how seriously Jean-Paul Sartre's *No Exit* was taken not long ago, with frequent relishing of Garcin's line at the end, "Hell is other people" *("L'enfer, c'est les Autres"—Huis-Clos* [Paris: Gallimard, 1947], p. 75).

105. As I am revising this chapter, I have just read an undergraduate paper on Romeo's final words in Act V, scene i, as he buys poison and goes off to use it at Juliet's tomb. The author remarks that "He has suddenly grown up to see the world as a cruel place rather than a storybook." Apart from whether this properly reads the speech (I think it doesn't), one may question the casual presuppositions: it is more mature to be grim about life; Romeo's desperate resolution to kill himself is an advance over his earlier bliss; joyful love is a fantasy that fades before the impact of realistic disappointment. My acquaintance with the paper's author is slight (it's still early in the school year at this writing) but does not divine any signs of habitual cynicism: this is merely the normal presumption of an educated and basically sophisticated North American twenty-year-old when trying to be serious.

106. Jean Piaget, *The Moral Judgment of the Child* (Glencoe, Ill.: The Free Press, 1948).

107. Ibid., p. 63.

108. I repeat the verdict of John Hick: "the 'bottom line' can, I believe, only be that none of the traditional theistic arguments finally succeeds" *(God Has Many Names* [Philadelphia: The Westminster Press, 1982], p. 23). Similar conclusions by other investigators of the question are cited in Chapter 4's note 56.

109. *Systematic Theology,* vol. 1 (Chicago: University of Chicago Press, 1951), p. 237. Tillich's critique of the theologizing of God's existence is presented in pp. 235ff. (Two thousand years earlier, the philosopher Carneades argued that it is impious to assert God's existence.)

110. Originally published in the *Proceedings of the Aristotelian Society* in 1944–1945, this seminal article is reprinted in his *Logic and Language,* vol. 1 (Oxford: Blackwell, 1951) and in his *Philosophy and Psychoanalysis* (Oxford: Blackwell, 1953).

111. In *New Essays in Philosophical Theology,* eds. Antony Flew and Alasdair MacIntyre (London: SCM Press, 1955), pp. 96–99.

112. Sir Francis Galton, a man of great practical curiosity, once undertook to see what would happen if he made a serious attempt to worship Punch (as in Punch and Judy), and reported that his efforts resulted in a mild but detectable temporary idolatry.

113. "Burnt Norton," in *Collected Poems 1909–1962* (New York: Harcourt, Brace & World, 1970), p. 176.

114. This is a routine fact, but not to be shrugged off. As you may know, there have been several experiments with special goggles that turn visual images so that the wearers see things upside down. After a while, but much less than a week, the wearers start perceiving things normally: the image is now, through the goggles, projected right side up on the retina, but the imagination compensates to put the

final seeing in place, business as usual. Try to remember your earliest experiences doing things in a mirror, and compare it to the rich finesse with which you now know how to move your mirror-observed hand in order to pluck an eyebrow or shave that last corner of your stubble. Impressive.

115. Jean-Paul Sartre shows us how to do this in the course of his aptly titled (but philosophically self-defeating) *Nausea,* in Roquentin's six o'clock meditation that psychologically (but not, despite the apparent intentions, metaphysically) sabotages a theoretically romantic Parisian chestnut tree in the park *(La Nausée* [Paris: Gallimard, 1938], pp. 126–35).

116. See Samuel J. Beck, *Rorschach's Test,* 3d ed., vol. 1 (New York: Grune and Stratton, 1961), especially chapter 10.

117. W. Grey Walter, *The Living Brain* (London: Gerald Duckworth & Co., 1953), p. 148. If you try this on others, I suggest that you drop the reference to the child's block, substitute something like "the external surface is colored" for "It is painted," and say "divide" rather than "cut," so as to keep the exercise maximally unprejudiced. I can guarantee that you will still get children's blocks, painting, and cutting from some of your subjects. But try it the original way too, as a way of smoking out the abstracters who automatically bring out their habitual Occam's razor to shave away the cues unnecessary to the solution of the problem at hand.

118. James Bieri, *Clinical and Social Judgment: The Discrimination of Behavioral Information* (New York: Wiley, 1966), p. 205, finds that those who process in a cognitively simple way are more confident of their judgment than complex-processors—until they run into incongruent information, whereupon they fall behind the latter in confidence. O. J. Harvey, D. E. Hunt, and H. M. Schroeder, *Conceptual Systems and Personality Organization* (New York: Wiley, 1961), shows evidence that cognitively concrete persons (e.g., eidetics) are less tolerant of ambiguity than abstracters, which probably also relates to simplicity vs. complexity in the process. Michael Smithson, "Interests and the Growth of Uncertainty," *Journal for the Theory of Social Behaviour* 10 (1980), pp. 157–68, offers a good critique, built upon such evidence, of the common sociology-of-knowledge assumption that societies strive for certainty and agreement, and a fairly persuasive argument in favor of the social value of unresolved uncertainty.

119. Thomas Natsoulas, "Concepts of Consciousness," *The Journal of Mind and Behavior* 4 (1983), pp. 13–59, offers six concepts of consciousness, drawn from both the history of the word's employment and from modern critical investigations in psychology and other fields. His observation that consciousness has been neglected by psychologists' research is echoed by Daniel A. Helminiak, "Consciousness as a Subject Matter," *Journal for the Theory of Social Behaviour* 14 (1984), pp. 211–30, but the latter argues that Natsoulas misleadingly telescopes his fourth type—nonreflexive awareness of self—into his third type, awareness of objects, and thus obscures that dimension of consciousness that validates a careful introspective method and provides the foundations for a more humanistic version of psychology.

120. Thomas Natsoulas, "The Subjective Organization of Personal Consciousness: A Concept of Conscious Personality," *The Journal of Mind and Behavior* 5 (1984), pp.

311–36, explores differences between a receptive/responsive consciousness and an originative/active consciousness.

121. Douglas M. Wardell and Joseph R. Royce, "Toward a multi-factor theory of styles and their relationships to cognition and affect," *Journal of Personality* 46 (1978), pp. 474–505, offer three styles of cognitive/affective integration (Rational, Empirical, and Metaphorical), based on analyses of eight categories of cognitive structuring, and correlate them with behavioral and personality characteristics.

122. E.g., Anthony Gale, "The Psychophysiology of Individual Differences: Studies of Extraversion and the EEG," in *New Approaches in Psychological Measurement,* ed. P. Kline (London: John Wiley & Sons, 1973), pp. 211–56. So far, the exploration of more precise understanding does not seem to have made much headway in getting nonpsychologists to spell *extraversion* the way Jung coined it.

123. See D. W. MacKinnon, "The Personality Correlates of Creativity," *Proceedings of the 14th International Congress of Applied Psychology,* vol. 2, ed. G. Nielson (Copenhagen: Munksgaard, 1962), pp. 11–39, and D. M. Quinlan and S. J. Blatt, "Field Articulation and Performance Under Stress: Differential Predictions in Surgical and Psychiatric Nursing Training," *Journal of Consulting and Clinical Psychology* 39 (1972), p. 517.

124. Herman A. Witkin and Donald R. Goodenough, *Cognitive Styles: Essence and Origins. Field Dependence and Field Independence* (New York: International Universities Press, 1981), p. 59.

125. Clifford Geertz has some telling remarks, made from an anthropological point of view, on the modern peculiarity of the sense of individuality that obtains almost universally in Europe and North America but virtually nowhere else and at no premodern time: see "From the Native's Point of View: On the Nature of Anthropological Understanding," in *Meaning and Anthropology,* eds. K. H. Basso and H. A. Selby (Albuquerque: University of New Mexico Press, 1977), pp. 221–37.

126. "September 1, 1939," quoted here from *Seven Centuries of Verse,* ed. A. J. M. Smith, 3d ed. (New York: Charles Scribner's Sons, 1967). (I quote this from there because it was the first book the library offered when I tried to check my memory— which turned out to be good except in specific punctuation—and also because the editor presents the poem in a way that suggests that he really knows, and cares about, editorial responsibility.) Auden eventually developed a perverse antipathy to this poem, first omitting one of its more impressive stanzas (and speaking scornfully about others' respect for it), and then repudiating the whole poem (with more disdainful remarks about it): it does not appear in his collected poems. I guess that most readers of the poem will agree with me, against Auden (if you want to check his trajectory on this question, trace "September 1, 1939" through the index of Humphrey Carpenter's *W. H. Auden: A biography* [London: George Allen & Unwin, 1981]), and that the result will be a sobering example of how our own judgments cannot be trusted and ought to be submitted to communal response for the sake of tradition. We often offer to tradition items—this book is in question, for instance— that the originator thinks quite fine and the community rebuffs. Sometimes the

originator is subsequently vindicated by a later, or different, community. Auden should be respected in what he once called his "professional" judgment in withdrawing "September 1, 1939." I try to respect that judgment, but I still can't think why I should join him in scrapping a poem that has been such a powerful guide to my imagination for so many years. Tradition is a difficult process, with unresolvable moral complexities. I think that one of the primary ethical rules is that no one gets to withdraw anything that has been submitted (and that word should be savored), though anyone should be allowed to withdraw *herself* from the submission—that is a different story. Such self-withdrawal ought to be respected, but its implications are not obvious within the deciding community. Let the community decide—but may the community please be more careful about how it decides.

127. Wayne Proudfoot, *God and the Self: Three Types of Philosophy of Religion* (Lewisburg: Bucknell University Press, 1976) deals with the correlation between the construct that is the idea of self and the construct that is the idea of God.

128. There were, of course, many other beginnings earlier, e.g., the division into flesh, soul, and spirit found in the Epistles of Paul, Plato's charioteer (and his *Republic),* the radically disintegrative Buddhist analysis into *skandhas,* etc.

129. A general, if somewhat breezy, survey of such matters may be found in Peter McKellar, *Mindsplit: The Psychology of Multiple Personality and the Dissociated Self* (London: J. M. Dent & Sons, 1979). For solider and more suggestive treatment, see Adam Crabtree, *Multiple Man: Explorations in Possession and Multiple Personality* (New York: Praeger, 1985).

130. Ernest R. Hilgard, *Divided Consciousness: Multiple Controls in Human Thought and Action* (New York: John Wiley & Sons, 1977), p. 1. This remarkable book surveys the history of investigation into divided consciousness and dissociation (including its unwarranted neglect for most of the present century) and presents compelling evidence, drawn from hypnotic experiments, for the view that normal personalities comprise a set of subsystems coordinated by an "Executive Center" which may yield to them, thus providing a shifting fluidity of personal forms. The hypnotic experimentation, amply described and documented in the book, discloses not only another grid of personal differences (the personal qualities of the hypnotically susceptible are differentiated from those of the nonsusceptible), but also grounds for postulating a subsystem which Hilgard calls the "Hidden Observer," who remains inactively aware of the various phases of the hypnotic episode even when the Executive Center is rendered inert and insensate. D. O. Hebb, according to Peter McKellar, has called Hilgard's work the most important in contemporary psychology. Given that Hebb's own work deserved that description twenty-five years ago, I suppose that his recommendation might be accorded rather more authority than mine, which is enthusiastic.

131. Gordon Willard Allport, *Pattern and Growth in Personality* (New York: Holt, Rinehart and Winston, 1961), p. 386.

132. Pronounced, incidentally, MAH-her, in case you're willing to care. It makes sense

if you know a bit about the perversities of Irish phonetics and late-medieval English orthography.

133. To anyone interested in this point, I recommend James Hillman, *Re-Visioning Psychology* (New York: Harper & Row, 1975), wishing that I had been organized well enough to meet it before I started writing this book rather than at the end. Still, it is a peculiar delight to find one's rudimentary insights so grandly and authoritatively supported.

134. I am thinking of the word in its older and more significant sense, deftly delineated by Ronald A. Knox in *Enthusiasm: A Chapter in the History of Religion* (Oxford: The Clarendon Press, 1961), in which it refers not to a rush of temporary celebration but a wholesale self-surrender to a particular mode of pursuing life, normally understood as inspired and guided by the Holy Spirit but usually channeled by those who preside over its recruits.

135. The literature of this strategy is already large. Some of its best accomplishments are sketched in Michael Goldberg's *Theology and Narrative: A Critical Introduction* (Nashville: Abingdon, 1982). The extent of its present influence is indicated by the fact that James Breech's thoughtful book *The Silence of Jesus: The Authentic Voice of the Historical Man* (Toronto: Doubleday, 1983) offers as an aside from its radical reconsideration of New Testament evidence, a projected application to "the question about what structures stunt and inhibit, and what structures enhance, the emergence of persons who live in story" (p. 220), without ever bothering to explain what that last phrase might mean.

136. This is sketched out both delightfully and persuasively by Stephen Crites, "The Narrative Quality of Experience," *Journal of the American Academy of Religion* 39 (1971), pp. 295–311.

137. For whatever it may be worth, I noted after writing this an account of Sri Ramakrishna: "After finding God as the Mother, He took God as His son and child. Just as a mother trains and disciplines a son and loves him, so Sri Ramakrishna saw God as an infant and found perfection in the expression of that emotion, in exalted spiritual realization. Then again, He worshipped God as Master and associated Himself as the servant . . ." (Swami Akhilananda, *Spiritual Practices* [Cape Cod: Claude Strak, Inc., 1974], p. 75). I claim nothing from the parallel, except that a frank recognition of the variability of our personal presence, and accordingly of the consequent variability in our needs and dispositions, ought at least to be considered in the formation of any spiritual diet and in any theologizing that attempts to be in touch with experience.

138. James Hillman, in *Re-Visioning Psychology* (New York: Harper & Row, 1975), makes a good Jungian case for the potential value of getting closer to the multiplicity than we are used to doing, and it is widely conceded that dissociation of personalities may be an indispensable stage in effective personal reintegration: but no one is likely to argue that it is a desirable permanent state.

139. Irvine Schiffer, "The Role of Illusion in Mental Life," *Union Seminary Quarterly Review* 36 (1981), pp. 83–93. See also, by the same author, *The Trauma of Time*

(New York: International Universities Press, 1978), especially pp. 81–117, and Karl A. Menninger, *The Vital Balance: The Life Process in Mental Health and Illness* (New York: Viking Press, 1963), pp. 357–400.

140. I am quoting myself, from Chapter 1, simply because I haven't in the meantime managed to think of a more adequate formulation. If you recognized the source, you are obviously an attentive reader. If you didn't, and are more interested in it this time than last time, then we are making progress. If you either did or didn't remember it from before, and find it disappointing now, I suggest that you brace yourself for more of the same: this is a stance from which the rest of this book will not retreat.

141. There are of course other ways: I have already dealt to some extent with historical and philosophical investigations, and will touch on some others later on. But this book is primarily concerned with the personal and the theological. I never said that there are *only* two.

142. In Greek antiquity, "theology" meant precisely the lore about the gods that was to be found in poems. The idea was revived in the late Middle Ages (see especially Boccaccio's *Genealogia Deorum Gentilium)* and found a new sponsorship and form in the late nineteenth century in the work of Matthew Arnold. (As I was working on this chapter in a café in Delhi, the café's hostess inquired what I was writing about. I said, "Theology." She asked what that was. When I explained, she smiled and said, "We call that mythology.")

143. There have been various attempts in modern times to confine theology to what is essentially a historical account, Bible-based, of the Mighty Acts of God, as if that is all we can know about God and the only way we can know it. For some of this and other variations, see James M. Robinson, *Theology as History* (New York: Harper & Row, 1967).

144. More on the word's background and early usage is helpfully presented in Kittel's *Theological Dictionary of the New Testament* and in Walter Bauer's *A Greek-English Lexicon of the New Testament.* For the legal dimension of traditional theological procedure, see T. Dzanfel-Licze, "The Alexandra Case: Samnite Dogmatic Argumentation and Claims to Ultimate Authority," *Bluebuff Law Review* 25 (1987), pp. 69–104.

145. As one indicative reminder of what Latin American liberation theology (one of the earliest and most productive tributaries to the stream) was up against, it may be noted that under the recent regime, the Argentinian bishops censored the Magnificat (Lk 1:46–55, often sung as a hymn in formal and semiformal Catholic liturgies) by omitting verse 52, with its reference to deposing those in power and exalting the humble (if we can trust the only source I have so far, which is *Le Nouvel Observateur* no. 1169 [3–9 avril, 1987] p. 46).

146. I have a basic sympathy with José Miranda's insistence that God is to be "perceived essentially as a demand for justice" *(Marx and the Bible,* trans. John Eagleson [Maryknoll: Orbis Books, 1974], p. 41), but I think this way of approaching God much too small, and implicit in the conception of God as truing. When he goes on

to say that "God . . . clearly specifies that he is knowable exclusively in the cry of the poor and the weak who seek justice" (Ibid., p. 48), he has lost me through what I take to be an insupportable valuation, and an indefensible reading, of the Bible, both of which faults are also to be found in what is apparently still the classic liberation theology text, Gustavo Gutierrez' *A Theology of Liberation: History, Politics and Salvation* (Maryknoll: Orbis Books, 1973). Schubert Ogden's thoughtful critique of liberation theology in *Faith and Freedom* (Nashville: Abingdon Press, 1979) has been met with considerable hostility but little relevant rebuttal. Osmundo Miranda, in a fine paper that as far as I know has not been published, likened liberation theology—to which camp he himself belongs—to disposable diapers. While that obviously does not characterize larger attempts like those of Juan Luis Segundo *The Liberation of Theology,* trans. John Drury (Maryknoll: Orbis Books, 1976), it strikes me as a wise thought for assessing the enterprise at present, which mainly does not pretend to deal in a comprehensive and universal fashion with the urgent problems it addresses. Much liberation theology, in fact, is not published at all but practically enacted in local situations. That too is one of its strengths, but limits its potential contribution to a large-scale theological reconstruction. The neglect of current biblical scholarship in this quarter is particularly ironic, in that the new wave of biblical scholarship is vastly more sensitive to troubled first-century social conditions than ever before, and constructs a view of Jesus that would be immeasurably more helpful to the liberation-theology cause than the easily dismissable proof-texting that now generally characterizes its appeals to the scriptural/ Dominical foundations. But it must be remembered that, especially for a major theological movement, liberation theology is extremely young—a mere twenty years ago, there was scarcely anything of the sort in print—and its present limitations are already in the process of being overcome toward more systematic and comprehensive versions of this valuable style, e.g., in the biblical competence being applied to feminist theology by such scholars as Elisabeth Schüssler Fiorenza.

147. Good surveys may be found in consulting Anne Carr, "The God Who Is Involved," *Theology Today* 38 (October, 1981), pp. 314–28, and *Journal of Ecumenical Studies* 17 (1980): issue title, "Consensus in Theology? A Dialogue with Hans Küng and Edward Schillebeeckx." (Published also as a book with the same title, ed. Leonard J. Swidler (Philadelphia: The Westminster Press, 1980).

148. "If Christ is the answer, what was the question?" is not a silly question in itself, but a calling to accountability of this style of theologizing. I have never heard or read an adequately persuasive reply. As I emphasized in my critique of classical apologetics in Chapter 4, accountability is not often instinctive, nor well done, within a theology or a religion that begins by supposing that it has the answers and only under pressure searches for the corresponding questions. It is perhaps too much to ask that theology begin with the questions (though interreligious dialogue, on which more is coming in Chapter 14, puts such a strategy close to being within reach), but it is not too much to ask that theologians be careful not merely to generate the questions from the answers, especially when the answers are experienced

within a culture that has already been formed in a traditional theological and religious image. And however much terms like "post–Christian Era" may be tossed around, no competent thinker would deny that the Western world still draws much of its value system, its categories of thought, its intellectual preoccupations, and a huge proportion of its general cultural presuppositions, from its inherited interpretations of Christianity. That biases the sense of both answer and correlated question into one another's potentially provincial arms, and plays out a large-scale analogue of the flaw inherent in Descartes' "I think, therefore I am," discussed in Chapter 9. For an example of how a biased grasp of the answer can corrupt the search for the question, consider the "What is the question to which this is the answer?" game that was popular in limited circles during the Kennedy administration in the United States. The best of the lot works well only orally, and works best when addressed to people used to driving cars in the Boston or Northern Virginia areas: the answer is "9-W," and (after a pause) the question is "Do you spell your name with a *V*, Mr. Wagner?" (The runner-up works in print too: "Strontium 90, Carbon 14" is the answer; the question is "What was the final score of the Carbon-Strontium game?")

149. David R. Griffin, *A Process Christology* (Philadelphia: The Westminster Press, 1973) offers a classic example of the virtues and (to my mind) vices of this mode. Wonderfully free of the presuppositions of usual theology, Griffin here plays deliberately into the hands of usual dogma. (His more recent work is promisingly different, apart from his *viva voce* stories.) After A. N. Whitehead, the major contributor to the enterprise has been Charles Hartshorne, whose work has still not received as much attention from Christian theologians as it deserves, despite the examples of such writers as Griffin, Schubert Ogden, and John Cobb, probably not only because it is not explicitly Christian but because it tends to come to conclusions, and to use modes of thought, that do not follow the standard Plato/Aristotle/ [Scholastics]/Descartes/Hume/Kant/Hegel/ [Kierkegaard]/[Nietzsche?]/Heidegger path of Western philosophical thought that set the dialectic for most theological developments, and therefore looks both odd and suspiciously unorthodox to many of those trained in that tradition. But that is of course one of the features that makes it most interesting and most capable of calling into useful and instructive question some of the provincial Western thought biases. I should think that liberation theologians could profit from absorbing more of this approach, for precisely that reason. Perhaps that will come.

150. Further examples may be noted in the multiauthored first number of *Communio: International Catholic Review* 6 (1979), under the general title "Approaches to the Study of Theology."

151. "Only say the word, and my soul shall be healed"—traditionally recited thrice by the congregation just before the distribution of the Eucharist.

152. While I am touching on this subject, I would like to recommend a striking essay by Peter Homans, "Toward a Psychology of Religion: By Way of Freud and Tillich," in *The Dialogue between Theology and Psychology,* ed. Peter Homans (Chicago: University of Chicago Press, 1968), pp. 53–81, which looks illuminatingly

into the common psychological tendency to swing between narcissism and self-abuse, and presses the matter theologically in a way that properly indicts our failure to believe what we pretend to believe about divine love and forgiveness. (I will say more on that subject later on. In the meantime, consider Hammarskjöld's astute observation in *Markings* to the effect that Narcissus is not a victim of vanity, but someone who responds to his sense of unworthiness with defiance.)

153. Presented in his *Pensées,* Section III, 233.

154. "From One Earth to One World," in the report of the World Commission on Environment and Development, *Our Common Future* (Oxford: Oxford University Press, 1987).

155. In the *Didache,* 9.2–3 (cf. 10.2). There will be more on this subject, with full quotations and more information, in Chapter 19.

156. [I put what follows into a note, despite the central relevance of its content, in order to spare the sensibility of my mother, who does indeed begin preparations for the next Christmas on 26 December if not earlier, and has been known to style herself "The Original Christmas Kid" (which eventually struck me as usurping a role that had already been taken). I operate on the presumption that if she reads this book at all, she will probably not bother with the notes, even those with exclamation points—hence the relegation of this to that category.] That the sheerly inventive dating of Christmas was a strategy to compete with—and, as it eventually turned out, replace—major pagan festivals is well known among those who have the sort of curiosity that inquires about such matters, but there is more to the curiosities of Christmas than the arbitrariness of 25 December. Almost all of the people who read this book (apart from my dutiful great-grandchildren, to whom copies will be bequeathed) are, I assume, more or less familiar with the components of the standard North American Christmas of [what we Christians so casually suppose everyone should refer to as] the late twentieth century. Many of these features appear in Christmases outside North America as well, and I think that there are few better ways of registering traditional Catholic-Christian adaptability than to observe a few facts about Christmas. (1) In popular North American Christianity, heir of Catholic precedents, Christmas is supposed to be the big event of the religious year, despite the fact that for the last few centuries it has, as I pointed out in Chapter 6, ranked third in formal liturgical ratings, after Easter and Epiphany; (2) No one I have ever known has ever shown serious religious discomfort about the fact that the rituals and symbols of Christmas especially involve a Santa Claus with little of sanctity about him, a tree borrowed not terribly long ago from remnants of northern European paganism (and which has never been successfully endowed with any Christian meaning), a regular incantation of "Deck the Hall with Boughs of Holly" (a song that has no Christian content whatsoever and promotes a pre-Christian religious ritual), and assorted other doings that neither originated with nor have been often offered to Christian meaning ("Yule" and "Yuletide" are pagan notions that would have become extinct some ten centuries ago, were it not for the reverent preservation of their now unintelligible names by Christian auspices—

specifically Catholic for most of that time, so Protestants are not excused from complicity if the Reformation failed to alienate Yule from Christmas and they themselves keep it up as an alternative name). (3) The Yule dimension of Christmas is faded into a dead word, mouthed but not understood, but the much more recent tradition is very much alive: ask yourself—and subsequently, under decent circumstances, friends who won't be offended by being caught out—how much venerable antiquity Santa Claus has in his present form. Chances are that they, and perhaps you, will think him part of the ancient inheritance (the last time I asked, one Protestant Evangelical respondent placed him earlier than the tenth century), perhaps vaguely identified with the Yule of the misty past, and will not have realized he is barely a century old, and that one of the problems of finesse in the last hundred Christmases has been how to transform the nearly definitive Santa of " 'Twas the Night before Christmas" (try to remember, as a trivial pursuit, the real title of the foundational poem) from the original diminutive elf to a full-sized, even portly, person, without compromising his ability to get down a chimney. It doesn't seem to have been difficult to do so: are you aware of any objection? Think about that. (4) Those of us who are old enough to remember (and in some cases, such as mine, to resent) the intrusion of Rudolph the Red-nosed Reindeer to dilute *our* established Christmas, quite complete as it was, thank you, with a solstice tree and a bunch of druidic mistletoe and a fat desanctified man who rode the sky by the power of reindeer alone, negotiated chimneys almost miraculously but with no evidence of piety about it, and left, ideally, elf-made toy machine guns and tawdry plastic jewelery as the record of his commercially faithful visit (none of this has any real relationship to Christianity), may be amused, and usefully informed about how tradition works, by questioning those who did not enjoy the privilege of having lived before the introduction of Rudolph. (Rudolph was evidently first offered to the tradition in 1939 by Robert Lewis May—who also gave us, less contagiously, *Benny the Bunny Liked Beans*—but got a big boost a few years later through the popularity of an astonishingly stupid song as rendered by Gene Autry, whose decline from the heroic position in which I had placed him for his cowboy achievements began at that point and for that reason.) Post-Rudolph informants are likely to presume, as many whom I have questioned have done, that he belongs to some sort of time immemorial, as least as old as fat (yet chimneyable) Santa himself, and will not appreciate your testimony about the joys of a pure, traditional, Rudolphless Christmas such as we once had.

All this, of course, provides the chance of an interesting exercise in assessing how tradition works. I am personally struck by the resemblance between the development of Christmas and the attitudes of Piaget's beginners at marbles. It is interesting and instructive to observe how thoroughly most of us remain, Christmaswise, at the first or low second level, close to beginners in the game despite the obvious historical and theological opportunities for advancement.

157. The Christianizing appropriation of the Hebrew Scriptures and of small writings on John the Baptist as heralds of Christianity goes back to the earliest days: I have

argued the impropriety of this in *Five Gospels*. It is well established that the popular medieval tale of Barlaam and Josaphat—not to be confused with the much later authentic Josephat of the Ukraine—is only an adjusted rerun of an Indian story of the Buddha. Anyone who compares the non-Christian Gnostic *Eugnostos the Blessed* with the Christian version *The Sophia of Jesus Christ* will conclude that the latter is a superficially Christianized adaptation of the former rather than the other way around (the two are presented in parallel texts by Douglas M. Parrott in *The Nag Hammadi Library in English,* ed. James M. Robinson [San Francisco: Harper & Row, 1978], pp. 207–28).

158. For example, Montmartre in Paris, like the parallel Montmartre in Avallon and St.-Michel Montmalchus in Poitou and various other sites dedicated to St. Michael, was once a shrine of the Roman god Mercury. Its original name, Mons Mercurii, was apparently not hard to adjust to a Christian-sounding deformation to support its rededication to St.-Denis, just as the attributes of its mercurial dedicatee as winged messenger were readily transferred to the leading archangel. See the article on "Montmartre" by H. Leclercq in *Dictionnaire d' Archéologie et de Liturgie,* vol. 11 (Paris: Librairie Letouzey et Ané, 1934), pp. 2673–74.

159. Earliest Christian art mainly transformed the meaning of available motifs that happened to be in the repertoire of available undistinguished artisans, and thus got a standard image of the god Hermes in his Criophorus (ram-bearing) form, who was conveniently reinterpretable as the Good Shepherd; for portraits of Jesus, there was no attempt at authentic memory—earliest forms use a routine Eastern icon of Hermes with short curly hair or a Greek hero/god with shoulder-length hair, both unbearded (the bearded form came into prominence later, derived from a Syrian form: see Charles Rufus Morey, *Early Christian Art,* 2d ed. [Princeton: Princeton University Press, 1953], pp. 63–66 and fn. 323; and the same author's *Medieval Art* [New York: W. W. Norton, 1942], pp. 43–44). The crucifix that later became, and still is, the classic Christian artifact came later still, probably not because of a lack of confidence in Paul but possibly because of a lack of competence in available artists, who worked with a repertoire of established conventional images and had surely never been asked before to represent such a subject. Isis with her child Horus, an image widespread in the eastern Mediterranean, was metamorphosed into what eventually became another classic, the Madonna and infant Jesus. (See V. Tran Tam Tinh, *Isis Lactans* [Leiden: Brill, 1973], a fascinating book in which the author's disinclination to complete the connection between the two traditions of meaning in his account seems to me to derive from motives distinct from those that properly guide a historian of art. It is difficult for me to imagine that anyone who looks at the Isis-Horus images he provides, and has even a modest competence in iconographical history, could doubt that Christians again in this case appropriated and reinterpreted a routine image that had at first virtually no theological or evangelical significance in the tradition but subsequently acquired great Mariological—though no successful Christological—power.)

160. For the absorption of pagan rites, see Hugo Rahner, *Greek Myths and Christian*

Mystery (London: Burns and Oates, 1963). This, of course, still goes on wherever Christian missions incorporate members of previously un-Christianized cultures, though sometimes in ways hidden from the missionaries. The development of the cult of the saints was amply fortified by this process. (But has sometimes produced ironic later collisions: Anglican and Roman Catholic missions in Africa experienced some difficulties when they evangelized tribes who spent considerable religious energy trying to keep their dead ancestors, who might be potentially mischievous or malevolent, as powerless as possible.)

161. The rosary, like the earlier St. Barlaam, may have been borrowed from Buddhist, or Hindu, custom, though the evidence is inconclusive. The early standard *orans* attitude of prayer, with arms spread apart, familiar to modern Catholics through the rubrical gesture used by the celebrant when saying *oremus* or "let us pray," was certainly taken from pre-Christian Hellenistic practice.

162. Christian monasticism, for instance, seems to have borrowed from the earlier Buddhist *sangha,* as well as from traditions that embraced Pythagoreans, Essenes, Therapeutae, and various eremitic types.

163. The theology of the Church Fathers is in many respects built on the contributions of Plato and of non-Christian philosophers of the Platonic tradition. The great tradition of medieval Scholastic theology could not have come about without the adoption of the work of pre-Christian Aristotle, which Christian theologians received gladly from Islamic philosophers along with those philosophers' commentaries on it and their own original speculative work. For a splendid treatment of various aspects of the subject, including these, see Étienne Gilson, *History of Christian Philosophy in the Middle Ages* (New York: Random House, 1955).

164. The Roman Catholic Church has always been wary, for good reason, of acknowledging any real change in its teaching, but anyone who investigates the history of Cyprian's notion that salvation is impossible except through the official church *(Extra Ecclesiam nulla salus)* will have difficulty denying that the meaning of the formula has changed considerably since its early days. Newman's celebrated *An Essay on the Development of Christian Doctrine* (1845) was, and has been cherished as, a defense of dogma's capacity to develop without changing, and is essentially an exercise in saving both historical appearances and Catholic face. The more candid admission would be that important positions have changed, usually a little more swiftly than geological eras but slowly enough to disguise the change from those who have no access to historical inquiry. Those who *do* have access are on the whole not fooled by the pretense. In fact, they can spot rather abrupt instances of official about-face: see the telling examples concisely given by Walter Principe—recently, until his conscientious resignation, a member of the Vatican's International Theological Commission—in *The Ecumenist* 25 (1987), pp. 70–73, entitled "When 'Authentic' Teachings Change." The examples include not only substantial changes in official teachings on marriage, reversals of formal condemnations of the "errors" of such teachers as Thomas Aquinas, and the enlarging of the defined limits of the pool of persons eligible for salvation, but also the abandonment of authentic teachings in

protection of the moral legitimacy of the institution of slavery—in 1965! (see John Maxwell, *Slavery and the Catholic Church: The History of Catholic Teaching* [Chichester: Rose, 1975], where the author argues persuasively that a major reason for this absurd delay was that the legitimacy of slavery had been Catholic doctrine for so long that it seemed to many traditionalists inappropriate to change it).

165. Catholic ashrams like Aikiya Alayam in Madras and Saccidananda (Shantivanam) just outside Tannirpalli are deliberately imitative of Hindu precedents and might fruitfully be imitated in turn outside India. The modern Catholic policy of inculturation (Fr. Ignatius Hirudayam of Aikiya Alayam prefers the more appropriate word—more consonant with his remarks cited in note 178 in Chapter 14—*conculturation)* has produced a multitude of examples, including the Indian liturgy from which I quote in Chapter 14 (p. 230).

166. In terms of texts, this is being impressively remedied for readers of English by the translations (and occasional English originals) of Christian spiritual classics published by Paulist Press and by Amity House; but much more needs doing, beyond present pioneering attempts, before the Christian classical tradition of spirituality can be brought into general practical use.

167. *Apologia I,* 46.

168. *Apologia I,* 5, 22, 23, 54, 62, 64, 66.

169. Especially pre-Christian varieties (see 55.1), but in an extraordinary passage (chapter 25), he seems to accord to the temple at Heliopolis an ongoing miraculous privilege.

170. *Relatio Symmachi Urbis Praefectif., Patrologia Latina* 16, 966–71; cf. Ambrose, *Epistola 18* (Ibid., 971–82).

171. *". . . non est nisi religio una in rituum varietate" (Nicolai de Cusa De Pace Fidei,* ed. R. Klibansky and H. Bascour [London: The Warburg Institute, 1956], p. 7).

172. E.g., in his well-known colloquy, *The Godly Feast (Convivium Religiosum),* Nephalius is made boldly to say "Saint Socrates, pray for us!" (See *The Colloquies of Erasmus,* trans. Craig R. Thompson [Chicago: University of Chicago Press, 1965], p. 68).

173. See *"Christianae Fidei brevis et clara Expositio,"* in *Huldrici Zuingli Opera,* vol. 4, ed. M. Schuler and O. Schilthess (Zürich: 1841), p. 65.

174. J. F. Raulin, *Historia Ecclesiae Malabaricae cum Diamperitana Synodo* (Rome: 1745), p. 85; cited in M. V. Cyriac, *Meeting of Religions* (Madras-Madurai: Dialogue Series, no. 3, 1982), p. 148.

175. On the Protestant side, two significant illustrative examples are Hendrik Kraemer, whose intransigent views as expressed in his *The Christian Message in a Non-Christian World* (London: Edinburgh House Press, 1938) were highly influential for at least a generation in the Protestant mission field (and among those back home who supported the missions), and Karl Barth, the dominant figure in the dominant Protestant theological movement of the same period, who wrote that Christianity "alone has the commission and the authority to be a missionary religion, i.e., to confront the world of religions as the one true religion, with absolute self-confi-

dence to invite and challenge it to abandon its ways and to start on the Christian way" *(Church Dogmatics,* I/2 [Edinburgh: Clark, 1956], p. 357). It is not difficult to find still more extreme examples, e.g., emphasizing the inevitable damnation of non-Christians.

176. My translation of the text as presented in *The Liber Usualis* (Tournai: Desclée & Co., 1952), pp. 703–04.

177. I quote this from the popular parish pamphlet-missal, *Living with Christ* (Ottawa: Novalis) in its Easter season edition. There are of course still some provincialities here, e.g., the characterization of the Jewish people as "the first to hear the word of God," but the advance renders them relatively trivial as limitations.

178. Ignatius Hirudayam, "Maturation of the Asian Church," *Bulletin: Secretariatus pro non Christianis* 53 [XVIII/2] (1983), p. 147.

179. *New Orders of the Mass for India* (Bangalore: National Biblical Catechetical and Liturgical Centre, 1974), pp. 35, 45, 59.

180. The Vatican's Secretariat for Non-Christians, founded after the Second Vatican Council, is predictably cautious about such developments, as may be seen in its position paper, "The attitude of the Church towards the followers of other religions," *Bulletin: Secretariatus pro non Christianis,* 56 [XIX/2] (1984), pp. 126–41. The subtitle is significant: it is "Reflections and orientations on dialogue and mission," and it is clear from the paper that dialogue is to be interpreted in the light of mission. That is also clear from the history of the secretariat, treated in Pietro Rossano, "The Secretariat for Non-Christians from the beginnings to the present day: history, ideas, problems," *Bulletin* 41–42 [XIV/2–3] (1979), pp. 88–109, in which the author pointedly remarks that "A Christian cannot place his own faith and other religions on the same level. He cannot hold that the Holy Spirit dwells equally in the Church, in Hinduism and in the dar-es-Islam" (p. 104). This too is not peculiarly Catholic: the analogous body in the World Council of Churches—Dialogue with Men of Living Faiths and Ideologies—is a bit younger than the secretariat, and its Guidelines for Inter-Religious Dialogue, formulated by its original director, S. J. Samartha, and published in 1972 (see "The Progress and Promise of Inter-Religious Dialogues," *Journal of Ecumenical Studies* 9 [1972], pp. 473–74), also deliberately manifest the theological caution appropriate to central bodies attempting to guide a wholesome consensus rather than to pioneer a dramatic breakthrough (see Paul F. Knitter, *No Other Name?* [Maryknoll: Orbis Books, 1984], p. 139).

181. There is considerable activity in the attempts to do so. On the Catholic side, some of the most promising developments may be found in Paul F. Knitter, *No Other Name?: A Critical Survey of Christian Attitudes Toward the World Religions* (Maryknoll: Orbis Books, 1985) and Hans Küng, *Christianity and the World Religions* (New York: Doubleday, 1986).

182. The precedent that will probably come to mind for many readers is medieval Córdoba, where Christian philosophers and theologians were deeply enriched in their understanding through their exchanges with their Jewish and Muslim counterparts. But I wish that the precedent that would come even more readily to mind

were the world of the first Christian generation, which offered an extraordinary opportunity that was engaged for a while but eventually went inadequately exploited on account of the same sort of suspicious reluctance and misplaced hostility and distorted self-understanding that inhibits Christians in our own time and prevents them from taking advantage of the ripeness of the moment. Try next time to think of the first Christian generation as the one that had the best shot at truing Christianity through hospitable attention to other religious ways, and got started on the project, but didn't move nearly far enough in that direction. Thinking especially of that missed chance, with appropriate forgiving regret, would be helpful to the cause of trying not to miss it this time around.

183. Particularly good on this insight is the work of R. C. Zaehner, e.g., *The Comparison of Religions* (Boston: Beacon Press, 1962) and *At Sundry Times* (London: Faber and Faber, 1958).

184. See Steven T. Katz, "Language, Epistemology, and Mysticism," *Mysticism and Philosophical Analysis,* ed. Steven T. Katz (New York: Oxford University Press, 1978), pp. 3–60, and "The 'Conservative' Character of Mystical Experience," *Mysticism and Religious Traditions,* ed. Steven T. Katz (New York: Oxford University Press, 1983). This is still a contested field, and loaded with defensive biases; but its advances beyond the romance of the mystical can be seen in Frits Staal, *Exploring Mysticism: A Methodological Essay* (Berkeley: University of California Press, 1975), which is sharply critical of the biases of some slightly earlier writers, and William J. Wainwright, *Mysticism: A Study of Its Nature, Cognitive Value and Moral Implications* (Brighton: The Harvester Press, 1981), which takes account of some of the more serious experiments with chemically induced simulations of mystical experience.

185. Ironically, the recent brouhaha over Martin Scorsese's rather innocuous, if somewhat dopey, film rendition of Nikos Kazantzakis' *The Last Temptation of Christ* seems to have been mainly over the thorough humanness of its Jesus, as if "thorough" (which is entirely orthodox) somehow implied "exclusive" (which the cherished pronouncement of the Council of Chalcedon took great pains to deny).

186. See, for instance, Sri Aurobindo, *The Mother* (Pondicherry: Sri Aurobindo Ashram, 1972), vol. 25 of the Sri Aurobindo Birth Centenary Library, pp. 47ff., which argues the divinity of Mirra Richard with an easy lightness unknown to Christian pondering of its own central thought.

187. *Phaedo,* 114c.

188. See Sebastian Moore, "Some Principles for an Adequate Theism." *Downside Review* 95 (1977), pp. 201–13, for a thoughtful and obviously experienced reflection on how contemplation trues and disciplines one's conception of God. Moore is firm about the independence of the conception, and argues that it should not be *drawn from* contemplative experience, only reshaped and reflavored by it. He also gives helpful suggestions about typical fallacies and near misses in the application of comtemplative experience to a normative notion of God.

189. There is a large literature on various forms of meditation, from which I cull a few worthy and readily accessible samples: Thomas Merton, *Seeds of Contemplation*

(originally Norfolk, Conn.: New Directions, 1949, with many editions since) and *Contemplative Prayer* (New York: Herder and Herder, 1969); William Johnston, *Christian Zen* (New York: Harper & Row, 1971); Morton T. Kelsey, *The Other Side of Silence: A Guide to Christian Meditation* (New York: Paulist Press, 1976); Bradley Hanson, *The Call of Silence: Discovering Christian Meditation* (Minneapolis: Augsburg Publishing House, 1980); John Main, *Moment of Christ: The Path of Meditation* (New York: Crossroad, 1984); Laurence Freeman, *Light Within: The Inner Path of Meditation* (New York: Crossroad, 1987). Three others deserve special mention: Theresa O'Callaghan Scheihing, with Louis M. Savary, *Our Treasured Heritage: Teaching Christian Meditation to Children* (New York: Crossroad, 1981), which does a remarkably fine job with a topic easy to bungle; and the classic by Reginald Garrigou-Lagrange, *The Three Ages of the Interior Life,* 2 vols. (St. Louis: B. Herder, 1947 and 1948)—a translation by Timothea Doyle of *Traité de théologie ascétique et mystique,* 2 vols. (Paris: Éditions du Cerf, 1938); and the fairly tough-minded inquiry into the subject in Douglas A. Fox, *Meditation and Reality: A Critical View* (Atlanta: John Knox Press, 1986).

190. Niels Bohr is reputed to have taken enough time off from physics to formulate a relevant law: you can't express yourself more clearly than you think. This is, I think, a useful complement to Aristotle's reminder that we should not expect more precision than the particular subject-matter allows.

191. See Otto Kurz, *Fakes,* 2d ed. (New York: Dover Publications, 1967); I find Part VI (pp. 116–41) particularly instructive. How William Henry Ireland managed to pass off his plays as the work of Shakespeare may mystify anyone who knows enough of literature to see how clearly eighteenth century they are, unless one (a) has read enough student papers to see how readily Shakespeare's work can be interpretively distorted even into a twentieth-century mind-set, and (b) has some awareness that one's own understanding of Shakespeare is, however archaeologically submissive in intent, certain to be full of indeliberate and unnoticed projections that a later age would easily detect as peculiarly typical of the period of Elizabeth II.

192. The word comes from the earlier English word *buhsum,* bendable, and is related to *bow.*

193. Cf. the recent popular game of inventing Sniglets, words that capture concepts that had not been verbally isolated (the word *Sniglets* being itself an obvious example). My favorite Sniglet candidate to date (still unnamed) was offered somewhat unplayfully by a witty university colleague in a public discussion of some suspect administrative proposals: when an administrator, whose academic discipline happened to be psychology, suggested that the suspicion was paranoid, he replied that there ought to be a parallel technical term to refer to a tendency to dismiss as paranoid an apprehensiveness about real dangers.

194. I say more on this subject in "Liberation (?) Theology (?) for North America (?)," in *Liberation Theology for North America,* ed. Deane William Ferm (New York: Paragon, 1987).

195. Gordon D. Kaufman, *The Theological Imagination: Constructing the Concept of God* (Philadelphia: The Westminster Press, 1981), p. 76.

196. Langdon Gilkey, "The Christian Understanding of Suffering," *Buddhist-Christian Studies* 5 (1985), p. 49.

197. Frank Whaling, "The Development of the Word 'Theology,' " *Scottish Journal of Theology* 34 (1981) pp. 289–312, surveys the use of the word from earliest Greek times to the present, and offers what seems to me to be a well-considered case for using its unadjectivalized form to denote the universal shared enterprise rather than a tradition-specific version of it. I have not come across a good study of what is really going on in the minds and hearts of those who are hostile to such a suggestion, and hope that somebody will produce one. In the meantime, I have taken sides.

198. This, if my procedural definition be accepted, is true even of those who think such language unwelcome and superfluous. They of course are unlikely to be interested in a theological project of any kind. But that hardly makes their contributions useless to those who are. Perspicacious critics of religious and theological views are important resources for a reconstructive theology, far from being deleterious to it.

199. I confess that I really wanted to say "impersonation" (i.e., the creative act of becoming and being a coordinated person) rather than "personhood," since it would better capture the dynamic nature of the reality in question, but I have so overtaxed the reader's patience with my verbal unorthodoxies thus far that I thought it best to let this one go, except to the extent that mentioning it gives me an occasion for renewing my gratitude to those of you who have done the extra mental work without grumbling.

200. *Republic,* Book III, 21–22; 414B–417B.

201. *Phaedo,* 107d–114c.

202. *Phaedo,* 114d.

203. Speaking of conventional certitude, have you ever wondered why sixty-five is the magic age for human obsolescence? If you track it down, I think you will find that Bismarck, in the course of instituting what was probably the world's first organized social-welfare program (inferior to the traditional extended-family social-welfare customs, perhaps, but a good move nevertheless) calculated on the basis of German demographical evidence that sixty-five was a good turning point, insofar as most respectable Germans were decorously dead by then and the few remaining could be afforded. We hang on to the age limit, mindlessly, because it is traditional, even though the actuarial tables have changed. Think about it.

204. A splendid combination of careful critical inquiry into and thoughtful interpretive reflection on the nativity stories will be found in Raymond E. Brown, *The Birth of the Messiah* (Garden City, N. Y.: Doubleday, 1977).

205. The texts are most readily accessible in Montague Rhodes James, *The Apocryphal New Testament* (Oxford: Oxford University Press, 1924) and, more recent and scholarly, E. Hennecke, *New Testament Apocrypha,* ed. W. Schneemelcher, 2 vols. (London: Lutterworth Press, 1963, 1965). The ox and ass come from the Gospel of Pseudo-Matthew (Hennecke vol. 1, p. 410), the clay birds from the Infancy Story of

Thomas (ibid., p. 393). Some of these texts were well known in the Middle Ages, and for a thousand years they had more influence on literature and art than the Bible did. Their present general neglect has resulted in the popular loss of another edifying image of the child Jesus, withering up a playmate who broke his artificial pools by the brook, and causing another lad to drop dead for making the mistake of bumping into his shoulder (ibid., p. 393).

206. For example: the Pontifical Biblical Commission, early in the current century, insisted on the literalness of Adam and Eve, the Mosaic authorship of the first five books of the Bible, the historical character of Genesis 1–3; Catholic scholars were forbidden to have any truck with positions to the contrary, and were explicitly informed that obsequious silence was inadequate (internal assent was required) and that to speak or write contrary opinions was a matter of grave sin. When the ban was lifted by Pius XII in *Divino afflante spiritu* (in 1943), it became clear that this heavy-handedness had successfully controlled the publication of counterideas, but not the thinking of them: the official position had quietly been abandoned by those Catholic scholars on whom it had been especially enjoined, and when they resumed public action, Protestant scholars were pleasantly surprised to discover that they had kept in shape during the darkened years and were now to be taken very seriously on matters of communal scholarly importance. On the more popular level, the public reception of and response to Paul VI's *Humanae vitae* is far too well known to require comment.

207. Since a few of the readers of this book will know me well enough to realize that the feeble and rudimentary condition of my Japanese must make this paragraph highly suspect, I refer them to Roy Andrew Miller, *Origins of the Japanese Language* (Seattle: University of Washington Press, 1980), pp. 28–29. The bits that I don't derive from Miller come from my having checked up on his remarks about *teisetsu* in conversations with Japanese professors while I was working in Nagoya. Trust me.

208. See, for early stages of the process, D. P. Walker, *The Decline of Hell: Seventeenth-Century Discussions of Eternal Torment* (London: Routledge and Kegan Paul, 1964).

209. This was an inspiration for much of the revisioning of Alfred North Whitehead, whose work in turn has inspired some of the most interesting Christian theology of our time.

210. E.g., note the use of Heidegger's work in the retheologizing of Rudolf Bultmann and many since. This is of course a type of imitation that is approximately as old as theology itself, and is often much more dramatic in its inception than it appears to have been later: in the long reign of the remarkable work of Thomas Aquinas over Catholic theology, it was not always remembered that his borrowing from the recently restored philosophy of Aristotle was sufficiently controversial to inspire the condemnation of Aquinas' works by Bishop Étienne Tempier of Paris in 1277.

211. Most recently, the Frankfurt School (especially Jürgen Habermas) has made a considerable impact on theological imagination, e.g., see Dennis P. McCann, "Habermas and the Theologians," *Religious Studies Review* 7 (1981), pp. 14–21.

212. Hegel's implicit invitations, such as his remark that art "enters into the same circle

with Religion and Philosophy, and is only a special mode and form of bringing the Divine, with the deepest interests of man and the most comprehensive truths of the spiritual life, to consciousness and expression" *(The Philosophy of Art* [New York: D. Appleton, 1879], p. 12), have not yet been followed by a large-scale reinterpretation of theology from that perspective, but there is considerable activity along these lines.

213. The Gentiles had their own ways of promising themselves such a grand finale, e.g., through the Mysteries of Eleusis, whose alumni seem to have been confident that they had an eternal happy future. But two alternatives were common. One was the conviction that death put an end to everything: many an ancient grave is decorated with the epitaph "I was not, I came to be, I am not, I care not." The other was an apprehensiveness ranging from uneasiness through anxiety to terror about what awaited ex-mortals in Hades. It is this feeling that inspires the aging Cephalus to try to get on the right side of the governing powers in his final days, and therefore to initiate an inquiry about what *dikaiosunê* (justice/righteousness) really is, the response to which is the rest of Plato's *Republic;* it is this feeling that Plato soothes with the myth of the True Earth at the end of the *Phaedo;* and it is this feeling that Lucretius addressed when he proclaimed Epicurus' doctrine of total extinction as a piece of good news. In this context, the Christian Gospel obviously offered much better news than the *Phaedo*'s hopeful stab in the dark, the *Republic*'s moral insurance policy with its uncertain backing, or the bleak euthanasia of Epicurus and Lucretius.

214. The judgment of the sheep and the goats in Mt 25:31–46 appears at first to look like a general resurrection, but in fact it never mentions any resurrection at all and is quite consistent with being read as a judgment of those who happen still to be alive when the Son or King arrives: the rewarded and the punished are those who have been kind or unkind to Christians, and the heroes and villains of the pre-Christian past are not brought into the picture. Rv 20:12–15 more clearly envisages a general resurrection, since the dead are given up out of the sea and out of death and hell and stand before God—but they are not actually said to be resurrected, and in the allusive and symbolic style of this book, it is not utterly clear that they are not merely being put on display before either being found in the Book of Life or sent back into the place of death and torment. Jn 5:28–29 offers what seems to be a general resurrection—out of the graves come those whose raising is to life and those bound for damnation—but this is not typical of the Fourth Gospel and is inconsistent with the view expressed only three verses previously. Acts 24:15 specifies a resurrection of both the righteous and the unrighteous, but beyond that there is not much unequivocal evidence—and that particular piece of evidence is not of much use (see next note).

215. Not the Paul of Acts 24:15, of course, who is not the real Paul (whom Luke evidently knew much less well than tradition would have it). Paul's own writings repeatedly emphasize the connection between Jesus' resurrection and the coming

resurrection of those who are made righteous in him (e.g., 2 Cor 4:14; Rom 4:25, 8:11; 1 Thes 4:13–17) and does not deal with a resurrection of the unrighteous.

216. E.g., Jn 6:39, 40, 44, 54 clearly raise up on the last day only those who have become eligible through association with Jesus. The general line is that special life is available through Jesus for those who respond appropriately to him, and everyone else dies permanently in their sin. Further difficulties with what the Fourth Gospel means by resurrection will be dealt with presently, but it seems clear that whatever it is, it isn't given to all.

217. Lk 14:14 refers explicitly to "the resurrection of the just," and Matthew reports (27:52–53) that it was the bodies of dead saints that were raised at the time of Jesus' crucifixion. Most of the Synoptic evidence is too oblique to help.

218. 1 Thes 4:14. The subsequent verses are not entirely clear, but seem to sustain the notion that the sleep is in heaven, and the rising—the usual verb for resurrection is used—takes place there, presumably in a spiritual body.

219. Jn 5:24, 8:24.

220. E.g., Rom 6:4–5, 8:10–11, and cf. Col 2:12.

221. See *Five Gospels,* pp. 278–84.

222. There, however, they are muted, quite plausibly in order to accommodate the alternative view reflected in Jesus' admonition to Mary Magdalene not to touch him (20:17) and in his ability to appear in a room whose doors are locked (20:19, 26): Jesus shows them his hands and feet, and invites Thomas to touch his hands and side, and offers bread and fish to his disciples, but it is never said that he ate, or that anyone touched him, or even what they saw when beholding his hands and feet. A close reading of 20:17 will disclose that whoever wrote it was evidently assuming that the risen Jesus did not appear to Peter and the brethren, but only (in a limited way) to Mary.

223. This movement has been sketched by Bernhard Lang, "The Sexual Life of the Saints: Towards an Anthropology of Christian Heaven," *Religion* 17 (1987), pp. 149–71, and will undoubtedly be further chronicled in his promised *Paradise Found: A Cultural History of Heaven,* which is still awaited at this writing.

224. Conversations with various educated and thoughtful Christians have persuaded me that this possibility is being pursued far more extensively than I had recently supposed. Examples of how and why may be found in John Hick, *Death and Eternal Life* (London: Collins, 1976), chapters 16–19 (pp. 297–396); Geddes MacGregor, *Reincarnation as a Christian Hope* (London: Macmillan, 1982); Ian Stevenson, *Twenty Cases Suggestive of Reincarnation,* 2d ed. (Charlottesville: University Press of Virginia, 1974), and *Cases of the Reincarnation Type,* 3 vols. (Charlottesville: University Press of Virginia, 1974–1979).

225. Earnest afterlife speculations among the Jews are not recorded until less than two centuries before the Christian era. The Hebrew Scriptures speak of resting in Abraham's bosom, but that seems to have been no more than a metaphor derived from the practice of interring bodies in the family tomb, and to have had no more clout than contemporary evasive phrases like "gone to her rest" and "passed away."

They also speak of Sheol, but that is no comfort: Sheol, quite appropriately translated as *Hades* in the Greek versions, is little more than a dustbin of human shadows, and is no fun. The only references to personal resurrection in the Hebrew Scriptures occur in their last-written book, Daniel (12:2). (Ezekiel's vision of the dry bones reconnected [Ez 37], according to the most informed scholarship, was meant, and was taken, as a metaphor for the restoration of Israel.) The Wisdom of Jesus Ben Sira, alias Sirach or Ecclesiasticus, written not long before Daniel, repeatedly (most forcefully in 14:11–19) reminds its readers—not polemically, as if correcting false hopes, but just pointedly, as if reminding them of what they already know—that there is nothing on the other side of death. The continuity of that view is probably what the Gospels and Acts mean by remarking that the Sadducees did not believe in resurrection, which was a doctrine associated with the Pharisees, as Acts 23:6–8 rightly suggests.

226. I have not yet found reincarnation congenial for a variety of reasons (most of which are not to my credit), but I think I have lost my original contempt for it (though I still think it a mistake to link it with personal karma, and accordingly resent its use as a tool for making people resign themselves to an unhappy lot as if they deserved it). And although I am skeptical about the memories of previous lives reported by various people, including a good and deeply intelligent friend, and remain unpersuaded by all the explanatory theories I know (including his), two considerations have caught my fancy with respect to the usefulness of entertaining reincarnation as a provisional component of a provisional afterlife-image. The first involves karma, unfortunately, but that need not be a problem in a private ideology. It is this: many of us (including me) are willing to engage in forms of self-deformation and self-destruction that we would not dream of extending to anyone else, and to suppose that someone else—i.e., the next reincarnation—may have to suffer for it might be usefully disciplining. The second is a Tibetan Buddhist theory and meditational practice that begins by supposing that "The cultivation of an aspiration to highest enlightenment begins with the recognition of all sentient beings as mothers" *(Instructions on the Three Principal Aspects of the Path,* by the Fourth Panchen Lama, in *Practice and Theory of Tibetan Buddhism,* trans. Geshe Lhunda Sopa and Jeffrey Hopkins [London: Rider and Company, 1976], p. 27) and proceeds through exercises in realizing that any creature at all was once, in the uncountable past incarnations, your mother, and should be responded to with appropriate practical compassion. That strikes me as worth considering. (And to those Freudians who suppose that they have got my dismissable number by deriving my preoccupation with God from my various bits of mother-talk, I feel that it is time for me to confess that part of my reason for including the latter was to tease them.)

227. John J. Heaney, "Some Implications of Parapsychology for Theology," *Theological Studies* 40 (1979), pp. 474–94, offers a fine survey, with citation of further helpful materials, of ESP, OBE, etc. (For OBE—"out-of-body experience"—see also Susan J. Blackmore, *Beyond the Body: An Investigation of Out-of-the-Body Experiences* [London: Heinemann, 1982] and Karlis Osis and Elendur Heraldsson, *At the*

Hour of Death [New York: Avon, 1977].) Alan Gauld offers a thoughtful and fair review of the overall state of the question of survival after death in *Mediumship and Survival: A Century of Investigations* (London: Heinemann, 1982). There is much current romanticism on this subject (I think it is relatively new in Western culture, an interestingly spontaneous response to the prevailing dreariness of currently governing assumptions, but that judgment may be wrong: there is little documentary evidence before the current century, but it may previously have been underground or have been carried by the assumption that the saints are released to make contact while the damned or the purgatorially confined are not. At any rate, there are analogues in antiquity, and it surely may be classified as a recurring motif, which says something in its favor). In the meantime, my view is starkly conditioned by a man whom I met in a pub in Southampton, who told me that he had died on the operating table (in the judgment of the surgeons, subsequently reported to him) and that the coordinate experience had changed his life much for the worse. *His* experience was not the glow of light, etc., reported by many others in similar circumstances. He was flung out to the cold and the darkness, and went miserably into what seemed to be an endless abandonment. He called God "the Cosmic Joker," and was morosely bitter about it, and had been so since the experience. I tried to help him abandon that god, by asking whether he had had any experiences of genuine love or joy. He admitted that this was the case, and under further cross-examination acknowledged that even a Cosmic Joker couldn't erase that from the happenings of the world, and that he himself was therefore entitled to the last laugh even in the face of a Cosmic Joker. That is where he could get a new start, I guessed, toward finding God beyond the one who had abandoned him, a god who was not truing enough to be thus entitled. His kind of evidence does not appear very often in the literature on those who have had what seems to be a taste of death, but it deserves to be taken as seriously as the alternatives. We just don't know what it's like. It is not necessary to know. We can be faithful without knowing: it is possible to do *now* well even if we can't be sure of what comes next. Doing *now* well may possibly require suspending caring about what comes next.

228. Origen thought it was from an Apocalypse of Elijah, but we don't know why he thought that.

229. Acts 10 is the *locus classicus,* with its story of how Peter, besieged by visions and voices and an angelic visitor and the spectacle of an outpouring of the Holy Spirit on Gentiles who were responsive to his gospel, finally succumbed to, and successfully promoted, the conviction that Gentile converts need not be concerned with circumcision and dietary laws. Mt 9:14–15 is more subtle, but cut from matching cloth: it is probably a fiction invented to justify the resumption of the practice of regular fasting, which had been temporarily suspended under the influence of Jesus.

230. The most obvious example is the countermission which Paul rebukes in Galatians, whose missionaries evidently advocated observance of circumcision even for Gentile converts.

231. For instance, 2 Tm 2:17–18 mentions Hymenaeus and Philetus as claiming that

the resurrection has already taken place—presumably a spiritualized reinterpretation of resurrection like that found in the Fourth Gospel (e.g., Jn 11:25–26), inspired by the tendency of Gentiles (and Jewish schools of thought that had absorbed Gentile ideas) to find a literal material resurrection rather bizarre (cf. Acts 17:32).

232. 2 Peter still clings to the claim that Jesus will come soon for the final judgment, but reports (very disapprovingly) that some now note that the world seems to be business-as-usual and scoff at the received promise (3:1–4). They were, of course, right: it was not to be soon, as history proved. That is, it at least was not to be soon in the form in which it had been promised: the Fourth Gospel's reinterpretive view that the final judgment has already taken place in a less spectacular fashion (e.g., 5:24) may have arisen from a combination of both motives.

233. See the rebuke in 2 Pt 2:1, and my general treatment of this movement in chapter 4 of *Five Gospels*.

234. Ex 1:7 bridges, in one verse, the gap between the death of Joseph and his brothers, which is where Genesis ends, and the time of Moses, which appears to have been roughly five hundred years later. The next nearly thousand years of the Jewish religious story is then told more or less continuously through various books of the Hebrew Scriptures.

235. Since the *Didache* is far less easily accessible than 1 Corinthians, and certainly deserving of equal time, I quote its eucharistic prayers from chapters 9 and 10: [over the cup] "We give you thanks, our Father, for the holy vine of your son David, which you made known to us through your son Jesus: glory to you forever! . . . [over the bread] We give you thanks, our Father, for the life and knowledge which you made known to us through your son Jesus: glory to you forever! As this broken bread used to be scattered upon the mountains and became gathered into unity, so may your church be gathered from the ends of the earth into your dominion: for yours is the glory and the power through Jesus Christ forever! . . . [after the ensuing meal] We give you thanks, holy Father, for your holy name which you tabernacled in our hearts, and for the knowledge and faith and deathlessness which you made known to us through your son Jesus: glory to you forever! You, all-ruling king, created all things for your name's sake, and gave both food and drink to humankind for enjoyment, that they might give you thanks that you are powerful: glory to you forever! Remember, Lord, your church, to deliver it from all evil and perfect it in your love, and gather its holiness from the four winds into your dominion which you have prepared for it: for yours is the power and the glory forever! Let grace come and let this world pass away. Hosanna to the God of David! If one is holy, let him [or her] come! if one is not, let him [or her] be changed. *Maranatha!* Amen."

236. The rules for eucharistic participation are strict in both cases. Paul insists that it is dangerous to share in the Eucharist unworthily (1 Cor 11:27–30), and the *Didache* explicitly excludes from it anyone who has not been baptized into formal Christian belonging, including hopeful catechumens (9.5), and enjoins repentance on anyone who is not holy enough to join in (10.6). The *Didache* text quoted in the previous

note is probably the earliest eucharistic prayer that survives. Paul presents an account of the original precedent-event in his account of Jesus' Last Supper in 1 Cor 11:23–25, but not in the form of a eucharistic prayer; and however obvious it may initially seem that the eucharistic presider would use Jesus' words, as they normally do now, it really isn't. The *Didache* Eucharist does not use them, and if our Eucharists had not habituated us to thinking it appropriate to do so, it might well appear more presumptuous than apt. Jean Daniélou's claim in *The First Six Hundred Years* (London: Darton, Longman and Todd, 1964) that Jesus' words were used by eucharistic celebrants in the first century is without foundation. I asked him for his evidence shortly after *L'Église des premiers temps: des origines à la fin du IIIᵉ siècle* (the original edition, vol. 1 of *La Nouvelle histoire de l'Église)* was published, and he had none. The earliest notice of such a practice comes from the middle of the second century, and the *Didache*'s eucharistic prayers are almost certainly earlier than that, probably of the first Christian century.

237. Which the *Didache* also enjoins, recording in 8.2 an evidently early version of it that differs slightly from those in our other earliest sources, Mt 6:9–13 and Lk 11:2–4.

238. This word is properly a noun, but its verb form was long since invented by those who were cramped by the failure of English to provide an equivalent of the corresponding Greek verb for interpreting the religious significance of something, especially a text. If you don't find it in your favorite dictionaries, you can find it readily enough in recent theological writings: it is a useful and long-overdue invention.

239. I am overusing *solemnly* and *solemn,* but they are unfortunately the only adequate words for carrying the transformational sense of *anamnesis* to the more ordinary nouns and verbs I have used them to qualify. English has unfortunately also neglected to supply a verb corresponding to the Greek *anamimnêskô,* and I feel that I should spare you the obvious coinage.

240. There is a wonderful line in David Kelsey's *The Uses of Scripture in Recent Theology* (Philadelphia: Fortress Press, 1975), p. 212: "Theology is 'done' as one of the activities compromising the life of the Christian community. Hence . . . it necessarily uses scripture to help authorize its proposals." I have long presumed that "compromising" is here a typographical error for "comprising," but perhaps Kelsey was just being candid. Even if my presumption is right, typos can obviously be an occasion of grace and insight.

241. For a little further elaboration, see *Five Gospels,* pp. 275–76.

242. Moses complains about inadequate instructions, and does a little instructing as an encore, in the dialogue with God reported in Ex 33:12–16. Cf. his remarks of grumpy discouragement in Ex 32:32, and his—successful—objections in Ex 32:11–13.

243. The story is in medieval French verse, retold in nineteenth-century prose by Anatole France. I quote, from possibly inaccurate memory, the epigraph used in *The Juggler of Notre Dame,* the university's undergraduate literary magazine which I

edited in long-bygone days. I don't know whose translation or invention it is, but I think it lovely, and theologically appropriate.

244. See details in John C. Meagher, "The Law, the Prophets, and the Development of People," *World Justice* 10 (1968–1969), pp. 54–77.

245. "Pictures at an Exhibition: Reflections on Exegesis and Theology" *(Journal of the American Academy of Religion,* vol. 47, no. 1, 1979, pp. 3–20). (This was the Presidential Address to the American Academy of Religion, 1978: the site was New Orleans, and I shared a wonderful penthouse suite overlooking the Mississippi, was delightedly amused by the juxtaposition of Royal and Bourbon Streets, and tried unsuccessfully to get fresh shrimp in restaurants. All of the above are of course potential sacramentals, a topic that I will take up shortly in another subsection.)

246. It is relatively little known even among Catholics (certainly not publicized by the Vatican!), and virtually unknown among Protestants, that Roman Catholicism of the Eastern Rite still has married priests. Marriage after ordination is not allowed, but the reverse order is still possible, though discouraged and difficult. This is all canonically quite in order, and a married Ukrainian priest is just as Roman Catholic as the celibate pope, and they recognize each other's full clerical legitimacy. And since I'm in a note anyway, I'll take the opportunity to throw in another historical antierotic tidbit: Pope Gregory I forbade sexual pleasure in marriage, and taught that married couples were not to receive the Eucharist after having sex.

247. The classic Protestant treatment is Anders Nygren, *Agape and Eros* (London: S.P.C.K., 1932–1939); its Catholic counterpart is Martin D'Arcy, *The Mind and Heart of Love, Lion and Unicorn: A Study in Eros and Agape* (London: Faber and Faber, 1945).

248. Probably needless to say, Aqiba's interpretation of the text was symbolic/allegorical, having to do with God's relationship with Israel (he objected to its being sung in banquet houses, presumably on the grounds that it should be kept above such profanation: see Tosefta *Sanhedrin* 12.10), but there is no indication that he tried to wriggle out of the erotic tonality in his reading of what the Song of Songs has to say on the subject. As for the standing of that book in the revelational scheme of things, Aqiba is quoted in the Mishna *(Yadayim* 3.5) as saying that "all the Scriptures are holy, but the Song of Songs is the Holy of Holies," and apparently said also (according to *Aggadat Shir Ha-Shirim,* as plausibly emended by E. E. Urbach in "The Homiletical Interpretation of the Sages and the Expositions of Origen," *Scripta Hierosolymitana* 22 [Jerusalem: Magnes Press, 1971], p. 250, n. 10) that "Had not the Torah been given, Canticles would have sufficed to guide the world." This latter opinion warrants reflective appreciation. (For a superb and thorough discussion of the Song of Songs, see the Anchor Bible commentary by Marvin H. Pope, *Song of Songs* [Garden City, N. Y.: Doubleday, 1977].)

249. The *Didache,* in a passage on discerning true from false prophets, remarks that a tried-and-true prophet is not disqualified even by acting out "a worldly mystery of the church" (11:11). Kirsopp Lake admitted that this passage "has never been satisfactorily explained," but hints at a perfectly satisfactory explanation in remarking

delicately—though with a reference to Hosea rather than the more illuminating Ephesians—that "it probably refers to a tendency among some prophets to introduce forms of worship, or of illustration of their teaching, of doubtful propriety" *(The Apostolic Fathers,* vol. 1 [London: W. Heinemann, 1912], p. 327). More recent commentaries retain or escalate Lake's diffidence and pretend that the passage is less clear in its drift, both about what the prophets were doing and about how the church was evidently thought to be loved by Christ (or by God, whose erotic love of Israel was read by the rabbis into the Song of Songs and may be the presumed lover of the church in these prophetic demonstrations), than it really is.

250. Still housed in Santa Maria della Vittoria in Rome, and often reproduced photographically not only in art books but in many other publications as well: only the relatively sheltered can be unaware of it.

251. Quoted from the third paragraph of the preface thereof.

252. This remained so until after the famous test case in the early 1960s, when Penguin Books was audacious enough to reprint *Lady Chatterley's Lover,* originally published in France and seized at many a customs office in various English-speaking countries in subsequent years. The editors of the OED then loosened up, and admitted in vol. 1 of the 1972 *Supplement* (pp. 704, 1170) that one of the omitted words had appeared in a textbook on surgery around 1400 and in a London street name ca. 1230, while the other one had made its way into a dictionary published in the sixteenth century (Florio's *Worlde of Wordes).*

253. I used this comparison once before, thirty years ago, to explain the difference to a Jewish classmate, and was rightly reminded by an older woman who was also in the conversation—and was an accomplished musician—that love and lust are not always as different as I seemed to be (pardon the expression) making out.

254. "Greenwich," by Isaac Watts and Daniel Read, in *The Sacred Harp* (Kingsport, Tenn.: Kingsport Press, 1971), p. 183.

255. One occasionally encounters modern smugness about how a dogged unreligious secularism has managed to win more leisure for workers than they could possibly have had in the dark days of religious superstition. A more informed understanding will realize that the medieval centuries were so besprinkled with liturgical feast days that workers had far more time off than they do now. It would of course be inconsiderate to suggest that this was one of the less respectable motives for some employers' support of the Reformation, but there is good reason to suggest that it would not be historically inaccurate.

256. I think here of a Jewish friend who told me a few years ago that almost all the synagogues on the North American continent observe a decorum that closely resembles that of Christian churches, though a few have failed to adopt it and retain the unruly and disorderly behavior of their nineteenth-century European counterparts. He complained that he had to drive more than thirty miles to attend one of the properly indecorous ones.

257. "O merveille, qu'on puisse ainsi faire présent de ce qu'on ne possède pas soi-

même, ô doux miracle de nos mains vides!" *(Journal d'un curé de campagne* [Paris: Plon, 1936], p. 188).

258. I have been impressed over the years by how commonly it is supposed among Christians that Jesus made up the two great commandments. Christian education has traditionally been antitraditional in its attempts to make Christianity seem brand spanking new, unprecedented and unindebted to previous Jewish Godwardness. If you have been thus abused in this case, remember the good intentions of your teachers and try to do what you can to see to it that your great-grandchildren are made aware that Jesus is quoting Dt 6:5 and Lv 19:18.

259. My understanding of Jesus' gospel is set out in chapter 2 of *Five Gospels* (Minneapolis: Winston Press, 1983). That account still represents what I think, though I inevitably have learned a few qualifying things since I wrote it.

. . .

And to those readers who have taken the trouble to work with me through the notes, thank you for your patience and I hope we get together again.

JOHN C. MEAGHER is a Professor of Theology, Religious Studies, and English at St. Michael's College of the University of Toronto. A former president of the American Academy of Religion, he has a B.A. from Notre Dame, an M.A. from Princeton, and three Ph.D.s, one from the University of London, one from Princeton University, and one from McMaster University. He is the author of several books, including *The Gathering of the Ungifted, The Way of the Word,* and *Five Gospels: An Account of How the Good News Came to Be.*